LANGUAGE, MIND, AND CULTURE

LANGUAGE, MIND, AND CULTURE

A Practical Introduction

ZOLTÁN KÖVECSES

Exercises written by
Bálint Koller,
Noémi Endrődi,
Sarolta Komlósi,
Rita Tóth,
& Zoltán Kövecses

OXFORD
UNIVERSITY PRESS

2006

OXFORD

UNIVERSITY PRESS

Oxford University Press, Inc., publishes works that further
Oxford University's objective of excellence
in research, scholarship, and education.

Oxford   New York
Auckland   Cape Town   Dar es Salaam   Hong Kong   Karachi
Kuala Lumpur   Madrid   Melbourne   Mexico City   Nairobi
New Delhi   Shanghai   Taipei   Toronto

With offices in
Argentina   Austria   Brazil   Chile   Czech Republic   France   Greece
Guatemala   Hungary   Italy   Japan   Poland   Portugal   Singapore
South Korea   Switzerland   Thailand   Turkey   Ukraine   Vietnam

Published by Oxford University Press, Inc.
198 Madison Avenue, New York, New York 10016

www.oup.com

Oxford is a registered trademark of Oxford University Press

Library of Congress Cataloging-in-Publication Data
Kövecses, Zoltán.
Language, mind, and culture : a practical introduction / Zoltán Kövecses ;
exercises written by Bálint Koller . . . [et al.].
p. cm.
Includes bibliographical references and index.
ISBN-13 978-0-19-518719-9; 978-019-518720-5 (pbk.)

1. Language and culture.   2. Psycholinguistics.   3. Categorization
(Linguistics).   4. Frames (Linguistics).   5. Metaphor.
6. Cognitive grammar.   I. Koller, Bálint.   II. Title
P35.K685 2006
306.44—dc22   2005044916

"A Very Short Story" in chapter 6 is reprinted with permission of Scribner,
an imprint of Simon & Schuster Adult Publishing Group, from
THE SHORT STORIES OF ERNEST HEMINGWAY. Copyright
1925 Charles Scribner's Sons. Copyright renewed 1953 by
Ernest Hemingway. "A Very Short Story" from The Short Stories of
Ernest Hemingway, published by Jonathan Cape. Reprinted by
permission of The Random House Group Ltd.

Printed in the United States of America
on acid-free paper

For those two rambunctious
little boys and Zsuzsi

Preface

This book is an attempt to provide a new way of studying how we make sense of our experience. To account for this, I minimally need to discuss the varied and complicated relationships between language, mind, and culture. Hence the title of the book: *Language, Mind, and Culture*.

I attempt to characterize the multifaceted relationship between the three elements of "meaning making" from the perspective of the relatively new field of cognitive linguistics—a new branch of cognitive science. This explains why I can claim that this is a "new" way of studying the relationship.

Although cognitive linguistics is a new field, several excellent introductions to it are available. However, these introductions concentrate on how cognitive linguistics can be helpful in studying *language* only—to the exclusion of culture at large. In the same way, there are of course a number of equally excellent introductions to linguistic anthropology and anthropological linguistics—the key disciplines to study the language-culture interface—but these introductions do not pay sufficient attention to the many cognitive processes that play a crucial role in our cultural meaning-making activity. In this sense, this book tries to bridge the gap between these disciplines.

The book is theoretical in its orientation, in that it attempts to provide the reader with a comprehensive theory of how we can account for meaning making. But at the same time, it is intended as a textbook for anyone interested in the fascinating issues that surround the relationship between language, mind, and culture. No prior knowledge of linguistics is assumed, and my hope is that students in a variety of disciplines, including not only linguistics but also anthropology, English, sociology, philosophy, psychology, communication, rhetoric, and the like, will use this book.

To complement and counterbalance its theoretical orientation, the book is also a "practical" introduction. Except for the first and the last chapters, each chapter contains a number of exercises that might help the student "digest" the theoretical points discussed. At the end of the book, there is a section that provides possible solutions to the exercises. To make the book even more "user-friendly," the reader can find a glossary of all the important terms used in the text.

In sum, somewhat contradictorily, this is a new theoretical-practical introduction to how we make meaning in our world. It is my hope that it helps us make sense of some of the important personal and social issues we encounter in our lives as members of particular cultures and also as human beings.

Acknowledgments

In writing this book, I have received a lot of help from a variety of people. First and foremost, I want to thank George Lakoff for his continued support and friendship over the years and his generosity in sharing his ideas with me. His work has been crucial in extending cognitive linguistics beyond the study of language.

My special thanks go to three colleagues who helped me generously with their many comments on draft versions of parts or the whole of the book, Seana Coulson, Ronald Langacker, and Mark Turner, and an anonymous reviewer for Oxford University Press. Conversations and professional contact with Ray Gibbs, Eve Sweetser, and Ning Yu have also shaped my ideas about the language-mind-culture complex. Discussions with my former doctoral students Réka Benczes, Szilvia Csábi, and Michael Kimmel have helped me in more ways than they know. Their help is much appreciated.

I owe a great deal of gratitude to my students at the Department of American Studies at Eötvös Loránd University, who prepared most of the exercises. My special thanks go to Bálint Koller for his smartness, knowledge, and generosity in working with me. Noémi Endrődi, Sarolta Komlósi, and Rita Tóth have also been instrumental in creating many of the exercises in the book. Réka Benczes and Susan Papdi generously provided most of the diagrams and made important comments. Other students who contributed in many different ways include Niki Köves, Zoltán Peterecz, Orsi Sági, István Fekete, and Rudi Sárdi. I really appreciate all their help.

Last but not least, I want to thank Peter Ohlin, senior editor for Oxford University Press, for his encouragement, understanding, and support.

Contents

LANGUAGE, MIND,
AND CULTURE

Meaning in Mind, Language, and Culture

The basic question that this book is seeking to answer is this: What relationships hold between the cognitive system, language, and culture? There
are many different ways to answer this question, in part because different
people mean different things by each of the concepts involved in the question. For the time being, it seems useful to assume that all of the three concepts have somehow to do with meaning—either with its creation, its communication, or human beings acting on meaning. We can perhaps assume as
a relatively safe starting point that meaning in its different facets is a crucial
aspect of the mind, language, and culture.

The General Goal of the Book

In this book, I will show that given the findings of cognitive linguistics in the
past several decades it is possible to offer a unified account not only of linguistic meaning but also of meaning in a wide variety of social and cultural
phenomena. I will suggest that cognitive linguistics is a much more comprehensive enterprise than it is commonly taken to be by many—both inside and
outside the field. Furthermore, I will claim that the comprehensive account
of meaning in many linguistic and cultural phenomena to be presented in
subsequent chapters is crucially based and dependent on cognitive capacities
that human understanders and producers of language possess independently
of their ability to use language.

To give an initial idea of this enterprise, what follows is a sample of the
cognitive processes and linguistic and cultural issues that I will be discussing
in the book:

Categorization: nature of concepts and debates concerning art
Knowledge organization: frame semantics and cultural issues

Metonymic thought: metonymy in language and social thought and behavior
Metaphoric thought: metaphor in mind, language, and politics
Image-schemas: the structure of mind and understanding literature
Figure-ground alignment: grammatical structure
Mental spaces: semantic anomaly and literary discourse
Conceptual integration: creativity in linguistic and conceptual structure, as well as in everyday activities and everyday objects, or "material anchors"

By discussing the cognitive processes and the various linguistic, social, and cultural issues, I wish to highlight the wide scope of cognitive linguistics. By providing a discussion of such a wide variety of linguistic, social, and cultural topics in terms of cognitive linguistics, my goal is to demonstrate that cognitive linguistics is far more than a theory of language; we can perhaps think of it as a theory of "meaning making" in general in its innumerable linguistic, social, and cultural facets, of which the preceding topics are just a handful of examples.

Overall, then, the general goal of this book is more theoretical than descriptive. Although I will describe several specific case studies taken from linguists, anthropologists, psychologists, and so on, whose work is compatible with the basic principles of cognitive linguistics as defined by foundational work by George Lakoff, Mark Johnson, Ronald Langacker, Charles J. Fillmore, Len Talmy, and Gilles Fauconnier in the late 1970s and the 1980s and developed into a loosely coherent complex paradigm of research in the past more than two decades, the main intention behind this project is to show the wide scope of cognitive linguistics and the possibilities that this view can offer in the study of the general meaning-making capacity of human beings in language but, even more important for my purposes, beyond it. It follows from this that this book cannot serve as a complete survey and cannot undertake to offer a complete bibliography of either cognitive linguistics or the neighboring fields that have the same goals (such as anthropology). The more limited goal is to outline this loosely coherent complex view *within* cognitive linguistics and draw out its potential implications for the study of not only language (customarily pursued by cognitive linguists) but also the more general study of *culture at large*.

The Kinds of Issues in a Theory of Mind

The book will approach the many issues that surround meaning from a particular perspective—mostly from a cognitive perspective as this is informed by the study of language. But there are many other perspectives to the study of meaning and mind, and they all have different methods, research goals, and results. In recent years, however, there has been a great deal of convergence among the fields that study the issues of meaning, mind, and culture. This convergence has resulted in a new interdisciplinary field: cognitive science. Cognitive science makes use of the results of a variety of fields that all study the mind in their own ways. These include cognitive psychology, artificial intelligence, neuroscience, linguistics, cognitive anthropology, and several others. Needless to say, there is no unanimous agreement among the practitioners of these fields concerning their main subject matter: the human mind and its workings, let alone its relationship to language and culture.

There is, however, a budding field among all these scholarly activities that tries to synthesize many of the results concerning the mind: It is the fledgling field of cognitive linguistics. We cannot, of course, be sure that all of its claims and suggestions are valid, but at least it provides a systematic answer to our basic question and attempts to offer a coherent view of meaning and its essential role in cognition, language, and culture.

But before I begin with some of the more specific issues in the discussion of meaning in this book, let me briefly describe in an informal way some of the more general aspects of the mind.

Some General Issues in Connection with the Mind

What is cognition?

The study of human cognition is concerned with certain essential issues. First and foremost among them is the nature of knowledge. Second, there is the issue of how we acquire knowledge. Third, and just as important, we have the issue of how knowledge is represented in the mind.

What aspects and faculties make up the mind?

The mind is not a unitary phenomenon, and it has never been treated as such. It has many distinct aspects, traditionally called the faculties of the mind. Different philosophers have offered different lists of the faculties of the mind throughout the ages. We can easily distinguish at least the following aspects of the mind based on our everyday experiences (and on the language we use): intentionality, attention, perception, emotion, dreams, personality. Other important (and overlapping) aspects of the mind include volition, thought (thinking), memory, belief, and learning. In addition, Freud made use of the notion of the unconscious, as opposed to the conscious mind. The "standard" traditional conception of the faculties of the mind operates with the following four aspects: reason-thought-thinking, morality, emotion, and willing-volition. Last but not least, there is language, and the question is whether language is a separate aspect, or faculty, of the mind or has a special status among the rest of the faculties.

Which cognitive operations run the mind?

A final basic general question that surrounds the mind is what the basic cognitive processes are that operate in the mind. We know a great deal about the cognitive processes that human beings make use of in the course of their interaction with the world. These include perception, attention, categorization, viewpoint, figure-ground alignment, image-schematic understanding, force dynamics, and several others that have been identified and studied by various disciplines through the ages. A more recent idea is that figurative devices of various kinds (such as metaphor and metonymy) play an equally important role in the operation of the mind and in shaping knowledge.

As was noted, these are all fairly general questions, and the answers to them are more or less accepted by most scholars. For example, not too many would want to deny that the mind is used to represent knowledge, that we are emotional beings, and that we categorize experience from the time we are born. Most of the differences in opinion enter when we ask more specific questions about the mind.

Some More Specific Issues in Connection with the Mind

Below are eight specific questions that are concerned with the mind in some of its facets, together with some possible answers. On the basis of the answers given, I will set up two broad views in the study of the mind, language, and culture.

1. Are different aspects of the mind governed by the same or different processes?

Given the several "faculties" of the mind, we can ask the following question: Are these distinct aspects of the mind governed by similar or different cognitive processes? In other words, is it the case that we have a mind that consists of "modules" each governed by a different set of cognitive processes or, alternatively, we have a mind that has a more global structure in terms of the processes that govern it? This issue is known as the distinction between a modular versus a holistic conception of the mind. The former view is commonly referred to as the "modularity of mind," while the latter is referred to as "holism."

2. What is the nature of reality?

Since most of our knowledge concerns external reality, it is crucial to be clear about what our view of this reality is. Do we think of the world as already structured independent of a human observer or do we think of it as an unstructured thing or mass that gains structure through the cognitive processes that human beings apply to it? In short, does the world come in a structured or unstructured form?

3. What is the relationship between the mind and external reality?

How do we view the relationship between the mind and external reality? There are basically two major views here. In one, the relationship is such that the mind reflects a preexisting reality, and in another, it is the mind that "creates," that is, provides structure for, this reality. The former conception describes the mind as some kind of a "mirror of reality." The latter gives more room for humans to create an idea of reality that can differ more or less from "actual reality"; that is, reality as it is, independent of human beings. Indeed, it is possible to claim in the second view that we can see only an "imagined," a "projected," kind of reality. In brief, the question is whether the mind reflects or creates reality. Clearly, these alternatives depend on one's views of external reality, as mentioned in the previous question.

4. What is the relationship between the mind and the body?

Human beings have both a body and a mind. What is the relationship between the two? We can ask if the mind is independent of the body or, just the contrary, if it is based on the body. If we adopt the first view, we would say that humans have a "transcendent" mind, that is, a mind that is abstract and goes way beyond the body, in that its real powers come precisely from those capabilities of the mind that have nothing to do with the physical body.

5. What is language?

What are the crucial aspects of human language? Should we think of it as highly structured form, especially syntactic form, or as meaning and conceptualization? Is grammar best conceived as a structured set of forms, as in the syntactic rules of the Chomskyan kind, or as form that serves the purpose only of conveying our conceptualized knowledge of the world? Is language essentially the manipulation of abstract symbols, analogous to a computer, or is it predominantly a process devoted to the conceptualization and communication of meaning? In short, is language mostly a matter of form or of meaning and conceptualization?

Furthermore, there is the issue of how we acquire language. In this connection, we can ask whether language is an innate or an acquired ability.

6. What is meaning?

If we see the mind as largely devoted to making sense of the world, then issues of meaning inevitably arise in connection with any discussion of language and mind. Indeed, foremost among these questions is: What is meaning? Can we define meaning in terms of truth conditions for the application of particular forms (e.g., words, sentences)? Do we know the meaning of the word *snow* or *tree* because we know the conditions on which the use of these words depends? Is there a checklist of features that we need to know if we want to use words and larger groups of forms in an appropriate way? Or, alternatively, can we identify meaning with the concepts we have in our conceptual system? In this case, the issue becomes how our knowledge that forms the basis of concepts is represented in the mind.

And then there is the even deeper question of how the forms (linguistic or otherwise) that we use become meaningful. Given a form (a sign), how does its meaning arise? Even more generally, we can ask how language acquires meaning. Is meaningfulness a matter of convention and reference (this sign will refer to this object, event, etc.) or something else? Is it conceivable, for example, that the human body plays a role in making forms and signs meaningful?

7. What is truth?

There is the issue of truth. Given language and the external world, can we maintain that truth is simply a direct relationship between a sentence and a state of affairs in the world?

8. What is the relationship between language and cognition?

The major issue here is whether language is an expression of thought or shapes thought.

These are some of the main issues that we hope to better understand in this book. They were listed here because the answers to them are systematically different in the different approaches. We will be primarily concerned with two of the rival approaches—the ones that dominate current thinking about these issues today. We can roughly gloss them as the "objectivist" and the "experientialist" approaches to the mind. The two differ consistently in the kinds of answers they provide to our questions. The descriptions of the two approaches that follow are intended as very rough characterizations (almost as caricatures) of two extreme positions that merely serve the purpose of giving the reader an initial idea of how we *can* think about the issues.

The Objectivist View

Let us begin with the conception of the mind we can call objectivist. Here are the ways in which the representatives of the approach would characterize the mind, language, meaning, and so on. (The letters *o* and *e* following the numbers stand for the objectivist and experientialist views, respectively.)

10. Modularity versus holism

The mind is modular. It consists of several separate modules that are each governed by different sets of cognitive processes. (But even in this view it is assumed, of course, that the various components or modules are connected and interact at a higher level.)

20. The nature of reality

Reality is structured. It comes in well-defined categories: categories of the world. There are categories of the world such as SNOW, TREE, CHAIR, CAT, RUNNING, BREAKING, and many other categories for objects and events. Each category of the world is defined by shared essential properties. For example, the category of TREE is defined by a set of such properties. In general, categories of the world are discrete entities and relations (events and states) defined by essential properties.

30. The mind-reality relationship

The mind is a mirror of external reality. Thought mirrors an objective reality. Thought is essentially literal.

In addition to categories of the world, there are also categories of the mind, that is, conceptual categories. These correspond to categories of the world. For example, corresponding to the category of TREE that exists in the world, there is also a conceptual category TREE. Conceptual categories are mental reflections of categories of the world.

40. The mind-body relationship

In the objectivist view, thought is independent of the body. Thus, the mind is transcendent, in that it goes beyond the body. Thought is also abstract; it consists of the manipulation of abstract symbols. The mind is like an abstract machine, on the analogy of a computer, that manipulates abstract symbols, where the mind is the software and the body (brain) is the hardware.

50. The nature of language

Language is a unique and independent faculty of human beings. It is one of the independent modules of the mind that is governed by its own rules.

Language is innate. We are born with a linguistic faculty that is characterized by a set of abstract universal rules. Given the innate universal language faculty, we can learn any language with equal ease. The only thing that matters is that we should be exposed to enough linguistic "input" early enough in our life.

In the study of language and thought, form (as abstract symbols and rules) is more important than meaning.

60. The nature of meaning

Meaning is a correspondence between symbols and things/events in the world (or, more precisely, between symbols and elements in sets). Meaning can be defined by a set of necessary and sufficient conditions. Take the word *square*.

It can be defined by necessary and sufficient conditions. For something to be a square, it has to be characterized by four equal sides and four equal angles. If either of these features is absent, the thing is not a square.

Forms and signs in general become meaningful because of their conventional connection with aspects of the world, consisting of objects and events.

70. The nature of truth

Truth and meaning are intimately connected. Meaning is based on truth. We can think of meaning as the truth conditions of a sentence—that is, the conditions under which the sentence is true.

8o. The language-mind relationship

The world is prestructured and the conceptual system reflects the structure of the world. Language with its categories merely expresses or reflects the conceptual system.

The Experientialist View

The experientialist answers to the questions differ systematically from the objectivist answers on all of these counts (see Johnson, 1987; Lakoff, 1987; Lakoff and Johnson, 1999).

1e. Modularity versus holism

In the experientialist view, the mind is holistic. Processes of the mind are seen as largely the same for the various aspects and faculties of the mind.

2e. The nature of reality

Reality does not come in a prestructured form and it is not viewed as something that exists independently of human beings. Nor does reality come in well-defined categories of the world. External reality does exist, but we have access to it only in our particularly human ways. We see categories in the world only as a result of our uniquely human experiences (through perception, interaction, etc.). The world, for us, is a "projected" reality that human beings "imaginatively" create.

3e. The mind-reality relationship

For an experientialist, the mind reflects the world *as* we experience and perceive it. Thus, the categories of mind do not fit categories of the world, that is, an objective reality. The world is "created" or built up by the mind in several imaginative ways. These include such cognitive processes as categorization based on prototypes, organizing knowledge in terms of frames, and understanding experience through metaphors. All of these can be and are differentially used, thus pointing to the fact that the "same" reality can be construed in alternative ways.

Experientialism does not accept the view that literality is an essential design feature of the mind. On the contrary, it claims that the mind is essentially both literal and figurative. Take, for example, an argument. When people see the participants of the argument as opponents and their behavior as defending and attacking, they interpret what is going on as war or battle. This understanding of what an argument is, is essentially figurative (metaphorical). Without metaphorically conceiving of argument this way, we would have a very different concept of "argument." It is in this sense that the mind is just as much metaphorical as it is literal.

4e. The mind-body relationship

In experientialism, the body is seen as playing a decisive role in producing the kind of mind we have. The mind is based on the body. In other words, the kind of body humans have influences the kind of mind they have. As a result, thought is taken to be embodied. As an example, take the conceptual category of TREE. How can the body play any role in our understanding what a tree is? For one thing, we understand a tree as being upright. This comes from how we experience our own bodies; namely, that we experience ourselves as being erect. For another, we see a tree as tall. The aspect of tallness only makes sense with respect to our standard evaluation of the body's relative height. A tree is tall relative to our average human size. In this way, categories of mind are defined by the body's interaction with the environment. We call such features of conceptual categories "interactional properties."

5e. The nature of language

Is language an independent module of the mind? In experientialism, it isn't. Language operates on the basis of the same principles that other cognitive faculties of the mind use. The cognitive processes of categorization, framing knowledge, figure-ground organization, and many others are just as important in language as in other aspects of the mind.

In addition, the key component of language is not form but meaning and conceptualization. Language serves the function of expressing meaning. In the study of language and thought, meaning is more important than form. Grammar serves the purpose of conceptualization; indeed, it is taken to be conceptualization.

6e. The nature of meaning

As the example of the category of TREE indicates, meaning derives from embodiment. Thought and meaning are thus embodied.

In addition, meaning is relative to how we frame experience. If I say, "I paid five dollars for the drink," I take the perspective of the buyer, but if I say, "I sold the drink for five dollars," I take the perspective of the seller. Different people can frame the same event in different ways, depending on their perspective. In other words, meaning is not simply a matter of conceptual content; it is equally a matter of how I construe some conceptual content.

7e. The nature of truth

In the experientialist view, truth is not a direct correspondence between a sentence and a situation. Rather, truth can only be assessed relative to a particular understanding of a situation.

8e. The language-mind relationship

The world comes largely unstructured; it is (human) observers who do most of its structuring. A large part of this structuring is due to the linguistic system (which is a subsystem of culture). Language can shape and, according to the principle of linguistic relativity (Whorf, 1956), does shape the way we think.

Universality versus the Relativity of Human Knowledge

Most of the issues I have just cited involve in some form and to some extent the relationship between language, cognition, and culture, but it is especially the last issue (number 8) that is relevant to its discussion. For this reason, it will be necessary to return to it several times in later chapters. However, it will be useful to get a flavor of what linguistic relativity involves at the outset in this chapter. The special significance of this lies in the fact that embracing linguistic relativity as our solution to the issue of whether language expresses thought or shapes it puts us on the side of relativity in the great historical and current debate over the universality versus the relativity of human knowledge.

A view of the universality of human knowledge would maintain the "psychic unity of mankind." We share the most significant knowledge about the world in the form of transcendental universal concepts. We have a universal faculty of reason. Such transcendental universal ideas make up the faculty of reason and are innate. Experience, including linguistic experience, is helpful only in triggering the acquisition of universal concepts and principles for their organization. By contrast, the view of the relativity of human knowledge would maintain that our knowledge of the world derives primarily from experience—experience that "is obtained through culturally mediated conceptual schemes, i.e., historically situated, contingent frameworks of meaning and understanding" (Foley, 1997: 169).

The Conception of Space: Universal or Relative?

Given this split in our thinking about the nature of knowledge, let us clarify the issue further by means of an example. Going through the example will allow us to discuss a number of important issues in the study of language, mind, and culture. Perhaps the most significant of these is the principle of linguistic relativity.

Benjamin Lee Whorf spells out the principle of linguistic relativity in an often-quoted passage (1956: 212–213):

> It was found that the background linguistic system (in other words, the grammar) of each language is not merely a reproducing instrument for voicing ideas but rather is itself the shaper of ideas, the program and guide for the individual's mental activity, for his analysis of impressions, for his synthesis of his mental stock in trade. Formulation of ideas is not an independent process, strictly rational in the old sense, but is part of a particular grammar, and differs, from slightly to greatly, between different grammars. We dissect nature along lines laid down by our native languages. The categories and types that we isolate from the world of phenomena we do not find there because they stare every observer in the face; on the contrary, the world is presented in a kaleidoscopic flux of impressions which has to be organized by our minds—and this means largely by the linguistic systems in our minds.

I will take up the issue of how Whorf's ideas have been received and the type of research they have generated over the past half century in subsequent chapters. Let us now see a specific example of a research program inspired by the principle of linguistic relativity. Stephen C. Levinson and his colleagues did important work that shows that, despite the many rejections Whorf's ideas have received over the years (see, e.g., Pinker, 1994; Pullum, 1991), his insights may turn out to be valid after all (see, e.g., Levinson, 1992, 1996; Lucy, 1992, 1996). Consider the conception of space in different languages. This example is especially interesting because SPACE is a domain that Whorf himself took to be universal (unlike TIME, which he showed to be very differently conceptualized in English and Hopi). This is what Whorf writes about the conceptualization of "space" (Whorf, 1956: 158–159):

> But what about our concept of "space," which was also included in our first question? There is no such striking difference between Hopi and SAE [Standard Average European] about space as about time, and probably the apprehension of space is given in substantially the same form by experience irrespective of language. The experiments of the Gestalt psychologists with visual perception appear to establish this as a fact.

In other words, Whorf did not see any significant difference in the conceptualization of "space" in English and Hopi, unlike in that of time. Moreover, he regarded space as "given substantially the same form by experience," that is, universal. Notice that Whorf's argument (mentioning the experiments of Gestalt psychologists) is perfectly consistent with the experiential suggestion in (4e), namely, that the mind is based on the body. Since we are spatial beings, it only makes sense for us to have a self- or ego-oriented spatial conceptualization that is based on "left-right," "in front of–behind," and so on, which are spatial coordinates that come from the human body. If we look at Standard Average European (SAE) languages, such relativist spatial orientations (i.e., relative to human beings) appear to be universal. But is spatial orientation indeed conceived in the same way in radically different languages?

John B. Haviland's (1979) and Stephen Levinson's (1992) research shows otherwise. Levinson describes a very different solution to the problem of spatial orientation in connection with a radically different language—the native Australian language of Guugu Yimithirr (1996: 180):

> Take, for example, the case of the Guugu Yimithirr speakers of N. Queensland, who utilize a system of spatial conception and description which is fundamentally different from that of English-speakers. Instead of concepts of relativistic space, wherein one object is located by reference to demarcated regions projected out from another reference object (ego, or some landmark) according to *its* orientation, Guugu Yimithirr speakers use a system of absolute orientation (similar to cardinal directions) which fixes absolute angles regardless of the orientation of the reference object. Instead of notions like "in front of," "behind," "to the left of," "opposite," etc., which concepts are uncoded in the language, Guugu Yimithirr speakers must specify locations as (in rough English gloss) "to the North of," "to the South of," "to the East of," etc. The system is used at every level of scale, from millimeters to miles, for there is (effectively) no other system available in the language; there is simply no analogue of the Indo-European prepositional concepts.

This is fascinating, but, more important for my purposes here, does this language have any consequence for the cognitive behavior of its speakers? As Levinson (1996: 181) makes clear (based on his own work [1992]), the consequences of such a spatial system for cognition are far-reaching:

> Every speaker must be absolutely oriented at all times, and when moving must dead-reckon all locations that may need to be referred to, or used as reference points. These cognitive processes can be demonstrated independently of language . . . : Guugu Yimithirr speakers can be shown during travel to be able to estimate the directions of other locations with an average error of less than 14°. It can also be demonstrated experimentally that they remember spatial arrays not in terms of ego-centric co-ordinates (like in front, behind, to the left or right), but in terms of the cardinal directions in which objects lie. Thus Guugu Yimithirr speakers appear to think about space in a fundamentally different way than we do.

The use of this "geocentric absolute spatial reckoning system" requires abilities that speakers of SAE languages do not possess as an everyday, natural ability. The Guugu Yimithirr must carry a mental map in their head of every-thing that surrounds them, with the map aligned for the four quadrants. With the help of such a mental map, they can identify the location of any object with a high degree of precision, far exceeding the ability of speakers of lan-guages that have a relativist system of spatial reckoning.

We can ask how such a system of spatial reckoning can have evolved. This would be a legitimate question since the conception of "space," as noted earlier, is one of the prime domains that is taken to have evolved from our most basic bodily experience as "ego-centric, forward-looking and -oriented bipedal primates wandering on a planet with significant gravity" (Levinson, 1996: 180). It can be suggested in response that a spatial reckoning system like the one found in Guugu Yimithirr is also motivated experientially—but that its motivation does not come directly from the human body but from the absolute coordinates that characterize the geographic space/environment in which human bodies function. In other words, the human body may under-determine the particular spatial orientation systems human beings use; never-theless, such systems are always well motivated and not arbitrary. That the human body plays an important role in establishing and motivating aspects of the conceptual system but may often underdetermine such aspects seems to be a well-established finding in cross-cultural research on language, mind, and culture (see Kövecses, 2005a, chap. 10; Lakoff and Johnson, 1999).

Conclusions

The main general goal of this book is to outline a theory of the relationships that hold between language, mind, and culture on the basis of some recent findings in cognitive linguistics. Although the book describes a large number of examples that relate to its subject matter, its major thrust is theoretical, rather than descriptive.

What connects the study of language, mind, and culture is the issue of meaning. The search for meaning in these realms requires the consideration of a number of specific questions. I used eight such questions and the answers given to them to distinguish two broad classes of schools in the study of meaning and meaningfulness in language, mind, and culture. We can roughly gloss the two approaches to meaning as "objectivism" and "experientialism."

Despite their many disagreements, the two views share a major finding. It is that most of thought is unconscious. Thought is here understood in a broad sense, including all our mental activities (one of them being speaking). When we speak or see, we are not normally paying any conscious attention to what we are engaged in. We perform everything automatically and without any effort.

Objectivism, as characterized here, is not a single unified school of thought but rather a variety of different ideas and philosophical orientations—admittedly a straw man created here to serve merely as the background to what we can call experientialism, a coherent system of thought as developed in the past two decades by George Lakoff and Mark Johnson, especially in Johnson (1987), Johnson and Lakoff (2002), Lakoff (1987), and Lakoff and Johnson (1980, 1999). Many others have contributed significantly to this work, and their contributions will be dealt with in the chapters to follow. This volume is intended as a relatively comprehensive and systematic attempt to broaden the approach to study how language, mind, and culture hang together in creating meaning for human beings.

In such an enterprise, the major issue on which we need to take sides is the universality versus the relativity of human knowledge. My experientialist orientation led me to side with relativity. At the same time, however, we will see that relativity does not exclude universality in human knowledge. Following Lakoff and Johnson's proposals, I will suggest that the experientialist solution to the issue not only does not exclude universality but requires it— but it requires it in a new form. The case study of space discussed in this chapter was an early indication of how this can be achieved.

2

Categorizing the World

Prototypes, Theories, and Linguistic Relativity

Together with many other higher-level organisms, humans are categorizing beings. We categorize all objects and events we encounter in the environment. Categorization is necessary for action, and it is essential for survival. Imagine that you want to read a book and in order to do that you want to sit down in a comfortable chair. You will see many things in the room, including, say, a dresser, a table, a couch, a chair, a stove, and the like. In order to be able to carry out your plan to sit down in a comfortable chair and read, you will have to categorize the objects that surround you. Of all the objects you see, you need to be able to pick out the object that is a comfortable chair. If you mistake the stove for the chair, you might be in trouble. For another hypothetical example, imagine that you encounter a tiger, but you mistake it for a big domestic cat. The consequence may be disastrous. Thus, in a very real sense, our ability to categorize the world has survival value.

The categorization of objects and events is taking place unconsciously most of the time. It is also a remarkably fast cognitive process. But despite the routine nature of categorization, it is not easy to explain what is happening in our heads when we categorize. Indeed, there are several competing theories to account for how we do it.

The conceptual categories we establish are the backbone of language and thought. Much of our meaning-making capacity depends on the system of conceptual categories we acquire. As we will see later in this chapter and throughout this book, conceptual categories can be identified with meaning in language. In addition, it is conceptual categories that make up a large part of thought.

The ability to categorize is shared by people everywhere—no matter where they live and which culture they belong to. As a matter of fact, most advanced organisms have the ability to categorize. Human beings categorize their environment in a wide variety of ways. Thus, while people all share the same cognitive capacity to categorize, the product of this categorization is far from being uniform.

At this point several important issues emerge: (1) How do we acquire the knowledge associated with categories? (2) What are the best-known theories to account for how we categorize? (3) Do languages with their different category systems determine how speakers of these languages view the world, or, the other way around, is it the world that comes with a particular structure and determines the categories that the speakers of different languages have? This chapter attempts to answer these questions from an experientialist perspective.

How Do We Acquire Our Categories?

Cognitive psychologist Lawrence Barsalou (1992: 26) describes the process of acquiring categories in five steps, as given here:

1. Form a structural description of the entity.
2. Search for category representations similar to the structural description.
3. Select the most similar category representation.
4. Draw inferences about the entity.
5. Store information about the categorization.

First, we perceive the most primitive properties of an entity we encounter. This may be perceptual information, such as lines, surfaces, weight, vertical or horizontal extension, roughness or softness, sweetness or bitterness, and so on. For example, in the case of a chair we can perceive the various surfaces that make up the chair (the seat and the back of a chair) and the particular configuration of these surfaces—namely, that they are perpendicular to each other.

Second, we search for category representations that are similar to the structural description we have arrived at. The rough structural description identified in step 1 may fit a number of distinct "category representations" in memory. The structural description of a chair may be similar to not only the representation of CHAIR but also a number of other representations, such as those associated with SOFA, STOOL, and TABLE.

Third, we have to make a decision about which category representation in memory best fits the structural description at hand (in the example, that of the chair). In most cases, we assign the entity to the category representation that is best suited to it. Thus, using the example of the chair, the category representation associated with chairs will be selected to categorize the entity in question.

Fourth, given the resulting categorization of an entity (i.e., whether we classify it as a chair, bed, couch, or stool), we can draw inferences based on the knowledge that is associated with the category. Thus, given that we have classified an entity as a chair, we know we can sit in it, given that if we have classified it as a bed, we know that we can lie down in it, and so on.

Fifth, every time we categorize something, the categorization process provides information that we make use of to update the category representation already in memory. We will rely on such memories when we encounter similar entities and categorize them in a particular way, for instance, as chairs.

We may note several important aspects of categories and the categorization process in this connection. To begin, we can see that what is meant by *category representation* is what we call a conceptual category. In this book, I will use the terms *conceptual category*, *category*, and *concept* interchangeably to refer to such mental representations of categories. Another important point is that, to use Barsalou's (1992: 25) apt phrasing, "categorization is usually not an end in itself." Rather, it is a cognitive process that we use to achieve some goal, such as sitting down to read. We can achieve such goals by examining and drawing the inferences from category knowledge. Finally, as noted earlier, the process of categorization takes place below the threshold of consciousness. With few exceptions, we do not pay conscious attention to any of the stages of the categorization process. It all happens very fast and automatically.

But the really challenging question is this: How are categories represented in the mind (and ultimately in the brain)? That is, what do category representations look like? This is an important issue because, as we just saw, we assign entities to categories on the basis of such representations and it is such representations that hold categories together. Not surprisingly, there are a number of accounts of category representations, including "classical" models, prototype models, exemplar models, spreading activation models, connectionist models, and intuitive theories (Barsalou, 1992). Of these we will briefly consider classical models, prototype models, and exemplar models in the sections that follow. Various mixes of such models are also available, but for our purposes it will be sufficient to look at the main features of classical, prototype, and exemplar models. I will briefly return to the role of intuitive theories in category formation in the next chapter.

Theories of Categorization

The issue of category representation amounts to the issue of how we define categories. We will distinguish three ways in which categories are defined: In one, categories are defined by certain essential features (classical models); in the second, categories are defined by prototypes (prototype models); and in the third, categories are defined by exemplars (exemplar models).

Classical Categorization

Much of what I will say about categorization in the rest of this chapter comes from the work of George Lakoff, especially his book *Women, Fire, and Dangerous Things* (1987), and from work by John Taylor in his *Linguistic Categorization* (1989/1995).

The so-called classical model of categorization is called the classical view because it represents the most traditional ideas concerning categorization, which go back to Greek antiquity. It was Aristotle's idea that things in the world (i.e., categories of the world) are defined by essential features. Thus, the corresponding conceptual categories are also defined by such features. It is these that hold members of a category together. This does not mean that categories can only have essential features; they can also have accidental, or peripheral, ones, but these latter ones do not play a significant role in making a category what it is. What makes a category what it is, is its essential features. For example, the category of MAN (in the sense of "humankind") is defined by certain essential features—say, the features of being a featherless biped (a two-legged animal without feathers). Others may find a different set of features to characterize the same category, such as man being a communicative animal or a rational animal. As a matter of fact, sometimes philosophical debates turn on which features of a category should be taken as essential. However, the point remains: Classical categories can be and are defined by a set of essential features, other, peripheral features playing no role in what a category really is.

But of course finding the essential features of categories is not the sole pursuit of philosophers. We all participate in this, and we have certain experts, such as linguists, lexicographers, scientists of all kinds, who are in the business of defining the categories that they use. For example, in what is known as "componential analysis," linguists, anthropologists, and others would define the other sense of the category of MAN (human males) as follows: HUMAN, ADULT, MALE. In other words, these are the features that are taken to be the essential properties in terms of which the word can be defined. The small capitals are used to indicate that the "components" of the meaning of the word (i.e., the essential features that define the conceptual category) are concepts, not words of the English language.

To see how componential analysis works in more detail, let us now take the contrastive category of WOMAN. In the classical view, it would be defined by the following features, or components of meaning: HUMAN, ADULT, –MALE (Katz and Fodor, 1963). (This definition of the word *woman* comes from the 1960s, when political correctness was not an issue.) Thus, the category of WOMAN is defined like the category of MAN except for the feature of MALE. Correspondingly, the category of GIRL would be defined as HUMAN, –ADULT, –MALE. In other words, componential analysis often works with a set of (contrastive) semantic features in its definitions of meaning. But not all features are contrastive and there are several additional characteristics of componential analysis, but they should not concern us here. The main idea for us is that conceptual categories (concepts or meanings) are defined by sets of essential features—more precisely, by a shared set of necessary and sufficient conditions for the application of a word. We can apply the words *man* and *woman* to individuals who share their respective sets of essential features, or necessary or sufficient conditions. The features are both necessary and sufficient because we can only call someone a man if he meets the conditions (i.e., the features are necessary to call him that) and because possessing the conditions makes someone a member of the category (i.e., the features are sufficient for him to be called a man).

What is the major goal of componential analysis? It is to minimally distinguish the meaning of every word from the meaning of every other word in the language. Componential analysis attempts to do this in the most economical way possible—by making use of a small number of essential properties that are minimally needed to distinguish one meaning from every other meaning in the language.

This is the single most important idea of the classical view of categorization, of which componential analysis is a fairly recent version. This general view of the definition of categories has certain implications that will be of important consequence for us later on in the chapter. Namely, given this view, it follows that

1. What holds together a category is that the members of the category all share the same features.
2. All category members have equal status.
3. Categories have sharp and rigid boundaries. (Taylor, 1989/1995)

First, if we adopt the view that categories are defined by sets of necessary and sufficient conditions, or features, it will be the case that all the members of a category will have the same essential features. If they did not, they would not be members of the category. That is to say, it is the sharing of essential features by all category members that holds together the category.

Second, if we assume that all members of a category are defined by the same essential features, we can reasonably assume that all the members are taken to be equally "good" members of the category. That is to say, no member is thought of as better than any of the other members.

Third, if categories are defined by a certain set of necessary and sufficient conditions, then we can expect categories to have sharp and fixed boundaries. That is, we can assume that essential features will tell us precisely where one category ends and another one begins.

Now we turn to the issue of whether these consequences actually hold up. If they do not, it is clear that we need a different account of how people go about categorizing the world around them.

Prototype Categorization

One scholar who took a serious look at the classical view of categorization and its potential consequences was the philosopher Ludwig Wittgenstein (1953). He asked us to consider the category of GAME. His arguments and suggestions could be summarized in the following way. (The structure of the argument that follows is based on proposals by Taylor [1989/1995].)

First, Wittgenstein asked if there are any features of the conceptual category (concept) of GAME that are shared by all members of the category. The category of GAME includes a large number of members, or instances—from ring-around-the-rosy, through hide-and-seek, to card games, to football or basketball. Potential candidates for essential features to define this extensive category include competitiveness, strategy, physical prowess, amusement, and so on. Let us try to see if any one of these is present in all instances of the category. Ring-around-the-rosy does not seem to have competitiveness, but it has amusement; card games and chess may possess strategy, but they do not possess physical prowess; American football is characterized by strategy, physical prowess, and competitiveness, but is it done by the players for their own amusement, as in the case of ring-around-the-rosy? Probably not. In any case, Wittgenstein came to the conclusion that there is not a single essential feature that characterizes all instances of the category of GAME. Instead, he suggested that what holds the category together is what he called "family resemblance" relations. This is a metaphor used by Wittgenstein. It suggests that members of a family have different properties, such as being blond, having green eyes, having large ears, having small feet, and so forth, but that not all members have all of these properties. Some of them have blond hair and large ears, others have green eyes and small feet, still others have blond hair and small feet, and so on. In other words, membership in the family is not defined by a fixed set of properties that each member of a family has. Instead, family members are held together to form a family by means of sharing a particular property with some members and sharing another property with other members. Family member A has properties x and y, family member B has properties y and z, and family member C has properties x and z. There is no single property that they all share, but they resemble one another and are members of the same family by virtue of sharing a property with only some family members but not others.

Second, in thinking about the category GAME, Wittgenstein asked us to imagine how we would teach the category to someone who is not familiar with it. What would be a good example to do this? If you want to teach people the category, would you teach them the game of dice? Probably not. Would you teach them ring-around-the-rosy or, based on Eric Berne's book *Games People Play*, "the games people play"? Probably not. We would be likely to teach people the category by using other games, such as playing a game of cricket, baseball, or basketball. This suggests that some games are better examples of the category of GAME than others.

Third, staying with the category of GAME, we can ask if it is a category that has sharp, rigid boundaries as predicted by the classical view. The category of GAME seems to be undergoing constant extension. For example, video games did not exist in Wittgenstein's time but today they constitute an obvious and clear member of the category. New kinds of games are constantly added to the category, and indeed this is what made it possible for Eric Berne to call some of the things that people do in their personal relationships the games people play.

If Wittgenstein is right, all three major consequences of the classical view of categorization become problematic and open to challenge: (1) It is not necessary and sufficient conditions (essential features) that hold the instances of a category together but what he called family resemblance relations among the different instances or members. (2) Despite the prediction of the classical view that the shared essential properties of category members ensure that all instances are regarded as equal by people, it turns out that some members of categories receive "preferential treatment"; that is, they are regarded as better examples of the category than others. (3) It seems that the sharing of a fixed set of essential properties does not lead to fixed, rigid category boundaries. Rather, categories can be creatively extended by adding new members (and also probably can be reduced).

If these suggestions are valid, we need to replace the classical view of categories. The new, rival view is called prototype categorization. In the new view, categories are defined not in terms of necessary and sufficient conditions but with respect to prototypes and various family resemblance relations to these prototypes.

So far I have discussed the everyday category of GAMES. The work of another philosopher, John Austin, can be seen as an extension of the scope of possible prototype organization in categories (Lakoff, 1987). Austin extended the notion of categories to the senses of words. In other words, he thought of the sense of words as being organized around a prototypical sense. For example, he showed by way of analyzing the different senses of the word *healthy* that one of the senses is central, while others are noncentral, or peripheral. *Healthy* can mean a 'healthy body,' and it can also mean 'productive of healthy body,' as in *a healthy exercise,* and 'resulting from a healthy body,' as in *a healthy complexion.* Thus, we have a category of senses with the sense "healthy body" in the center, that is, being the prototypical one, and two nonprototypical senses, "producing a healthy body" and "resulting from a healthy body,"' that both derive from the prototype. What is the relationship between the prototypical and nonprototypical senses? In this particular case, the extensions of the prototypical sense are motivated by "metonymic relations" (see chap. 7). One metonymic relation is that of a state (*healthy*) standing for a cause of that state (*healthy exercise*), the other being a state (*healthy*) standing for a result of that state (*healthy complexion*). As we will see in later chapters, it is very common for words to have a central prototypical sense, with the other senses deriving from that sense either through metonymy or metaphor.

Similarly, the notion of prototype was extended to "linguistic categories" by linguists (see Lakoff, 1987; Taylor, 1989/1995); that is, to the terms we use to describe language. Linguistic categories include NOUN, VERB, MODIFIER, PHRASE, CLAUSE, SENTENCE, and so on. The same question that can be raised in connection with everyday categories can be raised in connection with such grammatical categories: Are they defined by a set of essential properties or by certain prototypes? Recent work in this area suggests that it is reasonable to think of these categories as prototype based as well (Taylor, 2002). Take as a simple example the category of NOUN. We could ask, in the spirit of prototype approaches to categorization, which nouns we would be most likely to teach to a speaker of a foreign language: nouns such as *liberalism, constitution, institution, finance, beauty, morality*, and the like or nouns such as *bread, water, house, woman, school, bank, money*, and so on? Probably no one would deny that somehow it makes better sense to begin with the latter group, as most beginner-level foreign language textbooks attest. We all feel intuitively that such nouns are somehow better examples than the others, which means that they are more representative members of the category than the others. Actually, this observation makes sense of the old-fashioned definition of nouns as 'words used to describe people, objects, and places.' In the traditional view, nouns were defined in terms of the most prototypical instances of nouns—people, objects, and places—and not in terms of abstractions, such as liberalism and beauty. This makes sense of the old-fashioned definition but of course does not make it right. We can define categories through prototypes, but such definition will not cover all the members. To include these, we need to go on and systematically explore and analyze the (family) relations among the central and noncentral members. This way we could avoid the frustration that we find no similarity (i.e., shared essential features) among all the members of a category (such as that of noun).

It seems then that the notion of prototype-based organization in categories can be applied to three distinct levels, or areas of language:

Categories for everyday concepts
Categories for senses of words
Categories for linguistic concepts

We will see a number of examples for prototype-based categories at each of these levels in the sections that follow and in later chapters.

Experimental Evidence for Prototype Categorization

In the 1970s, it was mainly Eleanor Rosch and her associates who turned all these issues into an empirical one (see, e.g., Rosch, 1978; Rosch and Mervis, 1975). As cognitive psychologists, they conducted a large number of experiments to find out about the "internal" structure of categories. They were interested in seeing whether the ideas suggested by philosophers and anthropologists concerning the structure of categories hold up in light of rigorous psychological experiments. Rosch and her colleagues used a number of techniques to study categories. These included the following:

Production of Examples

Subjects were asked to list members of particular categories, such as FRUIT, TOOL, TOY, and BIRD. Items that were frequently mentioned within each of these can be taken to be better examples of the category than those that are mentioned with lower frequency. Order of mention is another valuable result here. If a certain item is mentioned toward the end of a list of items that belong to a category, it is likely to be a less central member than another that is given at the top of the list. For example, a consistent result was that hammer and saw were more frequently produced and came earlier on subjects' lists than items such as wrenches and drills.

Direct Rating

In this task, subjects were asked to rate how good an example of a category a particular item is. It was a consistent finding that, for example, robin and chicken were rated differentially for the category of BIRD. Among American college students, a robin was found to be a better example of the category than chicken. We can expect cultural differences in the rating of particular categories. In other cultures, a different kind of bird or a different set of birds may be judged to be the best example of the category. This shows that, unlike the domain of COLOR, the rating of best examples may differ for the same category in different languages/cultures.

Reaction Time

Subjects were also asked to press a button to indicate the truth or falsity of statements that included different members of a category. Statements like "A chicken is a bird" and "A robin is a bird" were responded to differentially in terms of reaction time. Subjects responded much faster to the latter sentence than to the former. They found the truth of "A robin is a bird" easier to accept than that of "A chicken is a bird." Thus, shorter reaction times correlated with central examples, while longer ones with less central examples.

Priming

In this kind of task, subjects are presented with a string of letters that is a word related to the one we are interested in. For example, if we want to find out whether the concept of "apple" is a good or poor example of FRUIT, we can present the word *fruit* to the subjects and then we can ask them whether an apple is a fruit. The prime (fruit) will speed up the response to the question about apple more than it will about another less prototypical fruit, like date. Again, this example shows that prototypicality can be culture-dependent. Dates may not be a central member of the category FRUIT in the United States or the United Kingdom, but they may be an absolutely central member in Tunisia or other North African countries (Croft and Cruse, 2004).

In all of the studies that Rosch and her associates conducted, there were consistent goodness of example (GOE) ratings. If a particular item ranked high in one kind of task, then it also ranked high in the other tasks. All the categories that were examined revealed clear prototype effects: certain items in each of the categories (such as FURNITURE, FRUIT, VEHICLE, WEAPON, VEGE-TABLE, TOOL, BIRD, SPORT, TOY, CLOTHING) were judged to be better examples than others. For example, in the category of FURNITURE items like chair, sofa, table, and bed received higher goodness of example ratings than other items within the same category, such as radio, clock, vase, and ashtray.

We can draw important conclusions from this experimental work. The conclusions give further support for the ideas advocated by Wittgenstein and, as we will see shortly, by Brent Berlin and Paul Kay (1969). First, we find that categories are defined by family resemblance relations among the members and not by necessary and sufficient conditions for the application of a particular term. Second, we discover that not all members of a category are equally good instances of the category. Categories have best, good, not so good, and poor examples. Third, we realize that category boundaries are typically not sharp and fixed once and for all but often fuzzy and expandable.

This does not mean, though, that we cannot have categories with sharp boundaries. We can, but what is remarkable about many of such cases is that we can have graded category membership in categories that have sharp boundaries. One example of such a category is that of BIRD. We can tell a bird from something that is not a bird, and yet within the category we find graded membership. A robin is surely a better example of BIRD in, for example, North America than an ostrich is. What this suggests is that graded membership within a category does not exclude clear and sharp boundaries for that category. Furthermore, we can also have categories with fuzzy boundaries that are characterized by internal graded membership. For example, categories like TALL and RED have fuzzy boundaries together with graded membership inside the category. Given the average size of people in, say, Northern Europe, a person who is 190 centimeters tall is a better example of a tall person than someone who is 180 centimeters, and the redness of the human blood is normally considered to be a better example of red than the redness of the nose due to cold weather.

Exemplar Models

In classical models categories are represented by a rulelike definition: For example, the category of MAN is defined as a 'person (human) who is adult and male,' GIRL is a 'person who is young and female (or not male),' and so on. By contrast, as we just saw, in prototype models categories are represented in the mind by prototypes. According to Barsalou (1992: 28), "a prototype is a single, centralized, category representation." Such single, centralized representations arise from properties that are representative of particular exemplars. In other words, we abstract the representative properties on encountering particular instances of a category and integrate them into an abstract prototype for the category. Thus, for example, we abstract the properties "small," "sings," and "can fly" on our encounters with birds and integrate these properties into an abstract representation, which we call the prototype of the category BIRD.

Exemplar models do not use either rulelike definitions or abstract centralized prototypes in the way they represent categories. Instead, they rely on specific exemplar memories. These are memories of specific exemplars of a category (Barsalou, 1992: 26). On this view, people do not generalize their exemplar memories into an abstract prototype but will have "a loose collection of exemplar memories." Such exemplar memories will be associated to a category name (Barsalou, 1992: 26). For example, my category for chairs will be a loose collection of my memories of all the chairs that I have encountered. In exemplar models, an entity is assigned to a category on the basis of its similarity to exemplar memories.

Research on category representation showed that people's representation of categories contains both abstract centralized knowledge and specific memories of exemplars of a category (see, for example, Barsalou, 1992).

More Recent Views of Categorization

Most scholars, including linguists, anthropologists, and psychologists, working within the experientialist mode of explanation use prototype categorization as their chief way of accounting for their data. However, it has been observed by several researchers (both working within and working outside the experientialist mode) that the "traditional" view of prototype categorization is problematic in a major way (e.g., Barsalou, 1983; Croft and Cruse, 2004; Gibbs, 2003b; Smith and Samuelson, 1997); namely, in its assumption that categories are stable abstract mental representations. This became especially clear in Lawrence Barsalou's work. Barsalou (1983) worked with categories that people make up "on the fly" for a given purpose. Such "ad hoc" and "goal-derived" categories include FOOD TO EAT ON A DIET, THINGS TO TAKE ON A CAMPING TRIP, CLOTHING TO TAKE ON A VACATION, and so on. These categories have no conventional names (in contrast to CHAIR, BIRD, HAMMER, DOLL, etc.) and they are created to achieve a given goal (i.e., to lose weight, to do things on a camping trip, etc.). A remarkable result of Barsalou's experiments was that such ad hoc goal-derived categories produced prototype effects just like "normal" conventional categories do, such as CHAIR, BIRD, and so on. For example, people came up with low-calorie items for FOOD TO TAKE ON A DIET, such as celery, tofu, and rice cakes, most frequently and easily. The prototype for this ad hoc category was created by people on the basis of the goal relative to the category. Given that goal, people easily use goal-relevant properties, such as "low in caloric value," to create the prototype for the category. But such prototypes cannot be stable mental representations because they are made up on the fly for an immediate purpose! This finding clearly goes against the view of prototypes as stable mental representations.

More generally, several researches began to see prototypes not as preexisting abstract mental representations but as variable structures that are created on-line (i.e., in real time) in context given the goal of the situation. We just saw how the goal of the situation can specify the creation of prototypes. Other experiments showed that prototypes vary according to context. As an example, I mentioned earlier that dates may be a highly prototypical fruit in Tunisia, but they are not in many other parts of the world, where apples, pears, oranges, and the like are much more prototypical. In addition, Gibbs (2003b) notes that tea is judged to be a more typical drink in the context of secretaries taking a break, whereas milk is considered more typical among truck drivers. I would add that there are interesting cross-cultural differences among nations with respect to what citizens judge to be their prototypical drink taken in a break. A case in point is the United States and England. In the United States coffee is the prototypical drink that people take in a break, whereas in England it is tea. Such differences between context-dependent prototypes commonly form the basis of stereotypical presentations of national, ethnic, regional, gender-based, and so on, groups.

Finally, it seems that there is a great deal of individual variation and flexibility in the way individuals construct their mental representations for categories. For example, Barsalou (1993) showed that when people list properties for categories, such as CHAIR and BIRD, only 47% of the features offered by a particular individual coincide with features offered by another individual. Moreover, even the same individual may define a given category by means of somewhat different features on different occasions. Barsalou reports that only 66% of the features used to define categories (such as CHAIR and BIRD) showed up again when individuals offered definitions for the same categories weeks later.

These results lead to the conclusion that many or most categories are not represented by stable abstract prototypes but by flexible and temporary mental representations produced by individuals in context. I will discuss one such case in some detail in chapter 4.

Prototypes in Culture: Two Examples

It was noted earlier that we have categories for everyday concepts, categories for senses of words, and categories for linguistic concepts. We also saw earlier that the prototypes we have for categories are greatly determined by the context and goal of categorization. This situation has far-reaching implications for several cultural issues, two of which I will consider here.

One of them is intercultural understanding. It is clear that if prototypes differ from culture to culture, subculture to subculture, and so on, this will affect how we understand members of other groups. Most of the prototypes we saw in this chapter involved physical objects, such as chairs and birds. But prototype-based categories involve all kinds of abstractions as well, including emotions (anger, pride, joy, etc.), personal relationships (marriage, friendship, privacy, etc.), evaluative and personal qualities (beauty, intelligence, etc.), political concepts (democracy, conservatism, etc.), and more. Cultural differences in both concrete and abstract concepts may be a source of mutual misunderstanding. One obvious area where this is crucial is the learning of a foreign language and the effective use of this language with native speakers of the language. Consider the following conversation between a native speaker (NS) of Canadian English and a Chinese non-native speaker (NNS) of English taken from Donald Qi's work on "cultural prototypes" in

a foreign language teaching setting (2001, *http://www.utpjournals.com/jour
.ihtml?lp=product/cmlr/582/582-Qi.html*). The conversation comes from an
experiment where an NS and an NNS respond to and discuss the sentences
"The stories written in the newspaper today are not entirely factual. They
are largely made up for certain political purposes. For me they are lies and
sheer _____." A part of the conversation is reproduced here:

NS: Oh! I have come up with a more exact word. 'Propaganda'!
Because it's for political purposes. It fits the sentence better.

NNS: But propaganda is not necessarily a lie. Sometimes it is a lie.
Sometimes it could mean a good thing. For example, it gives you
information, doesn't it?

NS: No. Propaganda has a very negative meaning, which means you
are biased and you are promoting something political for the government's
convenience.

NNS: Oh. In China we use the word very frequently to mean a lot of
positive things. For example, the government has propaganda division,
propaganda office, et cetera. It is obviously used positively in these
contexts.

NS: That's hilarious! In English it will cause an entirely negative
feeling.

NNS: Oh, I see. There's a big difference in the use of the word between
the two languages. What word would you use to describe such a
situation positively in English?

NS: Could be PR agent—Public Relation agents—or Press Attaché to
promote the image of a political figure.

NNS: Okay.

As can be seen, the category of PROPAGANDA is largely negative for the English speaker, whereas it is neutral for the Chinese speaker of English. Needless to say, such differences in cultural prototypes may be the source of misunderstanding between speakers of different languages.

"Propaganda" is a concept that belongs to our everyday repertoire of concepts. Let us now take what we called a linguistic category—that of SENTENCE.
How can such a linguistic category be interesting for appreciating the role
prototypes play in culture? We commonly observe that the language of literature tends to be different from ordinary language. When we try to spell
out the details of such differences, we often note, among many other things,
that literary language is richer in imagery, more evocative of feelings, more
condensed as far as meaning is concerned, and the like. But another difference lies in the more formal aspects of language: namely, that often the sentences typically used in ordinary language are somehow different in their form
from the "sentences" we encounter in literature (Stockwell, 2002). In other
words, one of the distinguishing features of literary language is in the form
of the sentences it uses. For everyday purposes, we consider a sentence as "fully

formed" if it has a noun phrase and a verb phrase that predicates something about the noun phrase (i.e., it expresses a predication); if it locates an action or event in time (i.e., it has a finite verb form to indicate tense); if it contains a positive assertion about the world (i.e., if it is not a negative but a positive sentence); if it is in the declarative mood (i.e., it is not a question, imperative, etc.); and if it contains definite reference (i.e., it does not operate with words like *a* or *some*) (Stockwell, 2002: 35). According to Peter Stockwell (2002), such differences between ordinary language and literary language represent various degrees of deviation from the prototype of SENTENCE in ordinary language—with lack of predication indicating the greatest degree of deviation and indefinite reference the smallest degree. Here are some examples from Stockwell's work to illustrate these points:

No predicates:
London. Michaelmas Term lately over, and the Lord Chancellor sitting in Lincoln's Inn Hall. Implacable November weather.
(*Bleak House*, Charles Dickens)

Nonfinite sentence:
Philomel, with lullaby, lulla, lulla, lullaby
(*A Midsummer Night's Dream*, William Shakespeare)

No positive polarity:
I know not whether Laws be right,
Or whether Laws be wrong.
("The Ballad of Reading Gaol," Oscar Wilde)

Imperative sentence:
Look on my works, ye Mighty, and despair!
("Ozymandias," Percy Bysshe Shelley)

Not definite reference:
Someone must have been telling lies about Joseph K., for without his having done anything wrong he was arrested one fine morning.
(*The Trial*, Franz Kafka)

Stockwell suggests that the type of sentence we commonly find in literature that does not contain predicates is the most deviant relative to the fully formed ordinary sentence, whereas the literary sentence type that shows the least deviation is the one that contains no definite reference. It is clear, however, that literary language cannot be fully characterized on the basis of its deviation from the fully formed ordinary sentence; this is just one of the several dimensions to be considered for its characterization. By presenting these examples through Stockwell's work I meant to show that the notion of prototype is absolutely necessary for understanding a wide range of cultural issues and phenomena—as diverse as foreign language teaching and the interpretation and appreciation of literature.

Color and Linguistic Relativity

In the late 1960s, two anthropologists, Brent Berlin and Paul Kay, designed a large-scale study to see how the domain of COLOR is structured in a large number of different languages. Color was chosen because the prevailing view was that color terms arbitrarily carve up the world and the boundaries of the use of color terms vary from language to language. That is to say, the claim was that a particular color term, say, *red*, covers a different range on the color spectrum in every language. This variation was taken to be arbitrary. In general, the claim was taken to support the view that languages structure the world in an arbitrary fashion; that is, they impose arbitrary boundaries for categories.

Berlin and Kay (1969) wanted to see if this is indeed the case. They distinguished between basic and nonbasic color terms. Which color term is basic and which nonbasic was determined on the basis of the following characteristics of color terms:

If a color term is monolexemic (i.e., contains only one lexeme), it is likely to be basic (e.g., *red, green, blue*).

A color term is basic if its meaning is not included within that of another color term (e.g., *scarlet*). *Scarlet* is not a basic color term because its meaning is contained within the meaning of *red*.

A color term is basic if its use is not restricted to a single object. For example, *blond* is not a basic color term because its use is limited to the human hair (and maybe a small number of other objects).

A basic color term must be generally known. While *yellow* is a basic color term, the related color *saffron* is not because it is not used extensively by people.

Given these criteria, Berlin and Kay found a number of basic color terms (such as *red, green, black, white*) in a large variety of different languages from different parts of the world. Their subjects were native speakers of these languages. Berlin and Kay had their subjects perform two tasks. One was the usual task in color research before them. They asked subjects to track the boundaries of basic color terms. However, the other task was new in color research. Berlin and Kay made an important methodological change in gathering their data. Instead of only asking the question "Where is the boundary of a particular color term?" they asked a new question: "What is the best example of the application of a particular basic color term?" Subjects consistently pointed to a particular shade of a given basic color term. Focal colors began to emerge. These were:

Black, white, red, blue, green, yellow, brown, purple, pink, orange, gray.

The focal colors are the best examples of basic color categories, which are named by basic color terms. There are eleven of them in English. Other languages may have fewer, but it seems that no language has more than eleven basic color terms.

The focal colors are universal conceptually—even if there is no name for them in every language. They were found in all the languages that were studied.

Just as interestingly, Berlin and Kay discovered an evolutionary sequence for basic color terms. This means that basic color terms emerge in a universal sequence in every language. It is as follows:

Black, white
Red
Yellow, blue, green
Brown
Purple, pink, orange, gray

This means that if a language has two basic colors, they will be black and white; if it has three, they will be black, white, and red; if it has four, they will be black, white, red, and either yellow, blue, or green; and so on. As was mentioned, not all languages have all of these basic terms. Sometimes languages have only one basic term to refer to two color ranges, such as blue and green. In such a case, the best example will be either blue or green, not turquoise—a color between the two.

Given these findings by Berlin and Kay, an extremely important issue arises: Why do we have just these basic colors? Based on Berlin and Kay's findings and findings by physiologists who specialized in vision, Lakoff (1987) provides the following answer: Two groups can be distinguished within basic colors: *primary* and *nonprimary* basic colors. The two groups of basic colors emerge in different ways. To begin, a large part of what colors we see has to do with wavelength. Another important factor that determines what we see concerns the human physiology of vision. We have four kinds of opponent response cells in our nervous system to deal with color: blue-yellow cells and red-green cells. These determine hue. For example, as Lakoff (1987) says, +R, −G cells fire above their base rate in response to a red stimulus and below their base rate in response to a green stimulus; in contrast, +G, −R cells fire above their base rate in response to a green stimulus and below their base rate in response to a red stimulus.

Thus, we get primary colors when the red-green cells show either a red response or a green response and the blue-yellow cells fire at their base rate; we get primary colors when the blue-yellow cells show either a blue response or a yellow response and the red-green cells fire at their base rate. Therefore, the primary colors that we have accounted for so far are red, green, blue, and yellow. But what about black and white? These are additional primary colors, but they emerge in a physiologically different way. Lakoff (1987) describes their emergence as follows:

Black is perceived when darkness-sensitive cells fire at their maximum rate and the light-sensitive cells fire at their minimum rates (and when the blue-yellow and red-green cells fire at their neutral base rates). White is perceived when light-sensitive cells fire at their maximum rate and when the darkness-sensitive cells fire at their minimum rates (and when the blue-yellow and red-green cells fire at their neutral base rates).

Given these primary colors, our mind/brain is capable of turning the primary colors of black, white, red, yellow, green, blue into nonprimary ones: purple, orange, pink, brown, gray. Again, as Lakoff explains: "When the blue-yellow cells show a blue response and the red-green cells show a red response, we perceive purple." In other words, purple is a combination of blue and red. Similarly, we get the further combinations:

Purple: blue + red
Orange: red + yellow
Pink: red + white
Brown: black + yellow
Gray: black + white

As this brief survey of research on color indicates, color categories are determined by four distinct factors. First, they are determined by the external physical world. This is how wavelength plays a role in color perception. Second, human biology (the structure of our nervous system) is crucially involved in how we see basic primary colors, such as black, red, and blue. Third, the human mind has the capability to combine primary basic colors into nonprimary basic colors, such as purple and pink. Fourth, culture is again a crucial factor in that it determines which color categories there are in a particular language and it also determines the boundaries of the use of color terms. This last point shows that previous research on color made partially valid observations, in that the boundaries of color terms are governed by cultural convention. The ranges of the application of color terms may indeed vary from language to language, culture to culture. However, this is just a part of the story, and it seems that it is not the most important part. The application of basic color terms appears to be universal when we use them of the best examples of color categories. People from a variety of different cultures have in mind the same range of the color spectrum when the focal colors are involved. In sum, color categories are exemplar-based categories—and they seem to involve both cross-culturally and temporarily stable exemplars.

However, the notion that focal colors are based on neurological structure and functioning remains just a hypothesis. (See, e.g., the interview with Paul Kay in *Scientific American*, April 2004, *www.sciam.com/article.cfm?articleID =00055EE3-4530-1052-853083414B7F0000*. The interview was brought to my attention by Alan Cienki.) Future research on higher-order neural processing will tell us whether the hypothesis stands or falls. At the same time, there is no other convincing alternative explanation for the universality of focal colors. (For further recent developments in color research, see, e.g., Kay and Maffi, 2000; *http://www.google.com/search?q=cache:JHjxktylVsAJ:www .psych.uchicago.edu/~regier/papers/cogscio5.8.pdf+kay+and+regier&hl=hu& client=firefox-a* and the references therein.)

The Sapir-Whorf Hypothesis

As mentioned in chapter 1, "linguistic relativity" is an influential hypothesis that concerns the relationship between the language we speak and the way we think and act. It was developed by a number of scholars, among them Edward Sapir, but it became best known through the writings of Benjamin Lee Whorf (1956), an American linguist who worked in the first half of the twentieth century; hence another name for the same view: the Sapir-Whorf hypothesis.

Linguistic relativity comes in a strong and weak version:

> *Strong version*: The language we speak determines the way we think.
> *Weak version*: The language we speak influences the way we think.

If the strong version were true, it would be impossible, or next to impossible, to learn a foreign language. We would be prisoners in the "prison house of our own language." But many people learn foreign languages, often several languages, and often acquire native or near-native competence in them. In addition, if our native language strictly determined the way we think, we could not translate from one language to another. Clearly, then, our cognitive abilities (such as learning another language and translation) are not limited in this strong sense by our native language. For reasons such as these, the strong version of the theory has minimal support among scholars.

But more interestingly, is the weak version of the hypothesis true? Does language shape thought in a less deterministic fashion? As we saw in chapter 1, opinions vary, and scholars adduce evidence both for and against it. How does prototype theory, and especially the study of color, bear on the linguistic relativity hypothesis? If anything, Berlin and Kay's study on color indicates that perception (a cognitive process) leads to the emergence of basic color terms. The perception of salient (focal) colors causes us to establish and name a particular set of color categories. That is, we have an effect that is the exact opposite of what linguistic relativity would predict: An aspect of thought (perception) influences language (establishing basic color terms), not the other way around.

Before Berlin and Kay's research it was widely believed that the domain of COLOR is an ideal area for showing effects of color language on color cognition. As Berlin and Kay's work also indicated, the boundaries of color terms vary greatly across languages (and even across individuals speaking the same language) and color languages can make very different distinctions in naming colors. For example, one language may distinguish between blue and green, while another may not. It can be demonstrated that if a color language has a certain vocabulary distinction, this will lead to an easier recognition of that distinction in actual color. In other words, the Whorfian effect of language structure on cognition (in this case, color recognition) was generally taken to be true. However, the Berlin-Kay finding that color cognition (the perception of salient colors) leads to the establishment of basic color terms dealt a first serious blow to the linguistic relativity hypothesis.

But how can we ever be sure that it is thought (color cognition) that influences language (the establishment of basic color terms), rather than language influencing thought? The only way to get around this problem in our research design would involve finding a language that has a minimal color vocabulary (i.e., that uses far fewer than eleven basic color terms) and if we can have the speakers of such a language learn names for the basic and nonbasic colors that their language does not name. Given this situation, our hypotheses could be the following:

1. If such speakers learn names for basic colors faster than for nonbasic ones, we have shown that color cognition (in this case, learning) influences color language (in this case, the establishment of a set of basic color terms).

2. If such speakers learn names for both basic and nonbasic colors at the same rate, we cannot be sure of such an influence and it is still an open question whether color cognition influences color language or color language influences color cognition.

In other words, several things must be done. We must find such a language and if we find it we must teach the speakers of such a language names for basic and nonbasic colors that their language does not have. Rosch (Heider [Rosch], 1972; Heider [Rosch] and Olivier, 1972; Rosch, 1973, 1974) found such a language—the Dani language spoken in New Guinea. Dani has only two color terms: *mili* (covering the dark-cool colors: black, green, blue) and *mola* (covering the light-warm colors: white, red, yellow). It lacks color terms for the eight chromatic colors (red, blue, etc.). She also managed to have speakers of Dani learn names for basic and nonbasic colors identified by standardized color chips. Since the Dani have only two color names, to teach them names for basic and nonbasic colors she used Dani tribal names.

The results of the experiments conducted by Rosch were unequivocal. The Dani systematically learned the basic color terms faster and with fewer errors than the nonbasic ones. This indicates that color cognition has systematic influence on color language—even in the case of a language that does not originally have color terms for the chromatic colors. This way, we get strong evidence against the Sapir-Whorf hypothesis that it is language that influences thought. The appropriate conclusion seems to be that, at least in the domain of COLOR, the theory of linguistic relativity appears not to hold.

Does it hold in other domains? As we saw in the first chapter, there is some evidence that it does. I will come back to the issue in several later chapters.

Conclusions

One of our most essential abilities to survive is the ability to categorize the objects and events around us. By creating conceptual categories we make sense of the world; when we encounter new objects and events we assign them to already-existing categories or create new ones to accommodate them. A large part of meaning making involves the process of categorization and the product of this process—conceptual categories. We set up and use categories unconsciously and without any effort most of the time. Thus, meaning making is also an unconscious and effortless activity most of the time.

As Barsalou (1992) explains, the way we form categories is a complex cognitive process. It involves the following five steps: (1) Form a structural description of the entity; (2) Search for category representations similar to the structural description; (3) Select the most similar category representation; (4) Draw inferences about the entity; and (5) Store information about the categorization.

How do we mentally represent categories in heads? We have considered three models of the mental representation of categories: the classical model, prototype categorization, and exemplar models. The classical model is based on rulelike definitions of categories that operate with what are called semantic features. This is known as componential analysis, since meaning is seen as being composed of systematic semantic components, such as HUMAN, ADULT, MALE. This way of thinking about categories and their mental representations goes back to Aristotle, who made a distinction between essential and peripheral attributes. In componential analysis, the mental representations for categories can be taken to be minimal definitions given in terms of essential features. In other words, in this view a category can be given in terms of the necessary and sufficient conditions for the use of the category. It is such necessary and sufficient conditions that hold categories together. If something does not have all the necessary and sufficient conditions, then it cannot be a member of the category.

The model of prototype categorization claims that instead of necessary and sufficient conditions categories are represented in the mind as prototypes, or best examples, for categories. These consist of an abstract idealization of category members. Thus, we have an abstract idealization for each of the categories BIRD, TOY, GAME, and the like. Categories defined by prototypes do not all share a single essential set of features. Rather, members of a category are held together by what Wittgenstein called "family resemblance" to a prototype. On this view, items may belong to a category even if they share only some (but not *all*) features with the prototype, that is to say, if they bear sufficient family resemblance to it. The view of prototype categorization as developed by Rosch and her colleagues was later criticized by several scholars, who suggested that in Rosch's view prototype was too abstract and static. New experimental evidence showed that prototypes are created in specific contexts for specific goals and thus cannot be conceived as abstract stable mental representations. Most of the prototypes we have are culturally determined prototypes. The term *cultural prototype* suggests that our mental representations of categories are both cognitive and cultural in nature.

Berlin and Kay studied the domain of color in a large number of languages. They wanted to check whether languages carve up the color spectrum in an arbitrary fashion, as was believed to be the case by most researchers at the time. In their research, they shifted attention from the question "Where are the boundaries of specific colors?" to "What is the best example of a particular color?" This methodological shift resulted in the discovery of basic colors denoted by basic color terms. In addition, they discovered that the emergence of basic color terms in the world's languages follows an evolutionary sequence from *black, white, red,* and so on, to *pink, orange,* and *gray.*

Since the basic colors may be at least partially based on universal aspects of color physiology, the existence of basic color terms may point to the conclusion that it is color perception that determines/shapes the naming of colors. Despite the initial optimism expressed in chapter 1, such a conclusion would go against the linguistic relativity, or Sapir-Whorf, hypothesis, which states that it is language that determines/shapes what we perceive. However, as we will see in later chapters, the domain of COLOR may be unique in this regard and other domains may yield "Whorfian effects" in which language does indeed shape thought.

Exercises

1. Conduct a little informal experiment. Ask as many people as you can (at least ten) the following questions and tell them to reply as fast as they can so they say the first word that comes to their mind. (If you want to exclude the possible influence of thoughts or ideas that may concern your respondents at the time of your experiment, you may resort to the technique of "reverse priming." Thus, instead of preparing a mental ground for your question by introducing the topic, you want your respondent's mind to be a "clean slate," a "blank page," as it were. You may achieve this psychological state by making them do mental operations that are completely unrelated to the area of your interest. For instance, right before asking question a, you could have your respondents do simple addition tasks several times in a row (e.g., six plus zero equals?, three plus three equals?, two plus four equals?, one plus five equals?). After a few of these, you should ask your question, which will this way be completely unexpected, and the answer will therefore reflect their true immediate associations.)

    a. What is the first vegetable that comes to your mind?
    b. Name a tool that a carpenter uses.

Write down what they say and ask yourself questions such as the following: Are there any items that occur with a significantly greater frequency than others? How do you account for this phenomenon? What theory do the answers prove? If you have managed to ask people with different cultural backgrounds and places of origin or residence, you might want to investigate the link (if any) between these factors and their answers.

2. Take the many uses of the noun *ring.* Which one is prototypical? What are some of the noncentral cases? How can you account for the meaning differences among the uses? Make use of the notions of "prototype," "noncentral

members of a category," "family resemblance," and "attributes" (or "semantic features"). Here are a few senses you may use to get you started (be sure to discuss at least **six total**; you may certainly include these):

a. Take this *ring* as a sign of my love and fidelity.
b. I want to buy some napkin *ring*s that match my tablecloth.
c. The FBI finally caught the leader of the smuggling *ring*.

3. Let's assume you want to study the category of TOYS and its internal structure (prototype effects, more central and peripheral category members). How would you go about planning an experiment that would be carried out among children? (Think of the number of participants, age, possible methods.) Do you expect any interesting results? Why? If you can, do your experiment with "real-life" participants and compare your results with your predictions and anticipations.

4. Ask ten people to list as many examples of the category of HOUSE as they can. Write down the examples in the order they were mentioned. Then try to see if different individuals mentioned the same examples. If they did, check to see if you can find a correlation between the shared examples and the order in which they were mentioned. What conclusions can you draw from this in light of what you have learned in this chapter?

5. In one interpretation, the Sapir-Whorf hypothesis claims that the language we speak determines the way we think. We have seen earlier that in the domain of COLOR this idea does not work. However, in other domains the theory may apply. Consider the following sentence: *One small step for man, one giant leap for mankind.* Ask several people how they interpret the sentence. Do they tend to imagine males *and* females or, rather, females *or* males only? What do your findings tell you about linguistic relativity?

Levels of Interacting with the World

Cognitive and Cultural Considerations

We can think of prototype-based categories as being on a "horizontal" level. Adjacent categories are "next to" each other; we have a prototype for CHAIR, a prototype for TABLE, and a prototype for SOFA. These are neighboring categories within the larger, more inclusive category of FURNI-TURE. When we look at the "highest-level" category and its "lower-level" members, we are dealing with a "vertical" level of categorization. The categories in such a vertical perspective are at different levels of generalization, or abstraction: The highest-level category is the most general, or abstract, with the categories below it being less general, or abstract. Finally, the categories at the various levels are related to one another in a hierarchy; that is, the highest member includes the members below it. We can call such hierarchies taxonomic hierarchies.

Such hierarchies are the products of both cognitive and cultural factors. This chapter discusses the theories we have for taxonomic hierarchies, the properties that characterize the different levels, and the role cultural factors play in shaping the cognitive processes that lead to the emergence of category hierarchies.

Theories of Taxonomic Hierarchies

Similar to the discussion of prototypes, here I will consider several theories of taxonomic hierarchies; in particular, what can be called the classical theory and what has become known as basic-level categorization. As a matter of fact, we will also look at a third and more recent theory that operates with "global categories" and is a critique of the view of basic-level categorization. However, the discussion of global categories will have to wait until we have reviewed the properties of basic-level categories in some detail.

Classical Theory of Vertical Categories

American psychologist Roger Brown noted in the 1950s that we can refer to things at various levels of generalization (1958). For example, if you have a dime in your pocket, you can use many different words or phrases to talk about it. You can refer to it as money, as a 1952 dime with a scratch, as a dime, as a metal object, or as a thing. We can arrange all these different ways of referring to a dime in the following hierarchy, ranging from the most to the least general:

> Thing; metal object; money; **dime**; a 1952 dime; a particular 1952 dime with a scratch

He also noted that in a neutral context the most natural way for people to talk about the coin in one's pocket is to call it a dime. (This is why the word appears in boldface.) Although this is an example of hierarchical categorization that is specific to American culture, the phenomenon it represents is very general. Observations like this by Brown and others concerning the existence of such an intuitively natural level of categorization led to an entire research paradigm in the study of human categorization.

Many taxonomic hierarchies have been examined by researchers. A consistent finding was that most of our categories can be placed at different levels of conceptual organization in such taxonomic hierarchies. Consider the additional examples of such taxonomies in table 3.1.

As with prototypes, we can ask what holds these taxonomic hierarchies together. According to the classical view, the hierarchies are held together by class inclusion. Level 1 classes include level 2 classes, and these include level 3 classes. The classes are defined by features. The features that characterize higher-level classes are included in the characterization of lower-level classes. For example, the features that characterize the category of VEHICLE are included in the characterization of CAR, and those of CAR are included in the characterization of SEDAN. The lower-level classes always have features in addition to the ones that they inherit from the higher levels.

Levels of Categorization in a Cognitive Framework

This neat picture based on logical inclusion fails to account for an important and, from the point of view of classical categorization, curious aspect of vertical hierarchies, namely, that there is a level in the hierarchy that seems to have a "superior status," in that, as was noted earlier, it seems to us to be the most natural level at which we engage with things in the world. Somehow the middle level is privileged; it is psychologically more important than the others (Rosch et al., 1976). This is the level at which people most readily name objects in the world. The general term that came to be used for this level is *basic level*. In a neutral context, when I am asked to identify a vehicle with four wheels with a driver driving it along a freeway, my most likely response

Table 3.1. Examples of Taxonomic Hierarchies

Level 1	Furniture		
Level 2	Chair	Table	Lamp
Level 3	Kitchen chair, living-room chair	Kitchen table, dining-room table	Floor lamp, desk lamp
Level 1	Vehicle		
Level 2	Car	Truck	Train
Level 3	Sedan, limo	Dump truck, garbage truck	Passenger train, freight train
Level 1	Emotion		
Level 2	Anger	Fear	Happiness
Level 3	Fury, irritation	Terror, fright	Gladness, euphoria

is that it is a car and not a vehicle or a limo. The three levels we distinguished earlier are the following:

LEVEL 1: SUPERORDINATE LEVEL: vehicle
LEVEL 2: BASIC LEVEL: car
LEVEL 3: SUBORDINATE LEVEL: limo

The same effect of automatically identifying objects at the basic level remains even if we consider more levels of categorization, as is customary in biological classifications. Plant and animal terms are commonly classified at a variety of additional levels (Lakoff, 1987). For example:

UNIQUE BEGINNER: plant; animal
LIFE-FORM: tree, bush, bird, fish
INTERMEDIATE: leaf-bearing tree, needle-bearing tree
GENUS: oak, maple, rabbit, raccoon
SPECIES: sugar maple, white oak
VARIETY: cutleaf staghorn sumac

In this case the psychologically privileged level is that of the genus. It is at this level where we most commonly identify things under everyday (nonspecial) circumstances. Above the level of the genus we have levels that correspond to the superordinate level; and below it, levels that correspond to the subordinate level. The level of the genus itself corresponds to the basic level. While anthropologists use a more varied set of levels, in cognitive psychology, and especially in work on categorization, it is more common to work with the three-way distinction that has the basic level in the middle of the hierarchy with the superordinate level above it and the subordinate level below it. For our purposes, it will also suffice to use the three-level distinction.

The categories at the different levels possess some general linguistic characteristics (Croft and Cruse, 2004). For example, categories at the superordinate level are often mass nouns, such as FURNITURE, FOOD, SILVERWARE,

FOOTWEAR. Other superordinate categories, however, are not, such as SPICES, including pepper and paprika, and METALS, including bronze, iron, and steel. Subordinate categories are linguistically often polymorphemic. They commonly represent modifier-head constructions (such as *kitchen chair*, *sugar maple*, and *sports car*).

Basic-Level Categories and Their Properties

Categories at the basic level are characterized by a number of consistent properties. I have mentioned one of these so far—namely, the property that it is the basic level at which people are fastest at identifying category members (e.g., oak, rose, grass, rabbit, pig, car, truck, train).

Second, this is the highest level at which category members have similar overall shapes. For example, we have a pretty good idea of overall shape of the basic-level object of chair, but we do not have any such clear shape in mind for its superordinate category, FURNITURE. It is hard to think of the shape of furniture that is not the shape of a particular kind of furniture, such as chair or sofa.

Third, this is the highest level at which we interact with category members using the same motor actions. We do not know how to act in relation to the category of FURNITURE in general, but we know precisely how we typically interact with chairs; that is, we can easily demonstrate the kinds of actions we perform in connection with chairs (as when we sit down on them). The same applies to many other basic-level objects and their superordinate categories. We smell flowers, kick or throw balls, stroke cats, and so on, but we find it difficult to demonstrate our motor actions in relation to plants, toys, or animals, in general.

Fourth, this is the communicatively most important level in a variety of different ways. This is the level with the most commonly used labels for category members. Basic-level terms like *cat*, *dog*, *flower*, *ball*, *wine*, *water*, and so on, are probably much more common in everyday language use than either superordinate or subordinate category names. The basic level is the first level used by children. It is the first level that appears historically in a language. It is the level with the shortest lexemes. And, finally, it is the level at which terms are used in a neutral context, a feature of basic level terms alluded to earlier. If I see a dog on the porch, I am much more likely to say, "There's a dog on the porch," than to say, "There's a mammal on the porch," or, "There's a wire-haired terrier on the porch" (Cruse, 1977).

Fifth, it is the highest level at which a large number of attributes are given for categories. In several experiments (e.g., Rosch and Mervis, 1975) subjects listed attributes for categories (such as "has four legs," "used to sit on," "has a back," etc., for CHAIR). The overall result was that very few attributes were listed for superordinate categories (such as FURNITURE), a large number of attributes were listed for basic-level categories (such as CHAIR), and only a few more were listed for subordinate categories (e.g., KITCHEN CHAIR) than were listed for basic-level ones.

In other words, a category is basic in terms of four important dimensions of experience:

In terms of PERCEPTION: We have a similar overall shape for basic-level categories. We do not have such overall shapes for superordinate ones.

In terms of ACTION: We perform similar motor actions in relation to basic-level categories. We do not perform similar motor actions in relation to superordinate-level categories.

In terms of COMMUNICATION: We have words for basic-level categories that are the shortest, are learned first, enter the lexicon first, and are used in neutral contexts.

In terms of KNOWLEDGE: We possess a large amount of knowledge (in the sense of knowing a large number of attributes) about basic-level categories.

Part-whole relations are especially important in determining the characteristics of the basic level. Part-whole relations determine most of the properties of basic-level categories. Take overall shape. Objects, either man-made or natural, have parts. Given the parts that make up an object and given the configuration of these parts that make up the whole, the object's overall shape will follow. For example, human beings have a head that is situated at the top of a canonical, that is, erect, trunk. These parts and this configuration will result in a characteristic overall shape for human beings. The same applies to motor activity. A car consists of many parts, one of these being the steering wheel, which has a circular shape and is rotatable. The motor action that primarily characterizes our relation to a car is that of using our hands in turning the steering wheel left and right. And much of our knowledge also comes from what we know about which parts make up the whole and from what we know about the parts themselves.

The Nature of Properties That Define Basic-Level Categories

If we look at the attributes or properties that define basic-level categories, we find that most of them have to do with perception, motor activity, function, or purpose. Consider, for example, the category CHAIR and some of the features that people are most likely to use to characterize chairs. Such features would include "has a particular shape (typical chair shape)," "has four legs," "has a seat," "may have arms and a back," "is used to sit on," "is used in homes and offices," and so on. Typical shape has to do with perception, that is, how we see the outline of chairs; having legs, arms, a seat, and a back determines the kinds of motor activities that we can perform in relation to chairs; the idea that we use chairs to sit on them indicates the function that they have for us; and using them in the home or office suggests the kinds of purposes to which we put them, such as working, eating, relaxing, and others. In other words, the features that characterize and define basic-level categories seem to reflect the interaction of human beings with these categories and do not appear to be inherent in the categories themselves.

Perception, motor activity, function, purpose, and other dimensions of human experience are concerned with the way we interact with the environment. Therefore, the attributes we use to define basic-level categories are "interactional properties" and not objectively existing properties inherent in the categories themselves. This is a crucial difference between experientialist and objectivist approaches to meaning and understanding. While objectivist approaches attempt to define categories in terms of objective features inherent in objects and events, experientialist approaches attempt to capture those properties that people intuitively use in defining and distinguishing their experiences.

A Challenge to Basic Level as the Entry Level

While the theory of basic-level categorization outlined earlier seems reasonable and makes intuitive sense, certain aspects of it came under criticism by a number of scholars. In particular, Jean M. Mandler and her associates challenged the view that it is basic-level categories that provide an entry level in the development of hierarchical categories (e.g., Mandler and Bauer, 1988; Mandler, Bauer, and McDonough, 1991). These scholars suggest that the first categories that appear in children are more general than what Rosch and her associates term *basic-level* ones; Mandler and her colleagues call these first categories global ones and distinguish them from superordinate categories of the kind we have seen earlier in this chapter. At the same time, however, Mandler and her associates also suggest that the more "sophisticated" superordinate categories of adults derive from the global ones developed by very young children.

Mandler, P. J. Bauer, and L. McDonough (1991: 295) characterize their rival theory in the following way:

> The data we have presented suggest that in the domains of animals, plants, and vehicles, and perhaps in other domains as well, basic-level categories, as formulated by Rosch and Mervis (1975) and Rosch et al. (1976), do not form the entry level in the development of hierarchical categorical systems. Rather, children appear to begin categorizing at a more global level; only gradually do these global categories become differentiated. We assume that such differentiation involves making conceptual distinctions that are initially absent, even when perceptual differentiation is present. The language adults use when labeling and talking about objects to children may provide some of the impetus toward the more detailed conceptualizations that basic-level concepts represent.

Mandler and her associates found evidence for the existence of such global categories in the second year, whereas most of the research on the basis of which initial basic-level concepts were proposed came from three- to-five-year-old children. These researchers also argue that previous research put too much emphasis on the notion of "similarity," especially "perceptual similarity," as the basis for forming categories in very young children (but also later on in life); that is, it may not be the case that children and adults form categories on the basis that certain objects look alike (i.e., based on their physical appearance). Instead, these researchers suggest that category membership crucially depends on judgments that concern what *kind* of thing an object is. In other words, the suggestion is that very young children unconsciously operate with "theories" for kinds of things. (On such intuitive theories, or the "theory theory" of category formation, see Murphy and Medin, 1985.) Global categories are based on "minitheories" that the child develops for purposes of categorization. For example, the category of ANIMAL might be defined in terms of a simple theory according to which it is 'an object that can move by itself'. In this mode of categorization, perceptual features do not play the most important role. The possible perceptual dissimilarity of different animals is less important than the fact that they are the same kind of thing as defined by the minitheory.

The view of global categories as the entry level of category development challenges an important aspect of basic-level categorization. However, it seems that it does not affect and challenge many other important aspects of the same theory. Most significantly, we can still see the basic level as the level where older children and adults primarily interact with the world.

Why Do We Need the Basic Level?

Finally, let us ask the most basic question in connection with the basic level: Why do we need basic-level categories at all? What was the point of establishing such a level at which to categorize things and events? We can provide an answer to this question if we consider the general goal of human categorization. We categorize the world under two contradictory pressures. On the one hand, we want to group together items in the world that we find similar to one another. This is why we have items that share properties such as "has a particular shape," "has a seat," "has four legs," "is used to sit on," and so on, in a category we call CHAIR. On the other hand, we also want our categories to reflect distinctions in the world. We want to distinguish chairs from tables and sofas. It is important for us to make such distinctions in the world. The level of basic-level categories can serve this double purpose in an ideal way: At that level we group together items that are maximally similar to one another and, at the same time, the resulting categories will be maximally different from one another. By contrast, at the superordinate level members of a category (such as FURNITURE) will be fairly different from one another (chair, table, sofa, clock, telephone). And also, at the subordinate level, although members of a category (such as KITCHEN CHAIR) will be similar to one another, the subordinate categories themselves will be similar to one another as well (such as kitchen chairs will be similar to living-room chairs). In other words, basic-level categories seem to be our best compromise to simultaneously satisfy the contradictory pressures of working with categories that minimize differences among category members, on the one hand, and categories that maximize differences between a category and neighboring categories, on the other hand. This means that we have a level of categorization at which we code maximal discontinuities in the world among objects, events, and so forth, and minimal differences among items that make up categories.

The Role of Culture in the Creation
of Basic-Level Categories

Given the characterization of basic-level categorization in the preceding sections, we may note two highly important additional features of human categorization. One is that it seems that what some people take to be the basic level may not be the basic level for others. In other words, there exists the phenomenon of basic-level nonuniversality. The other is that laypeople's basic-level categories coincide remarkably closely with the categories that scientists use, but on other levels there is a great deal of divergence in categorization. These two features clearly show that we cannot explain categorization only and simply as a *cognitive* process—culture plays an equally important role.

The Nonuniversality of the Basic Level

Consider the following problem that basic-level categorization runs into in many cases: When people are asked to list attributes for the category TREE, they tend to list a large number of attributes. This should not happen if TREE were a superordinate category (and OAK, PINE, MAPLE, etc., were basic-level). Superordinate categories, as we saw, are characterized by a small number of attributes, unlike basic-level ones, where most of the attributes for categories are given. Why did TREE become a basic-level category for people? The issue is further compounded by the suggestion that basic-level categories are defined by interactional properties. If interactional properties play such an important role in defining basic-level categories and human beings share cognitive capacities that give rise to such properties (perception, motor activity, function, etc.), how come often basic-level categories are not universal? After all, the level of genus is based on shared cognitive capacities. To put the question simply, if we have the same cognitive capacities universally, how come we find a lack of universality in levels of categorization? I provide an answer to this question along the lines of Lakoff (1987).

First of all, we should note that TREE is a basic-level category only in urban cultures. When indigenous people or people who live close to nature are asked to identify things in nature, they automatically respond with basic-level categories, such as OAK, MAPLE, and so on. Life in big cities has caused a loss in certain of our cognitive capacities. City dwellers seem to underutilize certain cognitive capacities, like gestalt perception. For most city dwellers all trees have a single characteristic shape, and they tend not to make finer distinctions in the overall shape of different kinds of trees, such as oak and maple. Thus, the underutilization of some cognitive capacities involved in categorization due to changes in human living can explain this form of nonuniversality in basic-level categorization.

Another form of nonuniversality occurs when some people use the level of the species as the basic level. Why does this happen? Take, for example, how certain people, such as horse breeders, use different kinds of horses as their basic level, where most people simply see "horse." In this case, the opposite of the previous situation occurs. The species is regarded as the basic level. In this case, cognitive capacities involved in categorization are "overutilized," not underutilized. This can happen due to the special training in certain subcultures, such as among horse breeders. The phenomenon is well known among many highly specialized subcultures, like those of skiers, surfers, and sailors, who can easily distinguish many different kinds of snow, waves, and wind. In their specialized lifestyles, what are subordinate (and mostly unnamed) categories for other people become basic-level categories for them.

Why Do Folk and Expert Categories Agree on the Basic Level?

As we have seen in this chapter, people see and use their categories at different levels of generality. This applies to both laypeople and experts. The distinction between laypeople and experts in connection with categorization is important because the system of categories used by everyday people, or laypeople, often does not correspond to the system used by scientists, or experts. We can call a system of categories for a particular domain used by everyday "folks" folk categorization; while a corresponding system of categories used by scientists, or experts, scientific categorization.

It is a common observation that categories that people use at the basic level fit categories that scientists use very accurately, but at other levels the categories fit much less accurately. Why is it that folk categorization fits scientific categorization at the basic level very well but not very closely at other levels? Both everyday people and scientists talk about apples, tomatoes, carrots, tigers, water, gold, and so on. Folk and scientific categorization correspond to each other at this level. This is the level that gives rise to what philosophers call natural kinds. However, when it comes to higher and lower levels of generalization, there are discrepancies between "folk" and "expert" classification systems. This is not particularly surprising, given the nature and sophistication of the scientific enterprise. What is remarkable is that folk classifications and scientific ones so remarkably agree at the basic level. What is the reason for this? Lakoff (1987) suggests that scientists set up the level of the genus (the level that corresponds to the basic level) by making use of most of the same psychological (perceptual and other) criteria that everyday people use. For example, Linnaeus used shape of the fruit as the basis for his definition of genus (Lakoff, 1987). Given the level of genus, it was assumed that differences between genera in scientific biology reflected real discontinuities of nature.

Conclusions

We have seen the main characteristics of three theories that are used to explain taxonomic hierarchies of conceptual categories: the classical theory, basic-level categories, and global categories. Essentially, the classical theory of hierarchic categories operates with the notion of "logical feature inclusion." Categories at the highest level of a taxonomy possess only a small number of features, while categories at lower levels possess the same features as the categories at the highest level as well as an increasing number of additional ones. On this view, it is difficult to explain why the middle of the hierarchy has a distinctive status for speakers. The theory of basic-level categorization accounts for the psychological primacy of the middle level by claiming that this is the level where categories can simultaneously meet two basic demands: the pressure for maximal similarity among category members and the pressure of maximal dissimilarity between neighboring categories. The theory of global categories criticizes the theory of basic-level categorization in respect to the issue of which categories serve as the entry level for the development of categories in very young children. Proponents of global categories suggest that children first develop not basic-level but global categories that later get differentiated into basic-level ones.

Basic-level categories are characterized by a number of distinctive features in four major dimensions, in particular, the dimensions of perception, action, communication, and knowledge. As far is perception is concerned, we have a similar overall shape for basic-level categories. We do not have such overall shapes for superordinate ones. The dimension of action is relevant in that we perform similar motor actions in relation to basic-level categories. We do not perform similar motor actions in relation to superordinate-level categories. As regards communication, we have words for basic-level categories that are the shortest, are learned first, enter the lexicon first, and are used in neutral contexts. The view of global categories denies that it is basic-level categories that are learned first by children. Finally, the dimension of knowledge is important because we possess a large amount of knowledge (in the sense of knowing a large number of attributes) about basic-level categories. The number of attributes provided for superordinate categories is far smaller, and it is just a few attributes more in the case of subordinate ones.

Categorization in general and levels of categorization for particular people is just as much a matter of culture as it is a matter of cognition. The cultural contexts in which the categorization takes place play a crucial role in why people categorize particular objects and events at particular levels of abstraction.

Exercises

1. Think about the popular game Activity. Which words would you be able to draw, mime, or explain in words more easily when playing this game?

You may want to test your anticipated results in real life as well. Explain your answer in relation to what you have learned in this chapter:

   a. animal, bird, or sparrow
   b. furniture, chair, or kitchen chair
   c. vehicle, car, or Porsche
   d. food, sausage, or pepperoni

2.
A. Complete the missing elements of this chart. In some cases the answer is subjective.

	GAME	
		PEN
BUS NR. 102		

The horizontal lines of the chart represent (downward) the superordinate, the basic, and the subordinate levels.

   B. Work in pairs. Try to act out with body movements the basic-level terms you have in your chart. Your partner should try to guess what your words are. Repeat the same task with sub-/superordinate terms. Was this last task easier or more difficult?

   3. Can a specific category change levels (e.g., the category COMPUTER shifting from basic to superordinate level), and if so, what enables that category to alter its levels and why? Can you think of any other examples for a similar phenomenon?

   4.
A. According to the color research of Berlin and Kay, which of the following definitions distinguish basic color terms from nonbasic ones? On reading the following statements carefully, try to decide the category (i.e., basic or nonbasic) to which they belong.

B = basic color term   N = nonbasic color term

   a. The color referred to by the term is contained within another
      color.   ____
   b. It is restricted to a small number of objects, such as hair, wood,
      and other things.   ____
   c. It consists of only one morpheme rather than more than one. ____
   d. It is rarely used and is generally not known. ____
   e. The central members of these color terms are not the same
      universally.   ____

   B. Based on the preceding statements, group the following colors into the appropriate categories.

   brunette, blue, pink, dark brown, blue-violet, black, ocher, saffron, buff

5.

A. Note that TREE is only a basic-level category in urban societies, where—due to changes in human living conditions—some cognitive capacities (namely, the need for distinction between different kinds of trees) have become underutilized. Can you think of any other possible examples of the underutilization of cognitive capacities that could result in a shift from superordinate-level categories to basic-level categories?

B. Think of the opposite procedure, when experts as a result of their wider, more specific knowledge use the names that denote subordinate levels as basic-level categories. For example, horse breeders (for horses), skiers (for snow types), surfers (for the curves of waves), and so on. Can you think of any other highly specialized subcultures in which a basic-level term in "mainstream" culture would "only" be at the superordinate level?

6. What can you see in Figure 3.1.? There are many ways to answer this question. (One may choose from a number of possibilities, like *Ciconia ciconia*; *white stork*; *stork*; *bird, animal*, etc.) Do this exercise with five to ten respondents, and write down what their answers reveal about basic-level categories.

Figure 3.1 What do you see?

Contesting Categories in Culture

Debates about Art

If prototypes are not mental representations that are fixed once and for all but can vary from group to group and even individual to individual, we can expect people to spend a great deal of time questioning, debating, challenging, modifying, and even negating one another's conceptual categories. We can refer to all of these activities with the general term *contestation*. Contesting one another's concepts is a prime cultural activity that people are likely to pursue in some form in every culture. Many of the concepts used in political discourse are especially clear cases of such "contested categories." Discussions and arguments concerning democracy, freedom, immigration, liberalism, nation, ethnicity, gender, sexuality, and many others often provoke heated debate in several contemporary Western societies, and, indeed, the positions and outcomes of these debates turn on what people mean by the concepts themselves.

In a way, of course, many of our categories are contested categories. We can debate, both as naive speakers of a language and as experts, the definition of almost any concept. In the chapter on prototype categorization, we saw, for example, how the concept of "man" (in the sense of "human") can be defined and redefined in different ways. But it seems that there are certain categories in every society that lend themselves to debate more readily than others. Political concepts were mentioned earlier as one example, but there are many others, such as the concept of "art." In the chapter, we will attempt to discover how and why this is not simply a contested category but an "essentially contested concept" (Gallie, 1956).

In what follows in the chapter, I will look at the concept of "art" and use it to demonstrate how everyday (i.e., nonexpert) definitions of art are primarily based on either essential features or basic-level categorization. Furthermore, I will show that ART cannot be defined in terms of essential features and that people have always taken it to be a prototype-based category in contemporary Western societies. I will suggest that the "traditional" definition of art functions as a deep-rooted cultural prototype. The prototype nature of the traditional view points to the possibility of treating ART as a contested category. Finally, we will see that if we apply W. B. Gallie's (1956) criteria for essentially contested concepts, we find that the criteria fit the concept of "art" closely, thereby making it an essentially contested concept.

Classical and Basic-Level Definitions of Art

To begin our discussion, it will be useful to try to define art and to look at some typical definitions of it. One tempting way to say what art is is as follows: "Art is what we see on display in an art museum, gallery, exhibition, and so on." Clearly, this is not a very good definition for several reasons. First, it limits art to some visible objects, the end product of a process, and thus it excludes the process itself that leads to the product. Second, it does not provide any deeper insight into what art is. It essentially says that art is what some people (i.e., the people who have the power to select certain items to be displayed in a museum) tell us it is. Nevertheless, we will see toward the end of the chapter that even this kind of definition plays a role in why ART should be taken to be an essentially contested category.

Some other definitions appear to be more adequate. Let us take the *Encyclopedia Britannica* definition (*Encyclopedia Britannicca Ready Reference*, 2003) as our first example: "[Art is a] [c]ombination of skill and imagination in the creation of objects, environments, or experiences." This definition seems to be a lot more appealing. The reason probably is that it is given in terms of what come close to necessary and sufficient conditions. On this definition, such conditions would include "using skill," "using imagination," "creating objects," and so on. This way of defining the category appeals to us because it is formulated as a classical definition and, given our training and education, most of us expect definitions to be given in terms of essential properties or necessary and sufficient conditions.

On this definition, sports and games that require the use of skill and imagination would also qualify as art because they certainly create new experiences. (Think of a movement in figure skating or basketball that has never been done before.) And it could be suggested that the term *art* also applies to science and engineering. These activities often create new objects or environments through the use of skill and imagination. It seems then that the features employed by the definition may be singly necessary, but they surely are not jointly sufficient to define art.

Webster's Dictionary defines art in this way: "4 a: the conscious use of skill and creative imagination esp. in the production of aesthetic objects; also: works so produced b (1): fine arts (2): one of the fine arts (3): a graphic art." This is also based on necessary and sufficient conditions. We find the use of skill and imagination here as well. The new idea is that these are used in the creation of "aesthetic objects." This makes the definition somewhat tautological because we find *aesthetic* defined as "artistic" in the same dictionary. We are back to art then, and the question remains: What is art?

To begin to investigate the issue further, it might be helpful to look at an additional definition provided by the *Encyclopedia Britannica*: "The term also designates modes of expression such as painting, drawing, sculpture, film-making, music, dance, poetry, theater, architecture, ceramics, and decorative arts, collectively known as the arts." As can be seen, this is a definition based on basic-level categorization. Art is taken to be a superordinate category, with painting, drawing, sculpture, and so on being basic-level. This type of definition lists examples of the category, but it does not provide any features for it. But at least this definition gives us an idea of what the members of the category of art are, and we can begin to search for features that characterize some or all of them. If "using skill" and "using imagination" are not sufficient to define what art is, it should be our goal to find out what other or additional features characterize the category. In other words, we should ask if art has any essential features that are permanent through the ages and are accepted by everyone in a particular period of time.

To find out, we can look at the category of ART in the course of its historical development. If we find features that are never challenged by groups of artists, it can be claimed that those features are essential for the definition of art. If, however, no such features can be identified, we should conclude that the category is inherently malleable and, indeed, contestable. It is important to bear in mind that this is simply a semantic exercise and no claim is made that in exploring the history of the concept we are engaged in the scholarly activity of art historians. We will not be doing art history; we will simply look at a concept (that happens to be art) and try to find out if it has any essential features as shown by the history of the acceptance or nonacceptance of its use. Our survey will be based on information concerning a portion of art history in the Western world as given in the *Encyclopedia Britannica* (*Encyclopedia Britannica Ready Reference*, 2003).

The Traditional View of Art
as a Prototype-Based Category

Our general strategy will be the following: We take a particular movement in the history of art and ask how that movement defines its own concept of "art" in relation to other historically prior or sociologically dominant contemporary positions.

Impressionism

Consider impressionism first. This was a movement in art in late-nineteenth-century France. The main characteristic of the work was the artists' attempt to "record the visual reality" of situations (landscape or urban scene) by making use of the effects of light on color and by using light colors and painting forms out of discrete dabs of color. They also moved out of the studio and painted outdoors. Some of the representative figures of the movement include Claude Monet, Auguste Renoir, and Alfred Sisley. Impressionist painters departed from the then-classical canon of painting by attempting to record their own impressions of visual reality. This effort was directed against the traditional ways of painting, in which the goal was to create a faithful model, or representation, of some objective reality (i.e., realism). This intent necessitated some changes in their use of materials (i.e., using lighter colors), their technique (painting dabs), and the place of their artistic work (moving outdoors).

Symbolism

The symbolists reacted against both realism and impressionism. They emphasized the "subjective, symbolic, and decorative functions" of art. Rather than attempting to give people objective and rational thoughts, they attempted to evoke in them "subjective states of mind." The Symbolists often "turned to the mystical and occult" to achieve this end. Famous artists commonly associated with the movement are Paul Gauguin and Vincent van Gogh. The traditional conception of art that the symbolists challenged was that art has objective, representational, and nondecorative functions, either in its realist or impressionist version. Moreover, by laying stress on symbolic forms capable of evoking subjective personal states of mind, they went against the traditional view of art that emphasized natural forms and figures.

Cubism

Cubism was started by Pablo Picasso and Georges Braque in the early twentieth century. Cubism rejects perspective and the modeling of reality. It makes use of the "flat, two-dimensional, fragmented surface of the picture plane" and "geometrical forms," drawing its inspiration from African sculpture and, later, works by Paul Cézanne. In doing this, it challenges major features of traditional style, namely, that an object of art must have perspective and that it should be characterized by the use of historically given, traditional forms and figures—that is, forms and figures as we find them in reality.

Expressionism

Expressionism was an especially influential art movement in Germany after World War I. Similar to other art styles, it challenged the traditional conception of art as a way of representing objective reality. Instead, its goal was to depict the "subjective emotions that objects or events arouse." One of the techniques used to achieve this goal was the "distortion and exaggeration of shape and the vivid or violent application of color." Early roots of the movement can be found in the works of van Gogh and Edvard Munch.

Constructivism

Constructivism goes back to the beginning of the twentieth century in Russia, where a number of artists began to use nontraditional ways of producing works of art. For them and their followers, art was the literal construction of works out of "plastic, glass, and other industrial materials." Their works reflected "modern machinery and technology." Thus, instead of using traditional ways of creating a work of art, they literally *constructed* their abstract works that depicted modern "machinery and technology" by using nontraditional materials for the purpose.

Surrealism

Surrealism dominated the European artistic scene between the two world wars. Its main idea was that objective reality is insufficient as a basis for dealing with the complexity of human experience. Its originator, the poet André Breton, suggested the joining of "dream and fantasy to everyday reality." He aimed at working with a more complete sense of reality this way, surreality, or absolute reality—a reality that includes the unconscious aspects of the human mind. One of the best-known surrealist painters was Salvador Dalí.

Social Realism

This trend originated in the United States in the 1930s. Its main idea was to get rid of the "great" traditional themes of the canon of art. Instead of focusing on the standard and often "eternal" issues of man, it treated social-political issues, largely inspired by issues of social conflict and problems in the United States at the time.

Abstract Art

Abstract art is the result of the convergence of a number of art movements, such as expressionism and cubism. It broke away with the idea of traditional art that art is "the imitation of nature." It aims to be "nonobjective" and "nonrepresentational." The first modern artist who is credited with producing a work of art in this style is Wassily Kandinsky, who painted "purely abstract pictures."

Pop Art

This form of art is regarded by many as a typically American phenomenon. In it, we find no "great" traditional themes, a feature it shares with social realism. It does not make use of "great" traditional techniques, either, a feature it shares with constructivism. Its audience is not assumed to be the "elite" of society. Its main materials are the "commonplace objects from the world of popular culture," such as soup cans, comic strips, Coca-Cola bottles, TV sets, and so forth. The effect of pop art was the destruction of the boundary between "high" and "low" art. Well-known American representatives of pop art include Jasper Johns, Andy Warhol, and George Segal.

Conceptual Art

At the core of the traditional conception of "art" is the existence of a physical object, a finished product of art. This idea was radically changed by conceptual art, in that advocates of conceptual art claim that the physical art object is much less important than the *idea* that such a physical object can evoke. The traditional notion that a work of art is made for exhibition or sale is also replaced by conceptual art, where it is suggested that the "true" work of art "consists of 'concepts' or 'ideas.'" Thus, works of art are made deliberately uninteresting so as not to divert attention from the concepts, or ideas, they express. One famous example of this is Joseph Kosuth's *One and Three Chairs*, consisting of a real chair, a photograph of a chair, and a dictionary definition of *chair*.

What Are the Emerging Features of the Traditional View of Art?

Given the preceding analysis, certain features of the traditional view of art emerge. The traditional conception is characterized by those features that are negated and canceled by the various movements of art discussed earlier.

- First, according to the traditional view, art imitates, represents, or models objective reality. It is also an aspect of this view that the more faithful the resemblance is, the better the work of art.
- Second, a work of art should evoke objective and rational thoughts. These come from the representations of objective reality.
- Third, a work of art is representational in the sense that it mirrors reality by representations (e.g., painted objects and events) that the audience can recognize and understand (e.g., the object represented is a man, a tree, a dog). In other words, the figures and forms of a work of art are natural figures and forms.
- Fourth, a work of art is such that certain canonical activities, techniques, and materials are used that lead to a final product—the work of art. For example, a painter *paints* a painting using certain materials and techniques, and a sculptor *sculpts* a sculpture using different materials and techniques.
- Fifth, works of art are *about* something; they have a theme. In the traditional view, the theme is often something elevated, such as death, freedom, love.
- Sixth, the themes typically belong to "high" culture, not "low" culture. In addition, the audience of works of art is generally the elite of society.

- Seventh, a work of art is typically for display or exhibition or sale in certain designated places, such as museums, galleries, auctions, concert halls, and so on.
- Eighth, a work of art is a physical object—an object that can be seen, touched, read, or heard.

Based on these features, it would be fairly easy for someone to say that we are dealing with art

> when someone models reality by means of certain natural representations of it by making use of certain activities, materials, techniques, and when the resulting physical product is about something important for especially those who are educated enough to understand it and who can experience the physical product in certain designated places.

In a way, this sounds like a plausible definition of the traditional view of art. We can claim that this is what "real" art is. We can think of the definition as providing the prototype, in the sense of chapter 2, of ART.

However, the point of the previous sketchy survey of art history was that there are always people who do not accept this definition. They can constantly challenge, undermine, or plainly negate every one of these features. In other words, these features are not essential ones for art. If they were essential, they could not be so easily challenged and canceled. Without them, the category of ART would collapse. But it does not seem to collapse. On the contrary, it thrives as newer and newer definitions are given for it. In sum, we can suggest that the concept of "art" has a central member—the traditional conception—and many noncentral ones. In other words, ART can be claimed to be a prototype-based category.

Let us see a summary of the assumed features of the traditional view and the art movements that cancel them:

A work of art:

Represents objective reality (canceled by impressionism, expressionism, surrealism)

Should evoke objective and rational thoughts (canceled by symbolism, surrealism)

Is representational, that is, consists of natural figures and forms (canceled by symbolism, cubism, abstract art)

Is made by means of certain canonical activities (canceled by constructivism)

Uses certain canonical techniques (canceled by impressionism)

Uses canonical materials (canceled by constructivism)

Uses canonical themes (canceled by constructivism, social realism, pop art)

Uses objects that are elevated, that belong to "high" culture (canceled by pop art)

Is for the elite of society (canceled by pop art)

Is for display (canceled by conceptual art)
Is a physical object (canceled by conceptual art)

As can be seen, even those features of art that many would take to be definitional for all forms of art (such as the one that art represents objective reality, the one that it is representational, and the one that it is some kind of physical object) can be explicitly negated and effectively canceled. That is, it is not simply the case that someone at some point challenged a feature of the definition, but that the challenge was actually successful to the degree that a new art movement was born out of the successful new definition.

As can be noticed, the process of "canceling features" can be both historical and contemporary. For example, the impressionists may have challenged the then-traditional view, thus achieving a historical shift for some people but not for others. And those who were "converted" may have been the target of the movement that followed them. This way, there can be more and more contemporary, or synchronic, fragmentation within the category as a whole as a result of historical change in the definition of art for some people.

Is Art an "Essentially Contested Concept"?

In light of what I have done so far, it seems clear that ART is a highly contested category. But we can further ask if it is an "essentially contested concept." The English philosopher of language W. B. Gallie (1956) provides seven necessary and sufficient conditions to define what he calls "essentially contested concepts." They are as follows:

1. The category must be appraisive or evaluative (must evaluate an achievement).
2. The achievement must be internally complex (consisting of a number of parts or aspects).
3. The explanation of its worth must make reference to the individual parts or aspects, but in doing so it can make reference to and assign different amounts of value to these parts or aspects; in other words, its value is describable in many different ways.
4. The achievement must be capable of indefinite modification, that is, must be "open" in character.
5. Each party recognizes that his or her definition is contested or challenged by others and each party is aware, to some extent at least, of the differing views of others; that is, the concept is used both "aggressively and defensively."
6. The category involves a concept that derives from an original exemplar whose authority is acknowledged by all the contestant users of the concept.
7. The continuous competition between contestant users enables the original exemplar's achievement to be sustained and developed.

The second feature of this definition is especially important. It suggests that for a category to be an essentially contested one it must have a complex internal structure. In our terms, this means that it must be describable in terms of a large number of features. If we have a category that can only be described by a large number of features due to its internal complexity, we can cancel each of these different features and can thus get a wide variety of different instances of the category. However, it should be noted that this is only one source of deriving alternative members for a category. Another is when the central member (the prototype) is very much underspecified and this leads to all types of conflicts in people's definitions of the category because they flesh it out in their different ways.

Let us now see how the traditional concept of art fits the seven conditions for essentially contested concepts, as laid out by Gallie:

1. *Art* is an appraisive or evaluative term; by using it, we evaluate an achievement.
2. The kind of achievement is internally complex: There is an actor (artist) and there is a receiver (audience, spectator). A work of art is created. The work of art:

   Represents objective reality
   Should evoke objective and rational thoughts
   Is representational, that is, consists of natural figures and forms
   Is made by means of certain canonical activities
   Uses certain canonical techniques
   Uses canonical materials
   Uses canonical themes
   Uses objects that are elevated, that belong to "high" culture
   Is for the elite of society
   Is for display
   Is a physical object

3. Given this complexity, we can describe art in many different ways.
4. We cannot at any specific time predict how the concept will change and what will be called art by some people.
5. Some people will argue for a particular conception of art, while others will argue against it.
6. There is always an "exemplar" with respect to which some people will argue for a particular conception of art.
7. The debates between a particular exemplar of art and its challengers help maintain the exemplar's achievement and its further development.

In other words, it seems that the necessary and sufficient conditions for essentially contested concept as laid out by Gallie apply readily to art. It is an evaluative category, it has a complex internal structure, this can lead to many different ways of describing it, and so on. Overall, this makes the category of ART an essentially contested concept.

What Gallie calls an exemplar here is what we call prototype. The prototype to be debated by different groups of people can be the traditional view or it can be a view that emerged as a result of the redefinition process. This is so despite the fact that we have taken the traditional view to be the prototype, or central member, of the category of art. We have adopted this choice because the traditional view is probably the most pervasive conception of art even today.

Conclusions

People in every culture are likely to contest many of their categories. They in fact suggest to each other something like "I don't think that that thing is what you take it to be." When they are engaged in this activity, they are calling into question each other's conceptions of reality. Contesting each other's categories, in this sense, amounts to challenging each other's reality. For this reason, in many cases the stakes can be high for the people involved in such contestations.

In this chapter, we used the concept of "art," which is a commonly contested concept. It may not seem like a concept whose definition can affect people's lives in a serious way. Yet when we look at the history of modern art, we often find that individual artists and groups of artists of various persuasions had to suffer as a consequence of either their own contestation or the contestations of others. In other words, the definitions of categories do seem to matter and may have a serious effect on people's lives.

Art can be and is defined in a variety of ways. The dominant folk or everyday definition of art is given either as a "classical" definition or as one based on basic-level categorization. The classical definition attempts to provide the essential features of art, that is, the necessary and sufficient conditions that we need to call something art. We saw, however, that there are no such essential features in terms of which the concept could be defined. The examination of a major part of contemporary art history shows that none of the features that have been taken to be criterial or definitional for the concept are indeed criterial. This led us to the conclusion that it is best to think of the features characteristic of art as comprising a prototype of the category.

Prototype-based categories are good candidates for contested concepts precisely because their features can be challenged, negated, and replaced. Classical definitions could not be altered in these ways by virtue of the nature of classical categories. But the concept of "art" is not simply a contested category but an essentially contested concept. We based this judgment on Gallie's seven criteria to determine whether a concept is essentially contested.

Interestingly, if we think of Gallie's criteria as essential features of essentially contested concepts, we use a classical definition to determine what counts as an essentially contested concept. It would probably be better to think of Gallie's criteria as merely defining *prototypical* essentially contested categories. This decision would make it possible for us to see concepts along a gradient from uncontestable categories (if there are any) to essentially contestable ones.

Exercises

1. In every culture there are contested categories, like democracy, freedom, immigration, nation, nationality, liberalism, etc. and so on. Love is also such a contested category. What makes LOVE a contested category? Is it also an *essentially* contested category?

2. If you were the leader of an experiment studying contested political concepts, *how* would you determine which factors are responsible for categories being contested besides those mentioned in this chapter? Gallie's (1956) prerequisite features for what he called essentially contested categories were: "appraisive or evaluative"; "internally complex"; "parts can be evaluated differently"; "'open' in character"; "can be used 'aggressively & defensively'"; "derives from an acknowledged original exemplar"; "constant competition sustains and develops the original exemplar's achievements" (see the chapter for details). Would you add anything to the list? Are there any other aspects that you regard as important?

3. Choose five pictures that symbolize five better-known art movements. One of the five should be a picture that depicts a classical work of art. Show your pictures to fifteen people of different ages and occupations, then compare their views to the features of the traditional view of art given in the chapter. Did their answers have any points in common? If so, what does this prove?

Organizing Knowledge about the World

Frames in the Mind

So far we have taken concepts to be lists of features. In other words, we have assumed that categories can be adequately described as feature lists—either as lists of essential features (as in "classical" approaches) or as lists of features that represent the central examples of concepts (as in prototype approaches). Such feature lists represent what we know about concepts. But the question is: Do feature lists represent all the contents of concepts at our disposal? The answer is clearly no. We possess a great deal more knowledge about concepts than what feature lists reveal (see, for example, Barsalou, 1992). Frames are representations of this large amount of underlying knowledge. As matter of fact, we can think of frames as including feature lists as well—feature lists that serve the representation of just the "tip" of a conceptual "iceberg" associated with a particular domain of experience.

But frames typically involve more than feature lists. Another problem with feature lists is that they do not show much of the structure of conceptual categories; they are simply lists of unrelated features. As such, they do not reveal the conceptual connections between the features, including spatial, temporal, causal, and other connections.

Frames, unlike feature lists, are typically constituted by a number of different parts—objects and predicates. Both objects and predicates can function as "attributes" and "values." For example, consider the feature "standard transmission" for "car." Now it is the case that standard transmission is a value of the more general attribute of "transmission." The attribute of "transmission" can be said to have the values "standard transmission" and "automatic transmission" (Barsalou, 1992).

In sum, while feature lists are possible candidates for the representation of concepts for some purposes, they are insufficient as a general strategy to represent what we know about the world. In particular, their insufficiency derives from at least three factors: first, their failure to represent all the information we have in connection with concepts; second, their failure to represent the structure of conceptual information we possess in connection with concepts; and third, their failure to represent attribute-value relationships between elements of concepts.

In exploring the issues connected with frames, I will proceed as follows. First, I take up the issue of how we can characterize frames in general. Second, I turn to the issue of the inherently cultural nature of frames. Third, I look at the many linguistic and cultural functions of frames in linguistics, philosophy of language, and cognition. The cultural application and importance of frames will be the topic of the next chapter.

What Is a Frame?

We can use the following working definition of frames: 'A frame is a structured mental representation of a conceptual category'. We will see many examples for this in the chapter. This definition is so vague and general that, as mentioned in the introduction to this chapter, it allows us to consider essential features (i.e., necessary and sufficient conditions) and feature lists of other kinds as a kind of frame also. After all, such feature lists can also be conceived of as structured representations of conceptual categories. The notion of "frame," however, is typically reserved for cases of mental representations that cannot be given as feature lists (see Fillmore, 1975, 1977a, b, c). A more comprehensive name for structured representations of conceptual categories in general, including both feature lists and frames proper, would be (cognitive) model, which is indeed often used as a generic term for the mental representation of categories of both kinds.

Roughly the same idea of what a frame is has been called by a variety of different names in the vast literature on the subject. These include, in addition to frame, script, scenario, scene, cultural model, cognitive model, idealized cognitive model, domain, schema, (experiential) gestalt, and several others (see, e.g., Andor, 1985). There is sometimes variation even within the same author as regards the terms used. The different terms come from different branches of cognitive science, and so the words used may have a slightly different meaning. In this discussion, I will use many of these interchangeably, because the basic idea is similar to each of them: They all designate a coherent organization of human experience.

In the classical approach, meaning is given in terms of necessary or sufficient conditions (i.e., by means of essential features). From the perspective of an experientialist cognitive science, meaning is defined by frames; as the best known formulation of this idea suggests, "meanings are relativized to frames/scenes" (Fillmore, 1975, 1977a, b, c). To see how this works in practice, let us take some examples.

We begin with the simplest kind of frame and ask how it contributes to the meaning of an expression. Consider the word *knuckle*, as discussed by Ronald Langacker (1987). It would be very difficult to define the meaning of this word in terms of essential features without evoking the larger frames of which it is a part. When we understand what *knuckle* is, perhaps the most important kind of information we know is that the knuckle is a part of the finger. Furthermore, we know that the knuckle-finger is a part of the hand and that the knuckle-finger-hand is a part of the arm and that the knuckle-finger-hand-arm is a part of the body. This knowledge concerning the ever more inclusive frames that contain the knuckle contributes significantly to what a knuckle is, that is, to our concept of "knuckle." A person without this knowledge could hardly be said to know the meaning of the word.

Let us take another example, the word *Friday*, which is discussed by Lakoff (1987). What is the mental representation of the conceptual category FRIDAY? Can it be defined in terms of features that are inherent in the concept of "Friday"? Could we propose something like "the fifth day of the week" as an inherent feature? Not really, because to say that it is the fifth day of the week only makes sense against the background of the concept of "week." Could we propose as an inherent feature that Friday is a day? No, because the concept of "day" itself only makes sense in a certain system of knowledge about the movement of the sun. The only thing we can do to define what Friday is, is say that the concept makes sense against the background of several frames: the natural cycle of the movement of the sun, and the seven-day calendric cycle. The former gives us an idea of what a day is; the latter tells us that there are seven units (days) in what we call a week. Against this background, we can provide a definition for "Friday": 'the fifth day of the week'. There are no inherent features here. The concept is defined in terms of two frames that exist independently of the concept. However, they are both necessary for its characterization.

An important property of frames is that they are idealized in several ways. One of them is that, often, what the frame defines does not actually exist in the world. For instance, in the case of the current example, there are no seven-day weeks in nature. In nature, we only find the alternation of light and darkness governed by the natural cycle of the movement of the sun. Frames are often idealized in this sense. To capture this aspect of frames, Lakoff (1987) calls such idealizations "idealized cognitive models," or ICMs for short. This feature of frames makes them open to cross-cultural variation. Particular frames may exist in only one or a few cultures, as is the case here, where the notion of our kind of calendric cycle is a peculiarity of the Western world.

Friday can also be "framed" in other ways. We can think of it as part of a SUPERSTITION frame, in which it is an unlucky day; as part of a WEEKEND frame, in which it is the day before the weekend; or as part of a WORKWEEK frame, in which it is the last day of the workweek (Radden, 1992). In other words, the meaning of a word seems to depend on the kind of frame within which we conceptualize it.

The Framenet Project

Many frames are richly structured by the elements they contain. The meanings of the sentences we use to talk about our experiences are based on such structured frames. The understanding of a particular sentence requires our knowledge of an entire frame. Charles Fillmore and his colleagues study such frames in what is called the Framenet project. (For some of the group's interesting results, see Fillmore and Atkins, 1992.)

Let us look at an example of one such underlying frame from the project's Web site—the COMPETITION frame. The COMPETITION frame contains a number of elements: the competition, participants, place, prize, rank, score, and venue. These elements are connected by particular events, such as lose, win, defeat, come in, play, and so on. The following is a brief illustration of the frame—with a short definition of the elements and some illustrative example sentences that contain the events that connect the elements (taken from the Framenet Web site: *http://www.icsi.berkeley.edu/framenet/*):

> **Name of frame element (FE):**
> **Competition:** name of the competition: Joe lost the [D]emocratic primary.
> **Participant 1:** identifies the first (or only) participant in the competition: Joe won the lottery. + Joe defeated Leslie at tennis.
> **Participant 2:** Joe defeated **Leslie** at tennis.
> **Participants:** **The Yankees** won the World Series.
> **Place:** where the event takes place: John's 3–0 win at **Wimbledon** (place or competition) surprised the crowd.
> **Prize:** the prize won in a competition: John won **a bronze medal.**
> **Rank:** the ranked results of a competition: John came in **third.**
> **Score:** the score in a game: The Yankees won the game **2–0.** + The Yankees won the game **by two [runs].**
> **Venue:** the venue of the competition: The Mets will play at **Shea Stadium** tonight.

The Framenet project defines competition in the following way:

> [P]eople (Participant 1, Participant 2, or Participants) participate in an organized rule-governed activity (the Competition) in order to achieve some advantageous outcome (often the Prize). Rank and Score are different criteria by which the degree of achievement of the advantageous outcome is judged.

The verbs *lose, win, defeat, come in,* and *play* link the elements in the frame and they take particular elements in a particular order, sometimes using additional prepositions. For example, a participant can *lose* a competition, a participant can *lose to* another participant, and a competition can *be lost,* but a participant cannot *be lost* or a participant cannot *lose* another participant. Such sentences (interestingly, even the unacceptable ones) evoke the entire frame of COMPETITION. That is to say, if I tell you that I lost the game, you will know that there was another participant, that I was engaged in some kind of rule-governed activity in a particular place and venue, and the activity had a potentially advantageous outcome for me, but based on the criteria that are used to judge the degree of achievement of the advantageous outcome, I did not achieve my goal. This is remarkable, given that all I say to you is, "I lost the game."

Some Additional Characteristics of Frames

After our general survey of what frames are, let us now turn to some additional and more specific characteristics of frames. In this section, I mention some of the most important ones (Fillmore, 1977c, 1982, 1985).

First, as was already mentioned, frames are evoked by particular meanings of words. Consider a sentence like *The teacher called on John to answer the question.* The word *teacher* evokes the frame of an institution where there are adults who teach children and where the adults have the right to call on the children to answer questions and where the children have the responsibility to answer them. The adult in the role of teaching children is the *teacher*. Conversely, the child who is taught is the *student* or *pupil*. While the verb *teach* "gives away" the role of teacher in this case, the role of student is not made explicit by it. Nevertheless, the word *student* can only be understood within the frame in which the word *teacher* is understood.

Second, particular elements of frames can be focused on, or "profiled." When we use the words *teacher* and *student*, particular elements of the school frame are profiled. Similarly, in the frame of a number of team sports (e.g., soccer, field handball) there are players, a playing field with two goals, and a ball and most of the players play in the field, while one of them plays in the goal. Now the particular player who plays in the goal is profiled within the frame by means of the words *goalkeeper* and *goalie*.

Third, frames often impose a certain perspective on a situation. In other words, speakers can often choose a particular perspective to talk about a situation and then the hearer is presented with that perspective in understanding it. One of Fillmore's famous examples is this:

(1)   a. John spent four hours on land.

      b. John spent four hours on the ground.

The first sentence provides a conceptualization of the situation from the perspective of a sea voyage, whereas the second provides a conceptualization from the perspective of air travel. If you travel somewhere by ship, you can say you spent four hours on land (but not "on the ground"), and if you travel somewhere by air, you can say that you spent four hours on the ground (but not "on land"). Notice that you can spend the four hours in exactly the same place (let us say in the same bar). This would not matter at all in deciding which expression to use. The only thing that matters is whether you travel by boat or by air.

Fourth, frames can provide a particular history. As an example, consider the word *widow*. When we use this word, it evokes the history of a woman who married a man some time ago and this man died at some later time. The woman who married the man who died is a widow. Thus, we can say, "She was a widow for three years." The history that underlies the word arises from a number of frames: especially, those of marriage, family, and death.

Fifth, certain frames assume larger cultural frames. Perhaps the best-known example for this is the word *bachelor*, as worked out by Fillmore. The basic frame for this word can be defined by a set of necessary and sufficient conditions; specifically, ADULT, MALE, NEVER MARRIED. The essential features define a category with rigid boundaries. Anyone who is not an adult, not a male, or married cannot be appropriately called a bachelor. But the definition of *bachelor* in terms of necessary and sufficient conditions leads to a problem. There are quite a few cases that do qualify as bachelors given these criteria, but we would hesitate to call them such. Consider the pope. The pope meets all the requirements for being considered a bachelor: He is an adult, he is male, and he has never married. And yet most people would not call him a bachelor! The same observation applies to other cases, like Tarzan, homosexual males, Muslims who could have four wives but have only three, and so on.

The way to get out of this dilemma is to suggest that the definition of *bachelor* works only in those cases that fall within a larger cultural frame: namely, that of the prototypical male life cycle. The most relevant aspects of this average life cycle include that there is a human society with the institution of marriage, that there is a marriageable age when males marry a woman, and that people are born male or female and the males live in relationships with only females. In other words, the definition of *bachelor* in terms of necessary and sufficient conditions only applies when the average life cycle also applies to the people in question. The pope is not called a bachelor because the average life cycle does not apply to him; the life cycle of the pope does not have marriage in it. Tarzan cannot appropriately be called a bachelor because he lived outside human society. Homosexual males are not considered bachelors because they live in relationships with other males. There are additional examples, but the point remains the same. The basic BACHELOR frame is insufficient for deciding whether someone is appropriately called a bachelor or not. We also need one or several larger cultural frames, or models, to help decide the issue.

Sixth, and finally, frames are idealizations or, to use another word for the same process, schematizations of experience. As we have seen in many of the earlier examples, frames do not correspond to, or fit, reality as it is; rather, frames constitute an idealized, or schematized, version of reality in the form of prototypes of various kinds: for instance, in the form of the average male life cycle, the typical school situation, stereotypical situations in a culture, and so forth.

Frames are intimately linked to prototypes (Fillmore, 1975). Let us take a specific example of how frames can define a prototype for a concept. Take the word *breakfast*. The understanding of the word requires a frame that contains a cycle of meals in the course of a day. The meal that one eats after sleeping through the night and has a somewhat unique menu is called breakfast (Fillmore, 1982). Breakfast is thus:

1. the meal we have after a period of sleep
2. the meal we eat early in the day
3. a meal that has a special menu

This is an idealization. There can be many deviations from this prototype in reality. For instance, you work through the night (canceling 1) and then you have scrambled eggs, toast, and coffee in the morning (maintaining 2 and 3); you sleep through the night and get up in the morning (maintaining 1 and 2), and then you have some cheesecake with a shot of bourbon (canceling 3); you go to bed at ten, sleep until two in the morning (maintaining 1), get up and have scrambled eggs, toast, and coffee (maintaining 3) at two o'clock (canceling 2). And when you go to a "breakfast all day" place at four o'clock in the afternoon and have scrambled eggs, toast, and coffee, both (1) and (2) are canceled. Nevertheless, all of these meals could be called breakfast.

The point is that the conventional frames we have primarily equip us to deal with an idealized, or schematized, version of reality from which many deviations are possible, but the deviations are defined with respect to such idealized, or schematized, frames. In this sense, frames are constructs of our imagination—and not mental representations that directly fit a preexisting objective reality. In short, frames are imaginative devices of the mind. Therefore, frame semantics contrasts with truth-conditional semantics. "Frame semantics" is the semantics of understanding, whereas the goal of "T(ruth-conditional)-semantics" is to determine under what conditions an expression may be used or a sentence may be true (Fillmore, 1985).

Frames as Cultural Constructs
and Cultures as Frames

Much of our understanding of the world comes through the frames we have associated with our categories. The frames constitute a huge and complex system of knowledge about the world. This large network of frames reflects the knowledge that we make use of in using language (e.g., figuring out meaning) and thinking about and acting in the world.

The frames that we use are not only cognitive in nature but also cultural constructs; hence the term *cultural model* for the same idea. Cultural models can differ cross-culturally, from group to group, and even from individual to individual. For instance, Hoyt Alverson insists that all experience is intentional, that is, it is conceived of "in a certain manner" (1991: 97). Experience that is conceived in a particular manner is captured by (often different) cultural models. At the same time, however, a large number of frames are shared by members of societies and groups within those societies. The fact that many frames are shared across people makes frames cultural products. Thus, frames represent a huge amount of shared knowledge that makes societies, subcultures, and social groups of various kinds coherent cultural formations. The shared character of frames has been recognized by many anthropologists, including Roy D'Andrade (e.g., 1995), Dorothy Holland, Naomi Quinn, and Claudia Strauss (e.g., Holland and Quinn, 1987; Strauss and Quinn, 1997), who propose that culture can be defined as a collection of shared understandings represented by frames, or cultural models.

A well-known example of one such shared frame is the RESTAURANT frame (Schank and Abelson, 1977), as it is used by many Americans. This frame serves to illustrate the kind of knowledge we have about going to a restaurant. This knowledge can be given as a series of events that follow one another. Another name for frames of this type is script. A script describes a stereotypical situation in a culture—a situation in which events unfold through time. The RESTAURANT-GOING frame, or script, involves the following events:

> Go to the restaurant
> Be seated
> Study the menu
> Order meal
> Waiter brings meal
> Eat the meal
> Pay
> Leave restaurant

Many members of American culture share this script about going to a restaurant. It enables them to understand conversations about restaurants. For example, if someone tells me that he or she went to a restaurant and paid way too much, I can legitimately assume that the person went through all the events listed here. Most important, I can assume that this person paid too much for a meal he or she had and not for buying a pair of shoes. I can be sure about this because the speaker and I share the script of what it means to go to a restaurant. Notice that these elements of the script are not essential features. They can all be easily canceled. I can tell you that I went to a restaurant, was seated, and looked at the menu, but I did not eat anything. At the same time, this script can vary in certain details from culture to culture. For example, in some countries you do not have to wait to be seated; you can go in and find a free table yourself. The cancelability of all these features can thus give rise to cultural variation.

Another source of cultural variation in cultural models is what we will call "frame-based" categories in the next section. Since ways of eating food can vary cross-culturally, the frame-based categories of selling food may vary from place to place. For example, it is common in Hungary for butcher shops to sell boiled meat and grated horseradish together in the same butcher shop. In other words, Hungarians have a frame that includes boiled meat and grated horseradish. This is because Hungarians commonly eat boiled meat with a horseradish dressing. This particular frame of eating meat in Hungary may not be found in other cultures.

Folk and Expert Theories

The frames we have in connection with objects and events of the world represent two kinds of knowledge: everyday, or folk, and expert knowledge. Our everyday knowledge is far more extensive than our expert knowledge. Everyday knowledge is knowledge that we use automatically, without conscious thought, and that we acquire without conscious learning or formal education. Our everyday knowledge is represented by "folk theories," while our expert knowledge is represented by "expert theories." On the one hand, we use folk theories (also called cultural models or naive understandings) of the world for most everyday purposes (such as going to a restaurant, reasoning about a particular topic, calling someone a bachelor, and understanding sentences). Expert theories (or scientific models), on the other hand, are used by specialists in a field. We can hold folk theories and expert theories about the same aspect of the world. It commonly happens that in such cases our folk and expert theories conflict with each other. For example, linguists have very different models about language than nonlinguists. In this case, we could say that laypeople's folk theories of language may differ considerably from the expert theories of language used by linguists.

We have seen a number of folk theories or cultural/cognitive models so far in this chapter. Taxonomies constitute another form of cultural/cognitive models of the world. As we saw in the chapter on basic-level categories, taxonomies have a hierarchical structure. Folk and expert taxonomies can differ considerably. For example, whales are commonly regarded as fish in folk theories of the natural world, whereas experts classify them as mammals. Most people—laypersons and experts alike—assume that there is only one correct taxonomy of anything. The fact that folk and expert theories often conflict casts doubt on this assumption. Just as important, expert theories can also clash with each other in attempting to explain a phenomenon, as incompatible scientific accounts of, say, language testify.

Moreover, cultural/cognitive models, or folk theories, are often inconsistent with each other. One example of this is the folk theory of "reference" in language. There exist two folk models of how linguistic expression refer to objects and events (Kay, 1987). The first is shown by the "hedges" *strictly speaking* and *loosely speaking*. Thus, when one says, "Loosely speaking, the first human beings lived in Kenya," one assumes that the meanings of words have certain semantic features and that the fit between the world and the words is not a very tight one; hence, the use of *loosely speaking*. In the second, we use hedges like *technically*. This is a hedge that makes different assumptions. Take the sentence *Technically, a dolphin is mammal.* Here there is the assumption that some people know better and/or have the expertise to designate things in the world in the proper way.

Thus, in the first folk theory of reference, words can refer to things in the world because they have certain inherent features on the basis of which we can apply words to things. In the second, however, words can refer to certain things on the basis of a certain body of knowledge. Now, given these different folk theories of reference, we find two corresponding expert theories that are also in conflict. In one, words fit the world by virtue of their inherent meanings. This is what can be called the Fregean tradition (named after the German philosopher of language who outlined its philosophical background). The clearest manifestation of this view in recent linguistics can be found in componential analysis (see chap. 2). In the second expert theory, there is a body of experts who decide what words should designate (see Lakoff, 1987).

Let's see what happens when we apply two hedges that are based on different folk theories to the same sentence. As was noted, the hedge *strictly speaking* is based on the first folk theory, while *technically* is based on the second.

Strictly speaking, a dolphin is a mammal. (folk theory 1)
Technically, a dolphin is a mammal. (folk theory 2)

Here we have the same truth conditions (specified by the words *dolphin, is, mammal*) but different folk theories (frames) of reference within which the sentence is conceptualized. While both sentences have the same conceptual content, they are looked at from a different folk theory, or frame, of reference. The hedges *strictly speaking* and *technically* are used to achieve the same communicative effect, but they "speak" from a different theory: the first from the perspective of the folk theory that reference is determined by semantic features, or truth conditions, whereas the second is from the perspective of the expert theory that reference is determined by a body of experts.

Much of our cultural knowledge comes from folk theories, or cultural/ cognitive models. Our folk theories may conflict with other people's folk theories, and they commonly clash with expert, or scientific, theories. As a matter of fact, the very same person may hold contradictory folk and expert theories of the same phenomenon. The two ideas that culture is largely composed of shared cultural/cognitive models and that there are two distinct type of cultural/cognitive models—folk and expert theories—go a long way in explaining our cultural functioning in the world.

What Are Frames Good For?

After the discussion of the general nature and some of the specific characteristics of frames, we can ask the inevitable question: What is the use of frames in how we speak, how we understand the world, and how we deal with important issues we encounter in our lives? What follows in this section is another brief survey of such uses. Let us begin with how we understand the meaning of words.

Frames Help Account for How We Understand
the Meanings of Individual Words

As we have seen in several earlier examples, each word evokes the entire frame to which it belongs. Many words may belong to a particular frame. The meaning of each word can be characterized in terms of a single schematized frame. The most celebrated example of this is Fillmore's COMMERCIAL EVENT frame. Consider the words that belong to this frame: *buy, sell, pay, spend, cost,* and *charge.* How can we characterize the meaning of these words? Fillmore suggests that the frame consists of the following elements:

Buyer—seller
Money—goods
Transfer of money and goods

The verbs *buy, sell, pay, spend,* and so on, focus on a different aspect of the frame. *Buy* focuses on the buyer and the goods; *sell* focuses on the seller and the goods; *pay* on the buyer and the money; *spend* on the buyer and the money; *cost* on the goods and the money; and *charge* on the seller and the money. Thus we get sentences such as:

(2)   I bought a car (from him).

(3)   He sold his car (to me).

(4)   I paid one thousand dollars (for the car).

(5)   I spent one thousand dollars (on the car).

(6)   The car cost one thousand dollars.

(7)   He charged one thousand dollars (for the car).

The central elements that the verbs focus on, or bring into perspective, are in subject and object position. Other elements can also be included in the sentences, as the phrases in parentheses indicate. The important point is that the different verbs are defined with respect to which aspects of the schematic commercial event they bring into focus. The verbs do not seem to have an inherent meaning isolated from one another; rather, their meaning depends on the particular aspects of a single frame that they profile.

Frames Help Account for Apparently Conflicting
Cases of Negation

A different application of frames can be used to show how we can account for apparently conflicting cases of negation. Take the sentence *He isn't stingy; he's thrifty.* This sentence contains an apparent contradiction because we cannot negate a word that means 'not liking to spend money' (i.e., say in effect that he likes to spend money) and at the same time assert of the same person that he "does not like to spend money." However, we can and do make sense of this sentence; we do not find it contradictory. In other words, there is only an apparent—not a real—contradiction involved. This is only a problem in objectivist semantics and cognition that has no place for the kinds of frames we are describing here.

We can distinguish between "frame-internal" and "frame-external" negation. For example, if I say, "He's not stingy," it means that it is not the case that he does not like to spend money. That is, I accept the STINGY frame but I negate what's inside it, the state of affairs in the world that it describes (i.e., that he does not like to spend money). In effect, I say that he does like to spend money. However, if I say, "He's not stingy; he's thrifty," I negate only the frame itself and say that the STINGY frame is not applicable. I leave the content of the frame intact (i.e., agree that he does not like to spend money) but at the same time suggest that his not liking to spend money is a good thing—and not a bad one, as the application of the STINGY frame would suggest. In other words, one kind of negation negates what's inside the frame (frame-internal negation); another negates the applicability of the frame itself (frame-external negation). This way we can account for apparently contradictory sentences that result from negation.

Frames Help Account for Problems with Analyticity

This type of explanation in terms of frames can also account for a problem that arises in connection with what philosophers of language call analyticity. Philosophers of language distinguish between two kinds of statement: "analytic" and "synthetic." Analytic statements are true by definition. The sentence *A bachelor is an unmarried man* is true by definition. This is so because it makes use of all the defining features of bachelor (ADULT, MALE, NEVER MARRIED). If we define a concept in terms of its essential features, the sentence that makes use of these features can only be true. Synthetic statements, however, are true with respect to the world. If I say that the house collapsed, this sentence is only true if it is really the case that the house collapsed. We can capture this distinction by saying that we assess the truth of analytic sentences "sentence internally" but that of synthetic sentences "sentence externally."

What does this have to do with frames? Notice that there is a problem with analytic sentences here. On the classical view (where concepts can be defined in terms of essential features), the sentence *A bachelor is an unmarried man* should be necessarily true; that is, if someone is an unmarried man, he should be a bachelor. But we just saw that this is not always the case. The pope is an unmarried man but not a bachelor. The notion of frames helps us overcome this problem with objectivist views of meaning and analyticity, in that larger cultural frames can delineate the situations within which the definition in terms of necessary and sufficient conditions applies.

Frames Help Account for Certain Problematic
Cases of Categorization

As I noted in previous chapters, most of our categories are based on similarity (especially family resemblance) among members of a category. That is, many categories are held together by family resemblances among the items that belong to a particular category. In this sense, most of our conventional categories for objects and events are similarity-based ones. For example, the things that one can buy in a store are commonly categorized based on their similarity to one another; thus, we find different kinds of nails in the same section of a hardware store. They form a similarity-based category. However, we can also find nails in other sections of the store. Nails can occur in sections where, for example, things for hanging pictures are displayed. Clearly, a nail is not similar to any of the possible things (such as picture frames, rings, short strings, adhesive tape, maybe even a special hammer) displayed in this section. How is it possible that certain nails appear in this section? Or, to put it in our terms, how is it possible that nails are put in the same category with these other things? The answer is that in addition to similarity-based categories, we also have "frame-based" ones. That is to say, categories can be formed on the basis of which things go commonly and repeatedly together in our experience. If we put up pictures on the wall by first driving a nail into the wall and then hanging the picture frame on the nail by means of attaching a metal ring or a string on the frame, then all the things that we use for this purpose may be placed in a single category. But this category will be frame based—not similarity based.

Frame-based categorization occurs on a large scale. For example, it explains why we often find fish sold together with lemon in many European and North American supermarkets. Fish is usually categorized with meat products, while lemon is categorized with fruits. This is similarity-based categorization. However, when fish and lemon are together in a supermarket, we get an instance of frame-based categorization. This frame emerges from the customary way of eating fish with lemon in Europe and North America. As an earlier example also indicates, food items are often categorized on the basis of the frames in which they occur.

Frames Help Account for Prototype Effects
and Some of the Boundary Issues That Arise
in Connection with Categories

The bachelor example we looked at earlier is a complicated one. It raises the following questions: Is the category of BACHELOR a graded category or not? Does it have clear boundaries or not? What we found was that there are many good examples of the category: A forty-year-old male who could be married but is not is probably an excellent example of the category. But he is only an excellent example if he fits the average male life cycle. Given the fit between an actual life cycle and the frame for the average male life cycle, the category does not seem to be graded; that is, if someone has the features ADULT, MALE, NEVER MARRIED, this person would be a hundred percent member of the category. But if someone does not have one of these or some of these features, the person would not be a member of the category at all. The category seems to be not graded but seems to have rigid boundaries instead. In other words, if the background frame, or idealized cognitive model (ICM), applies to particular cases, the category seems both to be not graded and to have clear boundaries.

However, when the background frame of the average male life cycle does not apply to particular cases, it seems that the category ceases to have clear boundaries. In every case (such as the pope, Tarzan, homosexual adult males, etc.) where there is some doubt about the applicability of the average male life cycle, we run into potential categorization problems. We have to ask: Is the pope, Tarzan, or a homosexual man appropriately called a bachelor? They have all the necessary and sufficient conditions, and yet we hesitate to call them such. This hesitation indicates that the category may be fuzzy; that is, it may not have clear boundaries.

Thus, frames are subtle devices with which we can explore some problematic issues in categorization. As in the case of BACHELOR, we can provide an explanation of why certain categories that seem to have clear-cut boundaries on the classical view may turn out to be fuzzy categories on the cognitive linguistic view based on frames.

Frames Help Account for Cases Where There Are No Necessary and Sufficient Conditions to Define the Category

But often we do not find any necessary and sufficient conditions for the use of concepts at all. How can we define and describe such concepts? As an example of a concept for which there seem to be no essential features, consider the concept of "mother." There are many different kinds of mother: stepmother, surrogate mother, adoptive mother, foster mother, donor mother, unwed mother, and so on. Do they share a set of necessary and sufficient conditions in terms of which we can define the category? Perhaps the most likely candidate for an essential feature for motherhood would be a woman having given birth to a child. But, as is immediately clear, stepmothers, adoptive mothers, and donor mothers do not give birth to a child and yet they are called mothers. In them, one of the features of motherhood is canceled: having given birth to a child. This means that the feature is not an essential one for calling someone a mother. It appears then that the concept of "mother" is not based on what can be called a birth model. The same goes for other potential features and the models they are based on. For example, let us take the feature having nurtured a child. It clearly applies to foster mothers, but not to all mothers, either. Your birth mother gave birth to you but may not have nurtured you.

Lakoff's (1987) solution to the problem is to suggest that the prototype of MOTHER is best characterized as a complex model that is constituted by five simple models:

The birth model: The woman who has given birth to a child is the mother.
The genetic model: The woman who has provided the genetic materials
  is the mother.
The nurturance model: The woman who nurtures the child is the mother.
The marital model: The wife of the father is the mother.
The genealogical model: The closest female ancestor is the mother.

When all simple models converge in a particular case, we have the prototypical mother. We can conceive of this as a complex frame that consists of several simple ones—with the prototype being characterized by the complex frame. The complex frame allows a great deal of variation, as many of the compounds that refer to various kinds of mother indicate.

Frames Help Account for Multiple Understandings of the Same Situation

This is perhaps the most powerful use of frames. With it, we can achieve several, often contradictory, understandings of exactly the same situation. Let us suppose that Bill does not like to spend money (see also a previous section on negation). Two of his friends can describe him appropriately as follows:

(8) Bill is stingy.

(9) Bill is thrifty.

Notice that we are talking about the same person, Bill, who does not like to spend money. One friend conceptualizes Bill as stingy and another conceptualizes him as thrifty. The first friend conceptualizes Bill in terms of the STINGY frame, the latter in terms of the THRIFTY frame. These are contradictory descriptions and contradictory frames: One suggests that the fact that Bill does not like to spend money is a bad thing, whereas the other suggests that it is a good thing. What we have here is what's called alternative construal of the same situation. Frames are often used for this purpose.

Alternative construals are especially common with evaluative terms, such as *stingy* and *thrifty*. As a matter of fact, the opposites of these terms, *wasteful* and *generous*, present us with the same kind of alternative understanding of situations. But alternative construals are not limited to evaluative terms. A clear example of this is how we understand the eggs of fish. In one frame, the eggs of fish are called roe, while in another they are called caviar. The first frame is based on the reproductive cycle of fish but the second on the frame of FOOD CONSUMPTION. In addition, we have seen in this chapter that multiple frames for the same thing play a major role in a wide range of important issues in language understanding and categorization.

Conclusions

Frames are structured mental representations of an area of human experience. They constitute a large part of our knowledge about the world. The knowledge we have about the world appears in highly schematic, or idealized, form in frames. In other words, frames capture our prototypes for conceptual categories. Frames have several additional characteristics. First, frames are evoked by particular meanings of words. Second, particular elements of frames can be focused on, or profiled. Third, frames can impose a certain perspective on a situation. Fourth, frames often suggest a particular history in a concept. Fifth, some frames assume larger cultural frames.

Frames are shared cultural products. Smaller or larger groups of people may share a large number of frames, or cultural/cognitive models. When this happens, we can define culture as a set of shared understandings embodied in cultural/cognitive models. It follows that cultures may be distinguished by the different cultural/cognitive models they use. Cultural/cognitive models can be factored into two types: folk theories and expert theories. Folk theories reflect laypeople's understandings of the world for everyday purposes, whereas expert theories reflect scientists' understandings of (a usually narrow aspect of) the world for some technical purpose. One folk theory may conflict with another with respect to an aspect of the world, and folk theories commonly conflict with scientific ones.

Frames have a variety of important uses, especially in the areas of language understanding, categorization, and the conceptualization of the world. In particular, as regards language understanding, frames help account for how we understand the meanings of individual words, they help account for apparently conflicting cases of negation, and they help account for problems with analyticity. As regards categorization, frames help account for certain problematic cases of categorization, they help account for prototype effects and some of the boundary issues that arise in connection with categories, they help account for cases where there are no necessary and sufficient conditions to define the category, and they help account for multiple understandings of the same situation. This last feature of frames is extremely important for cultural purposes. A large part of cultural behavior consists in negotiating situations that arise from people having different and contradictory cultural/cognitive models of the "same" area of experience. We will consider some examples of such situations in the next chapter.

Exercises

   1. In this chapter I discussed how certain concepts assume larger cultural frames. Consider the word *spinster* and decide what necessary and sufficient conditions define it. Then try to think of examples of the category that fit the necessary and sufficient conditions but for a certain reason you would not

call them such. Finally, compare the cultural connotations of SPINSTER with those of BACHELOR and decide whether the two frames differ in this respect.

2. Based on your knowledge of "script," explain the frame of GETTING MARRIED in a similar fashion to the explanation of the GOING TO A RESTAURANT frame in this chapter. Is the GETTING MARRIED frame regarded in the same way irrespective of the culture that talks about it? Ponder on, for example, the cultural differences between Indian marriage customs and the marriage customs of your own country.

3. A friend of yours is coming to your town on business and you arrange over the phone to meet him/her at his/her accommodation. He or she says, "I just checked in." What frame is evoked by these words in your head? What is the idealized, prototypical script of that frame? If you heard these words, "I just checked in" without a context, what other frames might these words evoke?

4. Collect a large number of sentences on the Internet concerning emotions (say fifty). Based on your examples, try to figure out the frame elements that are needed to set up a general (i.e., not emotion-specific) EMOTION frame. Give examples of the frame elements from your data. Then describe the EMOTION frame that can account for most of your example sentences. Finally, compare your frame with what you find on the Framenet Web site for EMOTION and describe the differences between your frame and the one given by the Framenet project. What do you think is the reason for the differences you can identify?

5. Explain the negation in the sentence *She's not skinny; she's slim!*

6

The Frame Analysis of Culture

Roughly three decades ago the eminent American sociologist Erving Goffman wrote a book with the title *Frame Analysis* (1974). Although he did not have exactly the same idea of frame as I do, Goffman's notion was fairly similar to mine and he applied it masterfully to the study of many aspects of (American) culture. In this chapter I will follow in Goffman's footsteps and apply the notion of "frame" as worked out in the previous chapter to the analysis of various issues in culture. In particular, with the help of frames I will first study the classification system of an Australian aboriginal language, Dyirbal. Then I turn to alternative conceptualization in the case of certain problematic cultural situations. This will be followed by an examination of the structure and understanding of literary works. Finally, I take up the issue of the role of frames in doing politics.

Classification Systems and Culture

We can think of a language as a large category system, in which there are thousands of categories. In some languages, the nouns must be classified according to particular classes they belong to. Languages where speakers need to mark the class of their nouns can be called "noun classifier languages." One well-known European language that does this is German with its required determiners before nouns: *der*, *die*, *das*. I will come back to the discussion of German in this connection later in this chapter.

The Case of Dyirbal

Another language where nouns are classified into larger classes, or categories, is the Australian aboriginal language Dyirbal (see Dixon, 1982; Lakoff, 1987). The Dyirbal nouns must be categorized into such larger classes, or categories. The words that the Dyirbal use to categorize their nouns are *bayi*, *balan*, *balam*, and *bala*.

An interesting feature of the Dyirbal classification of nouns is that in it women, fire, and dangerous things, together with others, are in the same class, or category. One of the foundational works in cognitive linguistics, George Lakoff's 1987, book, reflects this fact in its title: *Women, Fire, and Dangerous Things*. What Lakoff set out to do in his book, was explain how humans categorize the world, including how they set up larger categories to classify their nouns. Let us now see how Lakoff explains why the Dyirbal classify women, fire, and dangerous things together in the same larger category.

To begin, here are the four Dyirbal determiners that show the larger class, or category, of their nouns, together with some examples for each of them:

> *Bayi*: men, kangaroos, possums, bats, most snakes, most fish, some
>   birds, most insects, the moon, storms, rainbows, boomerangs, some
>   spears, and so on
> *Balan*: women, bandicoots, dogs, platypuses, echidnas, some snakes,
>   some fish, most birds, fireflies, scorpions, crickets, the hairy mary
>   grub, anything connected with water and fire, sun and stars, shields,
>   some spears, some trees, and so on
> *Balam*: all edible fruits and the plants that bear them, tubers, ferns,
>   honey, cigarettes, wine, cake
> *Bala*: parts of the body, meat, bees, wind, yamsticks, some spears, most
>   trees, grass, mud, stones, noises and language, and so on

At a first glance, it seems next to impossible to see a general pattern of categorization here. The lists look like completely random ways of bringing words together under particular categories.

Lakoff suggests that these examples can be reduced to four basic schemas as follows:

> *Bayi*: (human) males; animals
> *Balan*: (human) females; water; fire; fighting
> *Balam*: nonflesh food
> *Bala*: everything not in the other categories

In other words, the BAYI schema (or larger noun category) includes males and most animals, the BALAN schema includes females, water, fire, and fighting, the BALAM schema includes nonflesh food, and the BALA schema includes everything else. Lakoff's idea is that these are the prototypical examples of the schemas.

However, to account for the extensions, general principles are used. The most essential principles are the "domain of experience" principle, the "myth-and-belief" principle, and the "important property" principle. Lakoff (1987: 92–96) characterizes these as follows:

> *Domain of experience principle:* If there is a domain of experience
> associated with A, then entities in that domain will be in the same

category as A. (Most fishes are in the *bayi* category [they are animate], and because fishing spears and fishing lines are in the same domain, they will also be in *bayi*. This is despite the fact that spears are in the *balan* category.)

Like other peoples, the Dyirbal deal with their experience through frames. What the domain of experience principle shows is that the classification of some nouns depends on which frame they are included in. For example, since fishing spears are in the same frame as fish (fish are caught with fishing spears), fishing spears will be classified with fish—despite the fact that other spears are in another category.

> *Myth-and-belief principle:* If a noun has characteristic x (on the basis of which its class membership is expected to be decided) but is, through belief or myth, connected with characteristic y, then generally it will belong to the class that corresponds to y and not the one that corresponds to x. (Birds are believed to be spirits of dead human females, so they are classified with women. Some species of willy-wagtails are believed to be mythical men, so they are classified with men. The moon and the sun are believed to be husband and wife in myth, so the moon is in the first category, while the sun is in the second category.)

The Dyirbal have their myths and beliefs about the world. They assign certain nouns into the four categories on the basis of what these myths and beliefs are. Given that the moon is inanimate, we would think that it should probably go to class 4 (the EVERYTHING ELSE category). But because in myth the moon is the husband of the sun, it is in the BAYI category, together with other males.

> *The important property principle:* If a subset of nouns has an important property that the rest of the set does not have, then the members of the subset may be classified with a category other than the one where the larger set belongs. (Most birds are in category 2, but one subset of them, hawks, is in category 1—to mark it as a distinctive subset. The important property is dangerousness.)

This last principle is based on a property of a subset of entities. The property is regarded as highly important by the Dyirbal.

But we have not yet accounted for why women, fire, and dangerous things are in the same category to begin with—in BALAN, category 2. Lakoff offers the following explanation: First, women correspond to the sun in myth (based on the myth-and-belief principle); therefore, the sun is in the same category as women. Second, fire is in the same domain of experience as the sun. This is because it shares certain properties with the sun, namely, heat and brightness. This is based on the domain of experience principle. Third, fire is dangerous, and given the domain of experience principle, it is in the same category with other dangerous things. This way the Dyirbal end up with a particular classification of their nouns in which they have women, fire, and dangerous things. The category may sound strange, unfamiliar, or interesting to other peoples. However, it is natural and makes perfect sense to the Dyirbal, given the principles they use to categorize their world. This was Lakoff's main point.

Lakoff's analysis reveals a number of important general properties of human categorization.

First, as was noted in the chapter on prototypes, categories are characterized by "centrality"; this means that categories have basic members.

Second, there is also "chaining" among category members. This is the idea that the members of a category are linked to more central members via systematic principles. These two properties of centrality and chaining lead to what Lakoff calls "radial structure" within categories. Given this structure, most of our concepts are radial categories.

Third, we experience the world through experiential domains, or frames. In other words, experience comes structured by culturally given frames.

Fourth, we find "motivation" in our categories. Membership in categories is motivated, but it is not predictable.

Fifth and finally, there will be unaccountable cases. Often there remain arbitrary cases of classification that have to be learned item by item.

Framing and Linguistic Relativity

It is clear that inanimate objects have no sex, and yet in many languages words that refer to inanimate objects receive a gender marker, such as masculine, feminine, neuter, and so forth. As mentioned earlier, German is one such language. Given the marking of nouns that refer to inanimate objects, an interesting question arises: Will the speakers of languages like German actually think of these inanimate objects as masculine or feminine, as determined by gender markers? In other words, does gender marking result in a particular way of framing categories?

This is an interesting and important question because its resolution may shed new light on the linguistic relativity hypothesis we discussed in connection with prototype categorization. In that chapter, my conclusion was that language cannot determine the way we think; on the contrary, the way we think determines language. But, as mentioned in that discussion, the linguistic relativity hypothesis can be thought of in two ways: In one, language can be said to determine thought, and in the other, language can be said to merely influence thought. Let us now explore this second possibility with the help of some experiments conducted by Lera Boroditsky and her colleagues (Boroditsky, in press; Boroditsky, Schmidt, and Philips, 2003).

In one study, speakers of German and Spanish were asked to rate similarities between pictures of people (males and females) and pictures of objects whose names had opposite gender markers in German and Spanish. The main result was that both German and Spanish speakers rated inanimate objects with feminine gender markers to be more similar to females than to males and inanimate objects with masculine gender markers to be more similar to males than females. This finding shows that grammatical gender influences speakers' mental representations of objects, which is one form of thinking. The result was true even though the nouns that referred to the inanimate objects had opposite genders in German and Spanish.

In another set of studies, speakers of German and Spanish were asked to assign attributes to nouns that had opposite genders in German and Spanish. Again, the results demonstrated some "Whorfian effect." For example, the word that corresponds to the English *key* is masculine in German and feminine in Spanish. Speakers of German were more likely to describe *key* as hard, heavy, jagged, metal, serrated, and useful, whereas speakers of Spanish were more likely to use such words as *golden, intricate, little, lovely, shiny,* and *tiny* in their descriptions.

As a reverse of this situation, a word that is feminine in German but masculine in Spanish was chosen for study. The word that corresponds to the English *bridge* is feminine in German (*die Brücke*) and masculine in Spanish (*el puente*). The task was the same as before. Speakers of German described *bridge* as beautiful, elegant, fragile, peaceful, pretty, and slender. By contrast, speakers of Spanish used adjectives such as *big, dangerous, long, strong, sturdy,* and *towering* when describing bridge.

Both studies indicate that when a noun is classified as grammatically masculine, speakers are likely to use adjectives to describe it that fit the stereotype of males, and when the noun is marked as having feminine gender, they use adjectives that fit the stereotype of females. More generally, it seems that the gender-marking system of a language does indeed have some influence on the way people mentally represent inanimate objects. These studies show that language has an effect on how we think about things in the world.

Two Cultural Issues

As noted earlier, we can think of culture as a complex network of frames. Often, when we debate or argue about issues in a culture, we can frame the issues in several different ways. There is a wide variety of reasons that we frame experience in the way we do. Since we want to convince people of our truth concerning the issues, we frame the issues in ways that we believe will influence others. At other times, it is our emotional attitude to the situation that leads us to frame the situation in a particular way. And it is also possible that we redefine debated issues by introducing new frames or stressing frames that were previously unstressed in the discussion of the issue. There are many additional reasons for our choice of frames, but it is these reasons that we will consider here.

The Unborn Child and Abortion

One issue that we argue a great deal about in many modern societies is that of abortion. Essentially, two views can be distinguished. There are those who support legalized abortion and those who are against it. An interesting aspect of the debates is that those who are in favor tend to talk about the *fetus*, while those who are against it tend to talk about the *unborn baby* (Lakoff, 1996). It is clear that both sides are talking about the same "thing" (to use a third way of talking about it?/him?/her?), and yet they use different terms. Is this a random choice of terms or is there something deeper going on?

We suggest, together with others, that the choice of terms in the debate is not accidental but depends on framing. If someone uses the term *fetus*, he or she is likely to have a different frame in mind than the person who uses *unborn baby*. In other words, the word *fetus* profiles a concept in one frame, while *unborn baby* profiles a concept in another frame. The frame associated with fetus is that of MAMMALS, a frame above and including the concept of "fetus" in a taxonomic hierarchy. This is because all mammals can have a fetus. By contrast, the phrase *unborn baby* evokes two other frames: that of HUMANS and that of HUMAN LIFE. This is because babies are prototypically human beings, on the one hand, and because babies represent an early stage of the human life cycle, on the other.

But why do the two sides frame the same entity differently? The framing is different because different effects can be achieved with it. Profiling the entity in the MAMMAL frame makes it easier to argue for abortion. In general, people have less strong feelings concerning the killing of animals than the killing of humans. If, however, the profiling of the entity takes place against the background of the HUMANS and HUMAN LIFE CYCLE frames, it is easier to argue against abortion. Again, in general, people have stronger feelings concerning the killing of humans than the killing of animals.

In sum, we choose different words in debates because we profile them against different frames, and profiling them against different frames enables us to influence people according to our purposes and convince them of our "truth." Needless to say, "truth" becomes a relative notion in this view—a notion that is relative to the particular framing in which it is cast.

Who's the Mother?

That the issue of abortion is debated does not surprise anyone. But there are other categories where we would think that no debates can arise. For example, we would not seriously think that it can ever be an issue who one's "real mother" is. But it can and has a great deal to do with categorization and framing, as these notions were described in the previous chapters.

By way of illustration of such a situation, consider the story of a Hungarian-born couple living in the San Francisco Bay Area in California. The story was reported in the *San Francisco Chronicle* (May 10, 2003). A fifty-six-year-old woman, called Ilona, married a man called Istvan. This was her second marriage. She had two adult daughters from a previous marriage. Ilona and Istvan decided to have a child of their own, but their only option was for her to conceive through in vitro fertilization by having viable eggs implanted in her uterus. The egg donor was Ilona's older daughter, Cecilia, aged twenty-eight. Nine months after the successful fertilization, Ilona gave birth to a healthy baby called Monica. The *San Francisco Chronicle* writes: "In the giddy aftermath of the birth, by cesarean section, Istvan looked at his wife cradling the new-born swathed in blankets, smiled at his stepdaughter looking on from afar, and asked the question that many still pose: 'What is she, a mother or grand-mother?'" How come he wasn't sure? We have a situation here in which an adult man whose wife just gave birth to a child using his genetic materials does not know whether his wife is a mother! How can this be? In light of the previous chapter, we can suspect what the answer is. The complex frame of MOTHER-HOOD contains five submodels. The prototypical mother is the woman who gave birth to the child, who nurtures the child, who provided the genetic ma-terials, who is the father's wife, and who is one generation older than the child. The doubt can arise because Ilona did not provide the genetic materials of the child; it was provided by her own daughter, Cecilia. This shows that the lack of one feature that characterizes prototypical mothers can be sufficient grounds for questioning somebody's motherhood.

But there are further puzzles that emerge from the situation. How does Cecilia think of Monica? What is the relationship between Ilona's adult daugh-ter Cecilia and Ilona's new infant daughter, Monica? That this is not simply theoretical speculation can be gathered from the same article: "One look at Monica, and Cecilia's maternal feelings surfaced. She said she didn't expect such a reaction. Throughout the pregnancy, Cecilia referred to Monica as her sister. Afterward, she started feeling as if Monica were her daughter." Cecilia has real maternal feelings, although in many ways she is not the mother: She did not give birth to the child, she is not nurturing the baby, and she is not the father's wife. Is she entitled to such feelings? She can reasonably argue that she provided some of the baby's genes and so she is a mother. Would she also say that the baby has two mothers? We do not know, but that would not be an unreasonable idea, either.

Moreover, to complicate the situation further, Cecilia is expecting a new baby of her own. The birth of the baby will pose a question concerning the relationship between Cecilia's new baby and Ilona: Will Ilona become a grand-mother for the first time or second time? This will depend on whether we categorize Monica as Ilona's or Cecilia's child.

Finally, what will be the relationship between Cecilia's new baby and Ilona's baby, Monica? Will they be sisters, or will Monica be the aunt of Cecilia's new baby? Again, this depends on whether we take Cecilia to be Monica's mother or not.

As this example shows, categorization can have other than a referential func-tion and significance. How we categorize entities may determine how we feel, and, conversely, the feelings we have toward entities may influence the way we categorize them. All of this is possible because we have a flexible conceptual system, which can give rise to a number of different ways of conceptualizing or framing the "same" situation. Categorization, together with framing, is a way of thinking about the world, one of our most important "construal operations." I will discuss additional construal operations in subsequent chapters.

Literature and Frames

The notion of "frame as defining prototypes" can be put to good use in the study of literary texts. Following some suggestions by Mark Turner (1991, 1996), Patrick Colm Hogan (2003) conducted an extensive study of stories that people admire around the world. Hogan argues that these paradigmatic stories have a remarkable degree of structural similarity across cultures and that the universal patterns of the stories are built on cross-culturally shared emotion frames. Hogan cites evidence for his claims from a wide variety of unrelated literary traditions, including not only the Euro-American tradition but also many others, such as Indian, Japanese, Chinese, Middle Eastern, African, and Oceanic.

Let us now see the main ideas of this hypothesis. Hogan proposes and provides evidence for four specific hypotheses:

> *First hypothesis*: Emotion terms are prototype based in both their eliciting conditions and their expressive/actional consequences.

For example, we can define sadness in the following way: 'Sadness is what you feel when someone you like dies and what you express through weeping.' In general, emotions are embedded in stories and emotions are defined in terms of mininarratives. In other words, emotions have a causal part, the emotion as a response to a cause, and the expression of the emotion itself (i.e., the response that the emotion leads to). The cause and the consequence are prototypical of particular emotions. Such prototype-based emotion scenarios, or frames, function as mininarratives on which emotions are based.

> *Second hypothesis*: Prototypical narratives are generated largely from prototypes. They prominently include the prototype eliciting conditions for emotions.

Thus, in Hogan's view, prototypical stories are expansions of the micronarratives that define emotion terms. This means that stories follow the structure of emotion concepts in their general outline. They are largely "about" the eliciting conditions of emotions, the emotions that arise as responses to the eliciting conditions, and the emotional responses that emotions produce.

> *Third hypothesis*: Romantic union and social or political power are the two predominant prototypes for the eliciting conditions of happiness.

This hypothesis proposes that romantic union and social/political power are the prototypical outcomes from which prototypical literary narratives are generated. In other words, these are the goals that are most commonly sought by protagonists in prototypical narratives. The corresponding prototypes for sorrow are the death of the beloved and the complete loss of social or political power.

Fourth hypothesis: Two structures of literary narrative are especially prominent cross-culturally. These are romantic and heroic tragicomedy. Romantic tragicomedy is derived from the personal prototype of happiness (achieving romantic reunion) and heroic tragicomedy is derived from the social prototype for happiness (achieving social/political power).

Thus, happiness appears in two forms in literary texts: personal and social. The personal prototype for happiness defines romantic tragicomedy, while the social prototype defines heroic tragicomedy. In this scheme, a good example of the former is *Romeo and Juliet* and a good example of the latter is *Julius Caesar*—both by Shakespeare.

However, we should not imagine that paradigmatic stories in a culture (and, indeed, cross-culturally) can only be produced by "famous" authors. Many folktales and myths are stories that people consider prototypical narratives in many cultures. For example, "Cinderella" is just as much a paradigmatic story as *Romeo and Juliet* is. Hogan's main point in this connection is that the paradigm stories have a fairly clear universal structure based on very basic emotion scripts, or frames.

But there is more than this to Hogan's theory. He suggests that prototypical narratives have a telic (purposive) structure that includes an *agent*, a *goal*, and a *causal* sequence. (On this structure of stories, see Oatley, 1992.) The causal sequence connects the agent's actions with the achievement or nonachievement of the goal. Various emotions can be defined in relation to this telic structure. Thus, there are what Hogan calls *junctural emotions*. These define a certain juncture (interruption or pause) in the larger narrative. They include fear, disgust, anger, wonder, and mirth. Next, there are what are termed *outcome emotions*. Happiness and sorrow are the dominant emotions here. They represent the final evaluation points for junctural emotions. Finally, we have *sustaining emotions*. The two main sustaining emotions are romantic love and heroic perseverance. They sustain the plot. They help and cause the characters to go through the various junctural emotions until they reach a final outcome.

This allows us to see why the union of lovers is the outcome goal for a predominant and universal narrative structure—the comedy. This is so because it is the prototype-eliciting condition for personal happiness. The sustaining emotion in this type of narrative will be romantic love. In this view, tragedy is a transformation of comedy and not another genre of the same type. In general, we find the same type of romantic and heroic tragicomedies across unrelated traditions. This can be accounted for by the cross-cultural constancy of happiness. This constancy comes from the universal eliciting conditions for happiness: romantic union and social domination.

Hemingway's "A Very Short Story"

As an illustration of some of the preceding points, let us look at Hemingway's "A Very Short Story" and see the extent to which it conforms to the universal narrative structure outlined earlier:

One very hot evening in Padua they carried him up onto the roof and he could look out over the top of the town. There were chimney swifts in the sky. After a while it got dark and the searchlights came out. The others went down and took the bottles with them. He and Luz could hear them below on the balcony. Luz sat on the bed. She was cool and fresh in the hot night.

Luz stayed on night duty for three months. They were glad to let her. When they operated on him she prepared him for the operating table; and they had a joke about friend or enema. He went under the anesthetic holding tight on to himself so he would not blab about anything during the silly, talky time. After he got on crutches he used to take the temperatures so Luz would not have to get up from the bed. There were only a few patients, and they all knew about it. They all liked Luz. As he walked back along the halls he thought of Luz in his bed.

Before he went back to the front they went into the Duomo and prayed. It was dim and quiet, and there were other people praying. They wanted to get married, but there was not enough time for the banns, and neither of them had birth certificates. They felt as though they were married, but they wanted everyone to know about it, and to make it so they could not lose it.

Luz wrote him many letters that he never got until after the armistice. Fifteen came in a bunch to the front and he sorted them by the dates and read them all straight through. They were all about the hospital, and how much she loved him and how it was impossible to get along without him and how terrible it was missing him at night.

After the armistice they agreed he should go home to get a job so they might be married. Luz would not come home until he had a good job and could come to New York to meet her. It was understood he would not drink, and he did not want to see his friends or anyone in the States. Only to get a job and be married. On the train from Padua to Milan they quarreled about her not being willing to come home at once. When they had to say good-bye, in the station at Milan, they kissed good-bye, but were not finished with the quarrel. He felt sick about saying good-bye like that.

He went to America on a boat from Genoa. Luz went back to Pordonone to open a hospital. It was lonely and rainy there, and there was a battalion of arditi quartered in the town. Living in the muddy, rainy town in the winter, the major of the battalion made love to Luz, and she had never known Italians before, and finally wrote to the States that theirs had only been a boy and girl affair. She was sorry, and she knew he would probably not be able to understand, but might some day forgive her, and be grateful to her, and she expected, absolutely unexpectedly, to be married in the spring. She loved him as always, but she realized now it was only a boy and girl love. She hoped he would have a great career, and believed in him absolutely. She knew it was for the best.

The major did not marry her in the spring, or any other time. Luz never got an answer to the letter to Chicago about it. A short time after he contracted gonorrhea from a sales girl in a loop department store while riding in a taxicab through Lincoln Park.

We can note several points in connection with the story.

First, the story reflects the prototypical goal that people pursue in their lives: personal happiness. It is the attempt to achieve this goal that organizes much of the story.

Second, the goal of happiness can be achieved through romantic union between a man and a woman. In this story, the romantic union is given as marriage. In many cases, romantic union is a chief (prototypical) condition for enduring happiness.

Third, the man and the woman are in love with each other. Romantic love functions as a sustaining emotion in the story.

Fourth, eliciting conditions for romantic love include sexual attraction. The story begins with the (explicit and implicit) description of sexual attraction between the man and the woman.

Because of this structure, the story can be regarded as a romantic tragicomedy. The happiness-based sequence would be something like the following:

sexual attraction → romantic love → romantic union (marriage) → enduring happiness

In the sequence, the chief eliciting condition for enduring happiness is romantic union, the chief eliciting condition for romantic union is romantic love, and the chief eliciting condition for being in romantic love is sexual attraction. This is the idealization that underlies the story.

However, the actual story that is based on the idealized HAPPINESS frame is very different. In it, we find that the main goal of enduring happiness is not achieved by either the man or the woman. The romantic love between the man and the woman does not lead to marriage and hence to happiness. More than that, the woman's plans to marry the Italian major are not fulfilled and the American man contracts gonorrhea. Thus, instead of having the main characters achieve enduring personal happiness, the story ends in complete disappointment for both characters.

The main point of this brief analysis was to show that a story may evoke an underlying idealization—a schematized frame with respect to which the actual story can be said to belong to a particular genre. The underlying idealized frame and the actual story may be very different from each other. The reality of the story's world is set against the idealized version of reality. This difference may be responsible for much of the aesthetic and emotional effect that a story can have on readers.

Politics and Framing

Certain words are used to create a more or less "neutral" way of speaking about an issue. There is of course no neutral way. Neutrality in framing experience is an illusion. We conceptualize experience by means of the frames we get from a particular culture, and these frames are anything but neutral.

They have, built into them, a particular outlook on a situation. And yet we can say, at least in a loose way, that some of our framings of experience are more neutral than others. The phrasing *neutral way* is intended to suggest that some of the words we use evoke emotionally or otherwise less loaded frames than other words in connection with an issue.

One example of such a relatively neutral expression is *graduated income tax*. In taxation, health services, the educational system, and so on, such relatively neutral terms are frequently used (and create the impression of objectivity). However, these relatively neutral phrases can be, and often are, reinterpreted in such domains, and this is especially the case in political discourse. What this means is that politicians commonly reframe the ideas expressed in relatively neutral language; that is, they place the ideas in frames that were never intended to be used in conceptualizing the ideas. Lakoff (1996) provides a nice illustration of this process. He writes: "In Dan Quayle's acceptance speech to the Republican convention in 1992, he said, in a rhetorical question arguing against the graduated income tax, 'Why should the best people be punished?'" It seems that what Quayle did was reframe the relatively neutral expression *graduated income tax*. By means of his choice of words, he evoked several frames that allow a significant reinterpretation of this concept. First, he linked the concept to the notion of punishment. Second, he claimed that the people who pay the most taxes are the best people in the American system of progressive taxation.

This example raises an interesting issue in connection with framing. Can we reframe a concept in any way we like; that is, can we link it to, or place it in, just about any new frame? Obviously not. There is a clear constraint on doing this: The concept that we want to reframe must somehow fit the new frame. In our example, the idea that citizens are required to pay taxes by the government provides the possibility of and justification for linking progressive taxation to the punishment frame. In taxation, the government takes money from the people. But taking money from someone can be regarded as something dishonest or illegal. Given this, it makes it possible for Quayle to reframe progressive taxation as punishment. Notice that this reasoning is based on the assumption that the government has no right to tax citizens (at least the ones who have the highest income). The new frame for progressive taxation as punishment thus has all this information.

But why does Quayle say that it is the best people who get punished? The connection between the best people and punishment as regards taxation is based on another piece of reasoning within the frame, namely, that the quality of people depends on how successful they are financially. Those who are financially the most successful are the best people. Now in progressive taxation the people with the highest income pay the most taxes. Thus, these people (the best people) are punished.

This reasoning is clearly faulty. Since the money is taken away by the government not only from people who make the most money but also from others with a lower income, everyone with an income should be considered as being punished. But Quayle limits the group of people who are punished to those who make the most money and thus have to pay the most taxes. This kind of inconsistency is common in the application of frames and in reframing situations in especially political but also other types of discourse.

If, however, our basic assumptions are different, our reframings will also be different. If, for instance, we do not regard progressive taxation on the part of the government as unjustified but rather as fair and just, we will use other words to reconceptualize progressive taxation. People often do this and use phrases such as *paying one's fair share to society* or one's *civic duty to society*. These words assume a very different framing of progressive taxation—one in which the government has the right to impose the highest taxes on those with the highest income and that it is these citizens' duty to comply with the government.

The wordings and the frames the wordings evoke may distinguish the participants of the political scene. In this example, Lakoff suggests, the PUNISHMENT frame is typical of conservatives, whereas the CIVIC DUTY frame is most characteristic of liberals. These are clearly rough generalizations, but they point to the possibility of studying political discourse and thought by making use of frame theory.

Conclusions

If it is reasonable to think of culture, as I believe it is, as to a great degree being constituted by people's shared understandings of their world, we can study a large part of culture by analyzing the frames that underlie people's behavior. This chapter has looked at four areas of culture in which frames seem to play an important role in giving an account of human behavior.

The study of classification systems benefits from frame analysis in at least two ways. On the one hand, we can think of the broad gender-based categories of language as frames. Can we dismiss this kind of framing as merely an arbitrary linguistic convention? In other words, can we assume that, for instance, inanimate nouns that are marked for a particular gender do not play any role in the way speakers of such a language think about or "see" the world? Boroditsky's studies suggest otherwise. It seems that the gender-marking system of a language does shape the way people mentally represent inanimate objects. Her studies show that language does have an effect on how people think about things in the world. On the other hand, frames appear to be useful in explaining the specific details of such large-scale categorization systems. Why are particular items included in one category rather than another? The answer seems to be that cultures are not simply composed of frames with an arbitrary membership but also have certain higher-level principles that operate on frames and on the basis of which people assign items to particular categories. Cultures differ with respect to not only the frames they have but also the higher-level principles they have. In the case of Dyirbal, we mentioned the "domain of experience," the "myth-and-belief," and the "important property" principles based on Lakoff's (1987) work. In addition, the functioning of the "domain of experience" principle clearly involves a more specific use of frames. What the principle actually amounts to is that in Dyirbal many categories are frame based—rather than similarity based (as we used these terms in the sense of the previous chapter).

As a second application of frame analysis, we looked at a social issue and a problematic cultural situation in which the participants were at a loss to clearly identify their roles and those of others. What is common to the two applications is the possibility of construing the situations in alternative ways. We saw that in both cases alternative frames are involved. In the abortion example, we can apply very different frames, depending on whether we support or oppose legalized abortion. It could of course be suggested that frames merely serve rhetorical purposes here. However, in the other example no such argument could be made. At issue was the identity of the participants. Who is the real mother? Who am I? The analysis of the example by means of frames showed that the complexities in the use of frames can create complex dilemmas in human life.

By way of a third example, we saw how literary works may be based on particular cultural frames. Given the cross-cultural constancy of happiness, we find the same type of romantic and heroic tragicomedies in many unrelated cultures. For example, the union of lovers is the outcome goal for a predominant and universal narrative structure—the comedy. It is so because the union of lovers is the prototype eliciting condition for personal happiness. The sustaining emotion in this type of narrative will be romantic love. In other words, as Hogan's (2003) research shows, much of the structure of literary works relies on the frame associated with the emotion of happiness, in which the universal eliciting conditions include romantic union and social domination.

I demonstrated some of these points by looking at a short story by Ernest Hemingway. The analysis of "A Very Short Story" showed that the story evokes an idealized and schematized emotion frame. I pointed out that the underlying idealized frame and the actual story are very different from each other. Such differences can in part account for the aesthetic and emotional effect that stories have on readers.

My final illustration of cultural frame analysis involved politics. Politics is a domain where alternative framings and reframings are rife. Alternative framings and reframings largely depend on one's basic assumptions. This is what we saw in the case of progressive taxation. If one regards progressive taxation as unjustified (mostly out of self-interest), one will think of taxation as punishment. If, however, one regards progressive taxation as fair and just, one will conceptualize (i.e., frame) progressive taxation as "paying one's fair share to society" or as "one's civic duty to society." As George Lakoff suggests, alternative framings of this kind may distinguish the participants of the political scene.

I do not claim that the frame analysis of culture can explain each and every aspect of human behavior, but it can be used to account for a large part of human behavior. Subsequent chapters will discuss additional conceptual tools that are needed for a broader study of both culture and mind.

Exercises

1. Suppose that you want to start a business and decide to build and run a general department store (something like a Wal-Mart). You have a huge, empty, unstructured retail space. How would you arrange the different departments spatially? How would you further divide the different sections into subsections and possibly sub-subsections? What principles of organization would you use? What signs would you put up to guide your customers to their desired article as quickly as possible? How can you use your knowledge of the different levels of categorization to make the shopping experience as smooth and customer-friendly as possible? Would there be groups of goods that are difficult to categorize? For example, would you put men's perfume into the perfume section or among men's toiletries? What principles are there to help you?

2. Tales, as mentioned in the chapter, often have protoypical structures concerning the characters, their goals, and emotionally moving events. This is why they are so effective.

A. Try to make up a story that exemplifies some of these prototypical characteristics.

B. Based on what you have learned about prototypes, categorization, and frames, try to account for the success of prototypical or paradigmatic stories.

3. Given the huge success of *Star Wars*, try to account for it on the basis of what you have read about the suggestions of Patrick Colm Hogan (2003) concerning paradigmatic stories discussed in the chapter.

4. The concept of "marriage" has been changing throughout history and it differs from culture to culture even today. Do some research on the various contentious issues concerning marriage (e.g., monogamy-polygamy; same-sex marriage; marriage viewed according to Christian law vs. secular law, etc.). Explain how different frames can be utilized in support of or against these issues regarding marriage.

5. Similarly to the example of abortion mentioned in the chapter, examine how people view the case of HARMING ANIMALS. Recently many countries have passed laws that regulate and punish harming animals (e.g., in experiments). Nevertheless, two opposing groups still remain: those who disapprove of the laws and those who are for them. Do these two groups use the same pronouns and attributes in connection with animals when they give speeches regarding the issue? Can they have any underlying frames (or metaphors) that determine their way of thinking?

6. Collect examples where the same person, thing or notion is framed differently by different people "looking" at the same person, thing, or notion.

7. Consider the following situation: A child is stolen from her or his parents as a baby and is adopted by a family who believe the child is an orphan. After six years of living with this family the child is tracked down by the biological parents and they reclaim her or him. Who do you think the child would refer to as his or her parents? Who do you think are considered to be the "real" parents of this child? Ask ten people to answer the question and also ask them

to try to justify their answers. Think about your results and try to analyze your findings in terms of what you have learned about frames and their relationship to categorization.

8. Is your language a noun-classifying language?

A. If so, conduct a little experiment of your own, making use of Lera Boroditsky's work on nouns that denote inanimate objects in noun-classifying languages such as Spanish and German. See whether the nouns *key* and *bridge* (or some others) receive adjectives that are usually attributed to men or the adjectives listed are regarded as more feminine in your language. Compare your findings with Boroditsky's results.

B. If not, then you can do some work to "check" Lera Boroditsky's results. Do a survey, asking for adjectives attributed to the words *key* and *bridge*, and organize the adjectives according to their being more feminine or masculine (which you can also have judged by some people). Since your language does not classify nouns, there should not be too much asymmetry in the number of masculine / feminine adjectives that people list. Present your findings, and try to account for them.

7

Mappings within Frames

Metonymy as a Cognitive and Cultural Process

When we use words, we often mean something different from the primary meaning of the words used. One large class of such cases is called metonymy. Loosely speaking, metonymy is a "stand-for" relation: We use x to stand for y. For example, we use the head to stand for the person, such as in the phrase *head count*. Several questions arise in connection with metonymy.

First, we have to ask what metonymy more precisely is. I begin my discussion with this question and provide a new definition that is very different from the traditional one. In particular, I will point out that metonymy is not simply a linguistic device but also a conceptual one. As a conceptual device, it relies heavily on frames, or domains—a notion that was introduced in chapter 5.

Second, there is the issue of the variety of metonymies. Given the large number of different metonymic relationships between x and y, we should ask: What are the basic types? After offering a new definition of the concept, I provide a possible classification of metonymies, which also depends on frames, or domains, or idealized cognitive models.

Third, we need to find out about the nature of metonymy. Is it a purely cognitive or a purely cultural device or a combination of the two? I will argue that metonymy occurs not only in language but also in thought as well as in social/cultural practice.

There has been an upsurge in the cognitive linguistic study of metonymy in recent years. Clearly, this chapter can only provide some basic ideas and concentrate on issues that bear on the connections between metonymy and culture. (For extensive collections of essays, see Barcelona, 2000a; Dirven and Pörings, 2002; Panther and Radden, 1999; Panther and Thornburg, 2003. For individual essays that focus on metonymy, see, among others, Barcelona, 2000b; Brdar and Brdar-Szabó, 2003; Brdar and Brdar, 2003; Ruiz de Mendoza Ibanez, 2000.) Several sections of this chapter draw heavily on Kövecses and Radden, 1998, and Radden and Kövecses, 1999.

What Is Metonymy?

Let us begin with some celebrated examples of metonymy. Take the following sentences:

(1)   The ham sandwich spilled beer all over himself.

(2)   Washington denied the charges.

(3)   Nixon bombed Hanoi.

In all of these we have a "vehicle" and a "target." There is an entity, or element, that "stands for" another entity, or element. The element that stands for another element is the vehicle and the element for which it stands is the target. Thus, the preceding sentences have the following vehicles and targets:

(1)   a. The ham sandwich (vehicle) for the person eating it (target)

(2)   a. Washington (vehicle) for U.S. government (target)

(3)   a. Nixon (vehicle) for the U.S. Air Force (target)

Such "stand-for" relationships between elements are called metonymy. We know that the speaker talking about the ham sandwich is really talking about the person eating it; we know that the speaker talking about the city of Washington is really talking about the U.S. government; and we know that the speaker talking about former president Nixon is really talking about the U.S. Air Force.

How can these vehicle elements stand for these target elements? In other words, what enables us to use a particular element for another element? How do we know which element is connected with which other element? What makes this possible is the notion of "frame," as discussed in the previous chapters. The examples mentioned earlier are all based on a particular frame:

(1)   b. RESTAURANT frame: food for the person

(2)   b. GOVERNMENT frame: place for the institution

(3)   b. CONTROL frame: controller for the controlled

Since every frame consists of a number of elements, an element of the frame can stand for other elements of the frame. As we saw in chapter 4, the RESTAURANT frame consists of a variety of elements, including the person who goes to the restaurant, the restaurant itself, the food eaten, the waiter, and so on. Given this, the food eaten can be used for the person eating it. Similarly, the frame of the U.S. GOVERNMENT would include the president, the cabinet members, the place where the institutions are physically located, the actual buildings, and so on. For this reason, it makes sense that the place where the U.S. government is located, Washington, can stand for the U.S. government. Finally, given the taxonomic hierarchy of the chain of command in the U.S. Armed Forces, the president himself can stand for the U.S. Air Force that did the actual bombing. Since he is at the top of the chain, he has control over the elements underneath him, and this makes it possible for someone to use the element of controller (Nixon) for the element of the controlled (U.S. Air Force). In each case, we have a frame in which an element stands for another element of the same frame. By the cognitive process of "standing for" another element, the vehicle can direct our attention to the target in an indirect way.

Now we can provide a more precise definition of metonymy along the lines of Kövecses and Radden (Kövecses and Radden, 1998; Radden and Kövecses, 1999):

> Metonymy is a cognitive process in which a conceptual element or entity (thing, event, property), the vehicle, provides mental access to another conceptual entity (thing, event, property), the target, within the same frame, domain, or idealized cognitive model (ICM). We can conceive of this as a "within-domain mapping," where the vehicle entity is mapped onto the target entity.

Thus, for example, given the RESTAURANT frame, the speaker of *The ham sandwich spilled beer all over himself* directs attention, or provides mental access, to the conceptual element "person eating the ham sandwich" (target) through the use of another conceptual element "ham sandwich" (vehicle) that belongs to the same frame. However, this formulation leaves open the question of which elements of a frame can stand for which other elements of the same frame.

Given a frame, can any element of a frame stand for any other element of the same frame? Since frames are tightly organized conceptual structures with a manageable number of elements, it would seem that any frame element can stand for any other frame element. While this may be so theoretically, in practice we seem to pick those elements to stand for other elements that have a well-established, entrenched conceptual relationship to each other. Not all relationships are equally common in producing metonymies. Take, for example, the HUMAN FACE as a frame. It includes the nose and the mouth, among other things. The nose and the mouth stand in the relationship of spatial contiguity. Is this relationship sufficient to use the nose to stand for the mouth or the mouth to stand for the nose? It does not seem to. We cannot talk about someone's nose and mean his or her mouth, or conversely. In other words, given this frame, simple spatial contiguity does not seem to be sufficient for us to use these elements for each other. What are then the major metonymy-producing relationships between elements? I will survey some of the most important ones in the following pages.

Frames and Their Parts

As I noted in previous chapters, our knowledge of the world comes in the form of structured frames, or ICMs, short for idealized cognitive models. These can be construed as wholes with parts. Since frames are conceptualized as wholes that have parts, there are two general configurations of wholes and parts that give rise to metonymy-producing relationships: the "whole and its parts" configuration and the "part and part" configuration. A variety of specific metonymy-producing relationships can be observed within both configurations.

The "Whole and Its Parts" Configuration

This configuration leads to metonymies in a natural way. As we saw in the discussion of basic-level categorization, our interaction with parts of wholes is a crucially important aspect of "things." The relationship between whole "things" and parts of "things" is a major source of metonymies—in the form of either "whole for part" or "part for whole." Let us consider some specific relationships within this configuration.

The THING-AND-PART ICM

When we have a whole thing, this whole can be used for a part of the whole. This yields the metonymy WHOLE THING FOR PART OF THE THING. One example of this is the sentence *America is at war*, in which the (name of) the entire hemisphere (the Americas) is used for a part of it (the United States). This metonymy also works the other way around: PART OF THE THING FOR THE WHOLE THING. Here a part stands for the whole thing, as in *I'll go to England this summer*. England is a part of the Great Britain, and by mentioning it I may refer to the whole of Great Britain.

An interesting special case of the WHOLE THING FOR PART OF THE THING metonymy is what Langacker (1987) calls active zone. Consider the example "He hit me." In this sentence the whole person is taken to stand for a part of the person. The pronouns *he* and *me* indicate the whole person, but it is clear that the action of hitting is done by the hand (a part of the person) and that the hitting affects a particular part of the person, such as the jaw, the chest, the back—not the entire person. Thus, by making reference to the whole person the speaker of the sentence really means a part of the person—the part that Langacker calls active zone. This is the part that is most typically involved in the action denoted by a verb. Another example can be analyzed in the same way. Take the sentence *The car needs washing*. Although we mention the car as a whole, it is clear that the action of washing is directed at particular parts of the car—not the whole car. When we wash the car, we typically wash the external body of the car but not the seats, the steering wheel, the engine, or the battery. In other words, wholes have active zones that are unconsciously identified in the process of understanding sentences that involve certain WHOLE FOR PART metonymies.

PART OF THE THING FOR THE WHOLE THING metonymies are much more common or at least are much more commonly recognized as metonymies than WHOLE THING FOR PART OF THE THING metonymies. While active-zone metonymies are basically never consciously recognized as metonymies or as "figures of speech," the converse PART FOR WHOLE metonymies are often consciously created and recognized as such. The traditional name for such metonymies is synecdoche. An illustrative example could be "There are many sails out in the bay today," where the sails (part) stand for the sailboats (whole). This type of metonymy is especially common in classical literary texts.

Abstractions also commonly function as targets (wholes) for more concrete vehicles (parts). In the sentence *Most people prefer the ballot to the bullet*, the part "ballot" stands for the whole "democracy" and the part "bullet" stands for the whole "oppression." In this type of metonymy a more concrete vehicle stands for an abstract thing, the target. Thus, an abstract frame can include concrete elements, which can then stand for the whole frame.

We can think of places as parts of wholes. For example, institutions as wholes are typically located in physical places. Some examples for the PLACE FOR THE INSTITUTION metonymy include:

(4)   Washington denied the charges.

(5)   Wall Street is panicking.

(6)   Berkeley is firing professors.

In all of the examples, the place stands for an institution, which is a special case of the more general metonymy PART OF THE THING FOR THE WHOLE THING.

The SCALE ICM

What is called the SCALE ICM here is another instance of the whole and part configuration. It consists of a scale and an end point. The scale corresponds to the whole, while the end to the part. Consider two examples:

(7)   Harry was speeding again. (WHOLE FOR PART)

(8)   How old are you? (PART FOR WHOLE)

In the first, we have a speed-scale (whole) and an end point (part). The whole scale stands for the part, in that the generic concept of "speed" can be used to indicate the top of the scale, that is, high speed.

The reverse happens in the second sentence, where there is a scale of age (whole) and an end point—old age (part). In this case, we use the upper end of the scale (old age, part) to talk about the scale in general (whole). Notice that we would ask a person the same question (using "old," the part), regardless of his or her age (e.g., a young child).

The CONSTITUTION ICM

The CONSTITUTION frame is concerned mainly with the materials that make up objects. The object is whole; the constitutive materials are parts. The metonymy works both ways, either as WHOLE FOR PART or PART FOR WHOLE, as the examples show:

(9)   There was *cat* all over the road. (OBJECT FOR MATERIAL)

(10)   She disappeared in the *woods*. (MATERIAL FOR THE OBJECT)

In the first sentence, the whole object is used to talk about its constitutive part. Notice how the grammar of *cat* changes in this usage. It does not function as a count but as a mass noun in the sentence (no indefinite article; grammar of mass nouns).

In the second sentence, it is the constitutive material of trees/forests (wood) that is used for the whole forest. Notice also that the grammar of *wood* changes accordingly, assuming a feature of count nouns (plural *s*).

The COMPLEX EVENT ICM

Complex events are often conceptualized as wholes that have parts. All the subevents that make up a complex event are the whole, and the subevents, together with place and time, are the parts. One such complex event is getting treatment in a hospital. Take the following sentence:

(11)   She's in the hospital.

Mentioning the place where someone is, is used to indicate the entire complex event that takes place in that place. It is clear that when we say of someone that he or she is in the hospital, we do not simply mean that the person is just there. Our most common understanding of the sentence is that people are in hospitals to get treatment. Another potential meaning is that they are visiting someone in the hospital. In this latter case, we would still have the same metonymy, that is, PART OF THE WHOLE FOR THE WHOLE THING, except that here the whole would consist of visiting someone in a hospital. In other words, the same metonymy can be used to code, or talk about, two different situations.

Consider now the sentence *I speak Hungarian.* Speaking is a subevent for all the other events that are involved in knowing a language, such as understanding, reading, using it in the appropriate ways and situations, and so forth. We have a complex whole here of which a single subevent is singled out—speaking—and can be used to talk about the whole.

The same thing happens in an interesting type of complex events: indirect speech acts. In indirect speech acts a particular aspect of the whole event is singled out. Very often, this is a condition that has to be met in order to perform the action requested by, or otherwise involved in, the indirect speech act. Take the example "Can you pass the salt?" This is a request for passing the salt. However, instead of a direct request, the request is performed by asking a question about whether the person asked has the ability to perform the action. In our terms, this is a metonymy because the speaker makes a request by making reference to a part of an action—the hearer's ability to perform it. The metonymy can be put as ABILITY (TO PERFORM AN ACTION) FOR THE ACTION (REQUESTED). As can be expected, there are often cross-cultural differences in which an aspect of a complex indirect speech act is used to make the speech act.

A good example of such cross-cultural differences is given by Lakoff (1987). He argues that different parts of a frame can be used by speakers of different languages to talk about the same situation. Consider the example discussed by Lakoff. In response to the question *How did you get to the party?* speakers of English would most naturally say something like "I drove." Notice what's involved here. There is something like a GOING TO A PARTY frame. The frame is structured by some preconditions, like having the means or having access to some means to go to the party. In addition, certain initial actions must be performed, like getting into a vehicle, starting it up, and leaving. There will also be a central action, like traveling in a vehicle, driving, and so on. The central action must be successfully performed with the person arriving at the location of the party. Here he or she must get out of the vehicle. And when all these things are done, the person can be said to have arrived at the party. Now in response to the question *How did you get to the party?* speakers of Ojibwa, a North American Indian language, can say the equivalent of *I stepped into a canoe.* That is, they make reference to an initial prerequisite action (we can call it embarkation) in answering the question, whereas speakers of English typically use the central action—in this case, driving. In both languages, speakers will make use of the same PART FOR WHOLE metonymy, but the part made use of will be the central action in English and embarkation in Ojibwa.

The CATEGORY-AND-PROPERTY ICM

We can think of categories themselves as having a part-whole structure. In the case of categories, the most important part is the properties used to define the category. The category as a whole has properties as parts. In the sentence

(12)   Boys will be boys

the first *boys* indicates the category of BOYS as a whole, while the second indicates the typical qualities or features of boys, such as "unruly" (i.e., we have the metonymy CATEGORY FOR PROPERTY). That is to say, a quality or property of boys ("unruly") is made reference to by the second use of *boys* that captures the category as a whole. Incidentally, this analysis shows that sentences like *Boys will be boys* do not represent empty tautologies.

The reverse can also occur in the case of the CATEGORY-AND-PROPERTY frame. A property can stand for the entire category. Consider the following sentence:

(13)   African-Americans were once called blacks.

Here we have the metonymy PROPERTY FOR THE CATEGORY. As a matter of fact, the metonymy applies twice in the sentence—both *African-American* and *blacks* are instances of it. Euphemisms (as well as disphemisms) are often based on this specific type of metonymy. As the example shows, the conceptual structure of the euphemism is the same in both cases (i.e., PROPERTY FOR THE CATEGORY). What changes is the connotations that go together with the particular property that replaces the old one (*African-American* does not, as yet, have the negative connotations of *black*).

The CATEGORY-AND-MEMBER ICM

Another kind of metonymy involves a category and a member of the category. The category itself is viewed as a whole, while the members are the parts. The relationship between the whole category and a member is often reversible, as can be seen in the examples that follow:

(14)   She's on the pill. (CATEGORY FOR A MEMBER)

(15)   Do you have an aspirin? (A MEMBER FOR THE CATEGORY)

In the first sentence, the whole category of PILLS stands for a particular member of the category, namely, contraceptive pills, whereas in the second sentence a particular member of a category (i.e., aspirin) stands for the entire category of PAIN RELIEVERS. As we will see later, this type of metonymy is crucial in accounting for prototype effects and the impact of culture on such effects.

The "Part and Part" Configuration

So far we have looked at the configuration of frames that involves the whole frame and a part of it. Now let us turn to the other configuration that is also very productive of metonymic relations: the "part and part" configuration. We will mention some of the frames, or ICMs, that most clearly demonstrate the possibility that a part can stand for another part, namely, action, causation, control, and a kind of frame that arises in many different situations.

The ACTION ICM

The ACTION frame includes a variety of different frame elements that can stand for one another. What follows is a selection of some of the conventional possibilities that emerge for metonymic relations, each illustrated by one or more examples:

> *ski, shampoo* one's hair: INSTRUMENT FOR ACTION
> *butcher* the cow, *author* a book: AGENT FOR ACTION
> *snitch*: ACTION FOR AGENT
> *blanket* the bed: OBJECT INVOLVED IN THE ACTION FOR THE ACTION
> give me a *bite*: ACTION FOR THE OBJECT INVOLVED IN THE ACTION
> *sneeze* the napkin off the table: MEANS FOR ACTION
> *summer* in Paris: TIME PERIOD OF THE ACTION FOR THE ACTION
> *porch* the newspaper: DESTINATION FOR MOTION

As can be seen, most of the conventional metonymic relations take "action" as the target of the metonymy. However, in some of them we have "action" as the vehicle and some other part as the target.

The CAUSATION ICM

The CAUSATION frame minimally consists of a cause and an effect. These can be reversed in a metonymic relationship. For example, in Austin's famous examples ("healthy body," "healthy exercise," and "healthy complexion"), we find two causation metonymies: EFFECT FOR CAUSE ("healthy exercise") and CAUSE FOR EFFECT ("healthy complexion"). In the first, the exercise (cause) that produces a healthy body (effect) is described as *healthy*, whereas in the second the complexion (effect) that results from a healthy body (cause) is described as *healthy*.

There are many subtypes of the CAUSE AND EFFECT metonymy, as the following examples demonstrate:

(16) She's my *joy/pride*: EMOTION FOR THE CAUSE OF EMOTION

(17) The train *roared by*: SOUND FOR THE EVENT THAT CAUSED IT

(18) Have you seen my *Shakespeare*? + I bought a *Ford*: PRODUCER FOR PRODUCT

These are all very common and productive metonymic relations that are based on cause and effect.

The CONTROL ICM

We saw an example that was based on the control frame at the beginning of the chapter: "*Nixon* bombed Hanoi." In that metonymy the controller was used to stand for the controlled. But the relationship is reversible and the controlled can also stand for the controller: "The *presidential limousine* just arrived." Here we have the CONTROLLED FOR CONTROLLER.

The CONTROLLER AND CONTROLLED relationship also has some special cases. One such case is the POSSESSOR AND POSSESSED. The relationship between the possessor and the possessed is also that of control. The possessor has control over the possessed. Although the possessed does not have control over the possessor, it can still be used to stand for it. Here are some examples that make use of the relationship:

(19)   This is *Harry*: POSSESSOR FOR THE POSSESSED

(20)   marry *money*, marry *power*: POSSESSED FOR THE POSSESSOR

We use the first when we talk about a possession of Harry's among things possessed by other people, say, a bottle of milk in a shared refrigerator in a student hostel. We use the second when we indicate the person who has money or power by the possession itself.

ICMs That Involve Indeterminate Relationships

In a special type of metonymy, we have a frame, or ICM, in which there is a contextually highly relevant object or property that is connected to another element of the frame. In such cases, the contextually most relevant object or property can be used metonymically to stand for the element that is connected with it. One example of this was the sentence *The* ham sandwich *spilled beer all over himself*, which I discussed at the beginning of this chapter. In it, the contextually most relevant object is the food a person eats in a restaurant. This yields the metonymy THE FOOD ORDERED FOR THE PERSON WHO ORDERED IT. Some additional examples of this type of metonymy would be:

(21)   The violin sneezed during performance.

(22)   The appendicitis wants a glass of water.

Here we have a CONCERT frame and a HOSPITAL SURGERY frame. In the CONCERT frame, the situationally most relevant object that characterizes a musician is the instrument he or she plays (violin). In the HOSPITAL SURGERY frame, it is the kind of surgical problem that patients have (appendicitis). Given our knowledge and/or ability to establish the situationally most relevant objects or properties connected with other elements of the frame, we can easily create and understand such metonymies.

Culture, Cognition, and Metonymy

Despite the purely cognitivist definition of metonymy in the first section (i.e., metonymy being a cognitive process that provides mental access), there are good reasons to think of metonymy as just as much of a cultural as a cognitive phenomenon. In this section, I will consider some cultural factors in producing prototype effects, how cultural stereotypes are made, how and why

the human face comes to be used for persons in everyday thought and in art—
an exemplary aspect of culture—and the role of metonymy in the production
and understanding of everyday rituals.

Cultural Factors in Prototype Effects

The MEMBER FOR CATEGORY metonymy plays an important role in accounting for certain prototype effects. It seems that certain kinds of category members have a distinguished role in producing the kinds of effects I discussed in
chapter 2, where I observed that some members of categories are judged to
be better examples of categories than others. Now we can ask which members are likely to produce these effects. What follows in this section is a brief
survey of the kinds of category members that commonly cause prototype effects. The survey is based on Lakoff's (1987) work.

First, consider again the category of MOTHER. I noted that the prototype
of MOTHER is a woman who gave birth to you, who nurtures you, who provided your genetic materials, who is your father's wife, and who is one generation older than you are. In other words, when the basic models converge
in a particular case to form a complex model for mother, we have a very good
example of MOTHER. Here the prototype effect is produced by the convergence of the basic models. But let us assume that we have a large number of
such mothers where the basic models are all present and let us assume that
some of these mothers have a job and go out to work, while some others do
not have a job but are housewives. If we ask a large number of people whether
those mothers are better examples of the category who go out to work or
those who are housewives, the likely answer is going to be: the housewives.
Why is this the case?

The answer is that stereotypical members tend to be looked at as better
examples of a category than less or nonstereotypical members. The housewife
mother is one such stereotype. Thus, we have an additional source of prototype effects. Among all the members of the mother category who are characterized by the five basic models, some category members are better examples
than others: This is the housewife mother stereotype. This stereotype is defined
in relation to one of the basic models that characterize the category: the
nurturance model. Furthermore, this was an unnamed category member. When
Lakoff wrote *Women, Fire, and Dangerous Things* in the early '80s, there was
no conventional name for housewife mothers; Lakoff simply used the phrase
housewife mother to be able to talk about this particular category member, because at the time there was no fully conventional name to refer to such mothers.
However, the contrastive category member of mothers who go out to work did
have a conventional name: *working mother*. *Working mother* is defined in
contrast to the housewife mother stereotype. It is usually the case that more
prototypical members of a category do not have special, distinctive names,
whereas category members that are considered less prototypical do. This is what
happened in the case of housewife mother and working mother.

In addition to being additional sources of prototype effects, stereotypes also define many of our social expectations. This is why under normal circumstances we are more likely to use sentences such as *She's a mother, but she is not a housewife* than *She's a mother, but she is a housewife*. The conjunction *but* is used to cancel our expectations concerning what we expect mothers to be like. The same applies to many other categories, such as HUSBAND, BACHELOR, MOTHER-IN-LAW, ITALIAN, JEW, EASTERN EUROPEAN, and so forth.

But the linguistic situation has changed since the early '80s. Probably as a result of the need to be able to talk explicitly about mothers who are housewives in contradistinction to *working mothers*, a relatively recent name for housewife mothers emerged: *stay-at-home mom*. By now, this has become a fully conventional name for the housewife mother stereotype. In other words, there is now a conventional name both for the prototype defined by the stereotype (*stay-at-home mom*) and its opposite (*working mother*). We may wonder whether the fact that the "housewife mother" member of the category is now also named indicates a change in prototype and social expectations. Can we still say that it is the housewife mother stereotype that defines social expectations? The *but*-test seems to suggest that it is still the "housewife mother" stereotype that defines social expectations. Consider the sentences *She's a mother, but she goes out to work* (the case of *working mother*) and ??*She's a mother, but she stays at home with the child* (the case of *stay-at-home mom*). As the two question marks indicate, the latter sentence still sounds less acceptable than the former. As far as we can judge by this test, this shows that although both types of mother have acquired a conventional name, it is still the housewife mother stereotype (*stay-at-home mom*) that functions as the default case.

Second, if a category has some very commonly occurring members, these can acquire special status in that they can produce prototype effects. For example, in the case of the category of BIRD, such typical members include robins, sparrows, swallows, and so on, in North America. That is to say, typical members can stand for the category as a whole. Moreover, typical members play an interesting role in reasoning. In one experiment, people were told that there is an island where there are some typical birds (like robins and sparrows) and some nontypical ones (like ducks). The subjects were asked: If the robins and sparrows had a disease, would the ducks get it? The answer was yes. They were also asked: If the ducks had a disease, would the robins and sparrows get it? The answer was no. In other words, there was an asymmetry in making inferences based on prototypical and nonprototypical members. This is metonymy-based reasoning.

Third, ideal members within a category also have a special status. It is a common phenomenon that when we think of some category we have in mind an ideal member of that category. When we think about who we want to marry, we have ideal husbands and wives in mind; when we are teenagers, we want to have a special kind of love: ideal love; when we are planning to buy a car, we often think (or daydream) about an ideal car; and so on. That is to say, categories such as HUSBAND, WIFE, LOVE, CAR, and JOB, have ideal members and they can stand for the entire category. And as the examples show, we also use them to set goals. The ideal members of categories can often dictate how we act in the world and what emotions we have as a result of these actions.

Fourth, a single individual member of a category can also stand for the whole category. This happens in the case of paragons. A paragon is an individual who is an ideal. For example, in the United States the paragon of baseball players is still Babe Ruth or Joe DiMaggio for many people. Paragons also play an important cognitive role: We often imitate them and have a great deal of interest in them. Let it suffice to mention just a few additional examples of paragons: Princess Diana, Prince Charles, and Madonna. It is this interest in paragons that the business world often capitalizes on. Paragons can thus have a pervasive social effect.

Fifth, there are also members that Lakoff calls generators. These are central members of a category that work by the additional application of general rules. For example, single-digit numbers are central members of NATURAL NUMBERS. We can "generate" many noncentral members of the NUMBER category by the application of the rules of arithmetic to such single-digit numbers.

Sixth, we can have a special set of members of a category as the central ones. Powers of ten for NATURAL NUMBERS are one example. We call such a set a submodel. Another example is the basic emotions, including anger, fear, sadness, and happiness. We take these to be the most prototypical cases of emotion. Submodels are used as "cognitive reference points" (Rosch, 1975). They are commonly used for approximations. When used in such a way, they produce prototype effects. For example, it was shown that people much more readily agree to a statement like *98 is approximately 100* than to *100 is approximately 98*. Happiness and 100 are much better cognitive reference points for emotions and numbers, respectively, than euphoria and 98.

Seventh, and finally, categories often have "salient members." Salient members often stand out among category members by virtue of a particular property that they have. They can also determine how we think about other category members. If a particular type of airplane crashes (let us say a DC-10), people will avoid this type of airplane for a while as their means of travel, no matter how safe DC-10s in general are. In other words, salient members of a category are routinely used in thought: We generalize from salient examples to other examples of the category.

Cultural Stereotyping

Social groups have stereotypes about those outside the group and also about themselves. In-group stereotypes tend to be favorable, while out-group stereotypes tend to be unfavorable. Our stereotypes about others often result in prejudices. This makes stereotypes socially dangerous. There are many such stereotype-based prejudices in every society. Just to mention a few, there are prejudices against immigrants, against gypsies, against Muslims, against gays and lesbians, against intellectuals, against rural people, and so on. Correspondingly, people have prejudices against natives, against nongypsies, against Christians, against straight people, against working-class people, against city dwellers, and so forth. As the examples suggest, prejudices come in the form of structured opposites that correspond to relative in-groups and out-groups.

The metonymic nature of stereotype-based prejudices is clear in most cases. The general conceptual metonymy that underlies most of them is A MEMBER OF A CATEGORY FOR THE WHOLE CATEGORY. In other words, most stereotypes rely on particular members of a group who are used to represent the entire group. The main weakness (and the danger) of stereotype-based categorization is that the other members of the group who may be very different from the stereotypical one(s) in reality are presented as if there were no differences between the members. That is, this kind of categorization, which is ultimately metonymy based, glosses over individual members, making the category appear homogeneous when in fact it is not.

The FACE in Language and Art

There are several body parts that can be used metonymically to stand for the person; the relevant metonymy is BODY PART FOR THE PERSON. This is a PART FOR WHOLE metonymy that underlies more specific versions of it:

> HEAD FOR THE PERSON: We need some good heads on the project.
> HAND FOR THE PERSON: We need a good left hand on the team.
> FACE FOR THE PERSON: I saw some new faces in class today.
> . . .
> and so on

We use these conceptual metonymies for different purposes. When we are concerned with intellectual abilities, we use the head; when we are interested in certain physical aspects of the person, we use the hand. The human face behaves a bit differently when it comes to metonymic thought. It does not seem to be tied to a particular aspect of persons. Although we can talk about someone as a pretty face, we also can talk about her more generally as a person as such without further qualifications. It is this latter general usage that occurs in the idiomatic expression *come-face-to face with someone* and in the informal English word *whatsisface* to denote a person whose name we do not know. Szilvia Csábi (2005) notes in connection with THE FACE FOR THE PERSON metonymy that personification is also frequently associated with the face. She explains furthermore that the motivation for the metonymy in all probability derives from the fact that humans predominantly recognize and differentiate others by the face.

This aspect of THE FACE FOR THE PERSON metonymy was noticed by George Lakoff and Mark Johnson (1980), who suggest that this metonymy is active and pervasive in several of our cultural practices. Photographs of persons typically show the face of a person. This is a deeply entrenched cultural practice, as can be seen in passport photos, driver licenses, various identity cards, and so on. To appreciate the deeply entrenched nature of the metonymy, imagine a situation in which all these photos of a person would make use of other body parts, such as the leg, hand, shoulder, ear, or some other part. The ludicrousness of the very idea indicates that the face enjoys special status in representing human beings.

As a matter of fact, as Lakoff and Johnson also note, cultures have developed a form of art that is also based on THE FACE OF THE PERSON FOR THE PERSON metonymy; it is portrait painting. It does not seem to be accidental that it is the face that has acquired this status—as opposed to other body parts. We do not have an art form that is dedicated to representing entire persons through their legs, fingers, hair, chest, knees, and so forth. Portrait painting has been around for thousands of years possibly because the conceptual metonymy that underlies it is motivated by the most natural way for humans to recognize each other: through recognizing the face of another human being.

Everyday Rituals

Following Lakoff and Johnson (1980), we can take everyday rituals to be a kind of frame, or experiential gestalt. Everyday rituals are repeated actions with some special significance. What makes many everyday rituals meaningful for people is often one of the conceptual metonymies we have considered in this chapter. Take the everyday ritual of some Americans driving by the homes of Hollywood stars in Los Angeles (Lakoff and Johnson, 1980). This is an action that many visitors to Los Angeles like to perform. What is the meaning of this activity? What lends symbolic significance to it? A part of its significance derives from the metonymic association between people and their homes: The homes stand for the people who live in them. To use our terminology and notation, underlying the activity we have the metonymy HOME FOR THE PEOPLE. In other words, the people who engage in the ritual (unconsciously) take the homes of the Hollywood stars for the stars themselves. This is a specific-level version of the more general PLACE FOR THE PEOPLE LIVING IN THAT PLACE metonymy (as in *the whole town was asleep*). Without assuming this metonymy, it would be difficult to explain the ritual. At the same time, however, we do not claim that it is this particular metonymy alone that makes the behavior meaningful. There are some additional reasons for this. One of them is metaphorical conceptualization. In the example, people (again unconsciously) understand the situation *as if* they were personally familiar with the stars through their physical closeness to them. That is, we need both metaphor and metonymy in our account of the symbolic significance of many everyday rituals. Metaphorical conceptualization will be the topic of the next chapter.

Conclusions

At the heart of metonymy is the notion of frame, or ICM—a structured mental representation of a conceptual category (corresponding to some area of experience). In metonymy, we use an element of a frame to provide mental access to another element of the same frame, or ICM. We called this a within-domain mapping, in which an entity is mapped onto another entity within the same frame, or domain, or ICM. This is a conceptual, or cognitive, definition of what metonymy is; the fact that we use metonymic linguistic expressions when we speak and write follows from the essentially conceptual nature of metonymy.

Metonymies in thought and language come in a large number of specific kinds, including FACE FOR THE PERSON, PRODUCER FOR PRODUCT, and INSTRUMENT FOR ACTION. The diverse conceptual metonymies can be derived from two large configurations between the parts of a frame and the whole frame: the WHOLE AND PART configuration and the PART AND PART configuration. Within the first, two essential types of metonymic relations can be distinguished: WHOLE FOR THE PART and PART FOR THE WHOLE. The second configuration gives rise to PART FOR PART metonymic relations.

Metonymies are inherently cognitive and cultural at the same time. Prototype effects are partially determined by cultural factors, such as stereotypical members, ideal members, and paragons of categories. Moreover, not only can language be metonymic but also many of our cultural practices. In other words, metonymy can be found to underlie many forms of cultural behavior, as the examples of portrait painting and everyday rituals revealed. People in part find meaning in such activities because conceptual metonymies underlie their behavior.

Exercises

1. Read the political articles of a newspaper or magazine that are concerned with the United States or the United Kingdom and try to collect metonymies that have the PLACE FOR INSTITUTION and the CONTROLLER FOR THE CONTROLLED or the CONTROLLED FOR THE CONTROLLER structures. What important facts do your metonymies reveal about the political institutions of these countries?

2. Consider the following sentences:

   a. "I hate school." What kind of metonymic process(es) can you find in it?
   b. "Only Smith's hands were playing yesterday during the Brahms." What kind of metonymy is at work here and what other observations can you make?

3. What kind of metonymies can you identify in the following sentences? What are the vehicles and the targets?

   a. We painted the house last summer. It was tough work.
   b. The Big Stomach ate all the food in the fridge.

   c. The War of the Roses, the White Rose and the Red Rose, was a
     significant event in English history.
   d. The Redshirts fought persistently to capture the blue flag.
   e. Harvard is one of the most famous universities of the world.

4. Given the following linguistic metonymies, decide what their common
frame is:

Slow road
Sad book
She's my *ruin.*
He was *a failure.*

Then try to define the subtypes of the individual metonymies, using the
X (STANDS) FOR Y formula.

   5. As the preceding chapter explained, many cultural practices are based
on conceptual metonymies. Try to find additional examples of cultural practices that are metonymy based. Also, describe the particular conceptual metonymies involved.

Mappings across Frames

Metaphor

A s we saw in the previous chapter, metonymy is a mapping that applies between two elements of a single frame, or domain. Often, however, there are two frames, or domains, that we bring into conceptual interaction on the basis of some kind of perceived similarity. Initially at least, we can call such cases of interaction metaphor.

This chapter is primarily devoted to spelling out the most important aspects, or components, of the cognitive linguistic view of metaphor, and I will also offer a possible classification of metaphor within the same view. But the topic of metaphor will be pursued further in several subsequent chapters. The general argument of these chapters will be that metaphor plays a crucial role in the study of mind and culture. More specifically, in chapter 9 we will look at some of the cultural and social applications of metaphors; chapter 10 will take up the issue of cross-cultural and within-culture variation in metaphor; in chapter 11 we will ask whether it is reasonable to think of human thought as essentially literal; and chapter 12 will deal with the image-schematic basis of many metaphors.

This chapter proceeds as follows. First, I will take a closer look at what metaphor is. Second, I will go into some of the details concerning the many aspects or components of metaphor. Third, a classification of metaphor will be offered that is based on its conventionality, cognitive function, nature, and generality. Much of the discussion in the chapter is based on Lakoff and Johnson, 1980, and Kövecses, 2002.

What Is a Conceptual Metaphor?

Let us begin with how speakers of English talk about life—either their own or that of others. They say that some people have no direction in life, that they have to go through a lot, that they will go far in life, that some people have a head start, that some others carry heavy baggage, that they are at a crossroads, that they look back and think it was a bumpy road, that they are determined to reach their goals, and much else.

Underlying all these different ways of talking about life is the unifying concept of "a journey." Speakers of English commonly view the concept of life through the perspective of a journey. Thus, the particular linguistic examples they use to talk about life are based on a deeper connection between the two concepts of "life" and "journey." The concept of "life" is comprehended in terms of the concept of "journey." Moreover, the connection is systematic in the sense that we can observe systematic correspondences between the concept of "journey" and that of "life." Here are some of these correspondences:

JOURNEY		LIFE
traveler	→	person leading a life
journey/motion (toward a destination)	→	leading a life (with a purpose)
destination	→	purpose of life
obstacles (in the way of motion)	→	difficulties (in life)
distance covered	→	progress made
path/way of the journey	→	the manner/way of living
choices about the path	→	choices in life

As we can see, particular elements of the JOURNEY frame, or domain, correspond to particular elements of the LIFE frame, or domain. We call such correspondences between two frames conceptual metaphor. In other words, metaphor is a set of cross-domain mappings. It is customary to represent such relationships between two frames with the notation of A IS B, which would be "life is a journey" in this example. The concept to be comprehended is given first as A, while the concept used for its comprehension is given second as B. The IS between the two is used to indicate this relationship between the concepts.

Components of Conceptual Metaphors

In the cognitive linguistic view of metaphor, we can identify a number of aspects, or components, that characterize metaphorical connections between two concepts. These components include the following:

1. Source domain
2. Target domain
3. Basis of metaphor
4. Neural structures that correspond to 1 and 2 in the brain
5. Relationships between the source and the target
6. Metaphorical linguistic expressions
7. Mappings
8. Entailments

9. Aspects of source and target
10. Blends
11. Nonlinguistic realizations
12. Cultural models

I will now briefly describe each of these components of the cognitive linguistic view of metaphor that has developed from Lakoff and Johnson's (1980) work. (A book-length introduction to the past twenty years of the theory can be found in Kövecses, 2002.)

Source and Target

Metaphor consists of a source (B) and target domain (A) such that the source is a more physical and the target a more abstract kind of domain. In the preceding example, JOURNEY is the source domain and LIFE is the target domain. Thus we get the metaphor LIFE IS A JOURNEY. Further examples include source domains WARMTH, BUILDING, and WAR and target domains AFFECTION, THEORY, and ARGUMENT. Thus, we get additional conceptual metaphors: AFFECTION IS WARMTH; THEORIES ARE BUILDINGS; ARGUMENT IS WAR. What this means is that the concepts of "affection," "theory," and "argument" are comprehended via the concepts of "warmth," "buildings," and "war," respectively. (Linguistic examples will be provided later in the chapter.)

Basis of Metaphor

Why do particular target concepts go together with particular source concepts? The traditional answer to this question is that there is some kind of similarity between the two concepts; that is, concept A is similar to concept B in some respect. While we accept this kind of motivation for certain metaphors, we also take into account another kind of motivation for many other metaphors. The choice of a particular source to go with a particular target can also be motivated by some embodied experience.

Correlation in Bodily Experience

Consider as an example the metaphor AFFECTION IS WARMTH. We suggest that we find this metaphor natural because the feeling of affection correlates with bodily warmth. We experience such embodied correlation very early on in life. To be hugged and to be close to our first caretaker produces this kind of warmth that gives us comfort and eventually the feeling of affection. This example shows that the correlation between the experience of affection and that of warmth need not be conscious. As a matter of fact, it is characteristic of such embodied experiences that they are not conscious most of the time. We experience such correlations in bodily experience preconceptually and prelinguistically.

As another example, consider heat. Heat and warmth are of course related, in that they are both descriptions of temperature, but as far as bodily motivation for metaphor is concerned, they are quite different. That is to say, they motivate very different conceptual metaphors. Imagine the following situation. You are working hard, let us say sawing or chopping wood, or you are doing some vigorous exercise, like running or aerobics. After a while you're beginning to work up heat; you will feel hot and maybe begin to sweat. We can say that the vigorous bodily activity produces an increase in body heat. Typically, when you engage in vigorous bodily activity your body will respond in this way. Similarly, when you are very angry, or when you have strong sexual feelings, or when you are under strong psychological pressure, your body may also produce an increase in body heat that manifests itself physiologically in a variety of ways. In all of these cases, the increase in the intensity of an activity or state goes together with an increase in body heat, and your body responds this way automatically. The correlation between the increase in the intensity of the activity or the state, on the one hand, and the production of body heat, on the other, is inevitable for the kinds of bodies that we have. We can't help undergoing the correlation between intensity (of these activities and states) and body heat. This correlation forms the basis of a conceptual metaphor: INTENSITY IS HEAT. But the correlation is also at the level of the body, and it is in this sense that metaphor is just as much in the body as it is in language or thought.

Since "intensity" is an aspect of many concepts, the source domain of HEAT will apply to many concepts, such as "anger," "love," "lust," "work," "argument," and so forth. In general, we suggest that many conceptual metaphors (i.e., source and target pairings) are motivated by such bodily correlations in experience.

Similarity

As was mentioned, in the traditional view of metaphor similarity is the main motivation for bringing together two concepts in a metaphorical relationship. We do not deny that similarity is important, but we attach equal importance to correlations in bodily experience, as briefly described earlier. One of the favorite examples to justify the view that metaphors are based on similarity is "Achilles was a lion." It is proposed that Achilles and lions share a property, namely, that of being brave.

Let us look at some other examples where the basis of metaphor can be claimed to be some kind of similarity. Take a passage I have analyzed from the *San Francisco Chronicle* (Kövecses, 2005a):

> Last fall, in a radio interview with a San Diego radio station and later on CNN's "Larry King Live," [singer Harry] Belafonte likened Secretary of State Colin Powell to a plantation hand who moves into the master's house, in this case the White House, and only supports policies that will please his master, President Bush.

In the example, one of the things that Belafonte knows about Powell is that Powell is an African-American. Since slaves were also African-Americans, it is easy for Belafonte to set up the metaphor or, more exactly, metaphorical analogy. We can assume that this feature shared by Powell and the slaves helps trigger the particular analogy. In other words, a feature (being an African-American) that is shared by an element of the target (in this case, Powell) and an element of the source (the slaves) helps the speaker arrive at an extensive set of analogical relationships between source and target.

But in many other cases the shared element is not such an obvious feature. Often, the target and the source are characterized by similar structural relations—without any shared features of the communicative situation that might trigger the recognition of the shared relations (such as in the case cited earlier) (see, e.g., Gentner, 1983; Glucksberg and Keysar, 1993; Holyoak and Thagard, 1996). For example, we can find shared generic-level structure in such domains as HUMAN LIFETIME and the LIFE CYCLE OF PLANTS. This structure would include, for instance, something like "living organisms have a period of their existence when they are most active" (whatever this means either for people or for plants) and "living organisms decline after this period." This case is of course a highly conventional metaphor: THE HUMAN LIFETIME IS THE LIFE CYCLE OF A PLANT. But the same kind of cognitive process accounts for any number of similar metaphors. Take, for instance, the metaphor used by Harry Belafonte. We would not need any explicit triggers to say of an especially servile secretary of state or minister that he or she is a slave, thus evoking the GOVERNMENT IS A PLANTATION metaphor in which the president or prime minister is the master and the secretaries of state or ministers are the slaves. This is because we have the ability to recognize shared generic-level structure such as "inferiors are servile to superiors in order to please them" in distinct domains.

But what is recognized as shared between two domains need not be something as abstract as generic-level structure. It can be similarities of all kinds—most important, actual or perceived shared features. The literature on metaphor abounds in examples. Image metaphors of the kind described by Lakoff and Turner (1989) are based on shared features between source and target; for instance, the shared shape of a woman's waist and that of an hourglass. And the metaphor "She's a regular *fish*" would be a case in which there is some real or perceived similarity shared by a person and fish; namely, that they both swim well. The point here is that the recognition of (real or perceived) shared features between any two domains can create an infinitely large number of novel metaphors.

In summary, we can think of embodiment and similarity as different kinds of constraint on the creation of metaphor. Embodiment seems to be a stronger kind of constraint, in that it works automatically and unconsciously.

Connections in the Brain

The idea that metaphors can be motivated by correlations in bodily experience has given rise to a "neural theory of metaphor." It is the brain that runs the body, and if metaphor is in the body it must also be in the brain. Embodied experience results in certain neural connections between areas of the brain (these areas that correspond to source and target). For example, it may be suggested that when the area of the brain that corresponds to affection is activated, the area that corresponds to warmth is also activated.

The assumption in recent neuroscientific studies (see, for example, Gallese and Lakoff, 2005) is that when we understand abstract concepts metaphorically, two groups of neurons in the brain are activated at the same time; when one group of neurons fires (the source), another group of neurons fires as well (the target). This situation has given rise to the slogan "neurons that fire together wire together" (based on Hebb's law; see Hebb, 1949). We can then assume that, for example, neurons that correspond to intensity and heat, respectively, are activated together in the brain when we think about the abstract concept of "intensity" in connection with certain events, activities, and states. Similarly, when we think about abstract amounts, such as prices, the neurons that correspond to amount and those that correspond to verticality (up-down) are coactivated in the brain. These coactivations of groups of neurons yield what we know as the primary conceptual metaphors INTENSITY IS HEAT and MORE IS UP (LESS IS DOWN) (on "primary metaphors," see later discussion).

In short, conceptual metaphors are ensembles of neurons in different parts of the brain connected by neural circuitry. The ensembles of neurons located in different parts of the brain are the source and target domains, and the physical neural circuitry that connects them is the mappings. This allows us to see metaphor as physical (i.e., neural) structures in the brain. To learn a metaphor means that appropriate neural connections are "recruited" between different parts of the brain. This happens as a result of repeated and simultaneous neural activation of two brain areas. For example, as mentioned earlier in this chapter, the repeated and simultaneous neural activation of the EMOTION domain (region) and the TEMPERATURE domain (region) in childhood and later on in life leads to the establishment of the appropriate neural circuitry between the two domains, yielding, as one case, the AFFECTION IS WARMTH metaphor.

The question arises: In which parts of the brain are the two domains located? According to this paradigm of research, the source domain is located in the sensory-motor system, whereas the target domain is found in higher cortical areas. This idea is the neuroscientific version of the notion of the embodiment of metaphor, which states that source domains typically come from more concrete and physical sensory-motor experience, while target domains are less physical in nature.

The Relationship between Source and Target

The relationship of the source and the target is such that a source domain may apply to several targets and a target may attach to several sources. We call the former case the scope of the source, while the latter is the range of the target.

Scope of the Source

The *scope of the source* is the number of target domains to which a particular source domain applies. For example, the source domain of BUILDING applies to THEORY, RELATIONSHIP, ECONOMIC SYSTEMS, LIFE, and so on. The source domain of FIRE/ HEAT is commonly used to comprehend target concepts such as "love," "anger," "activities," "conflict," "life," and several others. As can be noticed, the scope of different source domains may include the same target domain (e.g., that of LIFE).

Range of the Target

There can be differences in the *range* of source domains in conceptual metaphors that a language/ culture has available for a particular target. For example, "love" is a highly metaphorized concept in English; it has over twenty different domains as its source, including JOURNEY, WAR, FIRE, GAME, and others. (Linguistic examples for love will be provided in the next subsection.) By contrast, a concept like "surprise" has only a few source domains, such as PHYSICAL FORCE ("I was *hit hard* by the news"). In other words, target concepts vary in the number of source domains that are used to conceptualize them.

Metaphorical Linguistic Expressions

The particular pairings of source and target domains give rise to metaphorical linguistic expressions, linguistic expressions thus being derivative of two conceptual domains being connected. The expression "a *warm* relationship" is an example of the AFFECTION IS WARMTH metaphor, while "*got around* a prob lem" comes from DIFFICULTIES ARE OBSTACLES (ALONG A PATH OF MOTION).

Many target domains are almost exclusively talked about metaphorically. Here are two extensive sets of metaphorical language that people use to talk about love and anger:

LOVE:
1. I am *starved for* love.
2. It's been *a long, bumpy road.*
3. We're *as one.* They're *breaking up.* We're *inseparable.* We *fused together.*
4. They're very *close.*
5. There is a close *tie* between them.
6. She was *overflowing with* love.
7. I am *burning with* love.
8. I'm *putting more into* this than you are.
9. She *swept* me *off my feet.*
10. I was *magnetically drawn to* her.
11. She tried to *fight* her feelings of love.
12. She *let go of* her feelings.
13. She *conquered* him.
14. He *made a play for* her.

15. I am *heartsick.*
16. He was *enchanted.*
17. I am *crazy about* you.
18. She is completely *ruled by* love.
19. I have been *high on* love for weeks.
20. Hi, *sweetie pie.*
21. Well, *baby,* what are we gonna do?
22. Don't *put* her *on a pedestal.* He *worships* her.
23. You're my *treasure!*

ANGER:
1. She is *boiling with* anger.
2. He's doing a *slow burn.* His anger is *smoldering.*
3. The man was *insane with* rage.
4. I was *struggling with* my anger.
5. He *unleashed* his anger.
6. He *carries* his anger *around* with him.
7. Don't *snarl at* me!
8. Here I *draw the line.*
9. He's *a pain in the neck.*
10. It was a *stormy* meeting.
11. That really *got* him *going.*
12. His actions were completely *governed* by anger.

In our view, metaphor is only derivatively a linguistic phenomenon. It exists in language only because it exists in the body/brain and thought. Linguistic metaphors (i.e., metaphors in language) are expressions of metaphorical concepts in the brain's conceptual system. So, on the one hand, metaphorical linguistic expressions make conceptual metaphors manifest, and on the other, we can use these metaphorical expressions to arrive at metaphors in thought by means of hypothetically assuming links between two domains that can, in turn, be put to the test in psychological experiments (as we will see in later chapters).

Since we often arrive at hypotheses as to what conceptual metaphors we have on the basis of linguistic usage, it is important to know what counts as a metaphorical linguistic expression. We can ask what the criteria are on the basis of which we can decide what counts as a linguistic metaphor. As anyone who has tried it can testify, the identification of metaphorical words and expressions is an extremely difficult task.

Basic Mappings

There are basic, and essential, conceptual correspondences, or mappings, between the source and target domains. As an example, take the conceptual metaphor LOVE IS A JOURNEY. We can set up the mappings as follows:

Source: JOURNEY		*Target:* LOVE
travelers	→	lovers
vehicle	→	love relationship

destination	→	purpose of the relationship
distance covered	→	progress made in the relationship
obstacles along the way	→	difficulties encountered in the relationship
and so on		

The mappings must be set up in such a way that they explain particular metaphorical linguistic expressions. The metaphorical expressions for the LOVE IS A JOURNEY metaphor overlap greatly with those of LIFE IS A JOURNEY. The mappings therefore also overlap—with one exception: vehicle → love relationship. Since in the LIFE domain there is only one person leading a life, there is no relationship as an element in the frame. However, relationship does belong to the LOVE frame by definition. When people say that "a relationship isn't *getting anywhere*," the relationship corresponds to the vehicle in this metaphor.

As another example, take the conceptual metaphor ANGER IS A HOT FLUID IN A CONTAINER. This shows up in such metaphorical linguistic expressions as "*boil* with anger," "*simmer* down," "*seethe* with anger," and so on. The basic mapping, or set of correspondences, that defines the conceptual metaphor that underlies these expressions includes:

Source: HOT FLUID IN A CONTAINER		*Target*: ANGER
the physical container	→	the angry person's body
the hot fluid inside the container	→	the anger
the degree of fluid heat	→	the intensity of anger
the cause of increase in fluid heat	→	the cause of anger

A conceptual metaphor is such a set of correspondences that obtains between a source domain and a target domain, where metaphorical linguistic expressions (i.e., linguistic metaphors) commonly make the conceptual metaphors (i.e., metaphors in the mind) manifest (though there may be conceptual metaphors that have no linguistic metaphors to express them).

Entailments and Entailment Potential

Source domains often map ideas onto the target beyond the basic correspondences. These additional mappings are called entailments, or inferences. Consider LOVE IS A JOURNEY again (Lakoff, 1993). If "love" is conceptualized as a journey and the vehicle corresponds to the relationship, then our knowledge about the vehicle can be used to understand love relationships. If the vehicle breaks down, we have three choices: (1) we get out and try to reach our destination by some other means; (2) we try to fix the vehicle; or (3) we stay in the vehicle and do nothing. Correspondingly, if a love relationship does not work, we can (1) leave the relationship; (2) try to make it work; or (3) stay in it (and suffer).

The rich knowledge we have about many source domains results in a large number of entailments that can be carried over to the target.

Aspects of Concepts That Participate in Metaphor

It is an important feature of the theory of conceptual metaphor that only certain aspects of either the source or the target participate in metaphors. That is to say, when we suggest that a conceptual metaphor can be given as A IS B, this does not mean that the entire concept A or B is involved—only select aspects of them. But this presents a problem: How can we tell which aspects of source and target concepts will be involved?

Let us introduce some terminology and approach the problem through an example. We will talk about metaphorical "highlighting" and "hiding" to indicate that only certain aspects of the *target domain* are focused on in metaphors. Correspondingly, we will talk about metaphorical "utilization" to indicate that only certain aspects of the *source domain* are utilized in metaphors.

Thus, we suggest that only certain aspects of the source domain are utilized and certain aspects of the target domain are highlighted in the following example (taken from Lakoff and Johnson, 1980):

AN ARGUMENT/THEORY IS A BUILDING
We've got the *framework* for a *solid* argument.
If you don't *support* your argument with *solid* facts, the whole thing
   will *collapse.*
You should try to *buttress* your argument with more facts.
With the *groundwork* you've got, you can *build a strong* argument.

As the examples show, three aspects of buildings are utilized: the process of building, the physical structure of the building, and the issue of the strength of the building. Correspondingly, only three aspects of arguments/theories are focused on, or highlighted: the construction of a (rational) argument or theory, its structure, and its strength. In other words, these are the basic mappings between the two frames. The metaphorical expressions used in the examples make this clear:

physical process of building	→	theory construction: *build*
physical structure of building	→	structure of theory: *framework, groundwork*
physical strength of building	→	strength of theory: *strong, support, solid, collapse, buttress*

But why aren't many other parts (aspects) of buildings utilized by the metaphor? We know a lot more about buildings than what the basic mappings suggest. For example, we know that buildings have windows, doors, hallways, chimneys, roofs, tenants, and many other things, but these do not seem to be utilized from the source, and consequently, they do not highlight aspects of the target, either. Why not? The answer was provided by Joseph Grady (1997a, b) who suggested that there are "primary metaphors" and "complex metaphors" and that the primary metaphors make up the complex ones. Here are the primary metaphors that Grady found important to explain why only select aspects of the source are utilized to highlight select aspects of the target:

LOGICAL STRUCTURE IS PHYSICAL STRUCTURE.
PERSISTING IS REMAINING ERECT.

In essence, the first one suggests that we conceptualize abstract logical structures as physical structures (e.g., framework) and the second one suggests that persistence, functionality, and so on, in general are conceptualized as a functioning object remaining erect (e.g., supporting a structure so it does not collapse). If we put together the two primary metaphors, we get

VIABLE LOGICAL STRUCTURES ARE ERECT PHYSICAL STRUCTURES.

Theories and (rational) arguments are one kind of viable logical structure that are conceptualized as a building, which is a kind of erect physical structure. Grady suggests, furthermore, that primary metaphors can explain the existence of complex ones that would be very difficult to motivate otherwise. In this example, it would be difficult to see any kind of correlation or similarity between buildings and theories, but the two primary metaphors can easily provide a motivation. There is "built-in" logical structure in every physical structure (like a house) and many physical structures are erect when they are functional (a house or a telephone pole that collapsed is not functional).

Blending Source and Target

The bringing together of a source domain with a target domain often results in blends, that is, conceptual materials that are new with respect to *both* the source and the target. As an example, take the sentence *He was so mad, smoke was coming out of his ears*. In this example we have AN ANGRY PERSON as the target domain and SMOKE (FUME) IN A CONTAINER as the source domain. The target (the angry person) has no smoke coming out of it and the source (the container with hot fluid) has no ears. But the example conceptually integrates the two: we have a container that has ears with smoke coming out of them. This is a conceptual blend that results from the conceptual integration of some of the elements of the source with some of the elements of the target (see, e.g., Fauconnier and Turner, 2002). We will deal more extensively with conceptual integration in a later chapter.

Nonlinguistic Realization

Conceptual metaphors often materialize, or are realized, in nonlinguistic ways, that is, not only in language and thought but also in social-physical practice and reality (Kövecses, 2002; Lakoff, 1993). Here is a simple example to demonstrate this component of conceptual metaphors. Given the IMPORTANT

IS CENTRAL conceptual metaphor and its linguistic manifestations (such as "the *central* issue"), at meetings and various other social events important people (e.g., people in higher social positions) tend to occupy more "central" physical locations in the setting than less important ones.

Cultural Models

Conceptual metaphors converge on and often produce cultural models, or frames, that operate in thought. These are structures that are simultaneously cultural and cognitive (hence the terms *cultural model, cognitive model,* and *ICM*), in that they are culturally specific mental representations of aspects of the world. Again, a brief example will have to suffice: An integral part of our understanding of time is that time is an entity that moves (passes). This is because much of our cultural model of time is based on (created by) the conceptual metaphor TIME IS A MOVING ENTITY. Hence, we talk about time *passing, coming, arriving, flying,* and so on.

As a matter of fact, even our most "sacred" scientific models may be based on metaphorical thought. For example, George Lakoff and Raphael Nunez (2000) argue that many of our basic ideas about mathematics are inherently metaphorical in nature.

The issue of whether abstract concepts can be *other than* metaphorical at all will be discussed further in chapter 11.

In summary, we can ask: What kind of "thing" is metaphor? It follows from what has been said so far in this chapter that metaphor is not only a property of words. One of the major claims of the cognitive linguistic view of metaphor is that metaphor is not an exclusively linguistic phenomenon. It seems to belong to language, thought, social-cultural practice, brain, and body. In other words, it can be suggested that metaphor is a

- linguistic
- conceptual
- social-cultural
- neural
- bodily

phenomenon and that it exists on all of these different levels at the same time.

Metaphor and Metonymy

In light of the discussion so far, we can see how metaphor and metonymy differ from each other.

First, while metonymy is a process used to provide mental access to an entity through another entity, the main cognitive function of metaphor typically is to provide understanding for a more abstract concept (the target domain) through a more concrete one (the source domain). The source domain structures the target domain and provides a particular perspective on it.

Second, while metonymy involves a single domain, or frame (e.g., CONTROL ICM, INSTITUTION ICM, ACTION ICM), metaphor involves two distinct domains, or frames (e.g., LIFE and JOURNEY, LOVE and FIRE).

Third, and related to the second, while metonymy is a relationship of contiguity, or proximity, metaphors are characterized by either resemblance or correlations. Contiguity results from the fact that metonymy occurs within a particular frame. In metonymy, the elements in a metonymic relationship are conceptually close to each other (e.g., the "producer" and the "product," the "place" and the "institution"), whereas in metaphor they are far from each other in conceptual space (e.g., "life" and "journey," "love" and "fire"), although they may "come close together" as a result of correlations in experience.

Kinds of Metaphor

There are several ways in which conceptual metaphors can be classified. We will look at four of these. We will classify metaphors according to their degree of conventionality, their cognitive function, their nature, and generality.

Conventionality

Earlier, I made a distinction between linguistic and conceptual metaphor. Conventionality applies to both types; both linguistic and conceptual metaphors can be conventional and unconventional. Conventionality is not understood here in the usual sense in which it is used in linguistics, where it refers to the arbitrary relationship between linguistic form and meaning. Rather, conventionality is conceived of as the degree to which either a linguistic or a conceptual metaphor has become entrenched in the course of its use. Thus, the metaphorical linguistic expressions *steal the show, be in the spotlight*, and *play a role in something* are all highly conventional for the conceptual metaphor LIFE IS A PLAY, whereas the Shakespearean lines "All the world is a stage / And all the men and women merely players. / They have their exits and their entrances" are unconventional for the same conceptual metaphor. Unconventionality is not necessarily tied to poetic or literary language. We can have much less conventional or clearly unconventional instances of the same metaphor in colloquial language as well, as in *it's curtains for him, take a bow*, or *face the final curtain*.

Conceptual metaphors themselves can be more or less conventional. While LIFE IS A PLAY is a conventional conceptual metaphor, LIFE IS A BOX OF CHOCOLATES is not. Similarly, LOVE IS A JOURNEY is fairly conventional, but LOVE IS A COLLABORATIVE WORK OF ART is not.

Cognitive Function

A useful way to classify metaphors is according to their cognitive function. Some metaphors are used to impose structure on the target, some to provide an ontological status for it, and some to make several targets coherent with one another (Lakoff and Johnson, 1980). These are different cognitive functions, but they commonly occur together.

In structural metaphors, the source domain imposes some structure on the target by virtue of the mappings that characterize the metaphor. Most of the metaphors we have seen so far were of this kind. LIFE IS A JOURNEY, LOVE IS FIRE, THEORIES ARE BUILDINGS, and so on, are all structural metaphors. They map structure from one frame, or domain, onto another.

Ontological metaphors provide a certain ontological, or existential, status for the target domain. As a result, intangible phenomena become metaphorical "things," visual perceptions become containers, actions become metaphorical objects, and states become substances. For example, the mind is viewed as an *object*, we give people *a call*, what we can see is *within* our sight, and we are *in* love. In such cases, we have a variety of ontological metaphors that specify the existential status of processes, actions, states, and so on.

Finally, orientational metaphors are used to make several metaphors coherent with one another. Since health, morality, rationality, consciousness, and control are all good "things," they are all metaphorically oriented UP-WARD, whereas their opposites are all metaphorically DOWN. Consider the examples "I came *down* with the flu" (SICK IS DOWN), "He's an *upstanding* citizen" (MORAL IS UP), "He's slow on the *uptake*" (RATIONAL IS UP), "She's not *up* yet" (CONSCIOUS IS UP), "I'm *on top* of things" (CONTROL IS UP). The source domains provide a coherent organization for a large set of concepts.

Nature

Our knowledge about the world comes basically in two forms: propositional and image-schematic knowledge. Consequently, our metaphors are also based on these two types of knowledge. Propositional knowledge is essentially knowledge that derives from the meaning of the sentences that we use to describe particular phenomena. For example, we have some knowledge about how computers work and this can be given in the form of propositions (corresponding to the meaning of our statements about computers), such as "computers have hardware and software," "the software runs the hardware," and so on. This kind of knowledge is the basis of the THE MIND IS A COMPUTER metaphor.

By contrast, image-schematic knowledge comes from our repeated and regular experiences of the world. We go inside and go out of containers, we manipulate objects, we experience certain things as being connected, we maintain our balance when we walk, we move around in our physical environment, we experience the force of wind, and many others. All these repeated and regular experiences give rise to image-schematic knowledge that can structure many of our metaphors. This is the type of knowledge that underlies metaphors such as STATES ARE CONTAINERS, RELATIONSHIPS ARE LINKS/CONNECTIONS, ACTIONS ARE MOVEMENTS, CAUSES ARE FORCES, and many others.

An interesting kind of metaphor is based on the second type of knowledge—but on its less schematic version. When we perceive more specific kinds of imagistic similarities between things, we have to deal with image-based metaphors (see Lakoff and Turner, 1989). Lakoff and Turner (1989: 93) provide an example taken from the English translation of André Breton's "Free Union":

(1)   My wife . . . whose waist is an hourglass.

There are two detailed images here: one for the body of a woman and one for an hourglass. The images are based on the shape of the two "objects." According to the metaphor, we take the image of the detailed shape of the hourglass and map it onto the detailed shape of the woman's body. Such image-based metaphors are commonly employed in poetry.

Generality

Metaphors can be classified according to their level of generality. Most conceptual metaphors are at a specific level, while some are at a generic level. This makes sense in light of what we saw in the chapter on basic-level categorization. We have many more basic-level concepts than we have higher-level ones.

Examples of specific-level metaphors include BIRTH IS ARRIVAL and DEATH IS DEPARTURE. Birth and death are specific instances of events, and arrival and departure are specific instances of actions. Some metaphors work at a higher level of generality. Take, for example, the metaphor EVENTS ARE ACTIONS. The source and the target domains are both generic-level (or superordinate) concepts. Such metaphors can be taken to be generalizations of specific-level ones, and, conversely, specific-level ones can be regarded as instances of higher-level ones. Thus, we can say DEATH IS DEPARTURE is an instance of the higher-level metaphor EVENTS ARE ACTIONS. Death is an event and the source domain of departure is an action. And the same applies to BIRTH IS ARRIVAL.

Generic-level conceptual metaphors often underlie what is termed *personification*. In personification certain human qualities are imputed to nonhuman things. For example, a computer is a nonhuman machine, and yet we can say that it can save us time or it can steal our time, as the case may be. The computer is simply functioning, it is producing a number of events that it was programmed to do, but we talk about it metaphorically as if it were a human being, who can perform actions like saving or stealing something. Personifications can be characterized by means of two conceptual metaphors: EVENTS ARE ACTIONS and THINGS ARE PEOPLE. Both are generic-level metaphors with a huge number of specific-level instances.

Generic-level and specific-level metaphors are also useful in accounting for a large part of the meaning of many proverbs. Proverbs are often metaphor-based sayings that represent the folk wisdom of a culture. As an example, take "Look before you leap." The proverb is based on two conceptual metaphors. The "leap" part is an instance of the AN ACTION IS SELF-PROPELLED MOTION generic-level metaphor (as in "That should be the next *step*"), whereas the "look" part is an instance of the THINKING IS LOOKING specific-level metaphor (as in "*Look*, we can't do it"). We understand the meaning of this proverb largely because it (consciously or unconsciously) reminds us of these two conceptual metaphors.

In general, generic-level metaphors are typically ontological, orientational, and image-schematic ones. This shows that the classification of metaphors presented here is a cross-cutting system; the classifications overlap with each other.

Conclusions

In the cognitive linguistic view, metaphors are cross-domain mappings. Metaphor is a phenomenon that is linguistic, conceptual, social-cultural, neural, and bodily at the same time. It involves two domains of experience that are systematically connected. The two domains come from distant parts of the conceptual system (and the brain). The connections between the two are set up either because the two domains display some generic structural similarity or because they are correlated in our experience.

By contrast, metonymy involves a single domain, within which an element of the domain stands for another element of the same domain. Metonymy allows speakers to give mental access to an element through another element related to it—where the relationship either is conventional in the conceptual system or can be easily figured out in a given context.

Conceptual metaphors are characterized by a variety of aspects, or components. Among the most important ones are the following: They have a source and target domain; the connection between the two is established by the metaphor's basis; corresponding to source and target there are connected neural structures in the brain; basic elements of the source are mapped onto elements of the target; each source has an entailment potential that can be mapped onto the target; based on such basic and extended mappings we have linguistic metaphors that "express" the conceptual metaphors; only particular aspects of the source and target participate in the mappings; the source and the target may be blended; many conceptual metaphors are realized in socio-cultural reality; and metaphors often define cultural models.

Conceptual metaphors can be classified according to their conventionality, cognitive function, nature, and generality. According to their degree of conventionality, they can be conventional or unconventional. The same applies to linguistic expressions. When the basis of classification is cognitive function, metaphors can be structural, ontological, and orientational. The nature of metaphor allows us to distinguish between proposition-based and image-based metaphors. Image-based metaphors can be skeletal and abstract; these are image-schema metaphors. Finally, according to their generality, conceptual metaphors can be generic-level and specific-level. These metaphors play an important role in personification and the interpretation of many proverbs.

Exercises

1.

A. Identify the source domain for the concept of "theory/argument":

   i. Is that the foundation for your theory?
   ii. The theory needs more support.
   iii. We need to construct a strong argument for that.
   iv. We need to buttress the theory with solid arguments.
   v. The theory will stand or fall on the strength of that argument.
   vi. So far we have put together only the framework of the theory.

B. On the basis of your solution in the first part of this exercise, work out the conceptual *mappings* of the same metaphor:

   i. _____
   ii. _____
   iii. _____
   iv. _____
   v. _____
and so on _____

_____
_____

2. The three following sentences share a conceptual metaphor. Read the following sentences carefully and find the shared conceptual metaphor.

   a. He was cut off in his prime.
   b. One day the Grim Reaper will come for you.
   c. Hundreds of villagers have been mowed down by the enemy.

Now establish the conceptual *mappings*:

   i. _____
   ii. _____
   iii. _____
   iv. _____

3. Which *orientational metaphors* are involved in the following expressions? What general conclusions can you make about the orientations? (That is, is there a "generic-level" orientational metaphor?)

    a. an upstanding citizen; a low trick; a low-down thing to do
    b. lofty position; to rise to the top; the bottom of the social hierarchy
    c. high spirits; to be depressed; to be low
    d. in top shape; to fall ill; to drop dead

4. Analyze the following excerpts taken from American colonial documents. Find the recurrent linguistic metaphors that describe the relationship between the colonies and Britain. What is the conceptual metaphor that underlies these examples? What does this knowledge highlight about the colonial period?

    a. "To put the Government and trade of all our colonies into so good and sound a state, that every one may have its due share of nutrient, and thereby be the better fitted and disposed for the uses and benefit of the whole body politic, *especially of Great-Britain, their head, mother, and protectress*" (1757).
    b. "It is a standing instruction, as a security of the dependence of the government of the colonies *on the mother country*, that no acts wherein the king's rights or the rights of *the mother country* or of private persons can be affected" (1764).
    c. "But this I consider in effect as a destruction of one of the most necessary mediums of communication between the colonies and the *parent country*" (1771).
    d. "That it is the true indispensable duty of those colonies to the best of sovereigns, *to the mother country*, and to themselves to endeavor by a local and dutiful address to his majesty" (1765).

5. Read the following poem, written by Emily Dickinson. Which conceptual metaphor does the poem evoke? What metaphorical entailments does the poem's central conceptual metaphor have? Concentrate on the LIFE IS A JOURNEY and the DEATH IS DEPARTURE metaphors and Dickinson's extensions of these metaphors.

> Because I could not stop for Death-
> He kindly stopped for me-
> The Carriage held but just Ourselves-
> And Immortality.
>
> We slowly drove-He knew no haste
> And I had put away
> My labor and my leisure too,
> For His Civility-
>
> We passed the School, where Children strove
> At Recess-in the Ring-

We passed the Fields of Gazing Grain-
We passed the Setting Sun-

Or rather-He passed Us-
The Dews drew quivering and chill-
For only Gossamer, my Gown-
My Tippet-only Tulle-

We paused before a House that seemed
A Swelling of the Ground-
The Roof was scarcely visible-
The Cornice -in the Ground-

Since then-'tis Centuries- and yet
Feels shorter than the Day
I first surmised the Horses' Heads
Were toward Eternity

9

Metaphoric Frames

Some Cultural and Social Applications

I have suggested so far that, to a large extent, culture can be thought of as a set of shared understandings of the world, where our understandings are mental representations structured by cultural models, or frames. We also saw in the previous chapter that metaphor is the interaction of two cultural models— a source and a target domain, where the source provides much of the structure of the target. It then follows that some of our shared cultural understandings of the world will be based on metaphorical frames, that is, cases where a given cultural frame is structured by another cultural frame, or model.

This idea has important implications for the study of culture. Methodologically, in the same way as we used frame analysis for studying a variety of cultural phenomena, we can use *metaphorical* frame analysis in studying additional phenomena. On the content side, we can approach a number of significant cultural and social issues by means of the theory of conceptual metaphor.

First, we can ask: How do we understand cultural symbols? It can be suggested that many (though not all) symbols are based on metaphors and that, at least in part, we understand the symbols by virtue of the conceptual metaphors evoked by them.

Second, the interpretation of history may also commonly rest on metaphors. It is important to find which particular metaphors are used for such a purpose and how these metaphors emerged in the minds of the people who provided interpretations of historical events.

Third, cultures typically do not use one coherent set of frames in understanding the world; the frames used for a particular area of experience may be contradictory or conflicting. Such situations often lead to cultural debates among participants of a culture. The domain of POLITICS is particularly conducive to such conflicts of opinion. We will show how metaphorical frame analysis can elucidate and sometimes even explain the nature of these debates (similar to debates concerning art, as discussed in chap. 4).

Fourth, metaphor is not only linguistic and conceptual; a chief feature of metaphor is that it can actually occur in the social-physical practice of a society. Metaphor can thus become embodied cultural practice. A large part of culture is made up of such embodied cultural practices defined by metaphor. We will consider one such case in some detail.

Fifth, metaphors may also play a role in cultural frames that underlie prototypical narratives. Such metaphors may partially be constitutive of what we mean by particular types of narratives. To see this, we return to Hogan's analysis of culturally important narrative structures.

Finally, we examine the issue of linguistic relativity in relation to metaphorical understanding. Since cultures commonly use different source domains to understand a particular target domain, such situations offer an ideal possibility to study how metaphorical understanding via different source domains affects thought in different languages and cultures. We will look at a series of experiments that was conducted with this goal in mind.

Cultural Symbols

Symbols in general and cultural symbols in particular may be based on well-entrenched metaphors in a culture. For instance, a common symbol of life is fire. This symbol is a manifestation of the metaphor LIFE IS FIRE, which also appears in mundane linguistic expressions such as *to snuff out somebody's life*. Thus, symbols can be the source domains associated with target domains.

To understand a symbol means in part to be able to see the conceptual metaphors that the symbol can evoke or was created to evoke. Consider, for example, my analysis of the the Statue of Liberty in New York City (Kövecses, 1995b, 2002). The statue was created to evoke the idea that liberty was achieved in the United States (together with its "accompaniments" —knowledge and justice). This is displayed in the statue by means of several metaphors—metaphors for free action, history, and knowledge. Since ACTION IS SELF-PROPELLED MOVEMENT, free action will be UNINHIBITED SELF-PROPELLED MOVEMENT. This arises from the fact that the statue steps forward as broken shackles lie at her feet. Also, a common conception of history is that it is a change from a period of ignorance and oppression to a period of knowledge and freedom. This is based on the metaphor that HISTORICAL CHANGE IS MOVEMENT FROM A STATE OF IGNORANCE TO A STATE OF KNOWLEDGE. What evokes this metaphor is the fact that the statue steps forward with a torch enlightening the world. The torch symbolizes knowledge. Thus, finally, we have the metaphor KNOWING IS SEEING, as exemplified by such everyday linguistic metaphors as "I *see* your point." Given these metaphors, the statue may be regarded as a physical embodiment of the metaphorical source domains: UNINHIBITED MOVEMENT, MOVEMENT FROM DARK TO LIGHT, and SEEING.

Interpreting History and the Creation of Metaphors

I have previously pointed out (Kövecses, 1994) that Alexis de Tocqueville in his *Democracy in America* analyzes American democracy as a highly defective person, whose defects have to be made up for and counterbalanced by external forces such as the legal system. This view of democracy depends crucially on the acceptance of the conceptual metaphor A STATE/ SOCIETY IS A PERSON. The metaphor emerges from the study of hundreds of examples in Tocqueville's book.

But what is the PERSON metaphor like in *Democracy in America*? We can characterize it by providing the major mappings and entailments I have found:

Mappings:

- The person engaged in emotional, physical, political, and/or economic interaction with his immediate environment is the democratic society as a whole.
- The nature and propensities of the person are the constitutive (essential) properties of the democracy.
- The behaviors of the person are the passions and activities that occur in the democracy.
- The dangerousness of the behaviors of the person is the harmfulness of the behaviors that occur in democracy to the democracy.

Entailments:

Source: The behaviors are produced by the inherent nature of the person.

Target: The behaviors that occur in the democracy are produced by the constitutive properties of the democracy.

Source: Because the person produces dangerous behaviors, he or she is a defective person.

Target: Because the democracy produces harmful behaviors, it is a defective social system.

Source: The dangerous behaviors of the person have to be counterbalanced (controlled, corrected, etc.).

Target: The harmful behaviors of the democracy have to be counterbalanced (controlled, corrected, etc.).

Clearly, this is just one of the many possible versions of the PERSON metaphor; we know a great deal about people. And the metaphor of the BODY POLITIC has been around for a long time for the understanding of society. How did this particular version arise for Tocqueville? The question is important because the metaphor must have affected Tocqueville's thinking about American democracy. It seems that the particular version of the metaphor must have had its source in Tocqueville's idea of an ideal (free, independent, autonomous) person: This is a person who lives in a small community and engages in a variety of interactions with his or her environment. This community appears to be the township with its municipal institutions. For Tocqueville, the township, especially the New England township, is the "cradle" of American democracy, as the following quotes make clear:

> In the laws of Connecticut, as well as in all those of New England, we find the *germ and gradual development* of that township independence which is the *life and mainspring* of American liberty at the present day. (p. 40; italics added)

> The independence of the townships was the *nucleus round which the local interests, passions, rights, and duties collected and clung*. It gave scope to the activity of real political life, thoroughly democratic and republican. (p. 40; italics added)

The main point of these quotes is not to show that Tocqueville considered the township as the mainspring of American democracy but to show that he was fascinated by the free and autonomous life of people in the township. We can propose that it was this fascination that had possibly led him to conceptualize democracy in terms of a free, independent, and autonomous person who participates fully in the life of a small-scale but full-fledged democratic community.

The cognitive mechanism of arriving at this particular version of the PERSON metaphor is interesting. What we find here is that a phenomenon (democracy in America) is metaphorically comprehended in terms of the cause or origin (the township) of the phenomenon. This occurs commonly in our conceptual system.

But this alone does not explain all aspects of the PERSON metaphor, as used by Tocqueville. In particular, we have no explanation why he laid so much stress on the passionate side of the person. We can suggest that this became a prevalent feature of PERSON as a source domain because of Tocqueville's exaggerated fear of intense emotions. His book contains a large number of examples that reveal this fear. It can be surmised that this fear was his response to Romanticism, which gave a much more positive evaluation of the emotions than we can find in Tocqueville's work. As a child of the Enlightenment, he may have rejected or may have been disappointed by the emphasis that Romanticism placed on emotion.

This factor provides another important dimension of how we construct our metaphors. Particular metaphors are created not only because we see similarities between entities or because there are correlations in experience but also, and in combination with these, because the particular communicative, cultural, and historical situations in which we think metaphorically shape the metaphors we create.

Metaphoric Framing

The frames that we use can be based on conceptual metaphors. Particular target concepts are framed by particular source concepts. I will discuss three such target domains: TAXATION, WAR, and MORAL POLITICS.

Metaphor and Taxation

Let us begin with one of George Lakoff's examples that he analyzes in a number of interviews on the Internet. It is the phrase *tax relief*, as used by the Bush Administration. The phrase is used by the Bush Administration to substitute for the expression *tax cuts*. Although the phrase *tax relief* looks like a fairly neutral way of talking about taxation, it is not; it is couched in a conceptual metaphor that makes people see taxation in a particular way. People normally talk about "relief" when there is some affliction that causes pain or other damage. The word assumes a frame with a number of elements: the affliction, the person who is afflicted, a person who gives the afflicted person relief, and the action of giving this person relief from the affliction. The frame includes other background knowledge as well. The most important of these is that the person who provides relief is a "good guy" and anyone who tries to stop the reliever from providing relief is a "bad guy."

Now when we talk about taxation by employing the phrase *tax relief*, we are talking and thinking metaphorically. On this account, the administration that tries to provide relief from taxes is a hero and those who try to prevent this are villains. The metaphor is based on a frame that makes people see taxation in a new light, namely, that tax cuts are absolutely necessary and the moral thing to do. Choosing and using the metaphor divides politicians and citizens into good guys and bad guys by placing people with opposing views into particular roles in the frame. This is standard procedure in politics and it is achieved through "metaphor-based reframings."

Metaphor and War

The frames that we employ to understand social events and life in a culture can be either specific or very general ones. Consider the current war in Iraq. Americans conceptualize the events by means of a Western philosophical-political frame that emphasizes rationality, as well as political, military, and economic interest. This emphasis leads inevitably to a deep misunderstanding between Americans and Muslims of the Middle East. The reason is that Muslims look at the situation in a very different light; they employ a religious frame and a national pride frame to make sense of the events. The application of very different frames to the same situation results in incompatible evaluations and actions.

The same differences in general interpretation were present in the Gulf War in 1990–1991, but there are, of course, different specific frames that characterize differences between the two actual situations. One such specific frame that was used in the United States during the 1990 Iraqi war was that of the "fairy tale." Clearly, this is a metaphor-based frame (Lakoff, 1992).

As George Lakoff showed in several publications (1992, 1996), American politics is largely structured by a variety of conceptual metaphors: POLITICS IS WAR, POLITICS IS BUSINESS, SOCIETY IS A FAMILY, SOCIETY IS A PERSON, and THE PRESIDENTIAL ELECTION IS A RACE. For example, given the POLITICS IS WAR metaphor, American society can be seen as composed of armies that correspond to political groups; the leaders of the armies correspond to political leaders; the weapons used by the army are the ideas and policies of the political groups; the objective of the war is some political goal; and so on. These metaphors can be widely found in the media and in the speech of politicians. Most important, they impose a particular order or pattern on political activities.

Once people conceive of a nation as a person, it then becomes possible to think of neighboring countries as "neighbors" who can be friendly or hostile, strong or weak, and healthy or sick. Strength corresponds here to military strength and health to economic wealth. This metaphor has certain implications for foreign politics. A country can be identified as strong and another as weak. Since strength is associated with men and weakness with women, a militarily strong nation can be seen as "raping" a weak one when it attacks the weak nation. This was the conceptual metaphor that was used in the Gulf War in 1990 when Iraq attacked and occupied Kuwait. The attack was interpreted in the United States as the "rape" of Kuwait (Lakoff, 1992). The United States was seen as a hero that rescued an innocent victim (Kuwait) from a villain (Iraq). This interpretation convinced most of the American public that the United States had the right to intervene. It thus provided moral justification for the United States to go to war against Iraq.

Metaphor and Moral Politics

American discourse about morality often involves two foundational conceptual metaphors (Lakoff, 1996): (1) MORALITY IS STRENGTH and (2) MORALITY IS NURTURANCE.

(1)
BEING BAD IS BEING LOW
BEING GOOD IS BEING UPRIGHT
DOING EVIL IS FALLING
EVIL IS A FORCE
MORALITY IS STRENGTH

According to this metaphorical system of morality, evil can act on an *upright* person who can either *fall* (become bad) or *remain upright* (remain good). The evil can be either an external or an internal force. External evil may be a dangerous situation that causes fear. Internal evil may be, for example, the seven deadly sins. In either case, a moral person would apply a counterforce in an effort to overcome the force of evil and would be successful in overcoming it. Thus, in this view, moral "strength" is based on the notion of "physical strength."

(2)

THE COMMUNITY IS A FAMILY

MORAL AGENTS ARE NURTURING PARENTS

PEOPLE NEEDING HELP ARE CHILDREN NEEDING NURTURANCE

MORAL ACTION IS NURTURANCE

In this second set of metaphors, morality appears to be more of an "other-directed" issue than a "self-directed" one. Whereas in the STRENGTH metaphor there is only a single moral agent, in the NURTURANCE version there are two—people who need help and people who have a responsibility to provide that help. As Lakoff (1996) notes, it is not the case that the two metaphors exclude each other in the actual practice of morality in everyday life. They are used together on most occasions, but different people may give different priorities to them. For some people, morality is primarily defined in terms of the MORALITY IS STRENGTH metaphor, whereas for others it is defined mostly in terms of MORALITY IS NURTURANCE.

In Lakoff's (1996) account, the different priorities that people give to the two metaphors explain two conceptions of American politics—conservatism and liberalism. On the one hand, if someone considers the MORALITY IS STRENGTH metaphor more important, this person is likely to be attracted to conservative ideas and ideals in politics. On the other hand, if someone considers the NURTURANCE metaphor more important as regards morality, this person is more likely to be a liberal as far as political issues are concerned. Why? The link between one's moral and political views is provided by a metaphor for the concept of "nation" mentioned earlier: A STATE/SOCIETY IS A FAMILY. Society is conventionally viewed as a family, with the state as parent and citizens as children. The two views of morality that were briefly outlined earlier are different conceptions of what a family is (Lakoff, 1996). In the MORAL STRENGTH metaphor, the family consists of independent and self-reliant individuals and morality is taught and learned primarily through discipline (to resist evil). Lakoff characterizes this view of the family in an interview as follows (*UCBerkeley News*, October 27, 2003):

The conservative worldview, the strict father model, assumes that the world is dangerous and difficult and that children are born bad and must be made good. The strict father is the moral authority who supports and defends the family, tells his wife what to do, and teaches his kids right from wrong. The only way to do that is through painful discipline—physical punishment that by adulthood will become internal discipline. The good people are the disciplined people. Once grown, the self-reliant, disciplined children are on their own. Those children who remain dependent (who were spoiled, overly willful, or recalcitrant) should be forced to undergo further discipline or be cut free with no support to face the discipline of the outside world.

By contrast, in the NURTURANCE metaphor the family consists of people who have a moral obligation to help one another to begin with. In this view of the family, morality is taught and learned less through discipline than through nurturance. Again in Lakoff's words (*UCBerkeley News*, October 27, 2003):

> [T]he progressive worldview is modeled on a nurturant parent family. Briefly, it assumes that the world is basically good and can be made better and that one must work toward that. Children are born good; parents can make them better. Nurturing involves empathy, and the responsibility to take care of oneself and others for whom we are responsible. On a larger scale, specific policies follow, such as governmental protection in form of a social safety net and government regulation, universal education (to ensure competence, fairness), civil liberties and equal treatment (fairness and freedom), accountability (derived from trust), public service (from responsibility), open government (from open communication), and the promotion of an economy that benefits all and functions to promote these values, which are traditional progressive values in American politics.

Now the priorities given to the two metaphors will have implications for one's political views because the two conceptions of the family and "morality" will influence one's view of the nation as a family. The metaphor-based notion of morality will have different consequences for one's political views. Morality and politics will fuse into *moral politics*; hence the title of Lakoff's book: *Moral Politics*.

Metaphors Made Real

Many conceptual metaphors are "realized" in social and cultural reality (Gibbs, 1999; Kövecses, 2002, 2005a; Lakoff, 1993). Therefore, the study of these conceptual metaphors is important in the study of society and culture. This property of metaphors has also been noticed and studied by several anthropologists, including Bradd Shore (1996), William Foley (1997), and Christopher Tilley (1999), although they may have used different terms for the phenomenon. For example, such nonlinguistic realizations are called instituted models by Shore and material metaphor by Tilley.

There are several possibilities for metaphors to be realized in other than linguistic ways. If we take a conceptual metaphor to be a pairing of domains A (target) and B (source), such that "A is B," then the realization can occur in at least the following ways (Kövecses, 2005a):

1. The source domain, B, can turn into social-physical reality.
2. The entailments of the source domain, B, can turn into social-physical reality.
3. The target domain, A, can actually become the source domain, B, and, at the same time, turn into social-physical reality.

By a conceptual domain "turning into" social-physical reality, I simply mean that the conceptual domain occurs not only as a concept or as a word but also as a more or less tangible thing or process in our social and cultural practice (i.e., as a social and physical object, institution, action, activity, event, state, relationship, and the like). In this sense, we can legitimately say that metaphors can be "made real" (Krzeszowski, 2002).

The first case—the source domain converting into physical reality—is extremely common in culture. We find it when metaphorical idioms are "enacted"; when a source domain is visually represented (e.g., in dance, painting, sculpture, gestures, cartoons); when people actually act out a source domain (either in real life or onstage or as a ritual); when the static pattern of a situation or relationship follows the conceptual structure of the source domain, and so on. To take just one example, consider the seating arrangements at a formal meeting. Important people tend to sit more centrally and higher than people who are less important. This follows the metaphorical structure provided by the conceptual metaphors SIGNIFICANT/ IMPORTANT IS CENTRAL and SIGNIFICANT/ IMPORTANT IS HIGH, together with their opposites LESS SIGNIFICANT/ IMPORTANT IS PERIPHERAL and LESS SIGNIFICANT/ IMPORTANT IS LOWER.

A special case here is gestures. Inspired by work on metaphor in the cognitive linguistic framework, David McNeill (1992), Charles Forceville (1996, 2002), Alan Cienki (1998), Eve Sweetser (1998), Sarah Taub (2001), and Phyllis Wilcox (2000) were among the first to systematically study this kind of metaphor realization.

The second case—the entailments of the source domain converting into social-physical reality—may be somewhat less common but equally important in the study of cultures. Lakoff provides a pertinent example (message on the Internet, January 29, 1993). He analyzed then-president Bush's Address to the Nation on Drugs. The address was dominated by three conceptual metaphors: DRUGS ARE EVIL SUBSTANCES FLOWING INTO THE COUNTRY, TO BE DRUG-DEPENDENT IS TO HAVE A DISEASE, and DRUG USERS ARE ENEMIES (TO BE FOUGHT AGAINST). These metaphors share some consequences, or entailments, and do not share others. The entailments may play a role in determining social policy. For example, the PIPELINE and DISEASE metaphors share the consequence that the problem of drugs is not a result of internal social causes. On the PIPELINE metaphor, the drug problem originates outside the country. On the DISEASE metaphor, it is not a social but a physical issue. Thus, in neither case is it an internal social problem. However, the DISEASE and WAR metaphors have very different consequences for deciding how to handle the issue. If taking drugs is a disease, people with an addiction have to be placed in hospitals and large-scale programs have to be set up for treating them. If, however, people who sell and take drugs are enemies in a war, they have to be fought, for example, by more police officers on the streets in areas of cities where drugs are most commonly used (the inner-city ghettos). Given these different entailments, the money for handling the drug problem would have to be spent on hospitals, research, and such in the former case and on beefing up the police force, jails, courts, and so on, in the latter. Thus, the two metaphors have distinct social consequences. In our terms, the different entailments of the two conceptual metaphors are realized in different social policies, that is, in differing social realities.

The third case—the target actually becoming the source and turning into social-physical reality—can be regarded as the extreme case of conceptual metaphors becoming real. It can probably be assumed that each culture is characterized by certain central metaphors, or, as Bradd Shore (1996) calls them, foundational schemas, which can then be realized as instituted models. Foundational schemas are large-scale conceptual metaphors that organize extensive portions of experience in a culture and may involve several more specific metaphors that are more limited in their scope. Central everyday metaphors can also form the basis of "ideologies" in cultures (see e.g., Goatly, forthcoming).

I (Kövecses, 2005a) have studied one such foundational metaphor in American culture, namely, the metaphor LIFE IS A SHOW or SPECTACLE or, more generally, ENTERTAINMENT. (What follows in the remainder of this section is based on this study.)

It can be suggested that the POLITICS IS SPORTS metaphor that is so prevalent in the United States is a specific instance of this more general foundational metaphor. However, it cannot be claimed that this metaphor is an American invention. Varieties of the metaphor go back to Greek antiquity and show up in a number of distinct ways throughout the history of Western civilization (Turner, 1991). Perhaps the most famous "popularizer" of the SHOW, or PLAY, metaphor was Shakespeare, who wrote these lines in sixteenth-century Europe:

> All the world is a stage,
> And all the men and women merely players.
> They have their exits and their entrances;
> And one man in his time plays many parts.
> (Shakespeare, As You Like It 2.7)

As Neil Gabler (1998) points out, at this time public life was a performance in Europe, in which one presented a self that one wanted to be perceived. Social intercourse was role-playing.

The widespread use of the LIFE IS A PLAY metaphor in America in recent times is shown by its high linguistic productivity, that is, by the many metaphorical expressions that are based on it in one way or another. Lakoff and Turner (1989) provide a long list of examples:

LIFE IS A PLAY
It's *curtains* for him.
She's my *leading lady*.
She always wants to be *in the spotlight*.
The kid *stole the show*.
That's not *in the script*.
What's your *part in* this?
You *missed your cue*.
He *blew his lines*.
He *saved the show*.
She *brought the house down*.
Clean up your act!
He always *plays the fool*.
That attitude is just a *mask*.
He *turned in a great performance*.
Take a bow!
You deserve a *standing ovation*.
He *plays an important role in* the process.
He only *played a bit part* in my life.
He's *waiting in the wings*.
I'm *improvising*.
It's *showtime!*
You*'re on!*

This metaphor can be found in every facet of American life and popular culture, pop songs being one of the best sources of examples. Elvis Presley sings,
"*Act one* was when we met," and Frank Sinatra has the famous line "And
now I face the *final curtain*."

The LIFE IS A PLAY metaphor is structured by the following set of
mappings:

Source domain: A PLAY		Target domain: LIFE
an actor	→	a person leading a life
fellow actors	→	the people with whom he interacts
the way the actor acts	→	the behavior of the person leading a life
the parts	→	the roles in life
the leading parts	→	the people who play main roles in one's life
the beginning of the play	→	birth
the end of the play	→	death
the script	→	the story of one's life as it should happen

Probably the most important correspondence between the two domains is
the one according to which parts in a play correspond to roles people "play"
in life. This seems to be the main meaning focus of the metaphor. As we saw,
this is a very old focus of the metaphor, but it became especially important in
early twentieth-century America. Taking up some ideas from Warren I. Susman
(1984), Neil Gabler explains the shift from a primarily "character-oriented"
to a "personality-oriented" culture in the American context:

> [T]he old Puritan production-oriented culture demanded and honored what he [Warren Susman] called character, which was a function of one's moral fiber. The new consumption-oriented culture, on the other hand, demanded what he called personality which was a function of what one projected to others. It followed that the Puritan culture emphasized values like hard work, integrity and courage. The new culture of personality emphasized charm, fascination and likability. Or as Susman put it, "the social role demanded of all in the new culture of personality was that of a performer. Every American was to become a performing self." (1998: 197)

The chief representative of this type of character was Fitzgerald's Great Gatsby —Jay Gatz, who, as Gabler remarks, was an invention of himself. He was a symbol of twentieth-century America. This was a culture of personality in which "playing a role was just as good as being the real person" (Gabler, 1998: 198).

But the PLAY metaphor gradually grew into something much more extensive in twentieth-century America. The concept of "life" began to be understood not just in terms of a theater play, but in terms of many different forms of entertainment, such as shows of all kinds, spectator sports, and spectacles. Indeed, life became entertainment in general in many ways, yielding the highly general metaphor LIFE IS A SHOW or ENTERTAINMENT. The process must have been motivated by the spread and popularity of spectator sports, the invention of films, radio, and television, and the availability and popularity of mass communication (and several other factors).

Aspects of life began to assume features of entertainment. At first, there was, we could say, only a metonymic—not a metaphoric—connection between the two. Neil Gabler (1998) tells us that even the seemingly mundane activity of shopping was often accompanied by events that chiefly characterize entertainment. In Gabler's words, "[d]epartment stores had elaborate window dressing, musical accompaniment, art shows, theatrical lighting and playlets to enhance the sense that shopping was just another form of entertainment" (1998: 199–200). The metonymy might be put as ENTERTAINMENT FOR CONSUMPTION. But then the metonymy started to give way to metaphor in which the boundary between entertainment and shopping was lost to the point that the two fused into a full-fledged conceptual metaphor that characterized the megamalls of the 1980s. In this kind of situation, celebrities advertised products and when one bought something advertised by a celebrity one became a celebrity as well (Gabler, 1998). In the metaphor of SHOPPING AS A FORM OF ENTERTAINMENT, or A SHOW, the ordinary shopper became a celebrity. Moreover, by means of personification, the products themselves, such as Ray•Ban sunglasses and Godiva chocolates, also became celebrities— celebrity products (Gabler, 1998).

Other aspects of life were not spared, either. POLITICS as a target domain was also comprehended as a show. And it was done to an extent unmatched by other countries that have similar political institutions. The election campaign is a prime example. In it, the candidates appear as putative stars; the primaries are like open casting calls; the campaign looks like an audition; the election itself is the selection of the lead; the handlers are the drama coaches, scriptwriters, and directors. In this kind of political atmosphere, it almost appears that the goal of politics is none other than providing good entertainment (Gabler, 1998). Gabler might overstate his case here, but there can be no doubt that in America POLITICS (and especially the ELECTION) IS A SHOW. A (for many) sad punch line of this argument is that, after the late President Reagan, another actor, Arnold Schwarzenegger, was elected the governor of California.

For many American teachers and university professors, the teaching process itself is a form entertainment. Many educators believe that teaching a class without at the same time "putting on a show" is unimaginable or at least much less effective in American schools.

Not only teaching but also dating and romantic relationships are imbued with the vocabulary and conceptual patterns of entertainment, especially those of spectator sports. As Lakoff and Johnson (1980) showed, LOVE IS A GAME, in which people sometimes "can't *get to first base*" but at other times "can *score touchdowns.*"

Not even the beautiful American landscape escapes being viewed as a form of entertainment, especially as theater. Perhaps the most common adjective to describe the California coastline and the Grand Canyon in National Park publications and descriptions to visitors is the word *dramatic*, as in "the *dramatic* California coastline."

But the domain where one would least expect the application of the SHOW or ENTERTAINMENT metaphor is that of WARFARE. War is usually thought of as the most serious activity people can conduct, and yet in America the ENTERTAINMENT metaphor is one of the chief ways of talking and thinking about war. Surprisingly, even those who are in the "business" of making war think about it this way. According to the *San Francisco Chronicle*, "[o]ne member of the Pentagon press corps even referred to it [the war in Iraq] as 'the show last night' during a briefing Saturday" (section A14, "Editorials," March 24, 2003). Some Americans find this conceptualization unacceptable or offensive. The same journalist has this to say about the use of the SHOW metaphor: "As transfixed as Americans may be to the TV coverage of war in Iraq, flicking as it does from aircraft carriers to tank battalions in real time, this is not entertainment. The soldiers are real, putting their lives on the line" (section A14, "Editorials," March 24, 2003). A few days later, a reader of the *New York Times* writes this in connection with the coverage of the same war on TV: "Feeding our seemingly unquenchable thirst to get an intimate view, this real-time coverage turns us into voyeurs and war itself into spectacle" (section A18, "Letters," March 26, 2003). Clearly, the SHOW or ENTERTAINMENT metaphor is a large part of the way many Americans talk and think about war and, we could add, also of the way they debate it.

It seems, then, that Americans have a certain predilection to understand their various experiences in life, including business, politics, education, landscape, love and dating, warfare, and several others, in terms of a show or, more generally, entertainment. But this predilection is perhaps most conspicuous in the current fad of reality TV. In reality TV, life as a whole becomes entertainment. The target domain becomes one with the source domain. The parts played by actors in the source turn inseparably into the roles people play in life. It seems that, in it, life loses its goal other than that given to it by a show, which is to entertain people. Life does become a play, a kind of entertainment, and we as spectators watch ourselves living our own lives.

Narrative Structure and Metaphor

How can the theory of conceptual metaphor be related to the theory of narrative structure that was discussed in chapter 6? It will be recalled that Hogan's main suggestion was that paradigmatic narratives are based on prototypes of emotion concepts—with happiness as the main "outcome" emotion. Hogan seems to assume the presence of certain "literal" concepts in his theory—without questioning their allegedly literal status. One such concept is that of romantic union as one of the predominant prototypes for the eliciting conditions of happiness. In other words, the theory suggests that being united with the beloved is the paradigm of happiness. But the notion of being united with someone is itself a metaphorical one. It is based on the central metaphor for love (Kövecses, 1988, 1991b): LOVE IS PHYSICAL UNITY (OF TWO COMPLEMENTARY PARTS). Can cognitive literary analysis and theory construction start, without first reflecting, with concepts that are themselves the result of prior metaphorical conceptualization?

In certain types of narrative, happiness derives from the transcendental union of God and people. This transcendental happiness is based on happiness that derives from the more concrete concept of "romantic union"; that is, the relationship between God and humanity is imagined on the analogy of the relationship between two people who love each other. Hogan (2003) offers a hierarchy for capturing this: Transcendental happiness derives from romantic union, which derives from PHYSICAL UNITY (OF TWO COMPLEMENTARY PARTS). In other words, there are conceptual metaphors, such as LOVE IS THE PHYSICAL UNITY (OF TWO COMPLEMENTARY PARTS), on which both emotions (transcendental happiness and romantic happiness) and, hence, certain types of narratives are based. Instead of assuming such a vertical hierarchy (transcendental unity, romantic unity, and physical unity), we could imagine the metaphorical structuring of both emotion concepts and the narratives based on them not as a vertical hierarchy but as a single conceptual metaphor that applies to any kind of abstract unity; the generalized (i.e., generic-level) conceptual metaphor would be: ABSTRACT UNITY (transcendental, romantic) IS PHYSICAL UNITY. In other words, an abstract unity of whatever kind could be seen as being conventionally conceptualized as a PHYSICAL UNITY (Kövecses, 2000b). This might be a general structuring principle of both the conceptual system and certain narratives.

Is this a peculiarity of the UNITY metaphor? That does not seem to be the case. As Hogan suggests, the prototypical narrative plot also involves time and space. Consider space for our next example. The crucial distinction of space in literary narratives is, according to the author, "home" versus "away from home." The concept of "home" is instantiated differently in different types of narrative. In romantic plots, home is the place where one lives with the beloved; in heroic plots, it is the nation; and in sacrificial plots, it is "a paradise of natural comfort and plenty." Now we can think of these last two kinds of spaces as metaphorically constituted according to the following conceptual metaphors: A NATION IS A HOME and PARADISE IS HOME. They are both based on the idea that home is where we like to be most with the beloved—the literal definition of home in romantic narratives. Again, we find that the notion of "home" applies metaphorically to any abstract target domain that can be brought into correspondence with the literal concept, that is, to which the generalized metaphor AN ABSTRACT HOME (nation, paradise) IS A REAL HOME applies. Given this, it seems that we have a tendency here that characterizes the conceptual system in general (see Kövecses, 1995a).

The Kind of Mind Involved in Narratives

What is the mind like that operates with such conceptual metaphors as we have seen earlier? More specifically, what kind of conceptual system can be assumed to underlie narrative structures and the emotion prototypes on which they are based?

We can have an idea of this if we examine one of the emotion concepts that Hogan characterizes in his book. He postulates the existence of several nonspecific "proto-emotions." One of them is *sensitivity*, whose eliciting condition is an excess of stimulation and whose actional response is withdrawal from stimulation. He suggests that temperature regulation is the prototypical case for this. Given this idea, he explains the source domains for some more specific emotions on this basis: HEAT is the source domain for LUST and ANGER, WARMTH for AFFECTION, and COLD for FEAR.

However, we can think about this in a different way that might replace or complement Hogan's approach. Instead of saying that these metaphorical concepts come directly from ambient conditions that require temperature regulation, we could suggest that these are body-based metaphors for emotions. Feelings of change in body temperature evoke the ambient temperatures as metaphorical source domains. If we think of the motivational basis of conceptual metaphors along these lines, it would give us the idea of a conceptual system in which many metaphors find their motivation in real bodily experience, such as body temperature. The kind of mind would be an embodied mind—a new conception of the mind in which abstract ideas are based on physical experiences of the human body (see Lakoff and Johnson, 1999). This idea was called experientialism in the first chapter, and we will come back to it in chapter 12.

Linguistic Relativity and Metaphor

Following Lera Boroditsky (2001), we can ask: Does metaphorical language people use to talk about time shape thought about time? More specifically, do speakers of different languages, such as English and Mandarin Chinese, think differently about time as a result of their habitual use of language about time?

In a series of experiments, Boroditsky studied the TIME IS HORIZONTAL (e.g., "*before/after/ behind/* etc. . . . [a day, month, year, etc.]") and TIME IS VERTI-CAL (e.g., "handing *down* knowledge from one generation to the next") meta-phors. She was interested in whether spatial metaphors can have an effect on how people understand (i.e., process) sentences that contain such metaphors—both on-line (i.e., in real time) and in the long run (i.e., based on long-term memory).

There are languages where time is conceived of as being oriented vertically as well as horizontally. One such language is Mandarin Chinese (as opposed to English, where time is metaphorically viewed as primarily horizontal). In Mandarin Chinese both metaphorical conceptualizations for time are present in a robust and systematic way. The words *qian* ('front') and *hou* ('back') as well as *shang* ('up') and *xia* ('down') are all commonly and systematically used to talk about not only space but also time. In English, this happens much less frequently and systematically (e.g., "hand *down* knowledge," "Christmas is coming *up*"). In other words, in contrast to Mandarin Chinese, English pri-marily relies on a horizontal conceptualization of time (e.g., *ahead, before, after, forward, behind*).

Boroditsky made use of two kinds of primes in her experiments: a prime for horizontal orientation (e.g., "The black worm is ahead of the white worm") and a prime for vertical orientation (e.g., "The black ball is above the white ball"). Subjects were given such spatial primes on a computer screen and were asked to answer a TRUE/ FALSE question in connection with the primes. This was followed by a TRUE/ FALSE question about time as can be found in sentences like *March comes before April* and *March comes earlier than April*.

It should be noticed that the former sentence contains a horizontal spa-tiotemporal metaphor (*before*), while the latter contains a purely temporal (nonmetaphorical) expression (*earlier*). The former type of sentence can be used to check on-line understanding of the sentences, whereas the latter type can be used to check people's understanding of time using long-term memory.

Let us begin with on-line processing. Half of the sentences used in the experiment had the spatiotemporal metaphors *before/after* in them. These words are based on a horizontal metaphorical conceptualization of "time." The hypothesis was that both the English and Chinese speakers should be able to understand the sentences that contain these words faster if they re-ceive a horizontal prime than if they receive a vertical prime. The prediction was proved correct. The response times to TRUE/ FALSE questions about time were shorter for both groups of speakers when they just saw a horizon-tal prime than when they saw a vertical one. This shows the effect of spa-tiotemporal metaphors on thinking about time; the presence of spatiotemporal metaphors in a sentence facilitates the processing of sentences that contain them. (However, on the average, speakers of English were faster than speakers of Mandarin Chinese at the task.)

As far as long-term understanding is concerned, the hypothesis was the following: Since English speakers use a preponderance of horizontal metaphors to talk about time, we can expect speakers of English to respond faster to questions about sentences with words like *earlier/later* when they receive a horizontal prime than when they receive a vertical one. Conversely, since Mandarin speakers frequently and systematically use vertical metaphors to talk about time, we can expect them to respond faster to questions about these sentences when they receive a vertical prime than when they receive a horizontal one. This prediction was also proved to be correct. The special significance of this finding is that native speakers of Mandarin Chinese performed better with vertical primes even though the language for which they were thinking in the experiment was English. The result thus shows "that habits in language encourage habits in thought."

Thinking for Speaking

The general theoretical framework in which Boroditsky's experiments about time are couched is known as "thinking for speaking" (Slobin, 1987, 1996, 2003). The main idea here is that a language may make us attend to certain aspects of experience through grammatically encoding these aspects while ignoring others.

A case in point is the source domain of MOTION IN SPACE in English and Turkish, as analyzed by Seyda Özçaliskan (2003a, b, 2004a, b, 2005). Özçaliskan showed that English primarily encodes manner into its verbs of motion (e.g., *walk, run, march*), whereas Turkish motion verbs in general lack this information concerning motion. Turkish primarily encodes direction into many of its motion verbs (e.g., verbs that correspond to the English *fall, come, spread, descend*). Thus, the domain of MOTION comes in at least two versions across languages: the manner-centered one (like English) and the neutral or direction-centered one (like Turkish). As Özçaliskan notes, this built-in difference in the kinds of information that the source domain of MOTION encodes may predispose the speakers of the two languages to attend to slightly different aspects of not only the source but also the target domain to which it is applied.

The phenomenon of thinking for speaking often leads to Whorfian effects; that is, to cases where the way we speak influences the way we think (Slobin, 1996, 2003). We will see further demonstration of such effects in later chapters, specifically, in chapter 13.

Conclusions

The discussion in this chapter allows us to make some general observations about metaphorical thought and its relation to culture. If we think of culture as a set of shared frames, then it seems that a large part of culture is constituted by frames that are understood in terms of other frames. For example, the understanding of cultural symbols largely depends on the conceptual metaphors we bring to their understanding. A cultural symbol may evoke particular non-metaphorical frames as source domains (such as MOTION, SEEING) that conventionally go together with some target domains (such as FREEDOM, KNOWLEDGE). The activation of such target domains provides an important level in the understanding of symbols.

Aspects of history can also be understood by means of particular metaphors that constitute a particular way of conceiving of that aspect. Tocqueville's chief metaphor for American democracy is a version of the BODY POLITIC metaphor of society in general. Tocqueville was fascinated by the free and autonomous life of people in the township. His fascination led him to conceptualize democracy in terms of a free, independent, and autonomous person who participates fully in the life of a small-scale but full-fledged democratic community. Why did he arrive at this particular metaphor? We can suggest that his target domain is metaphorically comprehended in terms of the cause or origin of the target. More generally, if a target domain A derives causally from domain B, we can say that they are involved in the same frame. Later on, however, the larger frame A can be metaphorically understood in terms of B. This situation often leads to the emergence of conceptual metaphors on a cultural basis.

Politics commonly uses the cognitive device of "metaphor-based reframings." Such reframings may be used in political debate about taxation or justifying war on the part of decision makers. It is typical to have multiple metaphor-based frames for a single cultural, social, or political issue. The choice of a particular metaphorical frame may divide members of a society into subcultures, political camps, and so on. Metaphorical frames are chosen on the basis of one's goals and/or ideology. They can also be chosen because of the different consequences that different frames have.

A major way in which metaphor's role is crucial in culture is that metaphors can turn into social reality. Three possibilities were mentioned: (1) The source domain, B, can turn into social-physical reality; (2) the entailments of the source domain, B, can turn into social-physical reality; and (3) the target domain, A, can actually become the source domain, B, and, at the same time, turn into social-physical reality. Cultures differ in and can be characterized by the conceptual metaphors that they make real on a large scale. In addition, the metaphors may lead to ideologies that may become cultural practice (Goatly, forthcoming).

Another major way in which cultures differ is the different source domains that are used to structure a particular target domain. Experimental evidence I have surveyed in this chapter shows that the different source domains in two different languages for the same target lead to differences in certain cognitive tasks that involve the target. In other words, differences in metaphorical language seem to shape the way people speaking different languages in two cultures think about the same target domain. Language appears to make us attend to different aspects of experience through grammatically encoding these different aspects. This is called thinking for speaking, a phenomenon that often leads to Whorfian effects (Slobin, 1996, 2003). Despite old and recent arguments to the contrary, language habits appear to shape the way we think.

Exercises

1. In this chapter, it was mentioned that many, especially American, university teachers think of education as entertainment and they also try to realize this metaphor in their work. Think about the word *infotainment*. What process is signaled by the morphological blending of the two words? Can you find instances within this specific area that display this unification of the source and the target in reality? Can you find other areas where a similar fusion has taken place?

2. In this chapter, we saw that much of American politics and policy decisions is rooted in the different metaphorical conceptualizations of a single issue. The way an issue is metaphorically framed will determine the action taken with regard to that issue in the real world (actions based on metaphorical entailments). What are the different policy consequences of the different ways of framing America as a nation metaphorically? (Think of "melting pot," "City upon a Hill," "salad bowl," "mosaic," etc.) Do you know any other issues in America or your own country that are heavily debated and whose different views are due to different metaphorical framings?

3. "Road movies" are a specifically American genre. What do you think makes them such? What American experience does this genre possibly stem from? Can you think of famous road movies? Is there any overarching, "narrative" metaphor involved in these movies (or their interpretation)?

4. Collect at least five metaphoric or metonymic expressions or images from TV or radio commercials. Find the underlying conceptual metaphor(s) or metonymies, and explain in each case how the metaphors or metonymies help the commercial to be more effective. How do commercials make use of metaphors or metonymies?

10

Metaphor Variation across
and within Cultures

The major goal of this chapter is to outline the basic components of a theory of variation and universality in metaphor. It is suggested that such components must minimally include the following: dimensions of variation, aspects of metaphor involved in variation, and causes of variation. (A book-length treatment of these and additional issues can be found in Kövecses, 2005a.)

Since cognitive linguists claim that metaphor is of the mind, the brain, and the body—aspects of people that are more universal than either language or social reality—many people who are familiar with the view of metaphor that originates from Lakoff and Johnson's (1980) *Metaphors We Live By* often expect that what we call conceptual metaphors are largely or mostly universal. They also often criticize this view for ignoring the apparent diversity of metaphors across and within cultures.

It is true that cognitive linguists have so far paid less attention to the diversity of metaphorical conceptualization across and within languages and cultures than to its universal aspects. They have been primarily concerned with the question: Why are certain conceptual metaphors universal or at least near-universal? My major goal in this chapter is to offer a balanced view that takes into account both the universality and diversity of metaphor. In this view, we have to be able to answer the following questions:

1. What are the dimensions along which metaphors vary?
2. Which aspects of metaphor are involved in metaphor variation, and how are they involved?
3. What are the main causes of variation?
4. How do the causes that produce variation interact with the causes that produce universality?

Before I begin the discussion of cultural variation in metaphor, it will be useful to briefly look at an example of universality in metaphorical conceptualization.

Universal Conceptual Metaphors

It seems that several unrelated languages may share several conceptual metaphors for particular emotion concepts. One of these emotion concepts is "happiness." There are a large number of conceptual metaphors for happiness in English (Kövecses, 1991a), but three of them stand out in importance: HAPPINESS IS UP ("I'm feeling *up*"), HAPPINESS IS LIGHT ("She *brightened* up"), and HAPPINESS IS A FLUID IN A CONTAINER ("He's *bursting* with joy").

The Chinese cognitive linguist Ning Yu found the same conceptual metaphors in Chinese (1995, 1998). Let us take HAPPINESS IS UP as our example. (Ning Yu used the following grammatical abbreviations: PRT = particle, ASP = aspect marker, MOD = modifier marker, COM = complement marker, CL = classifier, BA = preposition *ba* in the so-called *ba*-sentences.)

(1)   HAPPY IS UP
       Ta hen gao-xing.
       He very high-spirit
       He is very high-spirited/happy.

       Ta xing congcong de.
       He spirit rise-rise   PRT
       His spirits are rising and rising./He's pleased and excited.

       Zhe-xia   tiqi le   wo-de xingzhi.
       this-moment raise ASP my   mood
       This time it lifted my mood/interest.

Hungarian, a Finno-Ugric language, also has the same conceptual metaphors, as can be seen from the following examples:

(2)   HAPPINESS IS UP
       Ez a   film feldobott.
       this the film up-threw-me
       This film gave me a high./This film made me happy.

       Majd elszáll   a   boldogságtól.
       Almost away-flies-he/she the happiness-from
       He/she is on cloud nine.

It is a remarkable fact that the same metaphor exists in the three languages. After all, English, Chinese, and Hungarian belong to very different language families and represent very different cultures of the world, which presumably did not have much contact with one another when these conceptual metaphors evolved. The question arises: How is it possible for such different languages and cultures to conceptualize happiness metaphorically in such similar ways? Three answers to the question suggest themselves: (1) it has happened by accident; (2) one language borrowed the metaphors from another; and

(3) there is some universal motivation that enables the metaphors to emerge in these cultures.

If it is true, as cognitive linguists claim, that "simple" or "primary" metaphors (Grady 1997a, b; Kövecses, 2002) are motivated by universal correlations in bodily experience, we can be fairly certain that it is the third explanation that gives us the correct answer to the question. Indeed, when we are joyful, we tend to be up, moving around, active, and jumping up and down, rather than down, inactive, and static. These are undoubtedly universal experiences associated with happiness (or, more precisely, joy), and they are likely to produce universal (or near-universal) simple or primary metaphors.

The HAPPY IS UP metaphor is a generic-level metaphor. We know that metaphors tend to be universal or near-universal at this level. Specific-level metaphors tend to be different cross-linguistically. For example, a specific-level version of the metaphor HAPPY IS UP in English is HAPPINESS IS BEING OFF THE GROUND. As Ning Yu (1995, 1998) observed, this specific metaphor does not exist in Chinese.

Despite universality in metaphorical conceptualization of this kind, we find a great deal of cultural variation in metaphor. I now turn to giving an account of such variation in the remainder of this chapter.

Dimensions of Metaphor Variation

We can distinguish two kinds of dimensions along which conceptual metaphors vary: the cross-cultural and the within-culture dimensions.

Cross-Cultural Variation

The most obvious dimension along which metaphors vary is the cross-cultural dimension. Variation in this dimension can be found in several distinct forms. One of them is what we can call congruence. This is what obtains between a generic-level metaphor and several specific-level ones. Another is the case where a culture uses a set of different source domains for a particular target domain, or conversely, where a culture uses a particular source domain for conceptualizing a set of different target domains. Yet another situation involves cases where the set of conceptual metaphors for a particular target domain is roughly the same between two languages/cultures, but one language/culture shows a clear preference for some of the conceptual metaphors that are employed. Finally, there may be some conceptual metaphors that appear to be unique to a given language/culture. We will demonstrate congruence and alternative metaphorical conceptualization by some examples.

Congruent Metaphors

There is some evidence that THE ANGRY PERSON IS A PRESSURIZED CONTAINER metaphor may be near-universal. What is especially important about this conceptual metaphor is that it functions at an extremely general level. The metaphor does not specify many things that *could* be specified. For example, it does not say what kind of container is used, how the pressure arises, whether the container is heated or not, what kind of substance fills the container (liquid, substance, or objects), what consequences the explosion has, and so on. The metaphor constitutes a generic schema that gets filled out by each culture that has the metaphor. When it is filled out, it receives unique cultural content at a specific level. In other words, a generic-level conceptual metaphor is instantiated in culture-specific ways at a specific level. This is one kind of cross-cultural variation.

Consider the following three special cases. In one, Keiko Matsuki (1995) observes that all the metaphors for anger in English as analyzed by George Lakoff and me (Lakoff and Kövecses, 1987) can also be found in Japanese. At the same time, she also points out that there are a large number of anger-related expressions that group around the Japanese concept of *hara* (literally, 'belly'). This is a culturally significant concept that is unique to Japanese culture, and so the conceptual metaphor ANGER IS (IN THE) HARA is limited to Japanese.

Second, Ning Yu (1998) studied the PRESSURIZED CONTAINER metaphor in great depth and points out that Chinese uses a version of this metaphor in which the excess *qi* (i.e., energy that flows through the body) that corresponds to anger is not a fluid, like in English, but a gas. The gas is neutral with respect to heat, but it is capable of exerting pressure on the body container. The most remarkable feature of the Chinese ANGER metaphor is that it employs and is crucially constituted by the concept of *qi*—a concept that is deeply embedded in the long history of Chinese philosophy and medicine.

Third, Zulu shares many conceptual metaphors with English (Taylor and Mbense, 1998). This does not mean, however, that it cannot have metaphors other than the ones we can find in English. One case in point is the Zulu metaphor that involves the heart: ANGER IS (UNDERSTOOD AS BEING) IN THE HEART. When the HEART metaphor applies to English, it is primarily associated with love, affection, and the like. In Zulu it applies to anger and patience-impatience, tolerance-intolerance. The HEART metaphor conceptualizes anger in Zulu as leading to internal pressure, since too much "emotion substance" is crammed into a container of limited capacity. The things that fill it up are other emotions that happen to a person in the wake of daily events. When too many of these happen to a person, the person becomes extremely angry and typically loses control over his or her anger.

In all of the three cases, there is a generic-level metaphor and a specific-level one. The specific-level metaphors are instantiations of the generic-level one in the sense that they exhibit the same general structure. The lower-level instantiations are thus congruent with a higher-level metaphor. Where they differ is in the specific cultural content that they bring to the metaphor.

Alternative Metaphors

There can be differences in the *range* of conceptual metaphors (or, more precisely, the range of source domains) that languages and cultures have available for the conceptualization of particular target domains. This is what commonly happens in the case of emotion concepts as targets.

Chinese shares with English all the basic metaphorical source domains for happiness: UP, LIGHT, FLUID IN A CONTAINER. A metaphor that Chinese has, but English does not, is HAPPINESS IS FLOWERS IN THE HEART. According to Ning Yu (1995, 1998), the application of this metaphor reflects "the more introverted character of Chinese." He sees this conceptual metaphor as a contrast to the (American) English metaphor BEING HAPPY IS BEING OFF THE GROUND, which does not exist in Chinese at all and which reflects the relatively "extroverted" character of speakers of English.

As another illustration, let us take the concept of "life" as target. Later in this chapter, we will see that life is commonly and primarily conceptualized as "struggle/war," "precious possession," "game," "journey," and in several other ways by Americans and Hungarians. However, as work by Elizabeth M. Riddle (2001) shows, speakers of Hmong, a language spoken mainly in Laos and Thailand, conceptualize it very differently. They view life as a "string" that can be cut and broken. The word meaning 'cut', *tu*, can also mean 'to give birth', 'to die', and 'to kill'. Riddle presents evidence for the existence of the conceptual metaphor not only from language but also from social behavior. Although the Hmong metaphor LIFE IS A STRING resonates as at least vaguely familiar to members of the European cultural sphere who have a similar metaphor in Greek mythology (the three Fates spinning, weaving, and cutting the thread of life), the Hmong metaphor is much more clearly present among speakers of this language and seems to guide much of their linguistic and nonlinguistic behavior.

Large Scale Alternative Conceptualizations. In chapter 1, we saw that spatial orientation may be conceptualized in alternative ways. The two ways of conceptualization we saw were both literal. English uses an ego-centric relative system, while Guugu Yimitthir uses an absolute system of spatial orientation. Differences in spatial conceptualization can also be based on the use of systematically different metaphors. We find rich descriptions of such metaphor-based systems for spatial relations in work by Bernd Heine and his colleagues (see, for example, Heine, 1995, 1997; Heine, Claudi, and Hünemeyer, 1991). (This subsection uses materials from Kövecses, 2005a, chap. 10.)

Heine studied the conceptualization of spatial relations in a huge number of different languages. Since spatial relations are fairly abstract, they commonly derive from even more basic human experience. The basic human experience that leads to the conceptualization of spatial relations in literally hundreds of languages is the human body itself. The human body commonly serves as the source domain of spatial relations. The main spatial reference points that seem to be recognized in most languages include our concepts of "on," "under," "front," "back," and "in." In Heine's system (1995), ON is typically expressed by such linguistics expressions as *up*, *above*, *on*, and *on top of*, while DOWN is expressed by *down*, *below*, *under*, and *bottom*. The conceptualization of the "spatial reference points" is based on our understanding of the human body.

In figure 10.1 (taken and adapted from Heine, 1995), we can see how abstract spatial relations are conceptualized as various body parts in hundreds of African and Oceanic languages.

In addition to the several similarities in the conceptualization of spatial relations across African and Oceanic languages, there are some highly interesting differences. As Heine (1995) remarks, two such differences stand out. One is that UNDER is derived from the "buttocks/ anus" body region in Africa, whereas it is derived from "foot/leg" in Oceania. The other difference in conceptualization concerns the spatial relation IN. It comes from the body part "belly/stomach" in Africa, but in Oceania no particular body part serves this function. Instead, a number of body parts may be used, such as "tooth," "belly/ stomach," "heart," "liver," and "bowels" (Heine, 1995: 127).

Bálint Koller (2003) studied the expression of spatial relations in an extremely rich source of data provided by Bernd Heine and Tania Kuteva (2002). Koller concluded that there are three basic schemata that human beings use to conceptualize spatial relations: the BODY-ONLY schema, the BODY AND ENVIRONMENT schema, and the EXTENDED BODY schema. In the BODY-ONLY schema, it is the human body from which the conceptualization of spatial relations derives. In languages that conform to this pattern, the "head" will be used to mean 'up' and the "foot/leg" to mean 'down'. This is basically the schema that underlies the preceding two ways of deriving spatial relations as presented by Heine (1995). In the second schema, environmental landmarks are used for the purpose of understanding spatial relations. Languages that are based on this pattern will have words like *sky/cloud* meaning 'up' and

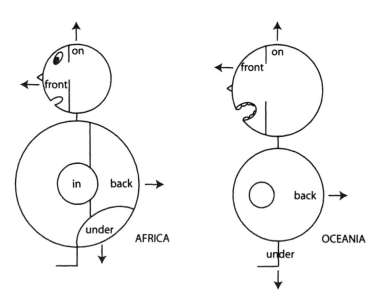

Figure 10.1 Conceptualizing spatial relations (from Heine, 1995, by permission)

words like *earth* meaning 'down'. In the third, called EXTENDED BODY schema by Koller, words primarily used to refer to aspects of the immediate human habitat, such as "home," "house," "roof," can give rise to words that mean 'at', 'to', 'with', and 'up' (Koller, 2003). This situation is represented in the following figures, taken from Koller (2003). Figure 10.2 corresponds to the BODY-ONLY schema, figure 10.3 to the ENVIRONMENTAL LANDMARK schema, and figure 10.4 to the EXTENDED BODY schema.

All the models make use of the body of a human being in upright position. This anthropomorphic model seems to be the most commonly used basis for the conceptualization of spatial relations in the world's languages. However, there are a small number of languages in which a zoomorphic model is used (Heine, 1995). In these languages, it is the animal body (a horizontally positioned body supported by four legs) that serves as the basis for conceptualizing spatial relations.

Within-Culture Variation

We know from work in sociology, anthropology, sociolinguistics, and so on, that languages are not monolithic but come in varieties that reflect divergences in human experience. It makes sense to expect metaphor variation in the varieties of language most commonly identified by these researchers. I will present

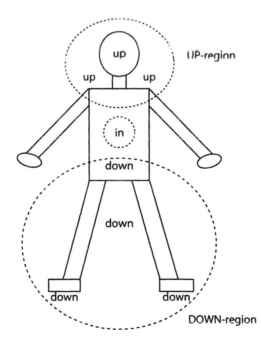

Figure 10.2 The "body only" schema (from Koller, 2003, by permission)

Figure 10.3 The "environmental land-mark" schema (from Koller, 2003, by permission)

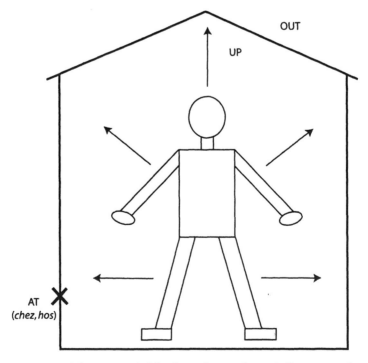

Figure 10.4 The "extended body" schema (from Koller, 2003, by permission)

evidence that, I believe, supports the idea that metaphors vary not only cross-culturally but also within cultures. This variation can occur along a number of dimensions, including the social, regional, ethnic, style, subcultural, diachronic, and individual dimensions. I conceive of this approach to metaphor variation as the cognitive dimension of social-cultural diversity. I will demonstrate with some examples how metaphors vary along some of these dimensions.

The Social Dimension

Social dimensions include the differentiation of society into men and women, young and old, middle class and working class, and so forth. Do men, the young, or the middle class use different metaphors than women, the old, or the working class? At present we do not have systematic studies from a cognitive linguistic perspective. But we do have some indication that some of these social factors might produce variation in metaphorical conceptualization.

One example of this is the men-women dimension. This dimension seems to be operative in several distinct cases: the way men talk about women, the way women talk about men, the way men *and* women talk about women, the way men *and* women talk about the world in general (i.e., not only about the other). In English-speaking countries (but also in others), it is common for men to use expressions such as *bunny, kitten, bird, chick, cookie, dish, sweetie pie,* and many others, for women. These metaphorical expressions assume certain conceptual metaphors: WOMEN ARE (SMALL) FURRY ANIMALS (*bunny, kitten*), WOMEN ARE BIRDS (*bird, chick*), and WOMEN ARE SWEET FOOD (*cookie, dish, sweetie pie*). However, when women talk about men they do not appear to use these metaphors of men, or use them in a more limited way. Men are not called bunnies or kittens by women. Neither are men characterized as birds or chicks, but they can be thought of as LARGE FURRY ANIMALS instead, such as *bears*. And women are more commonly viewed by men as SWEET FOOD than men are by women, although women can also sometimes describe men as FOOD, especially for sexual purposes.

The Regional Dimension

Languages often develop new metaphors when a language is moved by some of its speakers to a part of the world different from where it was originally spoken. American English is one example (see Kövecses, 2000a). Another is Afrikaans (Dutch spoken in South Africa). Afrikaans was carried from Europe to South Africa, and, as shown by René Dirven (1994), it changed its metaphorical patterns. It acquired many new metaphors based on natural phenomena and the animal world.

The Style Dimension

Style is determined by a number of factors, such as audience, topic, setting, and medium. All of these may influence the selection and use of metaphors in discourse. For example, slang is typically rich in metaphor and may be characterized by metaphors not found in other varieties of the language, such as the standard colloquial variety of a language.

The Subcultural Dimension

Each society and culture consists of a number of subcultures. Subcultures develop their own metaphors, and these metaphors may define the group. There is of course no subculture that defines itself through an entirely new set of metaphors, but some of the metaphors members of the group use may be new relative to the mainstream. For example, we can think of emotionally mentally ill people as one such group. Although depressed people share many of the metaphors for the concept of "depression-sadness" that "nondepressed" people have, like DEPRESSION IS DARKNESS, DEPRESSION IS HEAVY, DEPRESSION IS DESCENT/DOWN, they also have metaphors that are unique to the group. One such metaphor is DEPRESSION IS A CAPTOR (as shown by McMullen and Conway, 2002).

The Individual Dimension

Individuals often have their idiosyncratic metaphors. These can be entirely novel or they may be versions of already-existing conceptual metaphors. Thus, one can have a view of love relationships as the action of "pushing a wagon uphill," a metaphor based on LOVE IS A JOURNEY but adding to it the aspect of requiring a great deal of effort to maintain the relationship.

Aspects of Metaphor Involved in Variation

In the cognitive linguistic view, metaphor is seen as being constituted by a variety of components that interact with one another. In the chapter on metaphor, I identified the following components:

1. Source domain
2. Target domain
3. Basis of metaphor
4. Neural structures that correspond to 1 and 2 in the brain
5. Relationships between the source and the target
6. Metaphorical linguistic expressions
7. Mappings
8. Entailments
9. Aspects of source and target
10. Blends
11. Nonlinguistic realizations
12. Cultural models

For our purposes in this chapter, we can ask two questions in connection with these components: (1) Which of these aspects are involved in metaphor variation? (2) How are they involved in variation? The short answer is that all of them are involved—though in different ways (for more details, see Kövecses, 2005a). I will demonstrate the involvement of only some of the components in this section.

Source

Different construals of the same source domain may lead to cross-linguistic metaphor variation. Given a particular source, this source may be construed differently in two languages. A case in point is the source domain of motion in space in English and Turkish, as analyzed by Seyda Özçaliskan (2003a, b, 2004a, b). Özçaliskan showed that English primarily encodes manner into its verbs of motion (e.g., *walk, run, march*), whereas Turkish motion verbs lack this information concerning motion. Turkish primarily encodes direction into many of its motion verbs (e.g., verbs corresponding to English *fall, come, spread, descend*). This difference in the construal of motion events leads speakers of the two languages to comprehend target domains by means of a shared source domain that, for them, comes in two versions: the manner-centered one (for English) and the neutral or direction-centered one (for Turkish). In this case, the shared source is at a high level of abstraction, whereas the cross-linguistic differences are found at a specific level of conceptual organization. Moreover, as Özçaliskan notes, this built-in difference in the kinds of information that the source domain encodes may predispose the speakers of the two languages to attend to slightly different aspects of not only the source but also of the target domain; that is, we have Whorfian effects (see chap. 9).

Linguistic Expression

If two languages have the same conceptual metaphor, the linguistic expression of the conceptual metaphor in the two languages may follow a variety of different patterns.

As an illustration, consider some of the examples of the TIME IS MONEY metaphor in English and Hungarian (to be analyzed more fully in the next chapter):

(3) a. That flat tire *cost* me an hour.

    b. A   defekt egy órámba   került.
      The flat tire one hour-POSS-LOC cost-PAST

The pattern based on this example is: same literal meaning, same figurative meaning, same conceptual metaphor. (The asterisk in the next example is the conventional way to indicate ungrammaticality.)

(4) a. He's living on *borrowed* time.

    b.*?Kölcsönvett/hitelbe kapott időből   él.
      Borrowed   time-SOURCE live-3rd PERS

c. Minden nap ajándék számára.
   Every   day gift   him/her-DAT

d. Kapott   egy kis időt   ajándékba   az
   élettől.
   Receive-3rd PERS-PAST one little time-ACC gift-LOC/PURP the
   life-SOURCE

This example yields the following pattern in the expression of the same conceptual metaphor: different literal meaning, same figurative meaning, same conceptual metaphor.

(5)   a. How do you *spend* your time these days?

      b.*Hogyan   költöd   az idődet   mostanában?
        What-LOC spend-2nd PERS the time-POSS-ACC present-in

      c. Mivel/hogy(an) töltöd   az idődet   mostanában?
        What-INST/how fill-2nd PERS the time-POSS-ACC present-in

The Hungarian translation of *spend* is a verb (*tölteni*, meaning 'to fill') that is based on a different metaphor: TIME IS A CONTAINER, according to which you "put" activities into the time container. Thus, the emerging pattern is: different literal meaning, same figurative meaning, different conceptual metaphor.
   As in translation in general, the idea is to keep the figurative meanings the same. If we do that, we get a number of *patterns* for the translation of the English expressions into Hungarian. These patterns reflect the different possibilities for the construal of the same meaning. We can summarize them as in Table 10.1.
   Such patterns give us a way of *systematically* studying the differences between languages in the expression of metaphorical meaning. I will return to this issue in the next chapter.

Entailments

Both English and Zulu have FIRE as a source domain for anger, but speakers of Zulu make use of entailments, or inferences, concerning the metaphor in

Table 10.1. Patterns of Possible Construal of Same Meaning

Pattern/ Possibility for . . .	Literal Meaning	Figurative Meaning	Conceptual Metaphor
Example (3)	Same	Same	Same
Example (4)	Different	Same	Same
Example (5)	Different	Same	Different

a way in which speakers of English do not. In Zulu one can *extinguish* somebody's anger by pouring water on him or her (Taylor and Mbense, 1998). This potential metaphorical entailment is not picked up by the English ANGER IS FIRE metaphor in the form of conventionalized linguistic expressions. Notice, however, that the metaphorical entailment is perfectly applicable to enthusiasm in English, as when someone is said to be a *wet blanket* at a party.

Causes of Metaphor Variation

What causes our metaphors to vary along the dimensions and in the aspects that were discussed in the previous sections? I suggest that the causes can be grouped into two large classes: *differential experience* and *differential cognitive preferences*, or *styles*. In other words, the suggestion is that, on the one hand, many of our metaphors vary because our experiences as human beings also vary and, on the other hand, our metaphors vary because the cognitive processes we put to use for the creation of abstract thought may also vary.

Differential Experience

Awareness of Differential Contexts

When we use metaphors, we are (mostly unconsciously) aware of the context around us. The contexts that seem to have an influence on the metaphors we use include the physical environment, cultural context, and communicative situation. Let us look at cultural context and the communicative situation to demonstrate the point. This section is largely based on my previous work (Kövecses, 2002, 2005a).

Cultural Context. The broader cultural context simply means all the culturally unique and salient concepts and values that characterize cultures, including, importantly, the governing principles and the key concepts in a given culture or subculture. The governing principles and key concepts have special importance in (metaphorical) conceptualization because they permeate several general domains of experience for a culture or cultural group.

To demonstrate the effect of these differences on metaphor, let us first consider in some detail the near-universal PRESSURIZED CONTAINER metaphor for ANGER in a variety of cultures. We saw earlier that, at a generic level, this metaphor is very similar across many cultures. However, at a specific level we can notice important differences in this metaphor across certain cultures. How do these differences arise?

Dirk Geeraerts and Stephan Grondelaers (1995) note that in the Euro-American tradition (including Hungary), it is the classical-medieval notion of the "four humors" from which the Euro-American conceptualization of "anger" (as well as that of "emotion in general") derived. But they also note that the application of the humoral doctrine is not limited to anger or the emotions. The humoral view maintains that the four fluids (phlegm, black bile, yellow bile, and blood) regulate the vital processes of the human body. These fluids were also believed to determine personality types (such as sanguine, melancholy, etc.) and account for a number of medical problems, together with cures for them (like bloodletting). Obviously, then, the use of the humoral view as a form of cultural explanation extends far beyond anger and the emotions. In addition to being an account of emotional phenomena, it was also used to explain a variety of issues in physiology, psychology, and medicine. In other words, the humoral view was a key component of the classical-medieval cultural context and it exerted a major impact on the emergence of the European conception of anger as a fluid in a pressurized container.

In Japan, as Matsuki (1995) tells us, there seems to exist a culturally distinct set of concepts that is built around the concept of *hara*. Truth, real intentions, and the real self (called *honne*) constitute the content of *hara*. The term *honne* is contrasted with *tatemae*, or one's social face. Thus, when a Japanese person keeps his or her anger under control, he or she is hiding his or her private, truthful, innermost self and displaying a social face that is called for in the situation by accepted standards of behavior. The notion of *hara* greatly influenced the Japanese conception of anger over the ages.

Brian King (1989) and Ning Yu (1995, 1998) suggest that the Chinese concept of *nu* (corresponding to anger) is bound up with the notion of *qi*, that is, the energy that flows through the body. *Qi* in turn is embedded in not only the psychological (i.e., emotional) but also the philosophical and medical discourse of Chinese culture and civilization. The notion and the workings of *qi* are predicated on the belief that the human body is a homeostatic organism, the belief on which traditional Chinese medicine is based. And the conception of the body as a homeostatic organism seems to derive from the more general philosophical view that the universe operates with two complementary forces, *yin* and *yang*, which must be in balance to maintain the harmony of the universe. Similarly, when *qi* rises in the body, there is anger (*nu*), and when it subsides and there is balance again, there is harmony and emotional calm. Without the concept of *qi*, it would be difficult to imagine the view of anger in Chinese culture.

Thus, the four emotion concepts, *anger* in English, *düh* in Hungarian (the two representing European culture), *ikari* in Japanese, and *nu* in Chinese, are in part explained in the respective cultures by the culture-specific concepts of the *four humors*, *hara*, and *qi*. What accounts for the distinctiveness of the culture-specific concepts is the fact that, as we have just seen, the culture-specific concepts that are evoked to explain the emotion concepts are embedded in very different systems of cultural concepts and propositions. It appears then that the broader cultural contexts that operate with culture-specific key concepts account for many of the specific-level differences among the four emotion concepts and the PRESSURIZED CONTAINER metaphor.

The example of the PRESSURIZED CONTAINER metaphor for ANGER demonstrates how culturally unique key concepts fill out generic-level schemas in the creation of cross-culturally differential metaphors. We can expect such differences in key concepts to bring about differences not only in the production but also in the understanding of metaphors by speakers of languages that are associated with differential core values. Jeanette Littlemore (2003) shows that when speakers have conflicting core values (such as individualism-collectivism), they are likely to misunderstand each other's metaphors that are based on those values.

The Communicative Situation. I mentioned earlier that one of the factors in the communicative situation is topic. Take, for instance, the sentences described by Jean Aitchison: "Cougars *drown* Beavers," "Cowboys *corral* Buffaloes," "Air Force *torpedoes* the Navy," and "Clemson *cooks* Rice" (1987: 143). These headlines from articles describing American football games exemplify the case where the author of the headline can create a metaphor for the concept of "defeat" in sports on the basis of certain properties of the characters who participate in the "story." Since, for example, cowboys are in the business of corralling animals, the author is in a position to create a metaphor for defeat based on this property of cowboys.

History

Social History. One of my students, Nikoletta Köves (2002), showed in a small-scale study that Hungarians primarily use the LIFE IS WAR and LIFE IS A COMPROMISE metaphors for comprehending the concept of life in general, whereas Americans predominantly employ the LIFE IS A PRECIOUS POSSESSION and LIFE IS A GAME metaphors. Why do Hungarians use the metaphors they do for life, and why do Americans use different ones? The issue obviously has to do with the peculiarities of Hungarian and American history. Hungarians have been in wars throughout their more-than-one-thousand-year old history as a nation and state and had to struggle for their survival, as they are wedged between powerful German-speaking and Slavic nations. Given this history, it is not surprising that for many Hungarians life is struggle—and less of a game. To point this out is, of course, trivial as far as history is concerned, but it is not trivial as far as the study of the emergence of a particular metaphorical conceptual system is concerned.

Personal History. Personal history also plays a role in shaping metaphorical conceptualization. This is imperceptibly true of ordinary people, but it is much more clearly true of poets and other creative writers. We can suggest that the unique metaphor-based symbolic system that an author uses may be partially determined by his or her personal life history. For example, Sylvia Plath's metaphors come in part from the fact that her father was German and an entomologist who specialized in bees. Or take Hemingway's symbolic system. Hemingway did bullfighting in Spain, was a big-game hunter in Africa, and was a deep-sea fisherman in Florida. All of these activities became symbolic in his novels and short stories. Actually, in Hemingway's case it may be difficult to be sure whether the life story produced the metaphors, the life story was produced by a certain vision of the symbolic system itself, or the life story and the symbolic system envisioned simultaneously influenced each other and jointly emerged.

Human Concerns

I mentioned earlier the unique conceptual metaphors used by people diagnosed with episodes of depression. One of them was the metaphor DEPRESSION IS CAPTOR. Why don't nondepressed (i.e., "only" sad) people talk about sadness as CAPTOR? Most people do not normally talk about being trapped by, wanting to be free of, or wanting to break out of sadness, although these are ways of talking and thinking about depression in a clinical context. It makes sense to suggest that people with depression use this language and way of thinking about their situation because it faithfully captures what they experience and feel. Their deep concern is with their unique experiences and feelings that set them apart from people who do not have them. It is this concern that gives them the CAPTOR metaphor for depression.

Differential Cognitive Preferences and Styles

Many different cognitive processes are at work in metaphorical conceptualization. These include not only "seeing" some kind of resemblance between two things (metaphor) and/or blending them (see later discussion) and not only providing access to an entity through another (metonymy) but also elaboration, focusing, conventionalization, specificity, and transparency. All of these can be found at work in all languages and cultures, but the degree to which they apply to situations in which metaphorical conceptualization occurs can vary from language to language. We can think of these differentially applied processes as differential "cognitive preferences or styles." (My use of the term *cognitive style* is perhaps not the conventional one here as in customary usage in cognitive psychology, but this does not in any way affect the argument. On cognitive linguistic work in relation to metaphor understanding that uses the more customary sense, see Boers and Littlemore, 2000.) In this section, I will discuss two of these: experiential focus and metaphor and metonymy. I will discuss blending, or conceptual integration, in a later chapter.

Experiential Focus

Cognitive linguists emphasize that human beings share a great deal of bodily experience on the basis of which they can build universal metaphors. The question that inevitably arises is this: Is this universal bodily basis utilized in the same way across languages and cultures or even varieties? In light of the available evidence it seems that the answer is no. The universal bodily basis on which universal metaphors *could* be built is *not* utilized in the same way or to the same extent in different languages and varieties. The notion that I propose to get clear about this issue is that of "differential experiential focus."

What this means is that different peoples may be attuned to different aspects of their bodily functioning in relation to a target domain or that they can ignore or downplay certain aspects of their bodily functioning with respect to the metaphorical conceptualization of a target domain.

A case in point is the conceptualization of anger in English and Chinese. As studies of the physiology of anger across several unrelated cultures show, increases in skin temperature and blood pressure are universal physiological correlates of anger. This accounts for the ANGER IS HEAT metaphor in English and in many other languages. However, King's (1989) and Yu's (1995, 1998) work suggests that the conceptualization of "anger" in terms of heat is much less prevalent in Chinese than it is in English. In Chinese, the major metaphors of anger seem to be based on pressure—not heat. This indicates that speakers of Chinese have relied on a different aspect of their physiology in the metaphorical conceptualization of anger than speakers of English. The major point is that in many cases the universality of experiential basis does not necessarily lead to universally equivalent conceptualization—at least not at the specific level of hot fluids.

As a matter of fact, the conceptualization of "anger" in terms of heat has not always been the case even in English. Caroline Gevaert (2001, 2005) found on the basis of a variety of historical corpora that heat-related words accounted for only 1.59% of all the words that described anger before 850. The number of heat-related words for anger dramatically increased in the period between 850 and 950. Then the number of these words decreased between 950 and 1050 to 6.22% and then to 1.71% by around 1200 and then to 0.27% by around 1300. After 1300 the number started growing again, and after 1400 it became dominant in texts that described anger.

These numbers indicate that the conceptualization of "anger" in terms of heat is not a permanent and ever-present feature of the concept of "anger" in English. How can this fluctuation occur in the conceptualization of "anger" over time? Is it because people's physiology changes in anger throughout the ages? This obviously cannot be the case. I believe the answer is that universal physiology provides only a *potential* basis for metaphorical conceptualization —without mechanically constraining what the specific metaphors for anger will be. Heat was a major component in the concept of anger between 850 and 950, and then after a long decline it began to increase again at around 1400—possibly as a result of the emergence of the humoral view of emotions in Europe (see Geeraerts and Grondelaers, 1995; Gevaert, 2001, 2005). We can notice the same kind of fluctuation in the use of the domain of SWELL noted by Gevaert, which we can take to be akin to what we can call the "pressure" component in the conceptualization of "anger" today. Pressure was a major part of the conceptualization of "anger" until around 1300, but then it began to decline, only to emerge strongly again, together with heat, in the form of the HOT FLUID IN A CONTAINER metaphor centuries later. The point is that we should not expect any of the *conceptualized* responses associated with anger to remain constant in conceptualizing anger (and the emotions in general) throughout the ages.

Metaphor and Metonymy

Are there any differences in the way the cognitive processes of metaphor versus metonymy are used in different languages and cultures? The most systematic investigation along these lines is a study by Jonathan Charteris-Black (2003). He examined in great detail how and for what purpose three concepts— "mouth," "tongue," and "lip"—are figuratively utilized in English and Malay. He found similarities in metaphorical conceptualization. For example, in both languages the same underlying conceptual metaphor (e.g., MANNER IS TASTE) accounts for expressions like *honey-tongued* and *lidah manis* ('tongue sweet') and in both languages such expressions are used for the discourse function of evaluating (especially negatively) what a person says. However, he also found that the figurative expressions that involved the three concepts tended to be metonymic in English and metaphoric in Malay. In English more than half of the expressions were metonyms, while in Malay the vast majority of them showed evidence of metaphor (often in combination with metonymy). For example, while metonymic expressions like *tight-lipped* abound in English, such expressions are much less frequent in Malay. It seems that, at least in the domain of SPEECH ORGANS, the employment of these concepts by means of figurative processes is culture-specific. The reason for such a preference is important. Speakers of English tend to use language in a more straightforward manner in many situations than speakers of Malay. As Charteris-Black points out, the Malay preference for metaphor can be explained by the fact that members of Malay culture place a great deal of emphasis on saving one's face in social situations that involve a person's evaluation. This is more easily achieved by means of metaphoric devices than by metonymic ones.

Metaphor in Interaction with Embodiment,
Culture, and Cognition

In summary to this section, we have seen that embodiment (as in happiness and experiential focus), cultural experience, and cognitive preference interact with one another. The metaphorical systems that cultures produce will in general be coherent with embodiment, culturally defined experience, and certain cognitive preferences and styles. In many other cases, however, they will be coherent only with one or two of these (see, e.g., Kövecses, 2005a; Littlemore, 2003; Maalej, 2004, in press, for examples).

Love Is a Journey: A Case Study in Cultural
Differences in Metaphorical Expression

The issue that I will address in this section is how particular *cultural contexts* in which conceptual metaphors are embedded influence the linguistic expression of these metaphors. (The following case study is based on Kövecses, 2003, 2005a).

Two languages may share a conceptual metaphor and the conceptual metaphor may be expressed by largely overlapping metaphorical expressions, but the expressions can reveal subtle differences in the cultural-ideological background in which the conceptual metaphor functions. A good case in point is the metaphor LOVE IS A JOURNEY. This conceptual metaphor was introduced by Lakoff and Johnson (1980), who offered a number of American English examples for the metaphor. Following are the examples as given by these authors, together with their Hungarian counterparts:

LOVE IS A JOURNEY
(6) a. Look *how far we've come.*

   b.?Nézd/látod milyen messzire jutottunk.
      [Look/see how   far   reach-1st PERS PL-PAST]

   c.? Látod milyen messzire jutottunk?
      [See   how   far   reach-1st PERS PL-PAST]

(7) a. We're *at a crossroads.*

   b. Válaszút   előtt   állunk.
      [Crossroads before stand-1st PERS PL-PRES]

(8) a. We'll just have to *go our separate ways.*

   b.*Külön   utakra   kell   lépnünk.
      [Separate ways-on (LOC) must step-1st PERS PL]

   c. Elválnak   útjaink.
      [Separate-3rd PERS PL way-POSS-PL]

(9) a. We can't *turn back now.*

   b.*Nem fordulhatunk   vissza.
      [Not turn-can-1st PERS PL back]

   c. (Innen)   már   nincs visszaút.
      [(From-here) already none back-way]

(10) a. I don't think this relationship is *going anywhere.*

   b. Nem hiszem,   hogy   ez a kapcsolat
      vezet   valahova.
      [Not believe-1st PERS that (CONJ) this the relationship
      lead-3rd PERS somewhere]

   c. Nem hiszem,   hogy   ennek   a kapcsolatnak
      van értelme.
      [Not believe-1st PERS that (CONJ) this-POSS the relationship-POSS
      is   meaning]

(11) a. *Where* are we?

b. ?Hol   vagyunk/tartunk   most?
[Where be/keep-1st PERS PL. now]

(12) a. We're *stuck*.

b. *Elakadtunk.
[Get-stuck-1st PERS]

c. Kapcsolatunk   elakadt/   kátyúba jutott/ bedöglött.
[Relationship-POSS get-stuck/ get into mud/   become dead/
malfunction-1st PERS]

(13) a. It's been a *long, bumpy road.*

b. Hosszú, rögös   út   áll   mögöttünk.
[Long   bumpy road stand-3rd PERS behind-1st PERS]

(14) a. This relationship is a *dead-end street.*

b.?Ez   a   kapcsolat   zsákutca.
[This the relationship dead-end-street]

c. Zsákutcába   jutottunk.
[Dead-end-street-into reach-1st PERS PL PAST]

(15) a. We're just *spinning our wheels.*

b.*Csak   pörgetjük   a   kerekeinket.
[Only spin-1st PERS-PL the wheel-PL-POSS-ACC]

c. Ez   (már)   csak felesleges   erőlködés/kínlódás.
[This (already) only superfluous effort/agony]

(16) a. Our marriage is *on the rocks.*

b.*Házasságunk   sziklákon   van.
[Marriage-POSS rock-PL-LOC is]

c. Házasságunk   zátonyra futott.
[Marriage-POSS aground run-3rd PERS PAST]

(17) a. We've *gotten off the track.*

b.*Kisiklottunk.
[Get-off-track-1st PERS-PAST]

c.?Kapcsolatunk   kisiklott.
[Relationship-POSS get-off-track-1st PERS-PAST]

d. Kapcsolatunk   megfeneklett.
[Relationship-POSS run-aground-3rd PERS-PAST]

(18) a. This relationship is *foundering.*

  b.*Ez   a   kapcsolat   süllyed(őfélben van).
  [This the relationship founder-3rd PERS(ing-PROG)]

  c. Kapcsolatunk   megfeneklett.
  [Relationship-POSS run-aground-3rd PERS-PAST]

  d. Ez   a   kapcsolat   már   nem tart   sokáig.
  [This the relationship already not last-3rd PERS long]

As can be noticed, most of the American English examples translate into Hungarian in a straightforward way. In most cases where English has a metaphorical word or expression with a particular literal meaning, Hungarian also has a word or expression with the same or similar literal meaning. This would suggest that the conceptual metaphor LOVE IS A JOURNEY is expressed linguistically in much the same way in the two languages. While this is largely true, we can notice subtle differences in the details of linguistic expression. For example, in sentence (6) English uses the verb *come,* whereas Hungarian uses *jut,* meaning something like 'get to a place after experiencing difficulties', and in sentence (8) we find *we (have to go our separate ways),* with *we* in subject position, whereas in Hungarian it is *our roads (that separate).* The question we have to ask is this: Are these differences in detail isolated, accidental, and without any real significance in the study of metaphorical thought in culture, or, on the contrary, are they systematic, motivated and of significance in the study of this thought? I propose that the latter is the case. Larger cultural themes, or topics, that have the potential to distinguish different cultures manifest themselves and recur in many of the examples.

In several examples the American English sentences foreground active agents and deliberate action on the part of these agents, as opposed to the foregrounding of a passive relationship and relative passivity on the part of the people participating in the love relationship in Hungarian. In sentences (12) and (17), for example, we have a prototypical agent (humans) in English (*we*), whereas the corresponding Hungarian sentences foreground the relationship itself (a less prototypical agent) as a passive entity that undergoes some event (*getting stuck* in [12] and *getting off-track* in [17]). The difference may be suggestive of a more action-oriented versus a more passivity-oriented attitude to love and to life in general. In addition, in sentence 6, the active verb *come* is used in English, where Hungarian has the verb *jut* (corresponding to *reach*). The Hungarian verb emphasizes the difficult nature of, and hence the effort required in, making progress in the relationship; the English verb, by contrast, downplays any difficulties in the progress.

Other sentences suggest that decisions about relationships are influenced by internal considerations of active agents in English, while they seem to be influenced by external conditions in Hungarian. Decisions to act in certain ways are metaphorically understood in terms of choosing to go along one path rather than another. Thus, decisions about either staying together in the relationship or moving on with the relationship are conceptualized as choosing (or not choosing) certain paths. In sentence (8), in English two active agents (*we*) are making a(n internal mental) decision (probably based on some external factors), whereas in Hungarian it is the fork in the road (an external condition) that is forcing the agents to go their separate ways. We can find something similar in sentence (9), where in English decisions are made internally by the agents, as opposed to Hungarian, where, again, an external condition (that there is no road going back) is forcing the lovers to make the choice (of not going back). In other words, it seems that in English internal considerations of external conditions cause people in a love relationship to act in certain ways, whereas in Hungarian external conditions directly force the lovers to act in certain ways. Thus, the English LOVE IS A JOURNEY metaphor has agents who are involved in an internal way (mentally, conceptually) in making decisions, unlike the Hungarian metaphor, which has agents who are externally forced to make decisions about their relationship. In general, perhaps all this can be related to a more fatalistic attitude toward life in the case of Hungarians.

Sentence (15) suggests a further difference in culturally entrenched outlook on love relationships. In the English version, two active agents are trying to move the relationship ahead (by spinning wheels) despite the impossibility of the task (spinning wheels do not move the car forward). The wheels are spinning, but there is no motion forward. Spinning the wheels is an action intended to move the relationship (the car) forward. In other words, the agents are making a continued and concerted effort to achieve progress. Thus, in addition to goal-orientedness, this suggests optimism, determination, and perseverance in achieving one's goals. By contrast, the corresponding Hungarian sentence explicitly states what is only implied by the English one; namely, that superfluous effort and agony is spent on something that does not work. Hungarian, thus, attaches much less importance to the necessity of achieving one's goal, and it expresses resignation and a tendency to give in to forces that are beyond one's control. This difference might be related to a distinction between a more success-oriented and a less success-oriented attitude to problematic situations in life.

A final difference concerns the naturalness with which the people in the relationship evaluate "from the outside," as it were, the progress they have made. Sentences (6) and (11) constitute such objective evaluations. While these English sentences can easily be translated into Hungarian word for word, all the Hungarians who have been asked were of the opinion that the corresponding Hungarian sentences are not really used in everyday conversations in a natural way. In other words, it seems that Hungarians make explicit their evaluations of their love relationships with less ease than those Americans do whose language is characterized by sentences such as (6) and (11). This kind of self-evaluation may be related to an observation that was brought to my attention by Josephine Tudor, a native speaker of British English (p.c., November, 2002). Tudor observed that British speakers of English would primarily use the metaphorical expressions that belong to the LOVE IS A JOUR-

NEY metaphor of other people, rather than of themselves. Furthermore, on occasions when they do use the expressions of themselves, they tend to qualify them with all kinds of hedges, such as *rather, a bit, don't you think*, and so on. Thus, the American explicitness concerning one's success or difficulties in love relationships reflects a degree of extroversion that is not found in many other cultures, including Hungarian and British cultures.

As these differences in the subtler details of linguistic expression show, two languages or varieties may have the same conceptual metaphor, but the linguistic expression of the conceptual metaphor may be influenced or shaped by differences in cultural-ideological traits and assumptions that characterize different cultures. Subtle linguistic differences point to certain cultural-ideological traits that appear to be deeply entrenched and widespread in American and Hungarian culture. The LOVE IS A JOURNEY metaphor is a conceptual metaphor that is highly motivated cognitively. It consists of "primary metaphors" that are based on universal human experiences (e.g., Grady, 1997a, b), such as PURPOSES ARE DESTINATIONS. But the metaphor is not only cognitively but also culturally motivated. As characteristics of cultures change, so can the metaphor and its linguistic expression. In it, the cognitive and the cultural are fused into a single conceptual complex. In this sense, what we call conceptual metaphors are just as much cultural entities as they are cognitive ones.

In conclusion, I suggest that two languages may have the same conceptual metaphor, but the linguistic expression of the conceptual metaphor may be influenced or shaped by differences in cultural-ideological traits and assumptions that characterize the different cultures. Thus, in certain cases the linguistic expression of conceptual metaphors in different languages may reveal subtle but telling differences between cultures.

Conclusions

In this chapter, I have developed a view of conceptual metaphor in which the issue of metaphor variation is just as important as universal embodiment. It was demonstrated by means of a few examples that the basic components of such a theory include: dimensions of variation, aspects of variation, causes of variation, and the interaction of the causes that produce variation with universal embodiment that produces universality in metaphorical conceptualization.

Some conceptual metaphors may be universal because the bodily experiences on which they are based are universal. Many of the same conceptual metaphors may reflect certain culture-specific features at a more specific level of conceptualization. Other conceptual metaphors may be entirely based on unique cultural phenomena.

The two major dimensions along which conceptual metaphors vary are the cross-cultural and within-culture dimensions. Both can be further specified into subdimensions. Cross-culturally, metaphors vary because people can use alternative conceptualization for the same target domain. Within-culture variation occurs as a result of such subdimensions as the social dimension, regional dimension, subcultural dimension, individual dimension, and others.

Conceptual metaphors consist of a number of different components. These components are involved in cross-cultural and within-culture variation in different ways.

The causes of metaphor variation fall into two large classes: *differential experience* and *differential cognitive preferences and styles*. It seems safe to suggest that many of our metaphors vary because our experiences as human beings vary and because the cognitive processes we put to use for the creation of abstract thought may also vary.

Finally, we have seen that two languages may have the same conceptual metaphor, but the linguistic expression of the conceptual metaphor may be shaped by differences in cultural-ideological traits and assumptions that characterize the different cultures involved.

The components of metaphor variation that I have outlined here give us a cultural-cognitive theory of metaphor. The cultural-cognitive view complements other views where metaphor is regarded as being primarily based on universal bodily experience.

Exercises

1. At times we find metaphor variation across different languages in the domain of basic, image-schematic metaphors of spatial conceptualization. For example, whereas in English the "sky" is conceptualized as a three-dimensional entity ("clouds in the sky"), speakers of Hungarian talk about things being "on the sky" (thus, the sky is perceived as two-dimensional). What do you think are the consequences of such differences in spatial conceptualization? What methods could you devise to "unteach" native conceptualizations that are routinely being transferred to the target language (L2) in second-language acquisition? What other examples like the one mentioned earlier can you think of? (Knowledge of a language other than English might help here.)

2. A recent project was carried out on embodied metaphors by Raymond Gibbs and Heather Franks (2002), who interviewed six women recovering from cancer. The women talked about how they learned that they had developed cancer and spoke about their treatment. The interviews lasted for 20 to 35 minutes. The survey revealed 796 linguistic metaphors used by women, based on 22 conceptual metaphors.

Some of these linguistic metaphors were:

- Get through, get over, move into a new phase.
- Having a cancer was like walking off the face of the earth.
- Cancer is something that pulls you back to the core of life itself.
- Cancer forced me to begin stripping away a lot of things that don't matter.
- I had taken off the cloak of the disease.

Naturally, many of these are very strange metaphors for us, and only those under great mental and physical burden and pain can construct such metaphors. Your task is to identify the conceptual metaphors from the more concrete ones listed here. Try to make guesses regarding some of the abstract ones. What could these women have thought of when they used these expressions?

3. What follows is an extract from an interview between a client and a psychotherapist (Gibbs, 2002: 21–22). Howard, one of the characters, was fired one month previously by the hospital where he worked. He was accused of stealing some drugs. As he insisted that he was innocent, he was finally reinstated. Judy, his therapist, is talking to him now.

J: When you have a problem, what do you do with it?

H: I usually let it be a problem. I don't usually do anything much or I . . . I was thinking about that the other day.

J: Does the problem go away if you don't do anything about it?

H: No, it gets worse . . . or it just complicates things as you go further down the road.

J: Can you look at your own life, kind of on a continuum? Look down the road of that line and see what that's gonna do . . . in your life?

H: Look on down the road?

J: Yeah, . . . kinda visualize what on . . . your own life will be like if you don't deal with some of it . . . your problems . . . Can you see how it might complicate . . . your life?

H: It will just continue the way it is.

J: Kind of like a snowball . . . effect.

H: No, no not a snowball. Just kinda floating, floating down the river.

What metaphors can you identify in the extract? Try to define the underlying conceptual metaphor. What relevance does this extract have in connection with cultural variation? Do these metaphors have their counterparts in your own language?

4. Hungarian, a member of the Ugric branch of the Finno-Ugric languages, has developed a number of metaphorical expressions different from those of English and other Indo-European languages. Among these, juvenile slang terms are of special importance. Observe the following statement by a Hungarian high-school student:

A   magyartanár   ma   nagyon *pipa* volt; őrült *fásítást*
rendezett!
The Hun. Lit. teacher today very   pipe was; crazy planting trees
(organized)!
The Hungarian literature teacher *was a pipe* today; she was *planting trees* like crazy!

Preserving the figurative meaning, this sentence would translate into English as follows: "The Hungarian literature teacher was beside herself today; she was handing out Fs like crazy!"

    a. How do you think the phrase *the teacher was a pipe* arose? What conventional conceptual metaphor is behind this? Explain this particular set of mappings and the phenomena we are experiencing concerning metaphor variation.

    b. In the Hungarian educational system, the equivalent of an F is a 1, which often appears in colloquial usage as a *tree, stake, hoe,* or *harpoon.* Explain the second italicized expression in the sentence and write down the conceptual metaphor, its mappings, and entailments that you think would best describe a failing grade as presented in the example.

Meaning and Thought

Literal or Figurative?

W hat is the relationship between literal and figurative meaning, on the one hand, and concrete and abstract meaning, on the other? (The first half of this chapter is based on Kövecses 2005b.) Traditionally, the answer is that literal meaning goes together with concrete meaning and figurative meaning with abstract meaning. Thus, for example, the meaning of the word *ship* is both literal and concrete. We typically and normally talk about ships as *ships* and not as, say, *plows of the sea*, although exceptionally we can talk about ships this way. The second assumption is that figurative meaning commonly goes together with abstract meaning. Thus, for example, the abstract meaning of 'losing control over one's emotions' gains expression in such figurative phrases (or through such figurative meanings) as 'going crazy', 'becoming wild', 'flying off the handle', 'flipping one's lid,' 'blowing one's top', and 'going into a frenzy'. In other words, we have the following typical correlations between the kinds of meanings as given by the two distinctions:

Literal—concrete
Figurative—abstract

However, the association of figurative meaning with abstract meaning is often characterized by some additional assumptions in the traditional view; namely:

1. Literal meaning can *constitute* abstract meaning.
2. Certain figurative and abstract meanings are *understood* in a literal way under certain circumstances.
   Version one: The "dead metaphor" view.
   Version two: There are no conceptual metaphors involved in on-line interpretation.
3. Figurative abstract meaning in one language can be *expressed* by means of literal meaning in another language.

If true, these claims would provide us with a powerful and encompassing design feature of thought (meaning), namely, that the default property of thought (meaning) is literality.

This is precisely the view held by several philosophers and linguists. For example, John R. Searle (1969) formulated the "principle of expressibility," which is succinctly summarized by Tony Veale (2001): "Natural language has a rich and powerful literal substrate sufficient to express literally any possible speaker meaning" (retrieved from http://www.compapp.dcu.ie/tonyv/trinity/lit-moanifesto.html). Searle (1979: 96) expresses the idea as follows:

> Because in metaphorical utterances what the speaker means differs from what he says (in one sense of "say"), in general we shall need two sentences for our examples of metaphor—first the sentence uttered metaphorically, and second a sentence that expresses literally what the speaker means when he utters the first sentence and means it metaphorically.

Here are some examples of such literal paraphrases of metaphors from Searle's work (1979: 96–97) (MET means 'metaphorical' and PAR means 'paraphrase'):

1. (MET) It's getting hot in here.
   (PAR) The argument that is going on is becoming more vituperative.
2. (MET) Sally is a block of ice.
   (PAR) Sally is an extremely unemotional and unresponsive person.
3. (MET) I have climbed to the top of the greasy pole (Disraeli).
   (PAR) I have after great difficulty become prime minister.
4. (MET) Richard is a gorilla.
   (PAR) Richard is fierce, nasty, and prone to violence.

As Searle remarks, the paraphrases may not be completely adequate, but "the paraphrase or something like it must express a large part of speaker's utterance meaning, because the truth conditions are the same" (1979: 97). In other words, this view would give us the idea that thought (meaning), importantly including abstract thought, can be reduced to literal concepts and meanings. In this chapter, I will challenge the validity of such a claim.

As it turns out, the three assumptions have to do with three distinct, though related, aspects of linguistic meaning, as outlined in recent work by Raymond W. Gibbs (1998, 2003a). One aspect of linguistic meaning has to do with *why certain meanings emerge* in language. Another aspect of meaning concerns the (on-line) *processes* people employ *in understanding* the meanings of words and phrases. The third aspect of linguistic meaning concerns *speakers' intuitions* about why words and phrases of a language mean what they do.

The three assumptions mentioned here can be related to the three aspects of meaning discussed by Gibbs. Assumption (1), that abstract meaning can emerge from literal meaning, has to do with the emergence of linguistic meanings; assumption (2), that figurative-abstract meaning is interpreted on-line as literal meaning, rests on the issue of on-line processes of understanding;

finally, assumption (3), that figurative-abstract meaning can be expressed by means of literal meaning in another language, concerns people's intuitions about the meaning of words and phrases. Furthermore, these different aspects of meaning are typically studied by different methodologies: (1) by linguistic methods, such as etymology and historical semantics; (2) by psycholinguistic experiments, such as priming; and (3) by studying native speaker intuitions, such as translations. We will demonstrate each of these later.

The major claim of the chapter will be that the three assumptions in (1)–(3) can and should be challenged and replaced by what can be considered more reasonable suggestions in light of the evidence to be discussed; specifically,

1'. Only figurative meaning can constitute abstract meaning.
2'. All figurative and abstract meanings are understood in a nonliteral way.
  Version one: Once a meaning emerges as figurative abstract meaning, it will always be understood as figurative meaning and not as literal meaning.
  Version two: Figurative and abstract meanings are interpreted on-line as nonliteral meanings and not as literal ones.
3'. Figurative abstract meaning in one language can only be expressed by means of figurative meaning in another language as well.

The acceptance of these claims would lead us to a conception of thought (meaning) that is very different from the conception in the traditional views as characterized earlier; namely, it would lead us to the proposal that literality is not a default feature of thought (meaning) and that abstract thought (meaning) cannot be reduced to literal thought (meaning) in the three areas, or aspects, of meaning mentioned earlier. Let us now turn to the evidence.

Traditional Assumption (1): Literal Meaning Can Constitute Abstract Meanings

According to this aspect of the traditional view of meaning, there are linguistic expressions that have a literal meaning and yet they denote abstract objects, events, or states. In other words, their meaning is both literal and abstract. There are many words whose meaning can be characterized as both literal and abstract. Such apparently literal abstract words include *love, time, life, emotion, anger, sad, hate, fear, comprehend, theory, memory, morality, politics, argue(ment), know, fail(ure), success, think, might,* and hundreds of others.

It is immediately clear that the concepts that correspond to such words form the target domains of many well-known conceptual metaphors: LOVE or LIFE IS A JOURNEY, EMOTIONS ARE FORCES, COMPREHENDING/ UNDERSTANDING IS GRASPING, KNOWING IS SEEING, THEORIES ARE BUILDINGS, and so forth. But are these target concepts indeed literal? Do they fit an aspect of the world that is itself not metaphorically given? Evidence from historical linguistics along cognitive linguistic lines suggests that it is not the case.

First, Eve Sweetser (1990) showed that the concepts we take to be obviously literal today, relating to mental phenomena of all kinds, developed historically by means of many of the same conceptual metaphors that are still fully "active" today (such as UNDERSTANDING/ COMPREHENSION IS GRASPING and KNOWING IS SEEING). In addition, it is also common knowledge that the etymology of the word *emotion* suggests, and is based on, a major metaphor for emotions today: EMOTIONS ARE INTERNAL FORCES (COMING OUT OF A CONTAINER).

Second, work by Gábor Győri (1998) provides evidence that specific emotion words, such as *anger, fear, sad, happy,* and *love,* all derive etymologically from conceptual metaphors and metonymies that we can often find at work even today. For example, Győri shows that the English word *happy* derives from the Proto-Indo-European etymon **kob*—whose meaning was 'to suit, fit, succeed'. This meaning can be derived from the metonymy CAUSE FOR EMOTION, in which a situation where things suit us, fit our goals, and/or we succeed causes us to become happy. In this instance, it is the cause of an emotional state that "provides access to" and sanctions the use of a word with an apparently literal meaning. In other instances, it is the effect of an emotional state that does this. Consider the word *glad.* The Proto-Indo-European root of the word was **ghel-,* originally meaning 'to shine'. The metonymy that accounts for the change in meaning (from 'shine' to 'pleased') in this case is EFFECT FOR EMOTION. One of the obvious behavioral responses associated with happiness and joy even today is GLOW(ING) (or BRIGHTNESS) IN THE FACE. In other words, the historical development in meaning change in most instances follows the route of productive (or once productive) conceptual devices, such as CAUSE FOR EMOTION and EFFECT FOR EMOTION in many emotion words.

As we have seen, the traditional view maintains that the meaning of a word or phrase can be literal and abstract at the same time. At the conceptual level this view is clearly untenable. These words themselves were produced hundreds or thousands of years ago by the same conceptual metaphors and metonymies that are still being used (or were once used) for the conceptualization of the domains that they name today. Thus, the abstract meanings they express are figurative—not literal, as the traditional view of the essentially literal nature of all abstract meanings would have it.

Traditional Assumption (2): Certain Figurative and Abstract Meanings Are Understood in a Literal Way under Certain Circumstances

As Gibbs (1998) points out, understanding involves a number of distinct processes. Most important, we can distinguish the ultimate product of understanding from understanding that takes place on-line. Clearly, the two are related, but for my purposes the issue for us is to see whether people understand metaphor-based language as having literal meaning—in either mode of understanding. Let me start with the former issue: whether people's comprehension of conventionalized "dead" metaphors makes use of source domain concepts.

Version One: The Dead Metaphor View

The only way to decide whether the dead metaphor view is correct or not is to see whether people actually understand the meaning of formerly metaphorical expressions (meaning that was once figurative and abstract) as a literal one. For this reason, we have to turn to psychological experiments that have looked at examples of highly conventionalized metaphorical language (i.e., dead metaphors) and see whether people understand them without evoking the conceptual metaphors that gave rise to them in the first place.

One such expression is *to move forward a meeting*, as studied by Lera Boroditsky and Michael Ramscar (2002). Here the word *forward* is highly conventionalized and can be assumed to be literally understood—on a par with the expression *look forward to (an event)*, claimed by John Taylor (2002: 500–501) to be nonmetaphorically understood, and the words *branch* (as in the "local *branch* of the bank") and *flourish*, claimed by William Croft and Alan Cruse (2004: 205) to be literal. Boroditsky and Ramscar asked people who were riding on a moving train a question to find out how they were thinking about time. Notice that the train ride is the actual embodiment of one of the source domains for time: the moving observer in the metaphor TIME PASSING IS A MOVING OBSERVER, as in "We're *coming up on* Christmas" (as opposed to the metaphor TIME PASSING IS A MOVING OBJECT, as in "Christmas is *coming up on* us"). If people think and reason about time in terms of these metaphors and if the thinking or reasoning is influenced by embodied action people are actually engaging in during thinking and reasoning, in this situation people will choose and use the TIME PASSING IS A MOVING OBSERVER metaphor over the MOVING OBJECT metaphor in the course of their reasoning, since they are engaged in an action in which they are actually moving observers (i.e., they are riding on a train).

In this experiment, passengers on a train were presented with the following situation. They were told that a particular meeting that was scheduled to be held on the next Wednesday had been rescheduled and moved *forward* two days. Then they were asked the question: What day is the meeting, now that it has been rescheduled? If people use the MOVING OBSERVER metaphor in their reasoning, they must say that the meeting was moved to Friday; and if they use the MOVING OBJECT metaphor, they must say that it was moved to Monday. This is because *forward* is defined with respect to the moving observer and the moving observer reaches further points on the journey (or the corresponding later times) as he or she moves forward. That is, if the meeting was moved forward from Wednesday, then forward must mean Friday. However, if the person uses the MOVING OBJECT metaphor in his or her reasoning, the inference is different. In that case *forward* is defined with respect to the object that moves toward the stationary ego, and in that scenario *forward* means 'closer', that is, 'earlier' in time to the stationary ego. This must result in these people saying that the meeting was moved to Monday.

Overall, more people responded that the meeting was moved to Friday. This shows that the embodied experience of the train ride does play a role in how people think metaphorically about time and, more generally, that their understanding depends on embodied experience in context. However, for my purposes here the important point is that a highly conventionalized word, *forward* (which has to do with time and that could be assumed to be literally understood on the dead metaphor view), was understood in terms of a conceptual metaphor: either TIME-AS-MOVING OBSERVER or TIME-AS-MOVING OBJECT. The choice of the answer to the question asked could not be explained at all if people had not relied on either of these conceptual metaphors. The result of this experiment clearly goes against the assumption that dead metaphors are understood in a literal way (i.e., that *forward* in time is understood without recruiting knowledge about space).

Version Two: There Are No Conceptual Metaphors Involved in On-Line Interpretation

One of the greatest challenges to the cognitive linguistic view of metaphor is the claim that conceptual metaphors play no role in the process of on-line understanding (see Gibbs, 1998). The specific claim is that we process metaphorical expressions on-line without (consciously or unconsciously) evoking or relying on metaphorical mappings.

In a series of experiments that we discussed in connection with linguistic relativity (see chap. 9), Boroditsky (2001) studied the TIME IS HORIZONTAL/ VERTICAL metaphor by making use of two kinds of primes: a prime for horizontal orientation and a prime for vertical orientation. The distinction between horizontal and vertical primes is important because there are languages where time is conceived of as vertically, as well as horizontally, oriented. One such language is Mandarin Chinese (as opposed to English, where time is metaphorically horizontally oriented only). If the TIME IS HORIZONTAL/ VERTICAL metaphor is real in people's conceptual systems, then Mandarin Chinese speakers should perform better at certain tasks when they receive a vertical prime than speakers of English and speakers of English should perform better than Chinese speakers when they receive a horizontal prime.

In the experiment, half of the target sentences had a highly conventional spatiotemporal metaphor in them. The sentence was "March comes *before* April." The word *before* is a metaphorical expression that is based on the TIME IS HORIZONTAL conceptual metaphor (together with such expressions as *ahead of*, *after*, *behind*, etc.). It can be suggested that if conceptual metaphors immediately affect on-line understanding, then people will respond faster to a TRUE/FALSE question after receiving the horizontal prime than after receiving the vertical prime. The result of this part of the experiment was that both the English and Mandarin speakers performed better at this task after receiving the horizontal prime than after receiving the vertical prime.

In other words, both English and Mandarin speakers needed less time to respond to the questions when they were presented with a horizontal prime than with a vertical prime. This is because the horizontal prime was consistent with the conceptual metaphor underlying the metaphorical expression *before* in the target sentence "March comes *before* April" (i.e., with the conceptual metaphor TIME IS HORIZONTAL). The fact the speakers of Mandarin Chinese were affected in the same way as speakers of English shows that they also made use of the TIME IS HORIZONTAL conceptual metaphor in their on-line understanding of the sentence because this was the metaphor that was triggered by the metaphorical expression used in the sentence (*before*) and that was consistent with the horizontal prime.

As a matter of fact, the same experiment revealed that even literal words that belong to the abstract domain of TIME are understood metaphorically. Boroditsky hypothesized that speakers of Mandarin should be faster in saying that a sentence like "March comes *earlier* than April" is true after getting the vertical prime than speakers of English, and speakers of English should be faster than Chinese speakers after getting a horizontal prime. Both of these predictions proved to be correct. In other words, the influence of conceptual metaphors is so strong on on-line understanding that even literal words that pertain to an abstract domain are metaphorically understood on-line. (It might be claimed that this result by Boroditsky undermines the claim that all abstract meanings are figurative. Specifically, on this view, it should not be possible for the word *earlier* to be literal, since it belongs to the abstract domain of TIME. However, we can explain the literality of *earlier* by suggesting that it is based on time deixis; its meaning is defined relative to the speech event. Since deixis is a literal phenomenon in general, *earlier* is an example that is literal despite the fact that it is a word connected with the abstract domain of TIME.)

Traditional Assumption (3): Figurative Abstract Meaning in One language Can Be Expressed by Means of Literal Meaning in Another Language

There is a widespread idea in the comparison of metaphorical aspects of languages that figurative abstract meaning in one language can be expressed as literal meaning in another language (see, for example, Charteris-Black, 2002; Deignan, Gabrys, and Solska, 1997; Pontoretto, 1994). The theoretical background to this assertion comes from the view advocated by some philosophers that figurative abstract meaning can always be paraphrased by a literal meaning (see Searle, 1979). As far as this principle is concerned, it does not really matter whether we are talking about a single language or several languages. The question is: Is this principle true, and can figurative abstract meaning be expressed by literal meaning?

To investigate the issue, two abstract concepts frequently discussed in the cognitive linguistic literature have been chosen: "time" and "love" in English.

Both of these abstract concepts are talked about metaphorically in English. To see whether or not the abstract meanings that are expressed metaphorically in English are expressed metaphorically (more generally, figuratively) in another language, some English-speaking Hungarians were asked to translate English metaphorical sentences from Lakoff and Johnson's *Metaphors We Live By* that have to do with time and love. Students in two of my seminars (twenty students altogether) translated the expressions into Hungarian, and then we discussed all the cases where there was disagreement among us concerning the translations. In the course of the discussion, we tried to arrive at translation equivalents that were acceptable to all of us or at least to the majority. Thus, the translations that follow represent this majority opinion of twenty native speakers of Hungarian who also have a fluent command of English. This procedure was necessary because metaphorical expressions in one language are often assumed to be translatable into another language in several different ways (metaphoric, metonymic, literal, etc.). The two conceptual metaphors and their English metaphorical expressions were TIME IS MONEY (VALUABLE RESOURCE) and LOVE IS A JOURNEY, as these were first described in Lakoff and Johnson (1980).

When we study similarities and differences in the metaphorical expression of a conceptual metaphor, we need to take into account a number of factors, or parameters, including the literal meaning of the expressions used, the figurative meaning to be expressed, and the conceptual metaphor (or, in some cases, metaphors) on the basis of which figurative meanings are expressed. Thus, the following comments that explain the differences in linguistic expression between English and Hungarian will make use of the notions of "literal meaning," "figurative meaning," and "conceptual metaphor."

Given these notions, we can expect different patterns that characterize the differences, such as different literal meanings giving rise to the same figurative meaning, the same conceptual metaphor giving rise to the same figurative meaning, or different conceptual metaphors giving rise to the same figurative meaning. Each example will be characterized by one or several patterns in which I indicate whether the literal meaning is the same or different; whether the figurative meaning is the same or different (this is kept the same in an accurate translation); and whether the conceptual metaphor is the same or different.

First, let us see some examples of the TIME IS MONEY metaphor in English and Hungarian (the descriptions of the translation equivalents of all the Lakoff-Johnson examples can be found in Kövecses, 2005a):

TIME IS MONEY

(1)   a. That flat tire *cost* me an hour.

     b. A defekt egy órámba került.
       The flat tire one hour-POSS-LOC cost-PAST

The English sentence translates into Hungarian without difficulty. The Hungarian word that literally means the same as *cost*, *kerül*, can be used in the figurative sense. Thus, we get the pattern: same literal meaning, same figurative meaning, same conceptual metaphor.

(2) a. He's living on *borrowed* time.

    b.*?Kölcsönvett/hitelbe kapott időből él.
      Borrowed time-SOURCE live-3rd PERS

    c. Minden nap ajándék számára.
      Every day gift him/her-DAT

    d. Kapott egy kis időt ajándékba az élettől.
      Receive-3rd PERS-PAST one little time-ACC gift-LOC/PURP the life-SOURCE

The Hungarian verb *kölcsönvesz* (corresponding to English *borrow*) does not have the metaphorical application that the English verb *borrow* has (see [2a]), nor does its synonym, *hitelbe kap* (which translates into English as *receive as a loan*). However, a similar figurative meaning can be expressed by words with a different literal meaning that belong to the same metaphor. One of them is *ajándék* (*gift*), as in (2c) and (2d). *Pattern*: different literal meaning, same figurative meaning, same conceptual metaphor.

(3) a. How do you *spend* your time these days?

    b.*Hogyan   költöd   az idődet   mostanában?
      What-LOC spend-2nd PERS the time-POSS-ACC present-in?

    c. Mivel/hogy(an)   töltöd   az idődet   mostanában?
      What-INST/how fill-2nd PERS the time-POSS-ACC present-in?

The Hungarian literal equivalent of *spend*, *költ*, cannot be used in reference to time (see sentence [3b]). The Hungarian equivalent of the English metaphorical expression (3c), which is *tölt* (literally 'fill'), is based on a different conceptual metaphor: TIME IS A CONTAINER. The time-container is filled with actions; hence, ACTIONS ARE SUBSTANCES THAT GO INTO THE TIME CONTAINER. *Pattern*: different literal meaning, same figurative meaning, different conceptual metaphor.

On the basis of these examples of the TIME IS MONEY metaphor in English and Hungarian, it seems that there are three possibilities for the expression of the same figurative meaning:

- *Same literal meaning, same figurative meaning, same conceptual metaphor*, as in (1), in which words are used that have the same primary literal meaning, and the shared primary meanings are extended in the same way within the framework of the same conceptual metaphor;
- *Different literal meaning, same figurative meaning, same conceptual metaphor*, as in (2), in which words have different primary literal

meanings that are extended metaphorically within the same conceptual metaphor to yield the same figurative meaning;

- *Different literal meaning, same figurative meaning, different conceptual metaphor*, as in (3), in which the same figurative meaning is expressed by means of different words that have different primary literal meanings within different conceptual metaphors.

Table 11.1 summarizes these possibilities.

However, on closer analysis, and based on some additional examples, it could be claimed that there is yet another, a fourth, possibility for the expression of the same figurative meaning. Consider the following English sentence and its Hungarian translation equivalent:

(4)   a. I don't *have enough* time to *spare* for that.

      b. Nincs vesztegetni való időm (erre).
         [No lose-INF be-PURP time-POSS-1st PERS (this-LOC/PURP)]

      c. Nincs rá fölösleges időm.
         [No it-LOC/PURP superfluous time-POSS]

This possibility suggests that a figurative/metaphorical meaning can be expressed in a literal way. While, for syntactic reasons, Hungarian cannot have a straightforward translation equivalent of (4a), it can have a semantically equivalent translation, making use of the verb *veszteget* (roughly, 'to waste/lose') (see [4b]). In addition, Hungarians can also resort to a partly metaphorical, partly apparently literal sentence, as in (4c): *Nincs rá fölösleges időm* ('I have no superfluous time for that'). The metaphorical part comes from the translation of *I don't have*, while the apparently literal part from the translation of *time to spare*. The translation of this latter phrase is apparently literal, which means that a word that seems to be literal in Hungarian (*fölösleges* = superfluous) expresses a meaning ('superfluous') that is expressed by a metaphorical one in English (time to *spare*). *Pattern*: different literal meaning, same figurative meaning, same conceptual metaphor (for [4b]); same literal meaning, same figurative meaning, same conceptual metaphor for *I don't have*, plus different literal meaning, same figurative meaning, and [no metaphor] for *time to spare* in [4c]).

Table 11.1. Possible Patterns of Translating Abstract Meaning I

Pattern/ Possibility for ...	Literal Meaning	Figurative Meaning	Conceptual Metaphor
Sentences in (1)	Same	Same	Same
Sentences in (2)	Different	Same	Same
Sentences in (3)	Different	Same	Different

In other words, we now have four possibilities for the expression of an abstract meaning, as shown in table 11.2.

The interesting theoretical question for us is if abstract figurative meaning, such as that associated with the phrase *time to spare*, can be expressed in a literal way at all in another language. In other words, we have the question: Is the Hungarian phrase *fölösleges időm* ('superfluous time-my') in *Nincs rá fölösleges időm* ('I have no superfluous time for that') literal or metaphorical? I propose that it cannot be literal, only metaphorical. We can only think of the meaning of *fölösleges időm* if we think of time as some kind of valuable resource of which we can have enough, much, little, or more than enough. If we have more than enough, we can spare it. This is what the Hungarian expression means. The quantification (*much*, *little*), valuation (*enough*, *not enough*), and placement of time on a quantity scale are conceptual activities primarily applied to valuable resources. When we apply them to time, they suggest that we understand time metaphorically as a valuable resource, even though the Hungarian expression *fölösleges idő* ('superfluous time') appears, on the face of it, to be literal, and not metaphorical.

Let us now take some additional examples from the LOVE IS A JOURNEY metaphor:

(5)   a. I don't think this relationship is *going anywhere*.

     b.*Nem hiszem, hogy ez a kapcsolat megy valahova.
     [Not believe-1st PERS that (CONJ) this the relationship go-3rd PERS somewhere.

     c. Nem hiszem, hogy ez a kapcsolat vezet valahova.
     [Not believe 1st PERS that (CONJ) this the relationship lead-3rd PERS somewhere]

     d. Nem hiszem, hogy ennek a kapcsolatnak van értelme.
     [Not believe-1st PERS that(CONJ) this-POSS the relationship-POSS is meaning-POSS]

(6)   a. This relationship is *foundering*.

     b.*Ez a kapcsolat süllyed(őfélben van).
     [This the relationship founder-3rd PERS(ing-PROG)]

Table 11.2. Possible Patterns of Translating Abstract Meaning II

	Literal Meaning	Figurative Meaning	Conceptual Metaphor
Pattern/ possibility	Same	Same	Same
Pattern/ possibility	Different	Same	Same
Pattern/ possibility	Different	Same	Different
Pattern/ possibility	Different	Same [by means of literal meaning]	[No metaphor]

   c. Kapcsolatunk megfeneklett.
     [Relationship-POSS run-aground-3rd PERS-PAST]

   d. Ez a kapcsolat már nem tart sokáig.
     [This the relationship already not last-3rd PERS long]

Sentence (5c) is a metaphorical counterpart of the corresponding English sentence, while (5d) looks like a literal translation of (5a). Sentence (6c) is an approximate metaphorical counterpart of (6a), and (6d) again looks like a literal translation of the same English sentence. Are sentences (5d) and (6d) indeed literal? What can possibly point in the direction of an answer is if we ask how we attribute meaning to these sentences. Can we think of the meaning of the phrase *a kapcsolat értelme* (i.e., 'the meaning of a relationship') literally? Or do we need some conceptual metaphor to fall back on?

To say that a relationship has meaning means that the relationship has some purpose, use, or reason, and the like. I suggest that out of these it is the notion of purpose that is relevant here. When we think of the meaning 'the meaning of a relationship' as presented in the Hungarian sentence, we think of a goal or purpose associated with love. To think of a love relationship as having a goal or purpose is to think of the relationship as a purposeful activity. It is purposeful activities that have a clear purposive component. This is an act of interpreting the relationship in terms of an ontological metaphor, one in which an (originally passive and "goal-less") emotional state is attributed a goal or purpose. The STATE-AS-ACTIVITY ontological metaphor is made manifest by the specific LOVE IS A JOURNEY metaphor. If a journey has no destination, then it has no goal or meaning, given our folk theory of why we make journeys. It would seem that a clearly metaphorical proposition in (5c) gives rise to, or is the basis of, an apparently linguistically nonmetaphorical proposition in (5d) that seems to be based on the same conceptual metaphor nevertheless. We might perhaps say that there is a metonymic relationship between the metaphorical expression and the (superficially at least) nonmetaphorical one, where the nature of the metonymy is some weak causal relationship, an implication or entailment, between the two (something like LACK OF DESTINATION FOR LACK OF PURPOSE). If this way of thinking about the problem is correct, we can conclude that we have an expression (5d) that appears nonmetaphorical on the surface (linguistically) but metaphorical below the surface (conceptually), with the meanings of the two expressions being metonymically related.

A similar argument may be made with respect to sentence (6d). In this case we have the Hungarian expression *nem tart sokáig* ('not last long') that can be viewed as nonmetaphorical at face value. (We say "at face value" because the etymologically prior meaning of *tart* is not 'last' but '(physically) keep' and so it would be possible to argue for its metaphoric status on etymological grounds.) Notice that this was given as one of the two translation equivalents of the sentence *This relationship is foundering*. The conceptual connection between this sentence and its Hungarian translation (6c), on the one hand,

and (6d), on the other, can be explained as follows: If a ship founders, it is not likely to stay afloat long. This is an entailment in the JOURNEY domain. Given the JOURNEY metaphor for love, it will apply to love relationships: A nonfunctional love relationship will not last long, where nonfunctionality of the love relationship results in (or entails) the imminent end of the relationship. In other words, in this case as well there is a metonymic relationship between the metaphorical sentence and the superficially nonmetaphorical one.

But what happens in cases where one language simply does not have a metaphorical expression that corresponds to a metaphorical expression in another language? How do people arrive at a translation equivalent then? The previous examples do not really say anything about this situation because they have both a metaphorical and a superficially nonmetaphorical translation equivalent. As we saw earlier, one possibility for getting around such a situation is for language B to have a metaphorical expression y based on conceptual metaphor Y and language A to have a corresponding expression x based on a *different* conceptual metaphor X.

But sometimes not even this solution is available. If, in other words, a metaphorical expression x in language A cannot be translated into another language, B, by means of a corresponding metaphorical expression y having the same figurative meaning that is based on either the same or a different conceptual metaphor, then there is the problem of how people can find a translation equivalent for x. We have precisely this situation in one of the examples of the LOVE IS A JOURNEY metaphor:

(7) a. We're just *spinning our wheels*.

   b.?*Csak pörgetjük a kerekeinket.
      [Only spin-1st PERS-PL the wheel-PL-POSS-ACC]

   c. Ez (már) csak felesleges erőlködés/kínlódás.
      [This (already) only superfluous effort/agony]

My students and I have not been able to find an acceptable and obvious (or explicit) metaphor-based translation equivalent for sentence (7a) in Hungarian. The translation that reflected consensus was (7c). Again, it could be suggested that this is literal; on the face of it, there is nothing metaphorical about the phrase *fölösleges erőlködés* ('superfluous effort'). However, I claim that it is both metaphoric and metonymic.

It is metaphoric in the same sense in which the expression *fölösleges idő* ('superfluous time') was claimed to be metaphoric. When we apply the word *fölösleges* (*superfluous*) to actions (i.e., a set of efforts), we are turning actions into SUBSTANCES (cf. ACTIONS ARE SUBSTANCES) and, more specifically, into VALUABLE RESOURCES that we can have more than enough of. Further, it is metaphoric in the sense that the word *erőlködés* ('effort') that is used primarily of physical actions makes us conceptualize psychological and emotional phenomena as physical action via the metaphor PSYCHOLOGICAL/ EMOTIONAL IS PHYSICAL.

In addition, I also suggest that the finding of an acceptable translation equivalent in this case is again facilitated by metonymy. The meaning of the phrase *fölösleges erőlködés* ('superfluous effort') is metonymic relative to the meaning of sentence (7). It is metonymic because it is entailed by the meaning of sentence (7): Merely spinning the wheels does not make motion forward possible, and so it is unnecessary or superfluous to keep doing it. Hungarian seems to capture the situation by reference to one of the entailments (i.e., the RESULT) of the total situation as described by (7), while American English prefers to capture it via the CAUSE (i.e., the mere spinning of the wheels corresponding to psychological and emotional efforts that do not lead to progress in the relationship.) Thus, although Hungarian does not seem to have a ready and obviously (or explicitly) metaphoric translation equivalent for sentence (7), speakers of Hungarian are aided in finding a translation equivalent for the American English sentence with the help of conceptual metonymy—that is, by recourse to RESULT FOR CAUSE.

In sum, on the basis of these examples it seems to me that abstract meanings, such as the ones we looked at earlier, are expressed by figurative means in both English and Hungarian. Within the cognitive linguistic view perhaps a more general case can be made to the effect that abstract meanings can only be expressed in figurative ways in any language. As we have seen, in some cases the expression of an abstract meaning in one language happens with the help of (specific- or generic-level) conceptual metaphors (e.g., in the example of *fölösleges idő* 'superfluous time'), in other cases it is based on a combination of metaphoric and metonymic relationships (e.g., in *nem tart sokáig* 'not last long' or *fölösleges erőlködés* 'superfluous effort'), and in still others it is done primarily with the help of metonymies (*nem tart sokáig* 'not last long').

Can Cultural Models for Abstract Concepts Be Literal?

In chapter 8, on metaphor, I suggested that conceptual metaphors can produce cultural models, that is, a metaphor-based understanding of a domain of experience. The example that was given to illustrate this was the TIME IS A MOVING ENTITY metaphor. Indeed, could we understand time without metaphor? (On this issue, see Alverson, 1994.)

More generally, we should ask what the relationship between metaphors and cultural models is. More specifically, the issue in our context here is whether cultural models for abstract concepts can be literal at all. Our concepts for physical objects such as chairs, balls, water, rocks, forks, dogs, and so on, do not require metaphorical understanding (at least in our everyday conceptual system and for ordinary purposes). In fact, some scholars (especially some cognitive anthropologists) claim that literal cultural models do exist for abstract concepts; that is, they suggest that we can have a primary literal understanding of them (e.g., Quinn, 1991). Others, however,

claim that cultural models for abstract concepts are inherently metaphorical; that is, they are constituted by metaphor (e.g., Johnson, 1987; Kövecses,
1999, 2005a; Lakoff and Johnson, 1980; Lakoff and Kövecses, 1987). In
this section, the latter view will be defended, making use of some materials
from Kövecses, 2005a. (Several other scholars have participated in this
debate; see, e.g., Dirven, Wolf, and Polzenhagen, in press; Gibbs, 1994;
Palmer, 1996.)

Naomi Quinn (1991) suggests that, contrary to the claim made by George
Lakoff and me (Lakoff and Kövecses, 1987), metaphors simply *reflect* cultural models. In contrast, Lakoff and I claim that metaphors largely *constitute* the cultural model, or naive understanding, of anger, as based on our
study of American English.

Quinn bases her argument on her analysis of American marriage (see 1987,
1991). On Quinn's view, the American conception of "marriage" can be
characterized by a set of expectations: Marriage is expected to be shared,
mutually beneficial, and lasting (1991: 67). She points out, furthermore:

> that this particular constellation of expectations derives from the
> mapping of our cultural conception of love onto the institution of
> marriage and the consequent structuring of marital expectations in
> terms of the motivational structure of love. Because people want to be
> with the person they love, they want and expect marriage to be shared;
> because they want to fulfill the loved person's needs and have their own
> needs fulfilled by that person, they want and expect marriage to be
> beneficial to both spouses in the sense of mutually fulfilling; and
> because they do not want to lose the person they love, but want that
> person to go on loving them forever, people want and expect their
> marriages to be lasting. (1991: 67)

In this view, marriage takes over several properties of love, which then come
to define it (i.e., marriage). But the question then becomes: Where does the
abstract concept of "love" come from? Does it emerge literally or metaphorically? Quinn's answer is straightforward. It emerges literally from certain basic
experiences, and then these experiences will structure marriage. The particular basic experiences that Quinn suggests the American conception of "love
and marriage" derives from involve early infantile experiences between baby
and the first caretaker. Here is the relevant passage:

> I speculate that the motivational constellation that is part of our
> understanding of love and that provides marriage with its structure itself
> makes sense in psychoanalytic terms. Psychoanalysts since Freud, who
> characterized adult love as a "re-finding" of infantile love for the first
> caretaker, have theorized about the relation between the two. My claim
> is that Americans' distinctive conception of marriage takes the particular
> shape it does and has the force it does for us because of the cultural
> model of love mapped onto marriage and, thus, indirectly because of an
> infantile experience that Americans have shared and that underpins our
> conception of adult love. (1991: 67)

As can be seen, for Quinn, no metaphor is needed for abstract concepts to emerge. The expectational structure of marriage derives from the motivational structure of love, which in turn derives from the basic infantile experience between baby and first caretaker.

Quinn, then, goes on to say that marriage has some additional aspects. In her own words again: "The remainder of the cultural model of marriage reflected in the metaphors for marital compatibility, difficulty, effort, success or failure, and risk, derives from a contradiction that arises inevitably between the expectations of mutual benefit and that of lastingness." (1991: 67) She argues further that in voluntary relationships, if one's needs are not fulfilled one is free to leave the relationship. However, marriage is special in this respect: It is supposed to last. She adds: "A variety of situations can initiate a felt contradiction between the expectation of marital fulfillment and that of a lasting marriage."

If we characterize the essence of marriage, as Quinn does, as a set of expectations that can be viewed as being literal, Quinn's major claim stands: The core of the concept of "marriage" is literal, hence metaphors do not play a constitutive role in its understanding. More generally, abstract concepts such as "marriage" can exist without metaphors that constitute them. This analysis would support the Grounded Literal Emergence view (Kövecses, 2005a).

However, I believe that this analysis is incomplete and problematic. The problem is that we cannot take the expectational structure of marriage to be literal. Notice that Quinn's claim is that it is the motivational structure of love (i.e., that we want to be with the person we love, we want mutual need fulfillment, and we want love to be lasting) that provides the expectational structure of marriage. What Quinn does *not* say is how the concept of "love" itself is structured over and above its motivational structure. We should, therefore, first ask what love is before we discuss its expectational structure. And, ultimately, the question we have to face is whether the structure of the concept of "love" itself is derivable from the basic infantile experiences that Quinn mentions. Can the concept of "love" emerge literally from these basic experiences? My answer is that the basic infantile experiences play an important role in the emergence of the concept but are not sufficient for its detailed characterization. The insufficiency comes from the fact that the infantile experiences lack the detailed content and structure that characterize the concept of "love" in adults. In other words, the metaphorical source domain has structure and content that is additional to that found in the basic experience.

In her discussion it remains unclear whether Quinn equates the expectational structure of marriage with the concept of "marriage" itself. Nowhere does she describe or define marriage itself in terms of other than its "expectational structure." This leads one to believe that marriage is conceptualized by people in terms of this structure only. But is it? Don't people have an idea of what marriage is independently of and before they have an expectational structure of it? One would think that they do; yet this aspect of the concept of "marriage" does not show up in her essay. Marriage is presented by Quinn as an expectational structure, and all the other aspects of it that she discusses, such as compatibility, difficulty, effort, success and failure, and risk, are given as consequences of this structure. What, then, does the notion of "marriage" consist of independently of and before it acquires its particular expectational structure?

It can be argued that, first and foremost, marriage is some kind of abstract union between two people. To illustrate this, consider some definitions of marriage in a sample of American dictionaries:

> **marriage** 1 the state of being married; relation between husband and wife; married life; wedlock; matrimony . . . **4** any close or intimate union
> (*Webster's New World Dictionary*, Third College Edition)

> **marry** 1 a) to join as husband and wife; unite in wedlock b) to join (a man) to a woman as her husband, or (a woman) to a man as his wife **vi. 2** to enter into a close or intimate relationship; unite
> (*Webster's New World Dictionary*, Third College Edition)

> **marriage** 1 a: the state of being married b: the mutual relationship of husband and wife; wedlock; c: the institution whereby men and women are joined in a special kind of social and legal dependence for the purpose of founding and maintaining a family
> (*Merriam-Webster's Ninth New Collegiate Dictionary*)

> **marry** 1 a: to join as husband and wife according to law or custom 2 to unite in close and usu. permanent relation **vi 2** to enter into a close or intimate union (these wines—well)
> (*Merriam-Webster's Ninth New Collegiate Dictionary*)

> **marriage** 1. a. The state of being husband and wife; wedlock b. The legal union of man and woman as husband and wife
> (*The Heritage Illustrated Dictionary*)

> **marry** 1. a. To become united with in matrimony
> (*The Heritage Illustrated Dictionary*)

> **married** 1. United in matrimony
> (*Funk & Wagnalls Standard Dictionary*)

As these dictionary definitions show, a major component of the concept of "marriage" is the (legal, social, emotional, etc.) union of two people. This seems to be a large part of the notion that is independent of and prior to the expectational structure associated with marriage. In other words, the prototypical, or stereotypical, idea of marriage must include the notion that it is an abstract union of various kinds between two people.

As Quinn suggests, the concept of "marriage" is structured by the mapping of the American cultural conception of "love." However, she only finds this in the expectational structure of marriage. But now we can see additional structure in marriage that derives from love. This is the notion of unity that involves two people. As was shown elsewhere (Kövecses, 1986, 1988, 1991b), the concept of "romantic love" is, in large measure, understood and structured by the metaphor LOVE IS A UNITY OF TWO COMPLEMENTARY PARTS, as can be found in expressions like "You *belong to* me and I *belong to* you," "Theirs is *a perfect fit*," "We're *as one*," "She's *my better half*," "They *broke up*," "They're *inseparable*," and "They *match* each other *perfectly*." It is largely the functional unity of two physical parts that serves as the source domain for the abstract target concept of "marriage." But more generally, our understanding of nonphysical—social, legal, emotional, spiritual, psychological, etc.—unions derives from physical or biological unions. This is a perfectly regular way in which human beings conceptualize and, by conceptualizing, also build their nonphysical, abstract world.

In other words, we have the conceptual metaphor NONPHYSICAL (FUNCTIONAL) UNITY IS PHYSICAL (FUNCTIONAL) UNITY. (It is also significant that the etymological root of the words *union* and *unity* is the Latin word *unus*, meaning 'one'.) This is the metaphor that underlies the conception of various social, legal, psychological, sexual, political, emotional, and other "unities" and explains the use of such expressions as "*to join* forces," "the *merging* of bodies," "the *unification* of Europe," "to be *at one with* the world," "a *union* of minds," "a deep spiritual *union with* God," and so on. Obviously, the metaphor also applies to marriage as a nonphysical unity between two people. Some examples from the preceding dictionary definitions include "*to join* in marriage," "a marriage *union*," "the legal *union* of man and woman," and "*to be united* in matrimony"; hence the metaphor MARRIAGE IS A PHYSICAL AND/OR BIOLOGICAL FUNCTIONAL UNITY OF TWO PARTS. Not surprisingly, we also find examples of this metaphor in the data that Quinn presents. She names what we call the MARRIAGE IS A PHYSICAL AND/OR BIOLOGICAL FUNCTIONAL UNITY metaphor "two inseparable objects," as in "We knew we were going *to stay together*" and "an unbreakable bond," as in "That just kind of *cements the bond*" (1991: 68).

At this point it might be objected that my analysis is largely based on dictionary data and that Americans may not conceptualize "marriage" according to the UNITY metaphor. We have some evidence that they do. The evidence is both direct and indirect. In 1992 at Rutgers University, New Jersey, in an informal experiment I asked students in an Introduction to Anthropology course to write down linguistic expressions about marriage. They came up with dozens of various phrases and sentences, including "the ultimate *bond*," "She's *my ball and chain*," "They are *a match made in heaven*," "They've *tied the knot*," "She's *my better half*," "They *broke up*," "I can't *function without her*," "They're *getting hitched*," "They *dissolved their union*," and others. These are all UNITY metaphors or at least closely related to this metaphor. They suggest that the notion of "unity" is not alien to many Americans when they talk and think about marriage.

The indirect evidence comes from a set of interviews that a student of mine, Ted Sablay, conducted concerning romantic love in the summer of 1996 at the University of Nevada, Las Vegas. The interview subjects were seven male and seven female students from roughly the same white middle-class background. What the interviews reveal about romantic love should be taken seriously in dealing with marriage because, as Quinn herself claims, marriage is in many ways structured by our understanding of love. In his report on the project, Ted Sablay found that the most frequent metaphor for love is the UNITY metaphor for his interview subjects. This gives us some reason to believe that, at least for some Americans, the conception of marriage is still built on the idea of forming a unity with another and that this notion is not just a consequence of an antiquated dictionary definition.

What is the relationship between the idea of MARRIAGE-AS-NONPHYSICAL-UNITY and the expectational structure of marriage that Quinn describes? I suggest that the conception of marriage as a unity between two people is the basis, or the foundation, of its expectational structure, namely, that marriage is expected to be shared, beneficial, and lasting. The reason that marriage is expected to be all these things is that it is conceptualized as a unity of a particular kind: the physical unity of two complementary parts, which yields the metaphor MARRIAGE IS THE PHYSICAL AND/OR BIOLOGICAL UNITY OF TWO COMPLEMENTARY PARTS. The details of the UNITY metaphor for marriage can be given as a set of mappings:

1. the two physical parts → the married people
2. the physical joining of the parts → the union of the two people in marriage
3. the physical/biological unity → the marriage union
4. the physical fit between the parts → the compatibility between the married people
5. the physical functions of the parts in the unity → the roles the married people play in the relationship
6. the complementariness of the functions of the parts → the complementariness of the roles of the married people
7. the whole physical object consisting of the parts → the marriage relationship
8. the function of the whole object → the role or purpose of the marriage relationship

What we have here is a source domain in which there are two parts that fit each other and form a whole, where the particular functions of the parts complement one another and the parts make up a larger unity that has a function (or functions). This source schema of a physical unity has parts that are additional to the basic experience between baby and first caretaker. Unlike the infantile experience, here two originally separate parts are joined, or put together; unlike the infantile experience, there is a preexisting fit between the parts; unlike the infantile experience, the whole has a function that is larger than, or goes beyond, the functions of the individual parts. What corresponds to these in the target domain of MARRIAGE is that two separate people who are compatible join each other in marriage with some life goal(s) in mind. It is this structure that appears in the way many people (in America and possibly elsewhere) think about marriage. *But this way of conceptualizing marriage is simply a special case of the larger process whereby nonphysical unities in general are constituted on the analogy of more physical ones.* It is important to see that the PHYSICAL UNITY metaphor characterizes not just "marriage" but many other abstract concepts where the issue of NONPHYSICAL UNION arises, that is, abstract concepts that have "union" as one of their dimensions, or aspects. This dimension of NONPHYSICAL UNION emerges from the content and structure of what was called the source domain of PHYSICAL UNITY (OF TWO COMPLEMENTARY PARTS). In this sense, abstract concepts that possess the dimension of NONPHYSICAL UNION can only be metaphorical. This is for the simple reason that this abstract dimension inevitably emerges from the physical source of PHYSICAL UNITY. The application of this simple, constitutive metaphor to marriage is both transparent and important. Its significance lies in the fact that in the concept of marriage NONPHYSICAL UNION is a core dimension. Indeed, it is so fundamental that, as we will see shortly, the expectational structure that Quinn identified derives from it.

In Quinn's view, the basic experiences constitute cultural models (like those of abstract concepts in general and that of the concept of "marriage" in particular) and the cultural models select the fitting conceptual metaphors. In my view, it is the basic experiences that select the fitting conceptual metaphors and the metaphors constitute the cultural models. As we saw earlier, there are differences between what the basic experiences and what the conceptual metaphors can yield relative to abstract concepts. Basic experiences in themselves could not account for the entire content and structure of the concepts of "love" and "marriage" (just as they could not account for the cultural model of anger). The more that is needed is provided by such constitutive metaphors as NONPHYSICAL UNION (IN LOVE AND MARRIAGE) IS PHYSICAL UNITY.

This metaphorically structured understanding of marriage forms a definition of marriage and provides its expectational structure. The definition could be given as follows: "Marriage is a union of two people who are compatible with each other. The two people perform different but complementary roles in the relationship. Their union serves a purpose (or purposes) in life." This is, of course, a generic-level definition, which can be filled out with specific details in individual cases.

The expectational structure of marriage arises from the definition in the following way:

- Because a part by itself is not functional, people want to share their lives with others in marriage.
- Because only one or some parts fit another part, people want compatible partners in marriage.
- Because (to get a functioning whole) a part must perform its designated function, people want to fulfill their designated roles in a marriage relationship.
- Because wholes have a designated function to perform, marriage relationships must be lasting.

As can be seen, this is similar to Quinn's expectational structure, although there are also some differences. One difference is that in my characterization compatibility is a mapping in the unity metaphor, while in hers it is a consequence that follows from the expectational structure. Another difference is more substantial. It is that I have given the expectational structure of marriage as a consequence of a certain metaphorical understanding of marriage, one that is based on the metaphor nonphysical unity is physical unity. It is in this sense that we can claim that the concept of "marriage" is metaphorically constituted.

In sum, what Quinn calls the expectational structure of marriage results from a certain metaphorical understanding of marriage. Thus, marriage is not a literally conceived abstract concept, although the metaphor that yields the expectational structure is based on certain bodily experiences.

However, I do not want to suggest that Quinn is entirely wrong in her claims. As a matter of fact, I believe that both Quinn and I are right at the same time. How is this possible? We get a straightforward explanation if we consider the following.

A part of our conceptual system consists of abstract concepts that are metaphorically defined. The definition of abstract concepts by means of metaphor takes place automatically and unconsciously. This is the case when emotions are viewed as forceful entities inside us, when we think of abstract complex systems as growing (= developing), when we define our goals as "goals" (to be reached), and, indeed, when we believe that marriage is some kind of a union. We take these metaphorical "definitions" as givens that are literal. As we saw earlier in this chapter, they are not. There are many concepts like these that are defined or constituted by conceptual metaphors. And they are so constituted unconsciously and without any cognitive effort. Probably it makes sense to believe that this kind of definition of abstract concepts takes place at what I call the supraindividual level of conceptualization (see Kövecses, 2002: chap. 17). It is the supraindividual level in the sense that it consists of a static and highly conventionalized system of mappings between physical source and abstract target domains. Because of the automatic and unconscious nature of the mappings, we tend to think of these abstract concepts as literal and believe, as Quinn does, that the literal models of the concepts "select" the appropriate metaphors.

However, having said this, I can suggest that Quinn makes a partially valid point. When we actually use these metaphorically constituted concepts in *real* discourse, it is often the case that we choose metaphorical expressions that are *not constitutive* of our understanding of the target concept in question in discourse but that are *based on* an already-existing metaphorical understanding of a model of a target domain. In other words, we may agree that the way discourse understanding and production works often creates situations in which metaphorical expressions arise from a prior understanding of the target as a (metaphorically constituted but literally taken) cultural model.

As an illustration of this situation, let us consider Paul Chilton and George Lakoff's (1995) work on the application of the BUILDING metaphor to the

POLITICAL domain, in particular, Gorbachev's metaphor of the COMMON EUROPEAN HOUSE, that is, EUROPE IS A COMMON HOUSE. There exists the general metaphor ABSTRACT COMPLEX SYSTEMS ARE BUILDINGS (Kövecses, 1995a, 2000c, 2002). This metaphor has several mappings that can be given as submetaphors within the general metaphor, specifically:

THE CREATION OF ABSTRACT STRUCTURE IS BUILDING.
ABSTRACT STRUCTURE IS PHYSICAL STRUCTURE (OF THE BUILDING).
ABSTRACT LASTINGNESS IS THE STABILITY OF THE PHYSICAL STRUCTURE
    (TO STAND).

According to the standard cognitive linguistic view of metaphor, the source domain of BUILDING and the target domain of, in this case, POLITICAL STRUC-TURE are characterized by these mappings (see, e.g., Grady, 1997a, b; Kövecses, 1995a, 2000c, 2002). My claim, in line with the argument stated earlier, would be that the abstract target concept of "political structure" is constituted by these mappings. That is to say, the notion of "political structure" (as in the discussion of the unification of European countries into a single political entity) is in part defined by the metaphor ABSTRACT COMPLEX SYSTEMS ARE BUILD-INGS. And, indeed, we find numerous examples that are based on these mappings in the discourse on the integration of Europe in the 1990s, as analyzed by Andreas Musolff (2001). Here are some examples from his work:

"We want a Europe that's not just an elevated free trade area, but the construction of a house of Europe as laid down in the Maastricht treaty." (*The Guardian*, July 6, 1994)

"The common currency is the weight-bearing pillar of the European house." (*The Guardian*, June 3, 1997)

The first example is based on the submetaphor THE CREATION OF ABSTRACT STRUCTURE IS BUILDING, while the second is based on both ABSTRACT STRUC-TURE IS PHYSICAL STRUCTURE (OF THE BUILDING) (pillar) and ABSTRACT LAST-INGNESS IS THE STABILITY OF THE PHYSICAL STRUCTURE (TO STAND) (weight-bearing). These examples show that political structure is thought about in terms of the BUILDING metaphor and, more important, that certain aspects of this abstract entity (and of many additional ones), such as construction, structure, and strength, are inevitably constituted by metaphor. (Notice the unavoidably metaphorical character of the words *construction*, *structure*, and *strength* in relation to political structure.)

But in the course of the debate about the unification of Europe at the time many expressions other than those that fit and are based on these submeta-phors were used in the press (Musolff, 2001). Musolff provides a large num-ber of metaphorical expressions that were not supposed to be used (according to this view of metaphor), but they were nonetheless. There was talk about the roof, the occupants, the apartments, and even caretakers and fire escapes. If the BUILDING metaphor is limited to these predetermined aspects of the target domain (such as structure), then speakers should not talk about any of these things in connection with political structure. But they do. Let us see some of Musolff's (2001) examples:

> "We are delighted that Germany's unification takes place under the European roof." (Documentation by the Federal Press and Information Office, Bonn)
>
> "At the moment, the German occupants of the first floor apartment in the 'European house' seem to think that foreigners from outside the continent should be content with living in the rubbish bin." (*Die Zeit*, January 10, 1992)
>
> "What does he [Chancellor Kohl] need this house for, after so many years as Chancellor?—Well, it's obvious, he wants to become the caretaker." (*Die Zeit*, May 16, 1997)
>
> "[The European house is] a building without fire-escapes: no escape if it goes wrong." (*The Guardian*, May 2, 1998)
>
> "[It is a] burning building with no exits." (*The Times*, May 20, 1998)

Given these examples of metaphor usage, it seems that metaphors can do more than just automatically and unconsciously constitute certain aspects of target domains in a static conceptual system (i.e., at the supraindividual level). Once we have a source domain that conventionally constitutes a target, we can use any component of this source that fits elements of the target. Notice that there is a reversal here. In a dynamic discourse situation the activated target domain in the discourse can indeed select components of the source that fit a particular target idea or purpose. For example, if one has a negative view of the unification of Europe and has problems with, say, the difficulty of leaving the union in case it does not work out for a particular country, then the speaker can talk about a "building without fireescapes"—a part of the source that is obviously outside the conventionally used aspects of the source but that fits the target. (This account of metaphorical expressions in real discourse that should not occur but that do is similar to that offered by Grady, Oakley, and Coulson, 1999. The difference, though, is that while this account makes use of conceptual metaphor theory, their explanation makes use of the theory of conceptual integration, or blending. On blending, see chap. 11; Fauconnier and Turner, 2002.)

Lynne Cameron and Graham Low discovered a similar process that they call metaphor "attraction" (2004). In it, a particular "base" metaphor (as they term it) can attract different metaphors that just "happen to be on the same topic." When this happens, real discourse tends to display a high density of metaphorical expressions; that is, metaphorical expressions based on the same source domain will form clusters in the text.

Conclusions

In this chapter, I have looked at three aspects of linguistic meaning—creation/constitution of meaning, understanding of meaning, expression of meaning

—in relation to the question of whether human thought (meaning) is essentially and inherently literal. According to the traditional view, it is literal: Literal meaning can constitute abstract meaning; figurative abstract meanings can be understood as literal ones; and figurative abstract meanings in one language can be rendered as literal ones in another. Taken together, these assertions, if true, would lead to a conception of "thought (meaning)" as being essentially and inherently literal.

However, evidence I have surveyed here suggests otherwise. First, historical data show that abstract meanings are always *constituted* by figurative meanings. Second, experimental evidence shows that the *comprehension* of abstract meanings does, in fact, recruit metaphoric mappings—both for conventionalized metaphors such as *forward* and for abstract "literal" meanings such as 'earlier'. Finally, the in-depth study of translated sentences shows that figurative abstract meanings in one language are always *expressed* as figurative abstract (and not as literal) meanings in another.

If true, these conclusions would lead us to a conception of "thought (meaning)" as being in part literal and in part figurative—and not essentially and predominantly literal. In this conception, there would be a large part devoted to literal meaning (corresponding to physical objects and events) and an equally large part devoted to figurative abstract meaning (corresponding to abstract things and events). Importantly, there would be no claim in it that the realm of abstract figurative meaning can for the most part be reduced to literal meaning (in any of the three aspects of meaning mentioned), as the traditional view would have it. In other words, figurative abstract meaning seems to be just as much a design feature of thought as literal concrete meaning is.

Can cultural models for abstract concepts be literal? My answer was that they cannot. It was pointed out in connection with Quinn's analysis of American marriage that it leaves out of consideration a large and significant portion of this concept—the part that is metaphorically conceived and from which the expectational structure of marriage derives. The notion of "marriage" is partially based on and constituted by the generic metaphor NONPHYSICAL UNITY IS PHYSICAL UNITY. However, I also argued that in real discourse target domains can indeed select metaphors that are not a part of the conventional application of the source to the target. In other words, in real discourse target domains can, indeed, select the metaphors, albeit in a limited fashion. The selection of metaphors is limited because they come from a source that is already constitutive of the target. However, the rich target domain knowledge may select metaphors that are not conventionally used for the automatic and unconscious understanding of this target.

Exercises

1. According to "grammaticalization theory," a field of linguistics with close affinities to cognitive linguistics, much of what we consider today as a nonexpandable "closed class" of grammar words with fixed morphological

items like modal auxiliaries, prepositions, or suffixes can be etymologically derived from words that denote concrete, physical entities in the world. Through time, contextual reinterpretation, and phonological change, they came to be reestablished as "function" words. For example, although today we tend to think of *back*, *down*, *going to*, and *ahead* as grammatical function words with completely literal meanings, Heine and Kuteva (2002) in their *World Lexicon of Grammaticalization* show how these words (and hundreds of other grammar words) developed their abstract meanings through the processes of metaphor and metonymy. What theory of the nature of thought and meaning does the phenomenon of grammaticalization support? Can you find further examples in your native language where a similar process has taken place?

2. Translate the linguistic expressions of the TIME IS MONEY conceptual metaphor into another language in a way similar to what I did in this chapter. Try to establish the patterns of translation and see what the most and least frequent patterns are in the language you have worked on.

3. Choose another conceptual metaphor with a rich set of linguistic expressions (e.g., THEORIES ARE BUILDINGS, ANGER IS A HOT FLUID IN A CONTAINER, IDEAS ARE FOOD, etc.) and translate the expressions or have them translated into another language. Establish the patterns of translation and compare your findings with the results of the previous exercise. What are the most and least common patterns? Are there any cultural factors involved in any differences you find?

4.

a. It has been suggested that some seemingly literal words are non-literal in nature. Look up the following words in an etymological dictionary to find out about their original meanings:
   i.   Theory: _____
   ii. Fear: _____
   iii. Life: _____
   iv. Sad: _____
   v.   Succeed: _____
   vi. Comprehend: _____
   vii. Anger: _____

b. Identify the conceptual metaphors or metonymies that underlie the previous words:
   i.   Theory: _____
   ii. Fear: _____
   iii. Life: _____
   iv. Sad: _____
   v.   Succeed: _____
   vi. Comprehend: _____
   vii. Anger: _____

12

The Embodied Mind

The Role of Image-Schemas

As was noted in chapter 2, the first step in acquiring a category is forming a structural description of an entity. Structural descriptions consist of the most elementary properties of entities. As we saw, these elementary properties include lines, surfaces, weight, vertical or horizontal extension, roughness or softness, sweetness or bitterness, and so on. When these experiences occur repeatedly, certain schematic structures begin to emerge and get represented in the brain/mind. The structures that emerge this way are what are called image-schemas.

Mark Johnson defines image-schemas in the following way: An image-schema is "a recurring, dynamic pattern of our perceptual interactions and motor programs that gives coherence to our experience" (1987: xix). Image-schemas have several important properties. First, they are imagistic in nature—and not propositional. Second, they are highly schematic, or abstract. This means that they lack detailed images—either visual or kinesthetic.

What follows is a list of common image-schemas based on Johnson's work (1987). The ones that will be discussed in some detail in the next section are in bold.

CONTAINER
BALANCE
COMPULSION
BLOCKAGE
COUNTERFORCE
RESTRAINT REMOVAL
ENABLEMENT
ATTRACTION
MASS-COUNT
PATH
LINK
CENTER-PERIPHERY

CYCLE

NEAR-FAR

SCALE

PART-WHOLE

MERGING

SPLITTING

FULL-EMPTY

MATCHING

SUPERIMPOSITION

ITERATION

CONTACT

PROCESS

SURFACE

OBJECT

COLLECTION

These image-schemas are common, but the list is not intended to be exhaustive. Probably there are several additional ones—a good candidate being the image-schema of verticality. In our survey later, we will first introduce some commonly occurring *perceptual image-schemas* based on George Lakoff's (1987) study, and then in a later section we will look at some *kinesthetic* ones based on Leonard Talmy's (1988a) work.

Image-schemas, then, provide an important part of our understanding of the world. Without accessible image-schemas at our disposal, it is difficult to make sense of experience. This role of image-schemas serves as the solution to one of the major problems in connection with linguistic expressions and symbols in general. It is called the "symbol grounding" problem (Harnad, 1990). The general issue is this: How do symbols acquire their meaning? The corresponding specific issue is this: How do linguistic expressions become meaningful for us? The standard answer to this question in objectivist semantics is that meaningfulness is achieved through reference (Lakoff, 1987); that is, a linguistic expression referring to an entity in the world (or in a possible world or projected world). It is reference that makes expressions meaningful. We saw in the chapter on frames (chap. 5) that there are at least two folk and expert theories of how this happens. In one, reference is based on sense (or intension). Expressions can refer to entities because the semantic properties that constitute an expression's sense are true of a set of entities in the world. According to the other view, expressions refer by virtue of the fact there is a conventionally fixed relationship between the expression and a set of entities; that is, certain things were simply "baptized" by some experts in certain ways. Image-schemas, as we will see in this chapter, offer a radically new alternative solution to the problem of how symbols and expressions get their meaning.

Some Perceptual Image-Schemas

In the discussion of image-schemas in this section, I will follow the structure of Lakoff's (1987) presentation, in which first, he describes the kind of bodily experience that leads to the emergence of the image-schema; second, he lists the structural elements of image-schemas; third, he outlines the basic logic of the schema; and finally, he discusses some of the conceptual metaphors that a particular image-schema underlies.

The CONTAINER Schema

The bodily experiences that motivate the existence of this schema are varied, but they can be reduced to two general types of experience. First, we have bodies that are containers (of body organs, fluids, etc.). Second, not only are our bodies containers, but we also function within other larger objects as containers. Thus, these larger objects, like buildings, rooms, forests, and the like, contain us.

The CONTAINER image-schema has the following structural elements: "interior," "boundary," and "exterior."

The basic logic of the schema can be given as follows: Everything is either inside the container or outside it. Moreover, if B is in A and C is in B, then one can conclude that C is in A. Thus, the CONTAINER schema imposes a certain logic on us.

There are many metaphors that are based on the CONTAINER schema. For example, STATES ARE CONTAINERS, PERSONAL RELATIONSHIPS ARE CONTAINERS, and THE VISUAL FIELD IS A CONTAINER. This is why we can be *in* trouble, we are *in* love, and things come *into* view.

The PART-WHOLE Schema

The most obvious bodily experience that led to the existence of this schema is that we experience ourselves as wholes with parts. We conceive of our body parts as parts of the larger whole that we are.

The structural elements that characterize this schema include "whole," "parts," and a "configuration" between the parts or the parts and the whole.

The major and first feature of the basic logic of the schema is that it is asymmetric. This means that if A is part of B, then B is not a part of A. If the finger is part of the hand, the hand is not a part of the finger. Second, if the whole exists, then the parts must also exist. However, the parts must be in a particular configuration. If not, then we do not normally consider the parts to form a whole. Third, if the parts are destroyed, the whole is destroyed. Fourth, if the parts are located at P, then the whole is located at P. All kinds of gory scenarios can be imagined when these do not hold, but then we would probably not consider the parts as forming a whole.

A metaphor that is based on the WHOLE-PART relationship is PERSONAL RELATIONSHIPS ARE WHOLES WITH PARTS. For example, in Indian society society is a whole and the castes are parts. The highest caste corresponds to the head. The structure of society is the configuration in which the body parts are related. This imposes a particularly important piece of logic on the understanding of Indian society; namely, that society can only exist if the highest caste exists.

The LINK Schema

The bodily basis for the LINK schema is manifold. Bodily experiences that may have led to the emergence of the schema include the following: the umbilical cord; holding on to things; attaching things to each other by means of some connection.

The structural elements that characterize the schema include two "entities" and a "link" that connects them.

The basic logic of the schema involves symmetry. This means that if A is linked to B, then B is linked to A. Moreover, if A is linked to B, then A is constrained by B.

Given the elements and the basic logic, the LINK schema serves as source domain in several metaphors. For example, RELATIONSHIPS ARE CONNECTIONS, in which two entities are linked by a connection. Another metaphor is DEPENDENCE IS CONNECTION, which has examples such as *be tied to one's mother's apron strings*. Finally, LACK OF FREEDOM IS BEING TIED DOWN/INABILITY TO MOVE, a metaphor that I mentioned in connection with interpretation of the Statue of Liberty.

The CENTER-PERIPHERY Schema

The most important kind of bodily experience we have that motivates the schema is that we experience our bodies as having a center and a periphery. Thus, the trunk of the body is considered to be more central than, for example, the fingers.

The structural elements of the schema include "entity," "center," and "periphery."

According to the basic logic of the schema, the periphery depends on the center, but the center does not depend on the periphery.

There are many metaphors that are based on this schema. Theories, meanings, and categories are metaphorically assumed to have a central part, as we saw, for example, in the discussion of prototypes. In addition, we talk about the *central* part of a theory. Similarly, according to the metaphor A PERSON IS A CONTAINER a person is understood as having a center and a periphery. In addition, we have the generic-level metaphors IMPORTANT IS CENTRAL and UNIMPORTANT IS PERIPHERAL.

The SOURCE-PATH-GOAL Schema

The bodily experience that motivates the schema is the most common (and so unconscious) type of experience: Whenever we move, we move *from* a place *to* another place *along* a sequence of continuous locations.

The structural elements include "source," "path," "goal (destination)," and "direction."

The basic logic is also hardly noticeable: If you go from A to B, then you must pass through each intermediate point that connects A and B.

Again, several metaphors are based on this image-schema. I mention two. As was observed in the previous chapter, the complex metaphor of LIFE IS A JOURNEY assumes the SOURCE-PATH-GOAL schema. A mapping and a submetaphor of this complex metaphor is PURPOSES ARE DESTINATIONS, in which we also have a source, a path, and a goal. As a matter of fact, it is this second primary metaphor that provides some of the motivation for the more complex one. Complex events are also commonly viewed as involving an initial state (SOURCE), intermediate stages (PATHS), and a final state (GOAL).

In conclusion, image-schemas provide much of our understanding the world. This is true for both literal and figurative ways of conceptualization. Word meaning makes use of the same idea. The meanings of many words are based on image-schemas of the kind I dealt with earlier. Here are some examples of image-schemas and the words whose meaning is based on them:

CONTAINER: *in-out, inside-outside, leave, enter, through*
SOURCE-PATH-GOAL: *from, along, to, walk, run, swim*
VERTICALITY: *up-down, high-low, above, under, over*

However, we often need more than one schema to characterize the meaning of a word or the interpretation of a situation. We will see examples for this later on in this chapter and elsewhere in this book.

The Structure of Mind

The presence of image-schemas in our conceptual system has a major consequence for the folk theory of the structure of the mind. Lakoff (1987) suggests that image-schemas structure our conceptual system. He calls this hypothesis the "spatialization of form" hypothesis. What this means is that we have an embodied understanding of the structure (form) of our conceptual system.

Consider some of the aspects of the conceptual system that I have discussed so far. In the preceding chapters I talked about the structure of categories, frames, hierarchical structures of concepts, relational structures, radial categories, and foreground-background structure in frames. These aspects of the conceptual system make up a large portion of the mind. As it turns out, all of these aspects are characterized by some of the image-schemas that I have mentioned or described in some detail in this chapter.

Here is a list of which aspects are characterized by which image-schemas:

Categories: CONTAINERS with entities inside. Members of categories are commonly conceptualized as "entities inside containers."
Frames: WHOLES with PARTS. Frames are wholes that have elements. The elements are parts. Metonymy is based on the configurations "whole and part" and "part and part."

Hierarchical structure: PART-WHOLE, UP-DOWN. Taxonomies consist of wholes and parts that are arranged in hierarchical structures with an up-down organization.

Relational structure: LINK. Relational structures obtain either between categories or between members of categories. Either categories or members can be linked to each other.

Radial structure: CENTER-PERIPHERY, LINK. In radial structures members of categories are organized in such a way that some members are in the center, while others are on the periphery. The members can be linked by a variety of relations.

Foreground-background structure: FRONT-BACK. Frames are characterized by foreground-background structure. When an element of a frame is profiled (focused on), it will be in the foreground and the rest of the frame will be in the background.

This characterization leads to a remarkable consequence, namely, that a large portion of the conceptual system is structured by image-schemas that structure physical space and that we acquire through our most mundane kinds of functioning in the physical world. To put it simply, the structure (form) of much of our conceptual apparatus is provided by the structure of embodied spatial experience. It seems as if what we would take as a metaphor—CONCEPTUAL SPACE IS PHYSICAL SPACE—is not really a metaphor after all; it is indeed the case that our embodied spatial experience gives structure to our conceptual system. This can happen because spatial-image-schematic structure is mapped onto "conceptual structure." In this sense, we can claim that much of the structure of the mind is based on the structure of embodied spatial experience.

Moreover, even conceptual metaphors themselves can be seen as structured this way. Source and target domains can be viewed as containers, and mappings can be characterized by the SOURCE-PATH-GOAL schema, in which elements of the source container are mapped onto elements of a goal container along a path.

If these suggestions about the structure of our conceptual system are valid, they point to the conclusion that we cannot really talk about the body and the mind as distinct entities. Instead, what emerges is that the mind is embodied in a clear and straightforward sense: Embodied image-schematic experience provides much of the structure of what we call the mind. However, it is one thing to make this suggestion and another to prove it in the actual "stuff" of the brain. The problem is neatly captured by an eminent cognitive scientist, Gerald M. Edelman (1992: 209): "without an understanding of how the mind is based in matter, we will be left with a vast chasm between scientific knowledge and knowledge of ourselves." But, in an encouraging tone, Edelman continues: "This chasm is not unbridgeable. But biology and psychology teach us that the bridge is made of many parts. The solution to the problem of how we know, feel, and are aware is not contained in a philosophical sentence, however profound. It must emerge from an understanding of how biological systems and relationships evolved in the physical world."

And work along these lines has already started. Based on his own and other researchers' results, a leading neuroscientist, Antonio R. Damasio (1994), appears to support the notion of the embodied mind: "Mind is probably not conceivable without some sort of *embodiment*, a notion that figures prominently in the theoretical proposals of George Lakoff, Mark Johnson, Eleanor Rosch, Francisco Varela, and Gerald Edelman" (Damasio, 1994: 209; italics in the original). The notion of embodied mind might be a counterintuitive one to many. It might be objected that we are not sensing anything bodily as we think on-line. Damasio responds to this objection as follows: "the weight of my idea concerns the *history of development* of brain/mind processes rather than the current moment. I believe images of body state were indispensable, as building blocks and scaffolding, for what exists now. Without a doubt, however, what exists now is dominated by non-body images" (italics in the original).

Forces in the Mind

But the conceptual system is not only structured by image-schemas like CON-TAINER, WHOLE-PART, LINK, and so on. Major components of the folk theory of the mind are organized in terms of force-dynamics, that is, various image-schemas centered around the notion of "force," as described by Talmy (1988a). First, we will analyze the domain of EMOTION as an area where force image-schemas play a significant role, and then we will turn to morality and rational thought.

Emotion and Force

Talmy (1988a) observed that many aspects of language can be profitably described and explained by what he called force dynamics. He provides the following characterization of this notion:

> The primary distinction that language marks here is a role difference between the two entities exerting the forces. One force-exerting entity is singled out for focal attention—the salient issue in the interaction is whether this entity is able to manifest its force tendency or, on the contrary, is overcome. The second force entity, correlatively, is considered for the effect that it has on the first, effectively overcoming it or not. (1988a:53)

The description of an event in terms of force dynamics involves:

Force entities:	Intrinsic force tendency:
Agonist	toward action
Antagonist	toward rest (inaction)
Resultant of the force interaction:	Balance of strengths:
action	the stronger entity
rest (inaction)	the weaker entity

If we apply these force-dynamic notions to the domain of EMOTION, we get the following correspondences (Kövecses, 2000b):

Force Agonist (FAgo)   →   Emotion Agonist (EmAgo)
Force Antagonist (FAnt)   →   Emotion Antagonist (EmAnt)
FAnt's force tendency   →   EmAnt's force tendency
FAgo's force tendency   →   EmAgo's force tendency
FAgo's resultant state   →   EmAgo's resultant state

Two questions immediately arise in this connection: (1) What allows us to set up these correspondences? (2) Precisely what is the emotion agonist, the emotion antagonist, the force tendency of the emotion agonist, and so on? To answer these questions, we should examine the most basic and skeletal emotion scenario in our folk theory of emotion. In this scenario, there is a cause that induces a person (self) to have an emotion, and the emotion causes the person to produce some response. In a schematic way, this can be given as:

1. A cause leads to emotion.
2. Emotion leads to some response.

Since we know from the EVENT STRUCTURE metaphor (Lakoff, 1990) that causes are forces, we can regard "cause" in part one and "emotion" in part two as forces and apply force dynamics to the EMOTION domain.

Let us begin with the first part of the scenario. If we think of the agonist as an entity that has an intrinsic force tendency toward inaction, that is, to stay inactive or at rest, the corresponding entity will be the self in the EMOTION domain; and if we think of the antagonist as an entity that has an intrinsic force tendency toward action, that is, to overcome the inaction of the agonist, to cause it to act, the corresponding entity will be the cause of emotion in the EMOTION domain.

Now let us look at the second part of the scenario, using the same definition of agonist and antagonist as before. If we think of the agonist as an entity that has an intrinsic force tendency toward inaction, the corresponding entity will be the self again, who will produce some kind of response. And if we think of the antagonist as an entity that has an intrinsic force tendency toward action, the corresponding entity will be the emotion itself. In other words, in both cases the emotion agonist will be the self (in that it becomes emotional in part one and it produces a response in part two) and the emotion antagonist will be the cause of emotion in the first part and the emotion itself in the second part of the scenario.

These instantiations of the abstract force-dynamic schema will apply to the majority of emotion metaphors but not all of them. Table 12.1 shows how the various emotion metaphors instantiate the force-dynamic schema. Metaphors in group I focus on the second part of the scenario, metaphors in group II can focus on both parts, and metaphors in group III focus on part one. (A detailed analysis of all these metaphors in terms of force dynamics can be found in Kövecses, 2000b.)

Table 12.1 The Agonist and Antagonist in Emotion
Metaphors

Source Domain	Agonist	Antagonist
I		
Internal pressure	Self	Emotion
Opponent	Self	Emotion
Wild animal	Self	Emotion
Social superior	Self	Emotion
Natural force	Self	Emotion
Trickster	Self	Emotion
Insanity	Self	Emotion
Fire	Self	Emotion
II		
Hunger1	Self	Desire for emotion
Hunger2	Emotional self	Insatiable desire
Physical agitation1	Self	Cause of emotion
Physical agitation2	Body	Emotion
Burden	Self	Emotional stress
III		
Physical force	Self	Cause of emotion

Now let us take some conceptual metaphors of emotion and see how force dynamics applies to them. We can begin with EMOTION IS AN OPPONENT (IN A STRUGGLE). Consider some examples for this metaphor:

EMOTION IS AN OPPONENT
He was *seized by* emotion.
He was *struggling with* his emotions.
I was *gripped by* emotion.
She was *overcome by* emotion.

There are two opponents in this struggle. As the first and third examples suggest, one opponent is inactive (the one who is seized and gripped all of a sudden). This is the agonist. The other, the one who seizes and grips, is active and attempts to cause opponent one to give in to his force. This is the antagonist. There is some struggle in which opponent one tries to resist opponent two's force and opponent two tries to make him give in to his force. There is the possibility of either opponent one winning or opponent two winning. Corresponding to opponent one in the source is the rational self in the target, while corresponding to opponent two in the source is the emotion in the target domain. Corresponding to opponent one's force tendency in the source is the rational self's force tendency to try to maintain control over the emotion, and corresponding to opponent two's force tendency is the emotion's force tendency to cause the self to lose control. This force-dynamic interpretation can be represented in table 12.2.

Source: OPPONENT IN A STRUGGLE
Target: EMOTION

Next, let us take the NATURAL FORCE metaphor. When this is applied to emotion the underlying logic is that there is an extremely forceful entity (like a wind, wave, storm, etc.) that affects a physical object and this object can't help but undergo its usually disastrous effects. When people say that they are *overwhelmed* by an emotion or that they are *swept off their feet*, it is this kind of effect that they imagine. This metaphor encapsulates perhaps the most deeply seated belief about emotions, namely, that we are passive and helpless in relation to them, just as physical objects are passive and helpless in relation to powerful natural forces acting on them. Schematically again, table 12.3 captures all this:

Source: NATURAL FORCE
Target: EMOTION

The OPPONENT and NATURAL FORCE metaphors both focus on the second part of the skeletal emotion scenario—"emotion → response." Now let us take a metaphor that can work for both the second and first parts: EMOTION IS A PHYSIOLOGICAL FORCE. Physiological forces include hunger and thirst. Consider the following two examples:

EMOTION IS HUNGER/THIRST
I'm *starved for* affection.
His anger was *insatiable*.

Both examples are based on the mapping according to which: hunger → desire. The physiological hunger corresponds to emotional desire. But the two desires are very different. In the case of *"starved for* affection," the hunger for

Table 12.2. Force Dynamics Applied to EMOTION IS AN OPPONENT Metaphor

Metaphorical Mapping	Agonist's Force Tendency	Antagonist's Force Tendency	Resultant Action
Source	*Opponent One* Opponent one's attempt to resist opponent 2	*Opponent Two* Opponent two's attempt to cause opponent 1 to give in to his force	Either opponent two wins or opponent one wins
Target	*Rational self*: self's attempt to try to maintain control	*Emotion*: the emotion causing the self to lose control	Self either loses or maintains control

Table 12.3. Force Dynamics Applied to EMOTION IS A NATURAL FORCE Metaphor

Metaphorical Mapping	Agonist's Force Tendency	Antagonist's Force Tendency	Resultant Action
Source	*Physical object*: to keep being the same	*Natural force*: to cause an effect in physical object	Physical object undergoes effect in a passive way
Target	*Rational self*: to continue to behave as before the emotion	*Emotion*: to cause the self to respond to emotion	Self responds to the emotion in a passive way

food corresponds to the psychological desire for an emotion. In the case of *"insatiable* anger," the hunger for (more) food corresponds to the emotional desire for (more) revenge or retaliation. In other words, in version one of the EMOTION IS HUNGER metaphor we are talking about the first part of the emotion scenario ("cause → emotion"), whereas in version two focus is on the second part ("emotion → response").

The logic of version one, represented in table 12.4, says this: A nonhungry person does not want food. What causes a hungry person to want food is the hunger. Similarly with emotion: An emotionally desireless person (self) does not want emotion, but a desire for emotion makes the self want emotion.

Source: HUNGER
Target: EMOTION

The last metaphor of emotion that I use to demonstrate the workings of force dynamics in the conceptualization of emotions is the EMOTION IS A PHYSICAL FORCE metaphor. This metaphor tends to have its main focus on the first part of the emotion scenario—"cause → emotion." It comes in a

Table 12.4. Force Dynamics Applied to EMOTION IS A PHYSIOLOGICAL FORCE Metaphor

Metaphorical Mapping	Agonist's Force Tendency	Antagonist's Force Tendency	Resultant Action
Source	*Person*: for the (nonhungry) person not to want food	*Hunger (for food)*: to cause the person to want food	Hunger makes person go get food
Target	*Self*: for the (desireless) self not to want emotion	*Desire (for emotion)*: to cause self to want to have emotion	Desire causes self to have emotion

variety of forms (MECHANICAL, ELECTRIC, GRAVITATIONAL, MAGNETIC), which are illustrated with the following examples:

> EMOTION IS A PHYSICAL FORCE.
> EMOTION IS A MECHANICAL FORCE; EMOTIONAL EFFECT IS PHYSICAL
>   CONTACT
>   When I found out, it *hit* me *hard.*
>   That was a terrible *blow.*
>   She *knocked* me *off my feet.*
> EMOTION IS AN ELECTRIC FORCE
>   It was an *electrifying* experience.
> EMOTION IS A GRAVITATIONAL FORCE
>   Her whole life *revolves around* him.
>   They *gravitated toward* each other immediately.
> EMOTION IS A MAGNETIC FORCE
>   I was *magnetically drawn to* her.
>   I am *attracted to* her.
>   She found him *irresistible.*
>   That *repels* me.

In the source domain, there is a physical object with the force tendency toward inaction, that is, to continue to be as before. There is also another force-exerting entity here, a physical force that has the force tendency to produce some effect in the object. Correspondingly, there is a rational self that has the force tendency to stay as before (that is, unemotional), and there is a cause (of emotion) that has the force tendency to cause the self to become emotional. This situation is depicted by such examples as "The news *hit* me *hard*" and "I was *attracted to* her," where a cause of emotion acts on the rational self, causing it to become emotional. Again, table 12.5 presents this logic in diagrammatic form.

> Source: PHYSICAL FORCE
> Target: EMOTION

We can represent this interplay of forces in emotion as a conceptually richer version of our initial skeletal emotion scenario:

> 1. cause of emotion—force $\Big\}$ $\leftrightarrow$ $\Big\{$ rational self—force
>   tendency of the cause of emotion $\Big\}$ tendency of self
> → 2. self has emotion
> → 3. self's force tendency $\leftrightarrow$ force tendency of emotion
> → 4. self's emotional response

In this richer schema it becomes clear that the various components of the EMOTION domain are conceptualized as forces that interact with one another. The schema shows that there are two main points of tension in the experience of emotion: The first takes place between the cause of emotion and the

Table 12.5. Force Dynamics Applied to EMOTION IS A PHYSICAL FORCE Metaphor

Metaphorical Mapping	Agonist's Force Tendency	Antagonist's Force Tendency	Resultant Action
Source	*Physical object*: to remain unaffected by force	*Physical force*: to produce effect in object	Object undergoes effect
Target	*Self*: to remain unemotional	*Cause of emotion*: to cause self to become emotional	Self is emotional

rational self, resulting in the emergence of emotion. The second occurs between the self that has the emotion but is still in control over it, on the one hand, and the force of the emotion, on the other. This second force interaction prototypically results in the self losing control and producing an emotional response. Most emotion metaphors (though not all) can be described in a similar fashion as an interaction of forces. This leads us to the conclusion that there exists a single "master metaphor" for emotion: EMOTIONS ARE FORCES. A large number of emotion metaphors are specific-level instantiations of this superordinate metaphor, each playing a specific and different role in conceptualizing the EMOTION domain.

Morality and Force

Now that we have a general idea of the metaphorical structure of the EMOTION domain in terms of force dynamics, we are in a position to compare this structure with other domains, or faculties, of the mind. We can begin the comparison with morality. The domain of MORALITY was described in some detail based on work by Lakoff (1996). Lakoff also notes that of the several metaphors that structure the domain of MORALITY the dominant one is the MORAL STRENGTH metaphor (see chapter 9). For convenience, here is the metaphor again:

The MORAL STRENGTH metaphor:
BEING BAD IS BEING LOW
BEING GOOD IS BEING UPRIGHT
DOING EVIL IS FALLING
EVIL IS A FORCE
MORALITY IS STRENGTH

In this metaphor complex, a moral person is conceptualized as "up" (as in an "*upright* citizen"), whereas an immoral one is conceptualized as "down" (as in "That was a *low* trick"); doing evil as "falling" (as in the biblical *fall*); evil as a physical force acting on a person, while being moral as resisting the force of evil (as in "She *resisted* the temptation").

In other words, in the source domain there is a physical force, which has a force tendency for action (to produce some effect), acting on a (physical) person-body, which has a force tendency toward inaction (to continue to stay as before). Corresponding to this in the MORALITY domain there are two non-physical forces in interaction: some kind of evil (either internal or external) and a self. The self's force tendency is toward inaction, that is, not to give in to the force of evil, to maintain control over it; hence the self is the agonist. The force tendency of the evil is toward action, that is, to make the self lose control; hence the evil is the antagonist. Thus, given the predominant MORAL STRENGTH metaphor, the MORALITY domain can be represented in table 12.6 using the same notions as have been used for emotion:

Source: TWO PHYSICAL FORCES
Target: MORALITY

This picture is very similar to that of emotion: Two forces interact and the interaction takes place between the self (same as in emotion) and evil (instead of emotion). The major difference is in the resultant action component. If the self is moral, it does not yield to the force of evil; it successfully withstands this force. In emotion, however, the typical situation or case is one in which the self (1) does become emotional (i.e., yields to the cause of emotion) and (2) cannot maintain control over the force of emotion and does produce a response.

Rational Thought and Force

Let us now turn to RATIONAL THOUGHT. This domain was analyzed and described extensively by Olaf Jäkel (1995). Based on a detailed study of a huge corpus of English usage, Jäkel found that the most prevalent metaphor for rational thought is PHYSICAL MANIPULATION. (To be sure, as Johnson, 1987, Lakoff and Johnson, 1999, and Sweetser, 1990, show, there are many other metaphors for thought in English, but this seems to be the one that is dominant.) In English, one can *hammer out* a solution, can have an *incisive* mind, can *put* things *on the back burner* for a while, can *store*

Table 12.6. Morality and Force

Metaphorical Mapping	Agonist's Force Tendency	Antagonist's Force Tendency	Resultant Action
Source	*Physical body*: to continue to stay as before	*Physical force*: to produce an effect in the physical body	No effect
Target	*Self*: to maintain control over evil (i.e., to maintain morality)	*Evil*: to make self lose control over evil (i.e., to make him immoral)	Self maintains control over evil (i.e., maintains morality)

ideas in memory, can *work out* and *on* a problem. In other words, speakers of English talk and think about thought by making use of the metaphor RA-TIONAL THOUGHT IS PHYSICAL MANIPULATION. The metaphor is constituted by the following mappings:

workman	→	rational self
physical objects	→	objects of thought
physical manipulations	→	mental activities
tools	→	intellect
workshop	→	mind

What these mappings tell us is that, similar to emotion and morality, there are two forces at work here as well. In the source domain, there is a workman acting on physical objects in various ways. In the target, there is a rational self performing various mental activities on mental objects, such as ideas (cf. IDEAS ARE OBJECTS). The workman has a force tendency toward action, that is, to change the physical objects and in the target the rational self has a force tendency toward action, that is, to change the objects of thought. In contrast, the physical objects in the source and the objects of thought in the target are inactive; that is, they have a force tendency to resist change by the workman and the rational self, respectively.

Given this characterization, the agonists are the physical objects and the objects of thought, while the antagonists are the workman and the rational self. A schematic representation of rational thought in terms of force-dynamic notions is given in table 12.7.

How does rational thought compare with emotion and morality in force-dynamic terms? The major difference seems to be that in thought the rational self acts as antagonist, unlike in emotion and morality, where the self is typically the agonist. In addition, in successful acts of thought the "agonist thought objects" are changed by the rational self, while in emotion the self undergoes change (i.e., responds emotionally) and in morality the self withstands change despite a force acting on it.

Table 12.7. Force Dynamics and the MENTAL ACTIVITY IS PHYSICAL MANIPULATION Metaphor

Metaphorical Mapping	Agonist's Force Tendency	Antagonist's Force Tendency	Resultant Action
Source	*Physical objects*: to resist change by the workman	*Workman*: to change the physical objects	The physical objects undergo change
Target	*Objects of thought*: to resist change by the self	*Rational self*: to change the objects of thought	The objects of thought undergo change

Emotion, Morality, and Rational Thought in Comparison

I have argued that major domains of the mind are conceptualized metaphorically as an interaction of forces. Metaphorical language about EMOTION, MORALITY, and RATIONAL THOUGHT suggests that each of these domains is viewed and can be described in force-dynamic terms: agonists and antagonists in interaction with each other, both having opposite force tendencies, and their interaction resulting in particular outcomes (action and inaction).

While all three domains are constituted force-dynamically, there are subtle but significant differences among them. Given their basic cognitive structure, the rational "self-agonist" undergoes change in EMOTION, the rational "self-agonist" withstands change in MORALITY, and the rational "self-antagonist" causes change in THOUGHT. Obviously, everyone knows that emotion is different from morality and that rational thought is different from both. That is not my point. What is remarkable about my analysis is that it shows that the basic cognitive "architecture" of emotion, morality, and rational thought is so much alike. They are all constituted force-dynamically, and this shows that "superficially" very different domains, or faculties, of the folk theory of the mind have a deep underlying similarity on which the many obvious differences are based.

Understanding Stories

It is a well-established feature of thought that we can conceptualize situations by means of not just one but several image-schemas. For example, force-dynamic image-schemas can interact with perceptual image-schemas: As one instance, we can have a force inside a container. Forces inside containers are fairly common as metaphorical ways of conceptualizing the mind. I have shown (Kövecses, 1990) that this was a major metaphor used by Sigmund Freud in his psychoanalytic theory.

But we can find something similar in the case of the image-schematic understanding of stories. That stories and discourse in general are commonly understood by means of image-schemas was noticed in the cognitive linguistic literature, for example, by Gary Palmer (1996). Much subsequent work also relies on this general idea (see, for example, Kimmel, 2002).

As a demonstration of the role of image-schemas in understanding and remembering a plot, Michael Kimmel (2005) uses Joseph Conrad's novel *Heart of Darkness*. Kimmel describes the gist of the story as follows:

> In the novel, Marlow, a seaman and wanderer, recounts a steamboat expedition into deep African territory in search of the enigmatic Mr. Kurtz who is the company's agent at the "Inner Station," a trading outpost. The story is situated around the turn from the 19th to the 20th century in the Congo, which was at that time a private property of the Belgian King Léopold and marked by rampant forced labor and vicious exploitation of the natives. The narrative's thrust goes quite literally

towards Kurtz who is the goal of the gradual penetration into a strange, dangerous and unfathomable territory. Kurtz has imposed a surreal order of terror and charisma among the natives. He is a man of captivating and demonic force who has signed a Faustian pact and is being worshipped as a god, yet troubled. When Marlow finds him, he is on the verge of madness and death and experiencing great inner turmoil. Marlow himself is changed in the struggle to comprehend his experience with this once exceptional and now tormented man who has looked into his own nature, the dark side of his passions. Having succumbed to alien and yet strangely familiar forces in the zone of proximity between culturalized humanity and an archaic "Other," Kurtz dies with the words "The horror! The horror!" on his lips. Back from his experience Marlow visits Kurtz's fiancée in Brussels, but conceals the truth about his fall from grace and his last words from her. It is apparent that while the tale's overall structure is that of a literal journey, metaphorically it is a journey to the limits of the human soul, a double-entendre that becomes evident in the very title.

Kimmel suggests that "the most fundamental macrostructural function of image-schemas is the creation by readers of a condensed representation for use in plot recall." That is to say, as we read the text, we try to construct a network of image-schemas that are based on the description of the literal journey, the various force metaphors used, and the many symbolic meanings that transpire from the novel. Kimmel proposes a diagrammatic representation of our understanding of the text as shown in figure 12.1.

The line with an arrow image-schematically represents the literal journey into Africa. The circles image-schematically represent Europe and Africa, respectively. Europe is an "out-space" and Africa is an "in-space." Superimposed on the image-schemas of CONTAINER and SOURCE-PATH-GOAL, we find

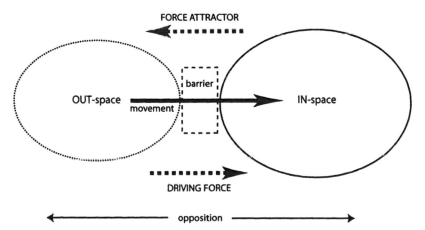

Figure 12.1 Superimposed image schemas in understanding the plot (from Kimmel, 2005, by permission)

a force-dynamic schema represented by opposing bold arrows. Marlow is both metaphorically driven and attracted by certain forces: the forces of intellectual curiosity and knowledge, on the one hand, and the forces of sensuality and passion, on the other. The push and the pull, as Kimmel calls them, find actual linguistic expression in the text of the novel. The following examples are taken from Kimmel's work:

PUSH ATTRACTOR / DRIVE
"driven toward the heat of fires"
PULL ATTRACTOR
"smiling, . . . inviting, mute with an air of whispering, Come and find out."; "beguiled his unlawful soul"

There are many more complexities to the analysis that Kimmel offers. One of them is the role of barriers as indicated by broken vertical lines in the diagram. I cannot present Kimmel's intricate system here. The main point of this brief demonstration was twofold: One was to show that image-schemas may have an important function in remembering and comprehending story plots. The second was to indicate that image-schemas may be superimposed on each other and may thus form complex structures that make sense of complex sets of events.

Conclusions

An image-schema is "a recurring, dynamic pattern of our perceptual interactions and motor programs that gives coherence to our experience" (Johnson, 1987: xix). Image-schemas are highly schematic, or abstract, structures.

Image-schemas can be described in terms of the kinds of bodily experience that lead to their emergence, their structural elements, their basic logic, and the conceptual metaphors that they underlie. I have briefly characterized five image-schemas in some detail: the CONTAINER schema, the PART-WHOLE schema, the LINK schema, the CENTER-PERIPHERY schema, and the SOURCE-PATH-GOAL schema. Not only do such image-schemas provide a large part of our general understanding of the world, but they also figure importantly in the meanings of many words. Many word meanings are based on image-schemas.

Image-schemas structure our conceptual system in general. This means that we have an embodied understanding of the structure (form) of our conceptual system. If correct, this conclusion points to the mind as being embodied, or as Mark Johnson (1987) put it, "the body [is] in the mind."

Our meaning-making activity makes extensive use of what Len Talmy (1988a) calls force dynamics. We can characterize a large part of the folk theory of the mind in terms of force-dynamic image-schemas. Most emotion metaphors (though not all) can be described as an interaction of forces. In a similar fashion, our conceptualization of morality and rational thought also relies on this image-schema. However, we also find significant differences in conceptualization. In thought the rational self is the antagonist, unlike in emotion and morality, where the self is typically the agonist. In addition, in successful acts of thought the "agonist thought objects" are changed by the rational self, while in emotion the self undergoes change (i.e., responds emotionally) and in morality the self withstands change despite a force acting on it. It would be possible to assign these force-dynamic roles to entities in thought, emotion, and morality in a different way. However, this would not change the main conclusion, namely, that the basic cognitive "architecture" of the folk theory of the mind is constituted force-dynamically.

Image-schemas appear to account in part for how we understand the plot of longer literary texts. Michael Kimmel's analysis of *Heart of Darkness* by Joseph Conrad showed that there are several image-schemas (such as CONTAINER, SOURCE, PATH, AND GOAL, FORCES) helping us understand and remember the plot of the novel. The image-schemas seem to be superimposed on one another, but through their simple general structure they enable us to keep track of a large number of specific-level events.

Image-schemas offer an alternative solution to the problem of how abstract symbols and linguistic expressions get their meaning. Since we rely on image-schemas in the conceptualization of the world and image-schemas are based on our bodily experience, symbols and expressions will be meaningful for us. This is because we bring our bodily experience to the conceptualization of the world around us. Since we are also part of the world, image-schemas will be used in understanding our own functioning as well. Image-schemas provide an important interface between the body and the world and, at the same time, allow us to understand ourselves "through ourselves."

Exercises

1. Think about the image-schema CYCLE. What are its structural elements and what logic applies to it? List ten examples from culture, mythology, society, or personal experience where the cycle is the central metaphor. Which conceptual metaphors make use of the natural cycle? Are all of these elements of the natural cycle mapped directly into those metaphors?

2. What image-schemas can you identify in the following English idioms? There may be more than one in each example.

   a. To spill the beans.
   b. All roads lead to Rome.
   c. To hate someone's guts.
   d. To pull ahead of someone.
   e. Off the beaten track.
   f. To reach an agreement with someone.
   g. To hit the bull's-eye.
   h. He was full of hate when he got to know what had happened.
   i. She is my better half.

    j. We are closer than we were before.
    k. He would be a good match for you.
    l. The girl stole the boy's heart.
    m. People have emotional ups and downs occasionally.

3. What everyday manifestations can you think of for the CENTER-PERIPHERY image-schema? Think of arrangements in metaphorical space or real-life, physical spatial arrangements that "realize" the IMPORTANT IS CENTRAL and LESS IMPORTANT IS LESS CENTRAL metaphor.

4. Think of the metaphor EMOTION IS A BURDEN. This focuses on the second part of the emotion scenario mentioned in the chapter: emotion → response.

    a. Try to fill out table 12.8 according to the force-dynamic interpretation of emotions.
        Source: BURDEN
        Target: EMOTION
        Agonist (target): self
        Antagonist (target): emotional stress
    b. Try to think of some linguistic realizations of EMOTION IS A BURDEN.

5. Find a (short) literary text that has, in your judgment, an underlying image-schematic basis. Analyze the text and try to come up with a diagram similar to Kimmel's. You might need to use additional image-schemas. Justify your analysis with linguistic examples and/or any other evidence.

Table 12.8. Force Dynamic Interpretation of EMOTION IS A BURDEN Metaphor

Metaphorical Mapping	Agonist's Force Tendency	Antagonist's Force Tendency	Resultant Action
Source			
Target			

13

Alternative Construals of the World

Construal is a way of understanding an aspect of the world (i.e., objects, events, etc.). It is used here in the sense of interpretation or conceptualization. When we say that an entity or situation is construed in a particular way, what we mean is that it is interpreted or conceptualized in some way. Often there are several different ways of conceptualizing the same "thing." We call such different ways of conceptualizing the same thing alternative construal. Alternative construal may be achieved by means of a variety of cognitive operations. As a matter of fact, we have seen several such construal operations, or processes, in the previous chapters, such as categorization, framing, metaphor, and others. We saw that we can often categorize, frame, or metaphorically understand the same thing in several different ways.

Construal operations have been discussed by a number of cognitive linguists. The four who proposed a classification, or taxonomy, of such mental operations are Ronald Langacker (1987), Leonard Talmy (1988b), and William Croft and Alan Cruse (2004). Here I will follow Croft and Cruse's classification in its general outline because theirs seems to be the most comprehensive one and takes into account the results of the other two authors. The examples to be discussed here come largely from these sources.

Croft and Cruse (2004) provide a four-way classification of construal operations. First, there are construal operations that have to do with *attention*. A second group is based on what they call *judgment* and *comparison*. A third group is organized around the operation of taking a *perspective* on an entity. Fourth and finally, a group of construal operations relies on how we establish the *overall structure* of entities and events. It is this classification that will serve as the basis of the discussion to follow. I will present construal operations based on this scheme with some minor simplifying modifications.

Attention

We use attention in a number of different ways to understand and talk about a situation, event, or entity. Following Croft and Cruse (2004), I will distinguish four such ways: the focus of attention, scope of attention, detail of attention (scalar adjustment), and dynamic or static nature of attention.

Focus of Attention

We can select, or choose, a particular facet, or aspect, of the situation, event, or entity. When we do this, we are focusing on that facet, or aspect. To use terminology from the chapter on frames, we can say that we *profile* a particular facet, or aspect of the situation, event, or entity. We call the facet so profiled the focus of attention (see fig. 13.1). For example, we can profile, or bring into focus, different facets, or aspects, of the CIRCLE frame by means of using the words *radius*, *arc*, and *circumference*. The arc, radius, and circumference represent different facets of the same frame. Another interesting case where we have a profile shift within a frame is when we focus attention on the agent or instrument rather than the action within the frame. For example, in the WRITING frame we have the elements of the person who writes, the action of writing, the instrument used in writing, the surface on which the person writes, the letters the person writes, and so on. We can focus attention on the action of writing. When we do, we use the verb *write*. We can also focus attention on the person who writes. When we do, we use the noun *writer*. The suffix *–er* indicates the choice of a particular facet of the frame. It shifts attention from the action of writing to the agent of writing. But the focus of attention does not need to be indicated by explicit grammatical elements like suffixes. For example, in the GOLD SEEKING frame we have the instrument of pan and the action of panning. Here the focus of attention can be indicated by the same word form, *pan*. However, there would be a difference in word class. When the action is the focus of attention we use the form as a verb, and when it is the instrument we use the form as a noun.

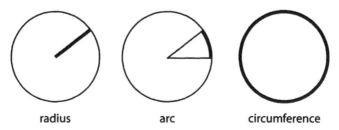

radius   arc   circumference

Figure 13.1 Profiling the radius, the arc, and the circumference against the background of the whole frame (CIRCLE)

Let us consider some additional sets of examples from Croft and Cruse (2004: 48):

(1) The *Chronicle* costs a dollar.

(2) The *Chronicle* called for his resignation.

(3) The *Chronicle* went bankrupt.

Although the same phrase, *the* Chronicle, is used in all three sentences, the different sentences indicate different aspects of the entity. The first focuses on the tome, the physical object itself, the second on the editor of the newspaper, and the third on the company.

In the second set of examples, although we are understanding the concept of "window" and we are using the same phrase, *the window*, the focus is different:

(4) The *window* is dirty.

(5) He came in through the *window*.

The first sentence profiles the windowpane, while the second profiles the frame of the window.

Finally, consider some well-known examples that can be thought of as metonymic in nature:

(6) They played lots of Mozart.

(7) She heard the piano.

(8) I'm in the phone book.

Recall my definition of metonymy in chapter 7: In metonymy, an element in a frame provides mental access to another element in the same frame. Thus, the first example provides mental access to the works of Mozart through the person Mozart (based on PRODUCER FOR PRODUCT). In our new terminology, we can say that the focus of attention is the product and that it is focused on by means of the producer. In other words, we can suggest that "providing mental access to something" means the same as "focusing on something."

The other two examples are cases of the active zone phenomenon, which I also discussed in the chapter on metonymy. Here the whole stands for a part. The piano (whole) focuses attention on the sounds made (part) and the personal pronoun *I* (whole) on the name I have (part). In such cases, the shift in profile, or focus of attention, is accomplished by the verb. We can't hear the piano, only the sounds made by it, and we can't actually be in the phone book, but our names can.

In all these cases, a particular aspect of a situation, event, or entity is highlighted.

Scope of Attention

The focus of attention is surrounded by the periphery of attention, or consciousness. This peripheral area of attention is called the scope of attention. The focus and scope of attention have consequences for the grammaticality of sentences. I mentioned an example of this in the discussion of frames. We conceive of knuckles as being parts of the finger, fingers as parts of the hand, the hand as part of the arm, and the arm as part of the body. Thus, it makes sense to say that the domain within which an entity becomes accessible to attention has an entity (Langacker, 1987: 119):

(9)   A finger has three knuckles and a fingernail.

But it is not really acceptable to say:

(10)   ???A body has twenty-eight knuckles.

The reason is that the concept of "knuckle" has as its immediate scope the "fingers" or the "hands," but the "body" is not within this immediate scope. In other words, this kind of statement is only possible when the immediate scope—but not when the more distant scope—is involved.

We also make use of the notion of the "scope of attention" when we construe the location of an entity in relation to other entities. For example, we can tell someone about the location of money in relation to the kitchen, which has a counter, which has a cabinet underneath it, which has shelves, and which has a meat grinder on the top shelf. We can express this as follows (Croft and Cruse, 2004: 50):

(11)   The money is in the kitchen, under the counter, in the lefthand cabinet, on the top shelf, behind the meat grinder.

The meat grinder provides the most immediate scope of attention and the kitchen the most distant scope. The sentence suggests a construal in which we start with the most distant scope of attention for the profiled entity, the money, and then we move on to successively narrower domains in which the profiled entity can be found.

Detail of Attention (Scalar Adjustment)

The notion of scalar adjustment has to do with how closely we attend to the details of the scene. This aspect of construal was studied extensively by Len Talmy (see, e.g., Talmy, 1983).

We can have a coarse-grained or a fine-grained view of the same situation, as can be seen in the following sentences (Talmy, 1983):

(12) She ran *across* the field.

(13) She ran *through* the field.

The first sentence looks at the situation "from a distance," so to speak. No details of the scene are suggested in any way. However, the second sentence indicates through the word *through* a more fine-grained view; it lets us imagine the field as having grass, weeds, bushes, and so on, through which the person runs.

The same idea can be exemplified with other sentences, taken from Croft and Cruse (2004: 52):

(14) We drove *along* the road.

(15) A squirrel ran *across* the road.

(16) The construction workers dug *through* the road.

As far as the degree of detail in construal is concerned, the basic difference among the three sentences is that they represent different degrees of attention to detail. In the first sentence, the road is merely a line, a one-dimensional object; in the second, it is a two-dimensional one; and in the third, it is three-dimensional.

Scalar adjustment is not limited to visual experience only. We can construe other types of experience with lower or greater degree of detail. When we say that "John's being silly," the construal is more fine grained than when we say that "John's silly." John's silliness is temporary in the former case with clear temporal boundaries, while it is permanent in the latter and it is taken to be a personality trait in the latter.

Dynamic or Static Nature of Attention

Our attention can scan a scene dynamically or statically. We can either move our attention across a scene or construe it as something static. This difference in construal has been applied to the state-process distinction by Talmy and to the predication-nonpredication distinction by Langacker.

Take the following sentence by Talmy (2000):

(17) The road *winds through* the valley and then *climbs over* the high mountains.

What we find here (indicated by italics) is what Talmy calls "fictive motion," that is, motion that does not really take place. When we use this sentence, we talk about observing a static scene. After all, the road does not move. However, we view this static scene dynamically, as if the road were moving.

Consider now Langacker's (1987) examples:

(18)   The Boston Bridge collapsed.

(19)   The collapse of the Boston Bridge.

In the first sentence, the word *collapse* is used in a predicative function; we say what happened to the Boston Bridge. That is to say, we have a dynamic scene viewed dynamically. Langacker calls this sequential scanning. The scene is dynamic because we can observe something happening through time.

By contrast, the second phrase construes the situation differently. It suggests what Langacker calls summary scanning. This is viewing the situation as a single static frame that somehow "summarizes" a whole series of events—not in terms of a process unfolding through time. The collapse of the bridge is an event, an essentially dynamic situation, but we choose to present it in a static way by making use of summary scanning.

Typically, dynamic situations are construed by means of sequential scanning and are expressed by means of verb phrases in sentences. The verb phrases are used predicatively. However, we can construe essentially dynamic situations by means of summary scanning and we can express them by means of noun phrases that we do not use predicatively. This is what happens in the case of *the collapse of the Boston Bridge*. But of course we can predicate something of such noun phrases; for example, we can say, "The collapse of the Boston Bridge was quick."

In general, the two kinds of scanning a situation (summary vs. sequential scanning) are used by Langacker to distinguish *things* and *relations*—the highest-level conceptual units. Things are expressed as nouns and adjectives, while relations are expressed as verbs, prepositions, and conjunctions.

Judgment and Comparison

Croft and Cruse (2004) argue that judgment and comparison are general cognitive operations that we constantly employ as we conceptualize the situations we are involved in. When we judge a situation in any way, we make use of comparison. What are the more specific cognitive operations that are based on comparison?

Croft and Cruse mention categorization, metaphor, and figure-ground alignment. Since I have already discussed categorization and metaphor in detail, I will treat them very briefly here.

Categorization/Framing

When we categorize an object, event, or situation, we compare it to prior experience. Most of the time, the prior experiences with any of these form categories and the categories will have a name. When I compare this animal that I notice on the street, I may have no difficulty assigning it to the category of DOGS. The unconscious process of comparing this particular animal to the others I have seen and have a category and name for will result in my placing the animal in the category of DOGS. But often the comparison will produce a much more dubious result. For example, some dogs look very much like cats. We may have a dilemma as to what to call the thing. Prototypes as represented by idealized cognitive models, or frames, can be helpful in taking care of such difficulties. We have seen a number of such cases in the chapters on categorization and framing.

Metaphor

Another cognitive operation that involves comparison is metaphor. When we have a target domain and ask what it is like, we are asking what source domain would serve our purposes best in a given situation. Since most target domains can be comprehended in terms of multiple source domains, metaphor is a cognitive operation that can easily provide alternative construal of the same situation. Take the following examples, used to talk about the exact same situation:

(20)   What's going on?

(21)   What's cooking?

When we use the first question we are conceptualizing events/happenings as moving objects, and when we use the second we are conceptualizing an event/happening as the process of cooking. This is trivial, but it is easy to imagine much more dramatic differences in viewing a particular target situation. Just think of a student who believes that school is a store of knowledge and another who believes that it is a burden. Or think of a couple, where one member thinks of marriage or love as a great opportunity to enjoy life and the other thinks that it is a prison.

In the preceding examples, people have alternative conceptual metaphors for a given target, but often alternative construal emerges within the same source domain. Take the following examples:

(22)   I spent most of the day playing golf.

(23)   I wasted most of the day playing golf.

Both conceptualizations are based on the TIME IS MONEY conceptual metaphor, but the choice of words (*spent* vs. *wasted*) portrays the situation as very differently conceived. The verb *spent* suggests that I did something valuable, whereas *wasted* conveys the opposite.

Figure-Ground Alignment

Like attention, figure-ground relations have been studied mostly by cognitive psychologists. What is called "figure-ground" alignment here is important if we want to account for how we talk about spatial relations in language. Language about spatial relations is pervasive in communication. We talk about how one entity is positioned with respect to another entity, how an entity moves in relation to another entity, and so on. For example, when we say that "the bus is coming," we have a figure, the bus, that is presented by the sentence as moving in relation to the ground, the speaker. The first cognitive linguist who studied this area of the interface between language and cognition in detail was Len Talmy (see Talmy, 1983, 2000a,b).

To begin, we should first note that figure-ground alignment is an asymmetrical relation. Let us assume that we have *bike* as figure and *house* as ground in the following sentences (Talmy, 2000a). Whereas one can naturally say:

(24)   The bike is near the house.

it is much less natural to say:

(25)   ??The house is near the bike.

This is because the figure should come first in the sentence, followed by the ground. The reversal of figure-ground alignment in the second sentence makes the sentence sound odd.

The same applies to the following pair of sentences:

(26)   a. The fly is on the ceiling.

b.*The ceiling is above the fly.

Why are *the bike* and *the fly* the figure and *the house* and *the ceiling* the ground? Talmy (2000a) characterizes figure and ground in the following way:

Figure:	*Ground:*
smaller	larger
more mobile	more stationary
structurally simpler	structurally more complex
more salient	more backgrounded
more recently in awareness	earlier on scene/in memory
location less known	location more known

These characteristics do not all have to be present in particular cases and we often decide on what the figure and ground will be on the basis on just one or two situationally important features. In the preceding examples, it is clear that the bike and the flea are smaller and more mobile than the house and the ceiling, respectively. This makes them good figures in the given context. In other contexts, however, they may become grounds.

We may ask what figure-ground alignment has to do with judgment/comparison. The simple answer is that in every situation we unconsciously decide which element of the situation is the figure and which one is the ground. We compare the elements in light of the characteristics suggested earlier. As a result of the comparison and judgment, we conceptualize the situation in a particular way (with the proper figure-ground alignment) and express it linguistically in accordance with this conceptualization.

The two examples we have seen so far involve static relations between two entities (bike-near-house and flea-on-ceiling). However, as our characterization of spatial relations earlier suggests, spatial relations also involve motion events, in which one entity moves in relation to another. This is exemplified by the sentence:

(27)   She went into the house.

In this case, we have a motion event, where *she* is the figure and *house* is the ground. The figure (*she*) moves in relation to the ground (*house*).

In addition to its application to static and dynamic spatial relations, figure-ground alignment can be seen at work in grammar as well. Complex sentences can be construed in terms of figure-ground alignment; the main clause corresponds to the figure, while the subordinate clause corresponds to the ground. Let us take the following sentences from Croft and Cruse (2004: 57):

(28)   I read while she sewed.

(29)   I read and she sewed.

The main clause *I read* is the figure and the subordinate clause *while she sewed* is the ground. The relation between the two events is construed asymmetrically in the first sentence but symmetrically in the second. This means that the reading event is viewed as occurring against the background of the sewing event. However, given the second sentence, no such relation is construed between the two events, which are seen as occurring independently of each other. This latter construal results in a coordinated syntactic construction (the two clauses connected by *and*).

In other cases, the two events can only be construed as an asymmetrical figure-ground relation. Since dreaming is contingent on sleeping, but sleeping is not contingent on dreaming (Talmy, 2000a: 325), we can have

(30)   He dreamed while he slept.

but not

(31)   *He slept while he dreamed.

While it is common in both cognitive science and linguistics to talk about "figure" and "ground," some cognitive linguists like Langacker prefer to use alternative terminology: They use *trajector* for figure and *landmark* for ground. For my purposes, I will use these terms interchangeably in this book.

Perspective

We conceptualize situations from our particular perspective. Although perspective is mostly spatial, it can also be extended to other domains, such as the knowledge we have and we assume others to have about situations. I now will consider several ways in which the notion of "perspective" plays a role; specifically: viewpoint, deixis, and subjectivity/objectivity.

Viewpoint

Consider first how an observer interprets and talks about a particular scene, or situation, in which there is, say, a ball and a tree and the ball is between the observer and the tree. In this situation, the observer might use the following sentence to describe the scene:

(32)   The ball is in front of the tree.

If, however, the observer goes to the other side of the tree and observes the situation from this new viewpoint, he or she would describe the scene with the sentence

(33)   The ball is behind the tree.

Notice that there is no change in the scene to be conceptualized and described: The ball and the tree do not move. The only change that occurs is in the viewpoint of the observer. As a result of that change, both the construal and the description change.

Deixis

Deixis can be viewed as alternative construal defined by the speech situation. The most basic elements of the speech situation include the time when the speech event takes place, the place where the speech event takes place, and the person who speaks. Accordingly, it is customary to distinguish three basic types of deixis: time, place, and person deixis. There are many linguistic items that are primarily used to signal the elements of the speech situation. What follows is a selection of them:

Time: now, then
Place: here, there
Person: I, you, he, she, we, they

Thus, for example, the pronoun *I* indicates the person who is speaking, *here* indicates where the speaker is located, and *now* indicates the time at which something is said. Every time these and other "deictic" words are used, the reference of the words changes. In one case it will be John and in another it will be Jill (*I*); in one case it will be John's home and in another it will be John's school (*here*); and in one case time reference will be to April 22 and in another it will be to April 23 (*now*).

It is not only particular words that can function deictically. What are known as the "tenses" also function as deictic elements. Thus when I say, "I'm missing you," the hearer will know that I am missing him or her at the time of speaking. And when I say that "I missed you," the hearer will know that I missed her sometime before the time of speaking. In other words, the present continuous tense and the past tense both mean what they mean relative to the time of the speech event; that is, they are deictic elements.

It is generally the case that the speech act situation (the time and place of speaking) functions as the "deictic center," that is, the time and place with respect to which we understand the time and place references of the speech event (the now and here). However, in some special cases a time or place other than the one defined by the speech act situation can become the deictic center. This displaced deictic center is suggested by the sentences taken from Croft and Cruse (2004):

(34)   He was coming up the steps. There was a broad smile on his face.

We have a displaced deictic center here that is defined by the time and place of the narrative of which the sentences are a part. The meaning of *come* is relative to a place in the narrative, and not the place of the narration itself; and the meaning of the past continuous tense is relative to a speech event time in the narrative, and not to the speech event of the narration. In sum, the deictic center provided by the time and place of the narration is displaced, and it is replaced by certain time and place coordinates in the narrative.

Particular construals of a situation depend not only on who says something when and where but also on how much knowledge we assume the hearer to have about a situation (Clark, 1996). Take the two sentences (from Croft and Cruse, 2004):

(35)   Did you see a hedgehog?

(36)   Did you see the hedgehog?

The difference between the two sentences is in the use of the indefinite article *a* versus the definite article *the*. They reflect different construals of the situation. Given the first sentence, the speaker construes the situation in the following way: Speaker assumes that the hearer does not share some information with him or her; namely, that the hearer does not know about the hedgehog. Given the second sentence, the speaker assumes that the hearer does know about the hedgehog. In other words, in such cases particular construals of situations (and their linguistic coding) may depend on the common ground that the speaker and hearer share.

Subjectivity/Objectivity

We can have either an objective or a subjective construal of a situation (Langacker, 1987). This has to do with how we present ourselves in the speech situation. The subjectivity of construal may take various forms.

In one, the speaker defines himself or herself by means of a deictic pronoun as part of the speech act situation. Contrast the following two sentences, in which a mother is talking to a child (Langacker, 1987: 131):

(37)   Don't lie to me!

(38)   Don't lie to your mother!

The first sentence represents subjective construal (the mother being part of the speech act situation), while the second represents an objective one, in which the speaker defines herself objectively independent of the speech act situation.

An entity that is not the speaker can also be presented in a subjective way. For example, when we look a photograph, we can say the following (Langacker, 1987: 132):

(39)   That's me in the top row.

The first-person deictic pronoun is used here, but it is not the speaker. By using the word *me,* we turn an element of the situation we're understanding into an element of the speech event. This is another form of "subjectification."

Finally, we can have cases in which the construal of a situation depends on whether an element of the speech event (subjective construal) or an objective element (objective construal) is utilized in describing a scene. Take, for example, the following sentences (Langacker, 1991a: 326, 328):

(40)   Vanessa is sitting across the table from Veronica.

(41)   Vanessa is sitting across the table from me.

(42)   Vanessa is sitting across the table.

The first sentence is a case of objective construal, in which an element (Veronica) of the external situation (and not that of the speech event) is utilized for spatially relating Vanessa in the scene. However, the second sentence does this by means of subjective construal: Vanessa is spatially located with respect to an element of the speech event (me). The third sentence does the same, except that here subjectivity is unexpressed—only implied.

Overall Structure

The final category of cognitive operations to be discussed includes operations that we use to make sense of the overall structure of entities and events in a scene. For this purpose, we have three extremely basic operations at our disposal: structural schematization, force dynamics, and relationality (Croft and Cruse, 2004).

Structural Schematization

One aspect of the operation of structural schematization is concerned with whether the entities in a scene are individuated or not (Croft and Cruse, 2004; Langacker, 1987).

For most purposes, we construe a hat, a chair, a star, and a leaf as individuated or "bounded entities." We see them as individuated entities in spatiotemporal reality. When we conceptualize "things" in this way, we code them linguistically as count nouns.

By contrast, things that we conceptualize as nonindividuated are "unbounded entities." Typical examples include dust, water, salt, and so forth. Such entities are linguistically coded as mass nouns.

When we perceive a large number of bounded entities, we can construe them as "multiple bounded entities." Multiple bounded entities appear as plural count nouns in language. Thus, we talk about hats, chairs, stars, and so on.

However, we can also construe many bounded entities as "unbounded entities." For example, if we see many leaves, we can alternatively refer to them as *foliage*. The word *foliage* is a singular mass noun that is unbounded. Similarly, we can think of several instances of chairs, tables, and so on, as furniture and refer to them by the singular mass noun furniture.

There is an interesting difference in construal between bounded entities conceptualized as bounded entities and bounded entities conceptualized as unbounded entities (resulting in mass nouns). The conceptualization of a large number of bounded entities as unbounded ones, such as furniture and foliage, suggests a coarse-grained construal, whereas the conceptualization of a large number of bounded entities, such as leaves, chairs, and tables, taken collectively, suggests a fine-grained construal. In short, to see a large number of bounded entities as a mass ignores many of the details that are characteristic of the conceptualization of individual entities.

Multiple bounded entities can also be construed as a singular bounded entity. For example, a team or a government consists of multiple bounded entities that we conceptualize as a unit. The conceptualization of multiple bounded entities as a unit results in singular count nouns, such as *team* or *government*.

Interestingly, the bounded-unbounded distinction can be extended to the analysis of states—and not just entities. Consider the following two sentences discussed earlier in the chapter (under scalar adjustment):

(43) He is silly.

(44) He is being silly.

The difference between the use of the "simple present tense" and the "present continuous tense" in the two sentences can be accounted for by the bounded-unbounded distinction. The simple present tense suggests the construal of the situation as unbounded (as in the first sentence), whereas the present continuous tense suggests the construal of the situation as bounded (as in the second sentence). What this means is that the simple present "draws" no temporal boundaries around the state, whereas the present continuous presents the state as having temporal boundaries relative to the "now" of the speech event.

Image-Schematic Structure

Another aspect of the overall structure of entities concerns their image-schematic structure, as discussed in the previous chapter. There we also saw that the understanding of situations in term of image-schemas can be metaphorical; that is, not only physical entities can be conceptualized in terms of image-schemas but also states and events. Since I dealt with this issue in a previous chapter, I will make only a few observations that seem relevant to the study of alternative conceptualization based on image-schemas (Croft and Cruse, 2004; Langacker, 1987; Taylor, 2002).

First, the same entity can be construed in different ways in different languages. Compare, for instance, the noun *tree* in English and Hungarian:

(45) There is a bird in the tree.
      Egy madár van   a fán.
      One bird   be-3rd PERS SING the tree-on
      There is a bird on the tree.

As these two sentences indicate, in English the entity tree is conceptualized as a container, whereas in Hungarian it is construed as a surface.

As a matter of fact, even two dialects of the same language can reveal alternative construal for the same entity. Let us take the entity street and how this is talked about in American and British English:

(46) She lives on this street.

(47) She lives in this street.

The entity is viewed as a surface in American English, whereas it is seen as a container in British English.

Second, the same image-schema-based linguistic expression can be differentially interpreted depending on context. Consider the preposition *under*.

When we say that someone stood under the tree, we think of a canonical position in which the person is standing under the lowest branches of a tree and is above the ground. Compare, however, the following two sentences:

(48)   He was *under the tree.*

(49)   He was buried *under the tree.*

Given the first sentence, we imagine the person to be standing in the canonical position, that is, standing (or sitting) above the ground under the lowest branches of the tree. However, the second sentence suggests another construal for the expression *under the tree*, namely, that the person is lying under the surface of the ground in the region under the branches of the tree. In other words, we may have a canonical interpretation for the expression in many cases, but in the appropriate context this canonical interpretation, or construal, can be significantly modified.

Let us take another example:

(50)   The cat was under the table.

Here again, when we hear the preceding sentence, we are inclined to imagine the cat as being under the tabletop—not under the legs of the table. That is the canonical, more conventional position for the cat to be in. In other contexts, though, such as a situation after an earthquake, one could imagine a cat as being under the legs of the table—not simply under the tabletop. In other words, the very same sentence can be used to denote very different situations.

Third, following Langacker, Taylor (2002) draws a distinction between "simple" and "complex relations." A simple relation is one where we construe a single relation between the trajector and landmark. (On trajector and landmark, see earlier discussion.) Take the phrase *the picture above the sofa* (Taylor, 2002: 217). We construe a single relation between the picture and the sofa. The word *above* represents a simple relation between the trajector (picture) and the landmark (sofa). Other words that designate simple relations include stative verbs, such as *be, stand, lie,* and *resemble.* If you say that someone resembles someone else, you are construing a static, unchanging relation between the trajector and landmark.

By contrast, complex relations involve the construal of multiple relations between trajector and landmark. As Taylor notes, the verb *leave* designates a number of relations between the two. First you as trajector are in an entity (landmark); then you move through a series of locations to a place that is out of the landmark entity. Dynamic verbs are good examples of words that construe the situation in terms of multiple relations between the trajector and landmark. Other examples include prepositions such as *across.* Compare the following two sentences (Taylor, 2002: 218):

(51) I walked *across* the field.

(52) He lives *across* the field.

In the first sentence we have a complex relation between the trajector (I) and the landmark (field). As I walk across the field, I occupy a number of different locations along the path of movement. These different locations represent a series of different relations between me and the field. In the second sentence, however, there is only a single relation—a simple one—between me and the field. As noted earlier, this is characteristic of stative verbs like *live*.

Force Dynamics

I briefly introduced force dynamics in the previous chapter, where I showed how we can interpret various emotion metaphors as the interaction of forces between the self and the emotion. Following Len Talmy (1988a), I distinguished two entities that affect each other in a force-dynamic interaction: the agonist (typically corresponding to the self) and the antagonist (typically corresponding to the emotion and the cause of emotion).

More generally, we can think of force dynamics as a cognitive operation that is used in the conceptualization of events. Whenever we interpret an event, we are interpreting the interplay of forces in the situation. The notions of "agonist" and "antagonist" are helpful in the discussion of how one entity affects or does not affect another entity in the same event. I can define the antagonist, in line with what I did in chapter 12, as the entity that causes another entity to change its force tendency (either to rest or to act). The entity that is caused to change its force tendency is the agonist. The agonist has a force tendency to either rest or action (motion), whereas the antagonist has a force tendency to cause change (action or motion) in the agonist.

Take the following sentences from Croft and Cruse (2004: 66):

(53) I kicked the ball.

(54) I held the ball.

(55) I dropped the ball.

We have three different kinds of causation involved in the three sentences: direct causation, causation as resistance to change, and causation as enablement. In the first sentence, *I* is the antagonist that causes the ball to move and the *ball* is the agonist that has a force tendency to rest. This is an example of direct causation. In the second sentence, the antagonist causes the agonist (which has a force tendency to move) to not move, meaning that the antagonist does not allow the ball to move (i.e., there is resistance to change). In the third sentence, the antagonist does not succeed in resisting the force tendency of the agonist, thus effectively enabling the ball to move. Thus, the antagonist actually causes change in the first sentence, resists change in the second, and enables change in the third.

This generalized pattern of causation in terms of force dynamics stands in contrast to cases where we do not construe the situation as involving forces in interaction with each other. These are stative situations, which we conceptualize as lacking any force-dynamic interaction. Compare the following two sentences (Croft and Cruse, 2004: 66):

(56)   The bowl was on the table.

(57)   The bowl stayed on the table.

When we use the first sentence, we do not construe the relationship between the bowl and the table as force-dynamically related. The sentence is simply the expression of a static spatial relationship between the two entities. However, the second sentence does imply a force-dynamic construal. It suggests that the bowl stayed on the table despite a force acting on it. What the force acting on the bowl is, is not specified by the sentence.

Although force dynamics as a construal operation is primarily used for the conceptualization of causation, it can also be applied to other domains. I will deal with these other domains that involve force dynamics in chapter 16.

Relationality

Conceptual entities can be construed as being related or unrelated to other entities (Langacker, 1987). The construal of entities as being unrelated, that is, conceptually autonomous, results in the grammatical category of NOUNS. The construal of conceptual entities as being related results in the grammatical category of VERBS, MODIFIERS, and PREPOSITIONS. They indicate entities that are not conceptually autonomous.

As an example, let us take the sentence

(58)   Runners run fast.

In the sentence, the noun *runner* is construed as a conceptually autonomous entity, while the verb *run* and the modifier *fast* are conceptually nonautonomous. In general, we can characterize verbs, modifiers, and nouns in the following way:

> *Verbs*: conceptual entities construed as *relational* and *sequentially scanned* (i.e., temporal): *run*
> *Modifiers*: conceptual entities construed as *relational* and *summarily scanned* (i.e., atemporal): *fast*
> *Nouns*: conceptual entities construed as *nonrelational* and *summarily scanned* (i.e., atemporal): *runner*

As can be seen, this characterization makes use of both the relationality of conceptual entities and the particular way of mentally scanning them (sequential vs. summary scanning), as discussed earlier in this chapter. Conceptually independent entities are "things," whereas conceptually dependent ones are "relations." These latter are processes in time. The two major word classes, nouns and verbs, correspond to things and relations, respectively.

In this view, the same situation can be construed as either a thing or a relation. When we talk about the *collapse of the Boston Bridge*, we construe a dynamic situation as thinglike, with static attention and summary scanning (vs. dynamic attention and sequential scanning, as in *The Boston bridge collapsed*), that is, as being nonrelational and atemporal. Another example for the same phenomenon would be the pair of sentences:

(59)   a. He suffered terribly.

      b. His suffering was terrible.

The first sentence conceptualizes an experience as a relational and temporal event, while the second views it as nonrelational and atemporal.

Thus, prototypical nouns are conceptual entities that profile things, are conceptually autonomous, and are time-stable. Good examples are nouns like *shoe*, *tree*, and *house*.

Finally, there are many nouns that refer to relations—not things. Such nouns include relational nouns, like *mother*, *father*, *sister*, *brother*, and so on. The phrase *the mother of Sally* (as in *Sue is the mother of Sally*) profiles a thing in a relation. The relation is between the entities, or "things," Sue and Sally, and it is that of being a mother. In other words, the noun phrase *the mother of* profiles a thing in the relation between two entities.

Grammatical Conceptualization and Linguistic Relativity

Several cognitive linguists have pointed out that grammar reflects ways of conceptualizing the world at a highly schematic level (see especially Langacker, 1987, 1991a). We can express the same kind of conceptual-experiential content by means of different conceptualizations, or construal operations. For example, the possessive relation between two entities can be expressed in several structurally different ways in different languages (Heine, 1997).

This idea takes us back to the issue of linguistic relativity. In Whorf's view, the grammatical structures we use habitually shape our thinking about the world. Thus, we can ask: Does grammatical conceptualization determine the way we think? Langacker (1987) suggests the following answer. He takes the different ways of expressing the same content in different languages. The example that he discusses in this connection is saying that one is cold. We find several grammatically different ways of doing this in different languages:

(60)   a. I am cold. (English)

     b. I have cold. (French)

     c. It's cold to me. (Modern Hebrew)

     d. I'm colding. (Hungarian)

All of these sentences express the same conceptual-experiential content. Can we claim that the different grammatical conceptualizations determine the way we think and feel when we are cold? Langacker suggests that we cannot because the different structures express the same conceptual-experiential content and that we speak differently as a result of differential conceptualization in grammar, for expressive purposes, but this does not affect the way we actually think, feel, or experience. In other words, the conceptual content expressed is basically the same, but its construal is different from language to language. It seems then that, on this view, language structure does not shape cognition, but we construe the same experience according to the conventional grammatical conceptualizations provided by the particular language we speak as native speakers. This idea is basically the same as that by Slobin (1987, 1996), who suggests that "we think for the way we speak." Using Langacker's terminology, this would be roughly equivalent to "we construe experience (for expressive purposes) in the way we speak about that experience."

Construal Operations and Culture

Is there any relationship between the construal operations we have seen earlier and culture at large? Aren't the operations just in our heads when we are engaged in the production and understanding of linguistic utterances? The answer is that they are not just cognitive operations used for language processing and that they are very clearly present in many aspects of culture.

Perhaps the clearest way to appreciate the importance of construal operations beyond their linguistic use is to consider various kinds of art. In many ways, the understanding of art relies on the same cognitive operations that we have discussed in this chapter. Obvious examples include perspective and figure-ground alignment. Perspective has been a major factor in painting. In a way, the history of painting and sculpting is the history of how the notion of perspective has changed throughout the ages. Also, in individual paintings we can get several different perspectives that carry important messages for the meaning of the paintings. Perspective and viewpoint play an obviously important role in the understanding of many literary works. As a matter of fact, an important way in which literary works and narratives in general can be distinguished from each other is whose perspective is taken by the narrator in telling the story. Figure-ground structure is equally crucial in many types of art. Clearly, all the visual arts rely heavily on it, but its role is just as pronounced in music. Certain sounds are more emphatic and are in the foreground against the background of other sounds.

That the use of construal operations extends way beyond language is almost a truism. A large part of literary and art criticism is in the business of exploring the absolutely crucial role of such cognitive operations in the reception and creation of art, as well as within individual pieces of art. Len Talmy (2000b) provides a systematic account of the implications of construal operations for the study of what he calls the "cultural system" and narrative structure.

Conclusions

Construals are particular ways of understanding the world. As we saw, the relationship between language (linguistic expressions), construal, and the world is manifold. The *same linguistic expression* may be used to refer to *different aspects of the same situation* (e.g., *window* can refer to the pane or the frame). *Different linguistic expressions* may be used to reflect *different construals of the same situation* (e.g., *walk across the field* and *walk through the field*). The *same linguistic expression* may be used to refer to *very different situations in the world* (e.g., *under the tree* may mean that someone is standing under the lowest branches of the tree but also that someone is lying buried under the ground in the region of the branches of the tree). All of these possibilities involve cases of alternative construal.

The main job of the embodied mind is the understanding of the world. The capacity of the mind for alternative construal is one extremely important aspect of the process of comprehending the world. There are many cognitive operations that we use for the purpose of alternative construal. Four large groups have been identified in this chapter: cognitive operations having to do with *attention, judgment and comparison, perspective* and *overall structure*.

The notion of alternative construal changes our conception of meaning. In the new view, meaning is not to be identified with conceptual content alone; it is constituted by *conceptual content, as well as the construal of that content*. In many cases, the construal aspect of meaning plays a more important function in discourse than conceptual content.

That we talk about the same experience by making use of different grammatical structures in different languages does not mean that the different ways of speaking determine or shape the way we think or feel at a deeper level. However, the different ways of speaking do seem to imply *different construals* of the same experiential content for that purpose.

Exercises

1.

A. Look at the following sentences and decide which ones illustrate a case of *objective* and which ones *subjective* construal:

I'm in the phone book.
The teacher is standing in front of Jerry.
The teacher is standing in front of me.
You can be sure that your grandma loves you.
Why don't you love me?
The teacher is standing in front of her desk.

B. Identify the construal operations in the following examples.

    i.   The football is under the table.
   ii.   We had a picnic in the field.
  iii.   Many thousands of soldiers remained dead in the field.
   iv.   Negotiation failed.
    v.   Failure of the negotiations.
   vi.   The glass is half-full
   vi.   The glass is half-empty.
  vii.   He is always complaining.

C. What kind of construal is represented by the following pair of sentences? Explain the difference in conceptualization.

    i.   Sue walked across the road.
   ii.   Sue is sitting across the table from Jim.

2. What are these sentences examples of? They exhibit differences in which category of construal operations?

  a.   University is expensive.
  b.   She entered the university.
  c.   The university has several departments.↔
  c'. *Europe has several departments.
(Even c". *Europe has several universities.)
  d.   She applied at an/the university.
  e.   The university cost several million dollars last year.

3. What construal operation(s) are the following examples of? Recall the chapters on categorization (chapters 2 and 3). How can they be connected to this chapter?

  a.   animal   —   cat
  b.   quadrangle —   rectangle
  c.   furniture   —   stool

4.
A. In this chapter I have discussed how Talmy distinguishes between figures and grounds. Look at the following pairs of sentences and decide which

sentence is acceptable in each pair. Then decide which entity is the figure and which one is the ground. Use Talmy's chart to state why.

A fly is under the president's nose.
The president('s nose) is above the fly.
The car was behind the Coliseum.
The Coliseum was behind the car.
A toy car was next to a millionaire's Ferrari.
The Ferrari was next to a toy car.

B. What is the difference between the following two sentences regarding the figure-ground relations:

i. The book is in front of the newspaper and the pencil.
ii. The book is in front of the newspaper and the newspaper is in front of the pencil.

14

Constructing Meaning in Discourse

Mental Spaces

Mappings operate not only within a single domain (metonymy) and be-tween two domains (metaphor) but also between what are called mental spaces—partial conceptual structures (frames or models) in the mind. With the help of mappings between mental spaces we can account for another cru-cially important aspect of meaning, namely, the way meaning is constructed in discourse.

The idea that "meaning is constructed" should be understood in a special way. Meaning construction is opposed to the view of meaning as somehow given or prepackaged in linguistic expressions. (This view is captured by M. Reddy's CONDUIT metaphor. See Reddy, 1979.) Meaning does not seem to be prepackaged in words waiting to be taken out by people participating in discourse. On the contrary, we are active participants in constructing mean-ing on-line in specific contexts. The expressions we use acquire their mean-ing as a product of how we build mental spaces and set up mappings between them in specific situations.

Meaning construction has several important features. First, it is happen-ing at lightning speed. Second, it is a part of our backstage cognition, which we are not consciously aware of. And third, human beings perform it with amazing ease. Most of the time, we do not find it at all difficult to produce and understand language when we communicate with others.

But similar to many of the other cognitive processes we have seen earlier in this book, the setting up of mental spaces and the conceptual connections between them are not limited to the understanding of language. We use men-tal spaces quickly, unconsciously, and with ease to think and to act in gen-eral. The masterful manipulation of mental spaces on our part pervades all of our efforts to find meaning in our experience.

We owe the idea of mental spaces to Gilles Fauconnier, and the account of the role of mental spaces in meaning construction to be presented in this chapter is based primarily on his work (1985/1994, 1997).

Characterizing Mental Spaces

A mental space is a "conceptual packet" that gets built up on-line in the course of communication. To use an analogy, we can think of mental spaces as small lightbulbs lighting up in the brain/mind. The area "lit up" corresponds to an activated mental space.

Consider some examples taken from Fauconnier (1997):

(1)   Richard is wonderful.

(2)   Liz thinks Richard is wonderful.

With the second sentence, we build a space for Liz's beliefs, namely, a belief space in which Richard is wonderful.

(3)   Last year, Richard was wonderful.

In this sentence, we build a space for last year. What is activated is a mental space set up by the expression *last year*, in which Richard was wonderful.

(4)   Liz thinks that last year Richard was wonderful.

This last sentence gives us even more complications. In it, we build a space for last year that is embedded in a belief space that is embedded in a "base space." In other words, several mental spaces can be embedded in one another. Ultimately, however, there must be a space from which other mental spaces derive. This ultimate mental space is called the base space. In example (1), it consists of the speaker of the sentence *Richard is wonderful* and the time (and possibly the place) when (and where) the statement was made.

Space Builders

One of the most important aspects of mental space theory is what we call space builders. Space builders help us set up particular mental spaces. One of the most commonly used ones is adverbials of time, such as *yesterday*:

(5)   Yesterday, I saw Susan.

Here there are two mental spaces: one for the speaker's present reality (corresponding to the base space, which has the speaker of the sentence and the time/place of the statement) and one for yesterday (corresponding to the yesterday mental space).

Other space builders include *Just imagine* (used to build an imagination space), *I would like* (used to build a desire space), *what if* (used to build a hypotheticality space), *imaginary* (as in *an imaginary illness*, used to build a fake belief space), and *would-be* (as in *a would-be actor*, used to build a hypothetical future space).

As can be seen from these examples and others, various grammatical forms can be used as space builders. Let us take some additional ones:

> in 1956, in that story, actually, in reality, in Susan's opinion, Susan believes, Max hopes, if it rains, and many others

In other words, space builders are not limited to a particular word class and they vary in their degree of frequency in discourse. The special importance of space builders lies in the fact that they *explicitly signal* the kinds of mental spaces we build in the course of communication.

The Treatment of the Same Phenomena in Formal Theories

Previous theories of meaning have also treated the kind of phenomenon that is handled by mental spaces. In formal theories of meaning the notion of "possible worlds" is used to account for roughly the same kind of phenomenon that mental spaces are used to account for. One major difference between possible worlds and mental spaces is that possible worlds are taken to be complete alternative universes, whereas mental spaces are thought of as partial cognitive models of some situation. Another difference between the two is related to this. Since possible worlds contain too many facts about the world, they cannot all be represented in the mind. For this reason, possible worlds do not seem to have any cognitive reality. We simply do not know where they are supposed to be. This is a major metaphysical problem with possible worlds. By contrast, because of their partial nature and smaller size as cognitive representations of the world, mental spaces can be claimed to be cognitively real. We can think of them as small activated areas of the brain/mind.

The Difference between Mental Spaces and Domains

On the one hand, mental spaces resemble domains, or frames, in that they are also structured areas of experience. On the other hand, they are different from them in several ways.

First, mental spaces are smaller than domains. The mental space of yesterday in the sentence *Yesterday, I saw Susan* contains just the speaker and Susan and the relationship of seeing between them.

Second, mental spaces are more specific than domains. The mental space in the previous sentence contains specific people: a specific speaker and a specific Susan. In domains, or frames, we have more general roles filled by specific entities.

Third, mental spaces may be structured by (several) domains, or frames. In the sentence *Yesterday, I asked Susan for her telephone number*, there are at least three participating domains that structure a particular mental space: the domain of TEMPORAL RELATIONS, the REQUEST domain, and possibly also a DATING domain. Let us now take another sentence:

(6)   Jack buys gold from Jill.

The sentence evokes a frame that we already saw in the chapter on frames: the COMMERCIAL EVENT frame. This structures the mental space that we build for the sentence. There are mappings between the frame and the space we use to make sense of the new space. These are as follows:

Buyer—Jack
Seller—Jill
Goods—gold

To understand the sentence, we unconsciously set up such mappings between the new mental space introduced by the sentence *Jack buys gold from Jill* and the COMMERCIAL EVENT frame.

Mappings between Two Mental Spaces

Such connections are often established not only between a new mental space and a frame but also between two mental spaces. Consider as an example the so-called "picture noun" context, as made explicit by the second sentence:

(7)   The girl with blue eyes has green eyes.

(8)   In the picture, the girl with blue eyes has green eyes.

There are two mental spaces here: the mental space of reality, as we represent it to ourselves, and the mental space of the picture, as we perceive it. The mental space of reality is the base space and the mental space of the picture is a "model" space (or picture space). To understand the sentence, the mappings go from the base space to the picture space. If we represent the girl as x, the eyes as y, and the blue color of the eyes as z, the mappings are as follows:

Base: $\rightarrow$ Picture:
girl (x) $\rightarrow$ girl (x')
eyes (y) $\rightarrow$ eyes (y')

However, the blue color (z) of x's eyes does not correspond to the green color of x's eyes. In other words,

blue (z) $\nrightarrow$ green (z')

This says that the blue color of the girl's eyes in the base space does not correspond to the green color of the girl's eyes in the picture space. But it is precisely what the sentence states: that the girl who has blue eyes has green eyes in the picture. Thus, we get a strange anomaly, or contradiction, to which I will return later.

Different Meaning Constructions for the Same Grammatical Structure

Yet another important property of mental spaces is that different meanings can be constructed for the same grammatical structure. Let us look at the sentence

(9) If I were your father, I would spank you.

To interpret the sentence, suppose Sue is a babysitter, Tom is the child, and Harry is the father. We have two spaces: (1) a presupposed reality, in which Sue is not the father and Sue is not spanking Tom; and (2) a counterfactual situation, in which Sue is Tom's father and is spanking Tom. There are several interpretations of this sentence, three of which I discuss briefly here. Let us call the first the lenient father interpretation, the second the stern father interpretation, and the third the role interpretation (Fauconnier, 1997: 14–17).

1. *Lenient father interpretation*: Sue is constructing a counterfactual situation in which the father's dispositions (leniency, weakness, etc.) are replaced by her own (strictness, etc.). Sue maps onto Harry with her disposition of strictness.
2. *Stern father interpretation*: The father is strict; Sue is lenient; Tom should consider himself lucky that he does not get spanked. Sue maps onto Harry and assumes Harry's disposition of strictness.
3. *Role interpretation*: If Sue had the role of father (disregarding Tom's real father), she would spank Tom. In this case, the real Sue would be the imaginary Sue in the role of a generic father. In this case, Sue would map onto Sue.

The remarkable conclusion here is that we get very different interpretations of a sentence, although the sentence does not change at all. This clearly shows that meaning is constructed by the cognitive processes of the human mind, such as the use of mental spaces and the mappings that connect the elements of mental spaces. In other words, meanings are not in the words or the sentences; meanings are creatively constructed by speakers and hearers.

The Role-Value Distinction

As the third interpretation of the preceding example indicates, we can distinguish interpretations based on *roles* as opposed to *values*. Take the following sentence:

(10) Adam wants to read a book.

This sentence has two interpretations: In one, there is a specific book, which is a particular member of the category of BOOKS. In the other, it can be any book, that is, any member of the category of BOOKS. This latter one reflects a generalized conception of roles as a generic category, such as that of FATHER.

Thus, the role is a generic category as a whole that can be instantiated in many ways by means of its individual members. By contrast, the value is a particular individual instantiation of the category.

On the specific reading (involving a particular book: x'), we have a base space that has Adam and a book (x) and there is a "want" space that has Adam and a corresponding book. That is, we have Adam in both spaces and the book in the base space corresponds to a book in the want space:

Specific reading:
    Base space: Adam; book(x)
    Want space: Adam; book(x')
Mappings between base and want space:
    Adam → Adam;
    book(x) → book(x')

This would be the "value interpretation" of the sentence, since the book is one particular member of the category of BOOKS.

On the nonspecific reading, there is Adam in the base space, but there is no specific book in that space. However, in the want space there is Adam and there is a nonspecific book. The interpretation can be represented as follows:

Nonspecific reading:
    Base space: Adam; NO book
    Want space: Adam; book(x')
Mappings between base and want space:
    Adam → Adam;
    NOTHING → book(x')

This would be the "role interpretation" of the sentence, since there is no particular book involved in the want space; it is any member of the category of BOOKS.

Many of our categories have a large number of members, and thus they lend themselves to the kind of role-value interpretation we have just seen for the sentence *Adam wants to read a book*. But some of our categories are such that they have only one member. These constitute special cases of the role-value distinction; in them, the roles are filled by just one individual. As an example, let us take the expression *the president of the United States*. In this case, a single but different individual fills the role over time. The president is the role, and the person filling it (Reagan, Clinton, Bush, etc.) is a value. There is only a single individual who can fill this role at any one time.

The Access Principle

A key principle of mental space theory is called the access principle. Informally, it states (Fauconnier, 1997): "an expression that names or describes an element in one mental space can be used to *access* a counterpart of that element in another mental space" (p. 41).

To illustrate, let us take again the sentence

(7)   The girl with blue eyes has green eyes.

In the base space, the expression *the girl with blue eyes* describes element 1. In the picture space, the same expression *the girl with blue eyes* describes a counterpart of element 1, that is, element 2: namely, the girl who has green eyes.

This is also based on the role-value distinction: There is a role in the base space (the girl with blue eyes) and a value of that role in the picture space (the girl with green eyes). Thus, we have

girl with blue eyes   =   role (in base space)
girl with green eyes   =   value (in picture space).

Given the role-value distinction, we reformulate the access principle in the following way (Fauconnier, 1997):

If a role description is used in mental space A to describe an element a, then that role description can be used to describe, or identify, a value, b, that is the counterpart of that element in mental space B; this can be done even if the role description in A does not fit the value in B. Strictly speaking, the role description of a, *the girl with blue eyes*, does not fit the value, b, the girl with green eyes, that is a's counterpart in mental space B.

How Mental Spaces Actually Work in Organizing
Our Understanding of Discourse

Consider the following simple story, taken from Fauconnier (1997), in which we find a great deal of space building:

Achilles sees a tortoise. He chases it. He thinks that the tortoise is slow and that he will catch it. But it is fast. If the tortoise had been slow, Achilles would have caught it. Maybe the tortoise is a hare.

Let us take the sentences of the text one by one: (The figures to follow in this section are taken and adapted from Fauconnier, 1997, by permission.)

Achilles sees a tortoise.

This sentence provides the base space (see fig. 14.1). The base space is structured internally by the ICM of SEEING, in which there is a seer and a seen. Achilles is the value assigned to the seer role, while a tortoise is the value of the seen role. Achilles must have been introduced earlier in the base space (definite expressions can't start discourse). The expression *a tortoise* is an indefinite noun phrase that indicates that the element designated by it is new in the space.

He chases it.

The sentence continues to elaborate on the base space by adding a new ICM: that of CHASING (see fig. 14.2). Based on our background information, we know that Achilles is human, and therefore we can identify, or refer back to, him by the pronoun *he*, and we know that the tortoise is an animal, and therefore we can refer back to it by the pronoun *it*.

He thinks that the tortoise is slow and that he will catch it.

Here a new space is set up relative to the base (see fig. 14.3). The sentence employs a space builder, *he thinks,* to create the new space. This is the space of his belief, in which Achilles believes something. The belief space is structured by the belief that the tortoise is slow. This belief leads Achilles to set up a new space (within and relative to the belief space) in which he will catch the tortoise. This is a future space introduced by the auxiliary verb *will.*

But it is fast.

This takes us back to the base space. In reality as represented by the base space (though not in Achilles' belief space), the tortoise is fast; so there is additional elaboration in this space. This conflicts with what the belief space contains. The word *but* signals this conflict between the base space and the belief space, and it cancels the expectation entertained in the latter space (see fig. 14.4).

If the tortoise had been slow, Achilles would have caught it.

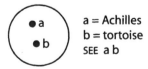

Base space

Figure 14.1 The base space
provided by the sentence
"Achilles sees a tortoise."

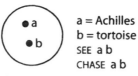

Base space

Figure 14.2 Further elaboration of the base space by the sentence "He chases it."

A further space is introduced by the space builder *if*: a hypothetical space (see fig. 14.5). The past perfect tense (*had been*) indicates that it is a counterfactual hypothetical space relative to the base space, which says that the tortoise is fast. The *if + had been* clause functions as a "matching condition": If something had had the property, then other things would have followed (if the tortoise had been slow, then Achilles would have caught it). The shift in mood (from indicative to conditional) is the grammatical signal that now the focus is on the counterfactual hypothetical space.

Maybe the tortoise is a hare.

The last sentence introduces yet another space by the space builder *maybe* (see fig. 14.6). It is a POSSIBILITY space that is set up relative to the base space. It is structured by a new identification relation (see the access principle

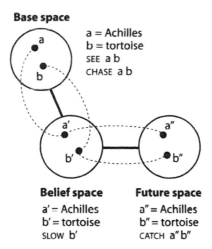

Figure 14.3 Setting up a belief and a future space by means of the sentence "He thinks that the tortoise is slow and that he will catch it."

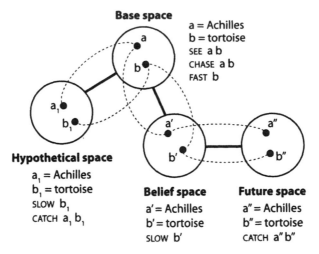

Figure 14.4 Still further elaboration of the base space by the sentence "But it is fast."

earlier), namely, that it is possible that the tortoise is a hare. That is, the counterpart of the tortoise in the base space is not tortoise in the possibility space, as was the case in the other spaces, but something else. The name of the element tortoise in the base space is used to access its counterpart in the possibility space. As I noted earlier in connection with the access principle, if the counterpart of b_1 in one space is b_2 in another space, then we can use the

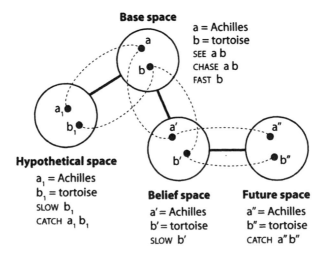

Figure 14.5 Setting up a hypothetical space by means of the sentence "If the tortoise had been slow, Achilles would have caught it."

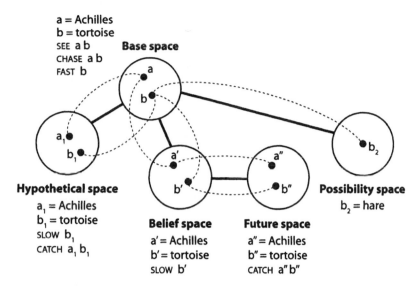

a = Achilles
b = tortoise
SEE a b
CHASE a b
FAST b

Base space

a₁ = Achilles
b₁ = tortoise
SLOW b₁
CATCH a₁ b₁

Hypothetical space

Belief space
a′ = Achilles
b′ = tortoise
SLOW b′

Future space
a″ = Achilles
b″ = tortoise
CATCH a″ b″

Possibility space
b₂ = hare

Figure 14.6   Setting up a possibility space by the sentence "Maybe the tortoise is a hare."

name, or description, of b_1 to identify, or access, b_2 in the other space. This is the case-specific version of the general access principle, according to which element b (here b_2) can be identified by naming its counterpart a (here b in base space).

Mental Spaces in Literary Discourse: An Application

One obvious way to make use of mental space theory is to apply it to complex literary texts. As Elena Semino (2003) notes, most of the examples that linguists interested in the theory use are somewhat artificial. In order to remedy this situation, Semino looked at a short literary work by Hemingway, "A Very Short Story"—which I have already discussed in chapter 6.

Semino demonstrates the usefulness of mental space theory (and its similarities to and differences from possible world theory) with respect to several issues, two of which will be briefly considered here: the issue of the kinds of mental spaces that make up a story and the issue of how to account for the literary effect of stories.

First, as Semino points out, the first two paragraphs of "A Very Short Story" consist mostly of temporal spaces introduced by such space builders as *One very hot evening in Padua*, *After a while*, and *After he got on crutches*. These spaces are related to a base space defined by the unspecified context of narration. In the story, these temporal spaces are anterior to the base space; they take place before the time of the narration. Beginning with the third paragraph, however, an increasing number of other kinds of spaces appear in the story. They are not simply temporally related to the base space but also related in several different ways, for example, as a wish space, hypothetical spaces, various speech act spaces (such as agreement), and so on. The temporal spaces of the story characterize the "reality," that is, what we can take to be the "facts," of the fictional world, whereas the other types of spaces represent what is not "real" in the story (i.e., only wished, hypothetical, spoken about, etc.). This latter type of spaces forms an important part of the story, in that such spaces are concerned with what the romantic dreams of the male protagonist and Luz are and the conditions that would have to be met in order for the dreams to come true.

Second, Semino raises the issue of how the story achieves its literary effect on readers. She sees a major role performed by mental spaces in this regard. In particular, she analyzes several sentences of the story in terms of their mental space structure. One of them is the sentence:

> They wanted to get married, but there was not enough time for the
> banns, and neither of them had birth certificates.

This sentence occurs in the third paragraph of the story. The first part of the sentence has the following mental space structure: There is a base space in which the story is told. There is also a separate reality space that precedes the time of the base space. It is with respect to this reality space that "they" have a wish—a wish, or want, space in which they get married. However, as indicated by the second part of the sentence, the conditions that are necessary for the wish space to come true are absent in the reality space of the fictional world.

Further complications are detailed by other sentences that Semino analyzes from paragraph 5, in particular:

> After the armistice they agreed he should go home to get a job so they
> might be married. Luz would not come home until he had a good job
> and could come to New York to meet her.

The sixth paragraph continues with further details of reality space. Most important, we find out that the major of the battalion stationed in Pordonone made love to Luz. This event is followed by an account of mainly Luz's mental spaces in the sixth paragraph:

> She was sorry, and she knew he would probably not be able to under-
> stand, but might some day forgive her, and be grateful to her, and she
> expected, absolutely unexpectedly, to be married in the spring. She
> loved him as always, but she realized now it was only a boy and girl
> love. She hoped he would have a great career, and believed in him
> absolutely. She knew it was for the best.

The passage contains a large number of mental spaces, introduced by space builders like *knew, expected, realized, hoped, knew* (again) on Luz's side and *would* and *might* on the male protagonist's side. These mental spaces have to do with Luz's and the male protagonist's new thoughts and ideas concerning their relationship—not with how reality space develops further in the story. By contrast, the last paragraph contains no such "epistemic" mental spaces but gives additional and highly negative further developments of reality space, such as the male protagonist contracting gonorrhea and Luz never getting married to the major. The sequencing of and interplay between different types of mental spaces may contribute to the effect that a literary work such as "A Very Short Story" has on its readers.

The Uses of Mental Space Theory in Solving Linguistic Issues

Mental space theory provides elegant solutions to and explanations of several difficult problems in logic, semantics, and the understanding of discourse. I will look at some of these areas here.

Semantic Anomalies

There are many sentences that contain an apparent contradiction. One example of this was the sentence we dealt with earlier:

(8)   In the picture, the girl with blue eyes has green eyes.

As we have seen, we can account for the apparent contradiction if we assume that there are two mental spaces here: a base space and a picture space. In the base space we have the girl with blue eyes, and in the picture space we have the girl with green eyes. The girl with blue eyes in the base space can be said to have green eyes in the picture space because, with the help of the access principle, we can refer to a counterpart of an element by means of the description of that element in another space (i.e., in the base space where the description is *the girl with blue eyes*).

As another example of a semantically anomalous sentence, consider

(11)   *I'm taller than I am.

This is clearly a semantically unacceptable sentence. However, by adding a space builder to the sentence we can easily fix it:

(12)   John thinks I'm taller than I am.

What makes the first sentence unacceptable and the second acceptable? We can say that there is only one mental space in the first sentence—current reality. There is only one point on the tallness scale that corresponds to an individual's height in a single mental space, but comparison involves two points. Therefore, the sentence is unacceptable. However, in the second sentence there are two mental spaces: reality space and John's belief space. The point on the height scale in John's belief space is higher than the point on the same scale in reality space. Since we have two points on the tallness scale (though in different spaces), as required by a comparison of height, the sentence is acceptable, and we do not feel that there is a logical contradiction.

Referential Ambiguity/Opacity

The following sentence provides an example of what is called referential ambiguity or opacity:

(13)   Oedipus wants to marry his mother.

There are two spaces here: a base space where Oedipus's mother is Jocasta and a want or belief space where Oedipus's mother is not Jocasta. This is because in the want/belief space Oedipus does not know that the woman he wants to marry, Jocasta, is his mother in reality. Thus, we have the following situation:

> Base space: O's mother = Jocasta
> Want/belief space: O's mother ≠ Jocasta

The sentence *Oedipus wants to marry his mother* has a true and a false reading. The true reading is based on the base space in which Oedipus wants to marry a woman, Jocasta, who is his mother. The false reading is based on Oedipus's want/belief space in which Oedipus's mother is not Jocasta.

Let us take another example:

(14)   The prime minister was ten years old in 1949.

This has two readings. On one reading, there are two spaces: a base space and a 1949 space. The base space has the prime minister now and the 1949 space has a ten-year-old child who corresponds to the prime minister now. That is to say, there is a mapping between the base space that contains the prime minister now and the 1949 space that contains the ten-year-old child. The mapping is between the prime minister now and the ten-year-old child in 1949.

Another reading is that there was a prime minister who was ten years old in 1949. On this reading, there is only one space, the space of 1949, and this contains the prime minister who was ten years old.

There are many such examples. As a final illustration, consider the following sentences, taken from David Lee (2001):

(15)   Ed thinks he's a hero.

(16)   In that movie, Ed thinks he's a hero.

The second sentence has two readings: In one, real-world Ed thinks that the character played by him in the movie is a hero. In the other, the character played by Ed in the movie thinks he is a hero. Within the movie space, either real-world Ed has a belief space (in which the character played by him is a hero) or the character played by Ed has a belief space (in which the character is a hero). In the latter reading, the name Ed does not refer to what it normally does (i.e., the real-world Ed) but to the character played by real-world Ed (i.e., Ed's character in the movie). We can see the access principle at work here. A description (*Ed*) used for an element (Ed) in one space (base space) can be used in another space (the belief space) to access, or identify, a counterpart of this element (the character played by Ed) in this second space.

In all of these cases, we can account for referential ambiguity by resorting to mental space theory. By taking into account the several mental spaces and the different possibilities for mappings between these spaces, we can work out the different interpretation of these sentences.

Change Predicates

Consider now what are called change predicates, such as *get bigger* (Sweetser, 1997). How can we account for the different interpretations of sentences such as the following?

(17)   Sue's house keeps getting bigger.

The sentence has two interpretations. One is what we can call the "normal" interpretation, namely, that Sue's house is becoming bigger and bigger (for example, by adding new rooms to it). According to the other interpretation, the meaning of the sentence is that every time Sue moves, she moves into a bigger house.

On the first reading, the phrase *Sue's house* refers to a single specific entity. Given the role-value distinction we made earlier, this would be the "value," or individual, interpretation of the sentence. On the second reading, the phrase has a "role" meaning that can refer to many values, that is, to all the different houses that Sue moves to.

In the sentence, the verb *keep* functions as a space builder: It creates a series of mental spaces in time. The conceptualizer (speaker/hearer) notes that in each successive mental space the house is bigger. He or she scans these successive mental spaces (in the sense of scanning introduced in the previous chapter). This process is independent of which reading we are dealing with.

Consider now the following sentences (taken from Lee, 2001, based on Sweetser's [1997] examples):

(18)   The trees get smaller as you go up the mountain.

(19)   The trees get taller as you go down the mountain.

Given the first sentence, we mentally scan subsets of trees as we go up. Given the second one, we mentally scan subsets of trees as we go down.

Some verbs allow only the value, or individual, interpretation. Take the following pairs of sentences:

(20) a. The trees get taller as you go up the mountain.

       b. ??The trees grow as you go up the mountain.

(21) a. The cars get three feet longer when you enter Pacific Heights.

       b. ??The cars lengthen by three feet when you enter Pacific Heights.

(22) a. Every time he buys a new car, it goes faster.

       b. ??Every time he buys a new car, it accelerates.

The second sentence in each pair is odd. (This is indicated by the double question marks.) They do not have both a role and a value reading. They only have a value, or individual, interpretation, which does not work in a situation that calls for a role interpretation. The value meanings for the three sentences could be given as follows:

(20) 'A particular set of trees grows in the short time you go up the mountain'.

(21) 'A particular set of cars all of a sudden becomes longer'.

(22) 'The cars suddenly accelerate when you buy them'.

Clearly, these meanings do not work because a set of trees does not visibly grow as we go up the mountain; a set of cars do not become longer, as if by magic, when we enter Pacific Heights; and it is not the case that when he buys a new car, it suddenly accelerates.

However, in a context that calls for a value, or individual, interpretation, the sentences that contain these verbs are acceptable. For example:

(20) The trees grew visibly as we watched them under the giant microscope.

(21) The cars slowly lengthened in the heat in the giant furnace.

(22) The cars accelerated in the finishing straight of the race.

In sum, when we have a context that calls for a value interpretation (i.e., when we talk about a particular set of trees), the sentences that contain the verbs *grow, lengthen, and accelerates* are perfectly acceptable, but when we place them in a context that calls for a role interpretation (i.e., when there are several different sets of trees that you pass by, when you see several different cars as you enter a place, and when you buy several different cars in the course of time), the sentences are unacceptable.

The Use of Tenses and Moods

Mental space theory can be used to explain some features of tenses and moods. Let us take some simple examples from David Lee (2001) to illustrate this.

First, consider the sentence

(23)   I hope Jean has green eyes.

The sentence is based on a hope space in which Jean has green eyes. The present tense expresses real hypothetical mood. The mood so expressed is not incompatible with reality: Jean either has green eyes or not.

The next sentence expresses unreal hypothetical mood:

(24)   I wish Jean had green eyes.

The unreal hypothetical is expressed by the past tense. In this case, what the sentence expresses is incompatible with reality: We know that Jean does not have green eyes.

In general, real hypothetical situations are expressed by the present tense, whereas unreal hypothetical situations are expressed by the past tense, as the following two examples indicate:

(25)   If Jean has green eyes . . .

(26)   If Jean had green eyes . . .

Given the first sentence, we do not know if she has green eyes; maybe she does. However, given the second, we know that she doesn't.

Languages may differ in the way they indicate different mental spaces in their grammar, as the French examples from Lee show:

(27)   a. Jeanne veut epouser quelqu'un qui **est** Norvegien.
            'Jean wants to marry someone who is [indicative form] Norwegian'.

      b. Jeanne veut epouser quelqu'un qui **soit** Norvegien.
            'Jean wants to marry someone who is [subjunctive form] Norwegian'.

The first sentence is in the indicative mood in French, whereas the second is in the subjunctive mood. The first sentence means that there is a specific Norwegian person in reality space that Jean wants to marry. The second one means that there is no such person in reality space, but that the person she wants to marry in the future will be Norwegian. In other words, Jeanne's want space contains someone who is Norwegian. As David Lee points out, the fact that one reality space does contain such an individual, whereas the second does not, is signaled by a difference in French grammar: by the indicative verb form *est* for the former case and by the subjunctive form *soit* for the latter.

The Global Cognitive Structure of Literary Discourse: A Further Use of Mental Space Theory

As we saw earlier in the case of Hemingway's "A Very Short Story," literary discourse is a prime area in which the author builds a variety of mental spaces. Furthermore, we observed that the particular distribution of the various mental spaces built may in part be responsible for the literary-aesthetic effect of a work. The mental spaces we dealt with were based on sentences that used particular space builders. These were relatively small spaces built by expressions such as *one very hot evening, knew, would, might, expected*, and the like. But the mental spaces that authors build in a literary work can be much larger. The identification of such larger spaces allows us to see the global cognitive structure of the work. Literary scholars often use the term (*possible*) *world* for mental spaces of this kind (see, e.g., Semino, 2003; Stockwell, 2002).

As an example, let us consider Thomas More's *Utopia* on the basis of Peter Stockwell's (2002) brief analysis of it. Stockwell gives us the gist of what happens in *Utopia* in the following way:

> It [the Utopia] embeds the description of the island of Utopia in a complex narratological framework, beginning with a letter from Thomas More to his friend Peter Giles, in which he describes being told by the Portuguese explorer Raphael Hythloday about his adventures. In the first part, Hythloday describes the abuses of property and the corrupt state of modern Europe. The second part is a description of the ideal island of Utopia, its geography and political economy. An Appendix reproduces four verses in the Utopian language, and the book ends with a note from the printer apologizing for not having any letters of the Utopian alphabet available, but promising to obtain some for the next impression. (2002: 99–100)

Given this description, Stockwell identifies four principal spaces, or worlds, in *Utopia*: (1) the historical actual world of 1515; (2) the world of Utopian poetry and printing in 1515; (3) the "knowledge" world of Raphael Hythloday in which Hythloday desribes actual modern Europe; and (4) the fictional account of the fictional Raphael Hythloday in which Hythloday desribes the fictional place of Utopia. The four worlds provide us with the general cognitive structure of *Utopia*. At a minimum, the understanding of the work requires us to understand at least this much about the work.

But there is also more cognitive work the reader needs to do. One of these is the identification of the real Thomas More in and across the four large spaces, or worlds. In other words, to properly understand the work we need to be able to "keep track" of the real Thomas More as we move from one space to another. This mental "tracking" takes place through the mappings that exist between the real world of 1515 and the respective other worlds. As Stockwell explains, the mappings are as follows:

In the historical actual world of 1515: Thomas More	→ the author of Utopia.
In the world of Utopian poetry and printing in 1515: Thomas More	→ implied author of Utopian poetry.
In the "knowledge" world of Raphael Hythloday in which Hythloday desribes actual modern Europe: Thomas More	→ the narratee (i.e., the person to whom the story is told).
In the fictional account of the fictional Raphael Hythloday in which Hythloday desribes the fictional place of Utopia: Thomas More	→ the narratee (i.e., the person to whom the story is told). (Stockwell, 2002: 100)

As we can see, Thomas More has a variety of "counterparts" in the four large spaces. As an additional minimum requirement of understanding the work, we need to be able to successfully track the various transformations of Thomas More in the four global spaces.

Conclusions

A mental space is a partial conceptual structure that we build up on-line in the course of communication. We set up mental spaces with the help of space builders. Space builders include adverbials of time, various adverbs, modal verbs, and several others. Mental spaces are cognitively real phenomena that we can think of as small activated areas of the brain/mind.

Similar to frames, or domains, mental spaces are also structured areas of experience, but they differ from frames in that they are smaller than domains and more specific than domains. At the same time, mental spaces may be structured by frames—often by several of them at the same time.

In actual discourse, mental spaces are connected by mappings between the elements of different but related mental spaces. A large part of our understanding of discourse is our ability to keep track of which mental spaces are set up and what the mappings are between the elements of mental spaces that we build.

Understanding, almost as a rule, involves multiple construals. We can build mental spaces and find connections between them in several different ways.

In a specific situation, the same word or sentence may receive very different interpretations. The remarkable conclusion is that meaning is constructed on-line in context by means of mental spaces and the mappings that connect the elements of mental spaces. Meanings are not in the words or sentences; meanings are creatively constructed by speakers and hearers.

Our interpretations may differ according to whether we interpret an expression based on roles or on the values associated with those roles. A role is a generic category as a whole that can be instantiated in many ways. A value is a particular individual instantiation of the generic category. The role-value distinction is important in what is called the access principle. This is the idea that an expression that names or describes an element in one mental space can be used to access a counterpart of that element in another mental space. By making use of the role-value distinction, we can state: "If a role description is used in mental space A to describe an element a, then that role description can be used to describe, or identify, a value, b, that is the counterpart of that element in mental space B."

The theory of mental spaces provides elegant solutions for a number of difficult issues in the study of language, including semantic anomaly, referential ambiguity/opacity, change predicates, and the use of tenses and moods.

Finally, mental space theory gives us a way to begin to make sense of our ability to manage discourse. Key components of this involve the many different kinds of mental spaces, the space builders that help us create them, the notions of base or reality space, counterparts, mappings between elements of spaces, and more (see Fauconnier, 1985/1994, 1997). Given such an apparatus, we can account for many aspects of how we understand everyday discourse in context, as well as literary works.

Exercises

1. Find the space builders in the following sentences and determine their function in terms of what mental spaces they build:

a. My mother believes that Kate is ugly.
b. My mother thinks Kate was not so ugly thirty years ago.
c. Just imagine, I cheated the last time we played.
d. If I had not cheated, I would have lost two thousand dollars.
e. My would-be husband is my elementary school friend.

2. For this exercise, you should do an explanatory analysis. Your job is to explain the mental space structures involved in the following text (you may represent the succession of the different mental spaces and embedded mental spaces in the form of a diagram like those you encountered in the chapter):

A little boy is in his bedroom with his puppy. He has a frog in an open jar. The little boy thinks the frog doesn't know it can get out of the jar. So he goes to sleep. But in fact the frog is going to escape.

Before you start your analysis, ponder the differences between *think* and *know* for mental space building.

3. Take a short passage from a newspaper or magazine article (five or six sentences) and analyze it in terms of mental spaces. Diagram your analysis, but also justify your analysis in writing.

4. Which sentence is correct? Which is not? Why? What are their interpretations? (Think about the distinction that was made in the chapter between role and value interpretations.)

a.
i. As the airplane lands, the fields on the ground grow bigger and bigger.
ii. As the airplane lands, the fields expand.
b.
i. As the exam period approaches, there is less and less time (for fun).
ii. As the exam period approaches, time lessens.
c.
i. The skyscrapers in Chicago became taller and taller.
ii. The skyscrapers in Chicago grew.

15

Conceptual Blends
and Material Anchors

When mental spaces do not simply map onto each other but partially blend their conceptual content, we talk about "conceptual integration" or, as the process has become commonly known, "blending." Conceptual integration is one of the newly developed areas of cognitive science. The leading figures in this paradigm of research are Gilles Fauconnier and Mark Turner, whose book *The Way We Think* (2002) serves as the basis of this chapter.

The theory of conceptual integration owes a great deal to the theory of conceptual metaphor but also complements it in important ways (see, e.g., Grady, Oakley, and Coulson, 1999). The most obvious difference between the two is that instead of working with only two domains (source and target) conceptual integration works with four or more spaces (input space 1, input space 2, blended space, and generic space). The resulting model of conceptual integration is often referred to as the Network Model. The name indicates the *network* of spaces (i.e., input spaces, blended space, etc.) that commonly participate in the creation of meaning.

The cognitive process of conceptual integration occurs on a large scale—and not only in the realm of the highly imaginative or fantastic. The large-scale presence of conceptual integration does not leave the social-physical world unaffected. It produces physical artifacts of all kinds, which are staple ingredients of cultures. Such physical products of blending and thought are called material anchors by American anthropologist Edwin Hutchins (see Hutchins, in preparation; Fauconnier and Turner, 2002). Material anchors embody thought and thought is embodied by material anchors. In other words, given this view, culture and cognition are inextricably fused.

First, to get a clear sense of what conceptual integration is and how it works, I will look at some well-known examples. Then, I move on to the issue of the different types of conceptual integration and its relationship to metaphor. Finally, I turn to some of the social-physical instantiations of conceptual blending: material anchors and cultural practices.

271

Some Examples of Conceptual Integration

In this section, I will briefly examine some well-known examples of conceptual integration, in particular, counterfactual conditionals, the boat race, and the surgeon-as-butcher examples.

Counterfactual Conditionals Again

In the previous chapter, we have seen some examples of hypothetical mental spaces. Because of their complexity, these examples require more sophisticated treatment than what we provided for them in that chapter.

Let us look at the following counterfactual conditional sentence (Fauconnier, 1997):

(1)   If I were you, I would hire me.

There are two mental spaces here: a reality space with a_1 as *you*, the employer, and b_1 as *I*, the worker, and a counterfactual space with a_2 as *I*, the employer, and b_2, as the worker. We have the mappings between reality space and the counterfactual space as follows:

Reality space (input 1):		Counterfactual space (input 2):
a_1: *you*, employer	→	a_2: *I*, employer
b_1: *I*, worker	→	b_2: worker

Or we can represent the same mappings in a visually more accessible way in diagrammatic form as in figure 15.1.

In addition, there is a mapping going from b_1 in reality space to a_2 in the counterfactual space:

b_1: worker   → a_2: employer-worker

This indicates that the employer in the counterfactual space adopts some of the dispositions of the worker in reality space. Specifically, the employer in

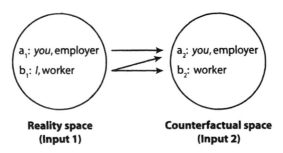

Reality space   **Counterfactual space**
(Input 1)   **(Input 2)**

Figure 15.1 Mappings between reality space and counterfactual space: "If I were you . . ."

the counterfactual space adopts the willingness of the worker in reality space to hire himself.

Notice that all of what has been said so far about the sentence is based on the part *if I were you*. The other clause, *I would hire me*, can be considered the conceptual integration of elements of reality space and elements of the counterfactual space in a new space. This clause prompts us to construct a space that is a blend of reality space and the counterfactual space. In particular, in it the employer from reality space who now has some of the dispositions of b_1 (worker) and is represented as a_2 (employer-worker) in the counterfactual space is willing to hire the worker-speaker, b_1, from reality space. The mappings are as follows (1/2 indicates that the element has counterparts in two spaces: reality space and the counterfactual space):

$$a_{1/2} \rightarrow a'$$
$$b_{1/2} \rightarrow b'$$

Or, again, in visual form in figure 15.2:

Thus, we have the new combined employer-worker a' from the counterfactual space hiring b' from reality space in a new space—the blended space. This is what the clause *I would hire me* states. In it, *I* corresponds to the employer-worker $a_{1/2}$ and *me* corresponds to the worker. In other words, three spaces are needed to give an account of this type of counterfactual conditional

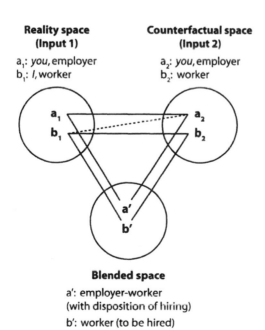

Reality space
(Input 1)
a_1: *you*, employer
b_1: *I*, worker

Counterfactual space
(Input 2)
a_2: *you*, employer
b_2: worker

a_1
b_1

a_2
b_2

a'
b'

Blended space

a': employer-worker
(with disposition of hiring)
b': worker (to be hired)

Figure 15.2 Blended space for "If I were you, I would hire me."

sentence: input space 1 (reality space), input space 2 (counterfactual space), and a blended space.

But why is the employer, a', in the blended space called I? In reality space, he or she was referred to by the pronoun *you*. We can account for this with the help of the access principle discussed in the previous chapter. The employer, a_2, in the counterfactual space has adopted some of the dispositions of the worker-speaker, I, in reality space (namely, his or her willingness to hire the worker). In this way, the employer, a_2, in the counterfactual space becomes in part the worker-speaker, I. Since a_2 becomes the *counterpart* (this relation is indicated with a broken line in fig. 15.2) of the element (worker-speaker) referred to as I in reality space, the expression I can be used to name the counterpart of this element (the employer) in the counterfactual space; hence the clause I *would hire me*, where the I refers to the worker-speaker-employer in the blend.

The Boat Race

Fauconnier and Turner describe the example of a boat race in several of their publications (e.g., Fauconnier and Turner, 1998; Turner, 1996). In a magazine article, a journalist reports on the passage of a catamaran, *Great America II*, from San Francisco to Boston in 1993:

> As we went to press, Rich Wilson and Bill Biewenga were barely maintaining a 4.5 day lead over the ghost of a clipper *Northern Light*, whose record run from San Francisco to Boston they're trying to beat. In 1853, the clipper made the passage in 76 days, 8 hours. (taken from Turner, 1996: 67)

There are two input spaces here: the passage of *Northern Light* in 1853 and the passage of *Great America II* in 1993. The two input spaces project several elements into the blended space. In the blended space, the two passages are conceived as a race. It is only in the blend that there can be a race between two boats that completed their journeys 140 years apart.

We also have a generic space here. The generic space includes a boat, a path, a departure point, a destination, and so on. These elements are shared by the two input spaces. Because of the shared elements, mappings can be set up between the two inputs:

Northern Light	→	*Great America II*
the path of *Northern Light*	→	the path of *Great America II*
departure point: San Francisco	→	departure point: San Francisco
destination: Boston	→	destination: Boston
date of journey: 1853	→	date of journey: 1993

As we can see, some of the mappings involve not simply counterparts but identical elements, such as the path, departure point, and destination. Such a proliferation of identical elements is an indication that we may not have metaphorical mappings here. Furthermore, the two spaces represent equally concrete events—a situation that again reveals the nonmetaphorical nature of the mappings.

Clearly then, we have a case of conceptual integration (blending) here that involves inputs that are not related to each other as source and target in conceptual metaphor theory. Blending, as Fauconnier and Turner suggest, is more general than metaphor; but, significantly, it includes metaphors.

Another interesting aspect of this example is that the blend very clearly contains emergent structure. The race in the blend is unimaginable in either of the input spaces; a boat cannot race against itself. The RACE frame consists of at least two entities (e.g., two boats) that perform an activity (e.g., sailing from A to B) measured by the same scale (e.g., time). The RACE frame is imaginatively constructed by the journalist who writes about the second journey. In this newly constructed space, there is a race between the boats and one boat can be said to be "barely maintaining a 4.5 day lead."

Finally, we can easily see how there can be "backward projection" from the blend into the input spaces. As further emergent structure in the blend, the crew of *Great America II* may beat the record set by *Northern Light*. Once this happens, they can then celebrate the breaking of the record. The celebration and the general mirth that results takes place in input space 2, that is, in that of the journey by *Great America II* in 1993. It is typical of emotions generated by a blended space to affect the counterpart participants in an input space (here, the crew in the space of 1993). In sum, conceptual structures may be projected back from the blend into the inputs.

The Surgeon-as-Butcher

In still other cases, we need the theory of conceptual integration because conceptual metaphor theory cannot solve certain problems. Consider a well-known metaphorical example:

(2)   This surgeon is a butcher.

What this sentence says is that we have a surgeon who is not very good at his job. Obviously, in the intended sense we are not literally identifying the surgeon with a butcher. So the sentence must express a figurative meaning. Let us now apply the "standard" cognitive linguistic analysis of metaphor to it. This means that we set up two domains: the word *surgeon* evokes the SURGERY domain, while the word *butcher* evokes the domain of BUTCHERY. Given these domains, we can set up the metaphor SURGERY IS BUTCHERY. Then we can work out the mappings between the two. It would be something as follows:

the butcher	→	the surgeon
the tool used: cleaver	→	the tool used: the scalpel
the animal (carcass)	→	the human being
commodity	→	the patient

abattoir   → operating room
the goal of severing meat   → the goal of healing
the means of butchery   → the means of surgery

While this is no doubt a valid analysis so far as it goes, it runs into a major difficulty: The analysis misses the main idea that the sentence is used to express; namely, that the surgeon is incompetent. In other words, there is no natural correspondence between the two domains that would capture this meaning. It would not really do to say that the butcher's incompetence corresponds to the surgeon's incompetence. This is not a good solution because butchers as such are not inherently or typically incompetent at their job. There is nothing about butchers that makes them inherently incompetent. But, then, if it is not legitimate to set up such a mapping between the incompetence of butchers and the incompetence of surgeons, how can we account for the fact that the sentence says that the surgeon is incompetent?

The theory of conceptual integration, or blending, offers a solution (see, e.g., Grady, Oakley, and Coulson, 1999). We can spell it out as follows:

- There are two input spaces: butchery and surgery. There is a set of mappings that characterize the relationship between the two.
- There is a generic space in which a person in a job role employs a sharp tool to a body for a purpose. The two input spaces share this structure.
- There is also a blended space. The blend inherits some structure from both the source input and the target input. It inherits from the target the surgeon, the patient, some tool, the operating room, and the goal of healing. From the source input it inherits the role of the butcher and the means of butchery.
- Thus, in the blend there is a surgeon (value) in the role of a butcher who uses a tool and the means of butchery for the purpose of healing a patient. This leads to the interpretation that the surgeon is incompetent. A surgeon cannot do a good job in trying to heal a human patient by using the means of butchery. A surgeon who does this can only do an ineffective, nonprofessional job and is thus incompetent.

In other words, the means of butchery is projected to the blended space from the BUTCHERY input and the goal of surgery (healing) is projected to the blended space from the SURGERY input. The clash between the means of butchery and the goal of surgery are blended in that space with the result that it is not possible for the surgeon/butcher to do a decent job in achieving the goal of surgery, that is, healing. For this reason, the blend gives rise to the idea of the surgeon's incompetence.

In conclusion, we can say that with the help of blending theory we can account for examples such as "This surgeon is a butcher" that would be very difficult to explain by using standard metaphor theory alone.

Types of Conceptual Integration

Conceptual integration of the kind that is prompted by the sentence *This surgeon is a butcher* is a highly sophisticated one. In it, both of the input spaces contribute to the creation of the blend. In other cases of conceptual integration, we have less complex (but no less important) cognitive processes at work in creating blends. We can imagine the various kinds of blends along a gradient of how many and what type of cognitive processes participate in producing blends. The example of the surgeon and the butcher is fairly complex and is at one end of the gradient. There are also fairly simple and transparent ways of producing blends, with many in-between cases. Along the gradient of "blend production" there are certain locations where we find characteristically different ways of blending that we can think of as the prototypes of conceptual integration. We can single out four such locations along the continuum: simplex networks, mirror networks, single-scope networks, and double-scope and multiple-scope networks (Fauconnier and Turner, 2002). These four different types of network represent increasingly complex systems of cognitive operations with which blends are created. (The rest of this section uses materials from Kövecses, 2005a.)

Simplex Networks

These are networks where it is hardly noticeable that there are several mental spaces and cognitive processes at work. Take kinship terms as an example. We have words like *father of, mother of, son of, daughter of*, and so on. All of these are organized into the frame of the FAMILY. It is the notion of the "family" that underlies kinship terms. It thus provides one of the mental spaces, or frames, in the network. The words in the frame have open slots waiting to be filled by certain elements (i.e., roles waiting to be filled with values): X is the father of Y, W is the daughter of Z, and so on. The elements that participate in this space, that is, the elements that fill out the open slots, are particular individuals (like Paul, Sally, etc.). So we can say that the other input space in the network is a set of individual people who do not form a frame (although they are in the same space). The people in this unframed space are connected by the values that are provided by the FAMILY domain. This means that the network has two input spaces: family and individual people.

But there is also a generic space with two kinds of people: man and woman. All the family members are either male or female.

And finally, we also have a blended space in which the two input spaces come together: Paul is the father of Sally, Sally is the mother of Sue, and so on.

In other words, we have a category system (kinship terms) that consists of a set of roles and we have a list of individuals (Paul, Sally, etc.) who fit one or several roles (kinship terms, categories) as defined in the system. When an individual fits one of the roles, we have a blended space with that role and individual combined. We get Paul as the father of Sally, Sally as the daughter of Paul, Sally as the mother of Sue, and so on.

Such simplex networks are commonly based on frames (with various roles defined in them) and elements (or values) that fit the roles of the frames. The frames and the sets of elements (that fit the roles) are input spaces. There is also a set of mappings between the two inputs: For example, the role of father corresponds to the individual Paul, the role of daughter corresponds to the individual Sally, and so on. The network of spaces involved is shown in figure 15.3. (This and all the rest of the figures in this chapter were made available to me by Mark Turner, p.c., May, 2003.)

What happens in the creation of this blend is something conceptually simple: The roles in the frame are filled out by individual elements in the other input space. This is an automatic and unconscious process. This is why we do not even notice that we have a blend here in which two input spaces are brought together. And this is also the reason that simplex networks are taken to be compositional and truth-functional. (The issue of compositionality will be discussed in some detail in the next chapter.) Unlike the example of "This surgeon is a butcher," there is no new emergent structure in the blend. We get straightforward combinations of roles and elements that we have in the

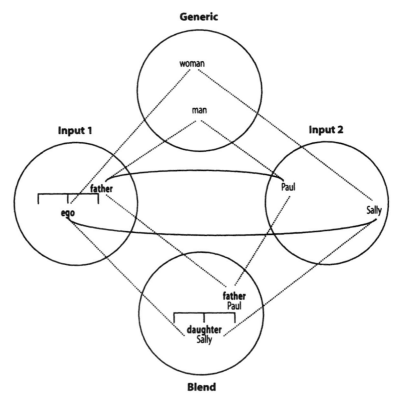

Figure 15.3 Simplex network (from Fauconnier and Turner, 2002, by permission)

two input spaces. And if it is true in the world that Paul is the father of Sally, then the combination of the role and the value as depicted by the sentence *Paul is the father of Sally* will also be taken to be true. That is, the blend will be taken to be true. This explains why compositional and truth-functional semantics mainly deals with such integration networks. However, the other blends we will see in the remainder of this chapter are not of this simple type.

Mirror Networks

In mirror networks, there is a single organizing frame that structures all the frames: the inputs, the generic space, and the blend. This organizing frame need not be exactly the same in every space, but there must be enough similarity. There are many cases like this. For example, suppose that you have a favorite basketball team now and suppose that there is an all-time all-star basketball team that is selected from the best players of the past one hundred years of basketball. Imagine now that your favorite team is playing a game against the all-time all-star team. If you can imagine this, you are running a blend in your head that is based on a mirror network.

Another case is the riddle of the Buddhist monk. It goes like this: A Buddhist monk starts at dawn to walk up to the top of a mountain. He gets there in the evening. He spends the night at the top of the mountain meditating. He starts walking down the mountain at dawn the following day and gets back in the evening. He takes the same path on both journeys. The question is: Is there a place on the path that the monk occupies at the same hour of the day on the two separate journeys?

Let us consider what conceptual work it might involve to figure out the riddle. People who find the "correct" solution often reason like this: Instead of imagining the monk going up one day and then separately imagining him coming down on another day, let's imagine the same monk going up and coming down on the same day. That is, the monk would start the walk up one day and his counterpart would start the walk down the same day at the same time. Since they both take the same path, they will meet at some location. This location will indicate the hour when they meet (because place is correlated with time). For most people this is a good solution. The argument here is that this reasoning is based on conceptual integration that involves mirror networks. Let us now try to lay out how we can arrive at the solution by the process of conceptual blending.

Clearly, we have two input spaces: one for the journey up and one for the journey down. These are structured in the same way, except that the monk walks uphill in one space and downhill in the other and the days of the journey are different.

There is also a generic space. The generic space contains all the information that the input spaces share. There is a moving individual, a path going from the foot to the top of the mountain, an unspecified direction of movement, and a day of travel. This information about the input spaces and the shared generic space is given in figure 15.4.

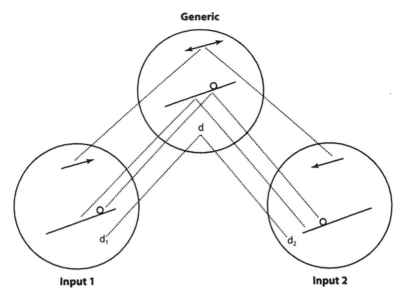

Figure 15.4 The "Buddhist monk" network: Generic space (from Fauconnier and Turner, 2002, by permission)

And, crucially, there is a blended space. The blended space has the two monks walking in opposite directions along the same path on the same day. This is emergent structure, since there is only one monk walking in both of the input spaces. What we find in this blend is one slope with one path and the same day, but we also find that instead of one monk walking (as in both of the inputs) there are two monks walking. This can be given as in figure 15.5.

Given these projections into the blend, we can imagine how the (by now) two monks walk along the same path in opposite directions on the same day and meet each other at some location. As we "run" the blend, we see a perfectly familiar situation of two people walking toward each other and meeting. The point of meeting along the path is represented in the blended space in figure 15.6.

Here the two monks meet (or, more precisely, the monk meets himself). This is a familiar frame that emerges as new structure from the inputs, which have only one person walking in his respective mental spaces. The location (and the time) of meeting is then projected back to the input spaces. The location (and time) projected back into the inputs offers the solution to the original question. Whatever location and time is projected back is the place and time where and when the monk will be on the two different journeys. By unconsciously creating a blend with a familiar frame of two people meeting at a particular time and place we come up with a natural solution to the riddle.

The more general point is this: Conceptual integration can involve spaces that are structured by the same frame. Mirror networks also involve map-

Input 1   Input 2

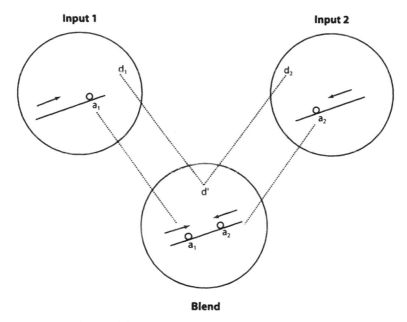

Blend

Figure 15.5 The "Buddhist monk" network: Blended space (from Fauconnier and Turner, 2002, by permission)

pings between the various spaces. Projecting elements and relations into the blend, we get a frame in the blend that is new relative to the frames in the input spaces. This is another form of creative thought, and it does not involve metaphor. Creativity does not necessarily require metaphorical thinking.

Single-Scope Networks

As we have seen so far in this section, the previous two types of conceptual integration—simplex networks and mirror networks—are not metaphor-based conceptual integrative processes. But the kind of conceptual blending I am about to discuss here involves, on this view, many of the standard examples of conceptual metaphor. In the theory of conceptual integration, conceptual metaphor is one kind of conceptual integration.

The label "single-scope network" comes from the notion that the network has a blended space whose structure derives from one of the input spaces. The two input spaces correspond to source and target in the "standard" metaphor view. In the theory of blending, it is the source domain (one of the inputs) that largely structures the blend. As an example of this, consider a sentence like *Murdoch knocks out Iacocca*. This sentence is based on the metaphor BUSINESS IS BOXING. The example and the metaphor can be thought of as a case of blending in the following way.

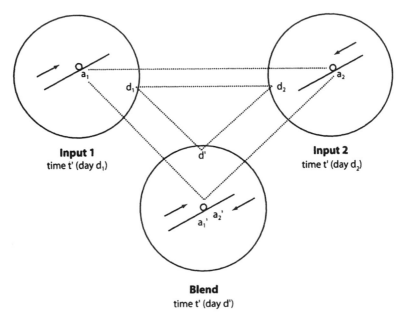

Figure 15.6 The "Buddhist monk" network: Emergent structure in the blend (from Fauconnier and Turner, 2002, by permission)

There are two input spaces (boxing and business), a generic space, and a blended space. There are systematic correspondences between the elements of the source input and those of the target input:

boxer 1   → Murdoch
boxer 2   → Iacocca
knocking someone out → defeating someone (in business)

Since both boxing and business are forms of competition in which two people or organizations compete with each other, the generic space contains the skeletal information "competition between competitors."

Finally, in the blend we have the frame of BOXING in which Murdoch knocks out Iacocca in the business world. The important observation here is that the blend has the frame of one of the input spaces (here, boxing) in which certain roles of that frame are filled out by elements of the other input space (here, business). Murdoch and Iacocca come from the target input, while the action of knocking someone out comes from the source. What makes the understanding of the sentence possible is the set of conventional correspondences between source and target: the boxers corresponding to businessmen and the act of knocking someone out to defeating someone in the business world. Figure 15.7 has all this information.

The source domains of conceptual metaphors impose their structure on the blended space. By means of filling out, or instantiating, the roles in the

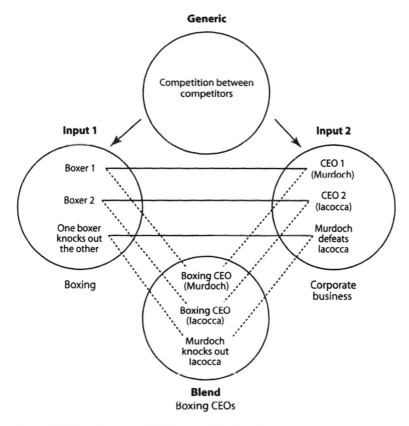

Figure 15.7 The "boxing CEOs" network: Blended space (from Fauconnier and Turner, 2002, by permission)

source frame by elements in the target frame, we get a blend that is both old and new with respect to the inputs. Its newness derives from the fact that individuals in the target (e.g., Murdoch and Iacocca) will participate in the "old" BOXING frame as boxers. This is a general phenomenon in the case of single-scope integration networks and an additional way of producing novel figurative thought.

Double-Scope and Multiple-Scope Networks

With "double-scope networks," the target domain plays an important role in contributing to the frame structure of the blend. Selective parts of both the source and target domains make up the emergent frame structure of the blend. We can illustrate this with an example that we have seen in chapter 8: ANGER IS A HOT FLUID IN A CONTAINER. Take the sentence:

(3)   God, he was so mad I could see the smoke coming out of his ears.

This is a novel elaboration of the metaphor ANGER IS A HOT FLUID IN A CONTAINER. In it, an element of the source is blended with an element of the target. There are no ears in the source and there is no smoke in the target, but in the blend both are present at the same time as *smoke coming out of his ears*. A frame is created with smoke and ears in it that is novel with respect to both the source frame and the target frame (Fauconnier and Turner, 2002).

What happens here is that an angry person's head with the ears becomes the container in the source and the smoke (steam) in the source will be seen as coming out of the ears (and not through the orifices of the container). This is a true conceptual fusion of certain elements of both source and target in the blend. The blend goes beyond simply instantiating existing frame roles in the source with participants in the target frame, as we saw was the case with single-scope networks.

Given the new emergent structure, the blend can be developed further. One can say, for example (see fig. 15.8):

(4)   God, was he ever mad. I could see smoke coming out of his ears—I thought his hat would catch fire!

To understand this sentence, we need the SMOKE COMING OUT OF ONE'S EARS frame, plus knowledge based on how intensity is conceptualized in the net-

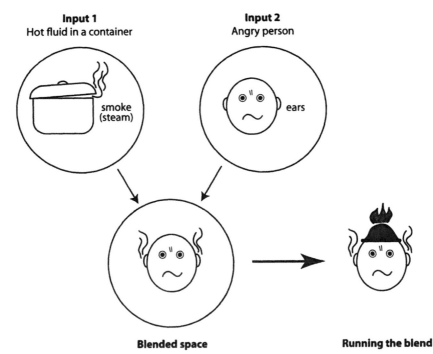

Figure 15.8 Running the "smoke was coming out of his ears" blend

work. A submapping of the ANGER IS HEAT metaphor is INTENSITY OF EMO-
TION IS DEGREE OF HEAT. One of the entailments of this metaphor is that a
high degree of heat may cause fire (corresponding to "intense anger may cause
a dangerous social situation"). But how does "hat" get into the blend? The
fact that it does shows the almost infinite creativity of blends: We can develop them further and further, bringing about new conceptualizations that
depend on old ones, as well as the application of systematic cognitive processes. In this particular case, the "hat" emerges as we run the previous blend
with the "smoke coming out of one's ears." The head container with the ears
metonymically evokes the hat, which is typically worn on the head. Due to
the entailment of the INTENSITY IS HEAT metaphor ("high degree of heat may
cause fire"), the hat can be seen as catching fire. This would indicate an overall increase in the intensity in the person's anger.

But many networks have not just two but many input spaces. One of the
celebrated examples of such a "multiple-scope network" is the Grim Reaper—
the symbol of death. This network contains multiple input spaces: the HAR-
VEST domain, the domain of HUMAN DEATH, the domain of KILLING, and the
domain of CAUSAL TAUTOLOGY. A crucial part of the network is the metaphor A HUMAN LIFETIME IS THE LIFE-CYCLE OF A PLANT or, more specifically,
DEATH IS HARVESTING. The metaphor involves the input domains of DEATH
and HARVESTING. In this metaphor, the plant that is cut down by a reaper
corresponds to the person who dies. Here are the correspondences in detail:

reaper	→	death-in-general
the grain (plant)	→	the person who dies
being cut down	→	the event of dying
reaping	→	causing death

Can this set of mappings by themselves explain the Grim Reaper as the
symbol of death? There are two major problems with these mappings that
require us to assume that there are two additional input spaces involved in
understanding what the Grim Reaper is (Fauconnier and Turner, 2002).

One is that according to the mappings it is "death-in-general" that causes
death. This is an obvious tautology. The tautology is a general one that can
be called Empty Causes. In it, the cause is the same as the result; death causes
death. This is a general process that shows up everywhere; it's cold because
of the cold, we see "blueness" as a result of something being blue, and so on.
Thus, Empty Cause is another input space in the network.

The other problem is that in the blend the Grim Reaper "kills" a person,
an act that does not follow from the mappings, where only the agricultural
activity of reaping is performed. Thus, we need a fourth space, namely, that
of a killer, who intentionally kills a specific human being.

Again, the network can be represented by a diagram, as shown in figure 15.9.
If we blend the Death as Empty Cause with the killer, we get death as a killer
who causes human beings to die. This is a case of personification. This per-
sonified death as a killer is further blended with the harvesting space. When

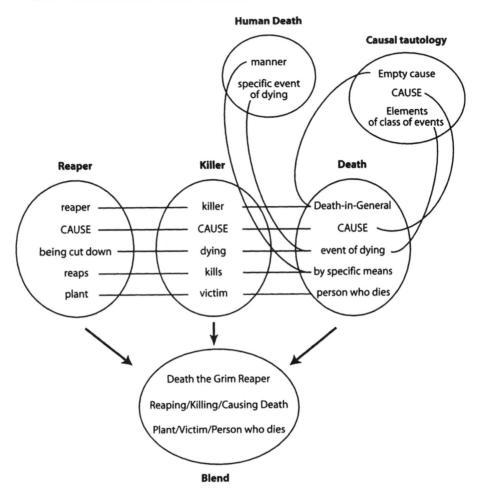

Figure 15.9 The "Grim Reaper" network (from Fauconnier and Turner, 2002, by permission)

this happens, death will be integrated with the reaper and the action of killing with reaping, the victim with the grain, and the instrument used by the killer with the scythe that is used by the reaper. There are other possible sequences to arrive at the same blended entity, but the result would be the same: the Grim Reaper.

Now we can see why an account of the Grim Reaper along the lines of conceptual integration is necessary and why metaphor analysis in itself would be insufficient. The Grim Reaper of the blend has authority over human beings, and no one has authority over him. There is only a single and definite Grim Reaper. He is also eternal; he is not replaced by other Grim Reapers. The Grim Reaper kills a specific person and does not kill indiscriminately. And the Grim Reaper is grim because death is grim for us. The Grim Reaper is different from real mortal reapers, and this is what makes him a blended entity—and not an entity simply projected from the HARVESTING domain onto human death.

Furthermore, we also get an account of why the particular words that make up the expression *Death, the Grim Reaper* are used. Specifically, *Death* comes from the domain of DEATH as one of the input spaces. The word *the* is used because there is a single definite Grim Reaper; the word *grim* is used because the emotion that we feel in connection with death makes the reaper grim as well (via the metonymy RESULT FOR CAUSE); and the Grim Reaper is a reaper because there are reapers in the HARVESTING input who correspond to killers and death in the other inputs.

There are additional aspects of the Grim Reaper that the preceding analysis does not touch upon (see, for example, Turner, 1996). For example, no mention was made of the Grim Reaper's cowl or of the fact that the Grim Reaper is a skeleton. In order to deal with these aspects of the complex concept of "the Grim Reaper," additional spaces or extensions of already-existing spaces are required. Take, for example, the fact that the Grim Reaper is a skeleton. The skeleton is the result of the long process of the "story" of dying. To begin, there is the stage of being about to die, then expiring, the burial, the decay of the body, and finally the skeleton itself. We find in this long chain two kinds of compression: a temporal and a causal one. The skeleton is the final stage in a long temporal and causal process. The actual "embodiment" of the Grim Reaper as a skeleton compresses the temporal and causal process into its last stage: the skeleton. Accordingly, death will be seen as a skeleton that compresses the temporal and causal story into a "timeless" and "causeless" part-for-whole structure. A part of the story (the last stage of death) and a part of the dead person (the remaining skeleton) will come to symbolize death itself.

We should note a final important point in connection with this example. Although many examples of blending occur in on-line communication and thought (and as such they are short-lived constructions), many of the blends that we use are deeply entrenched in culture and language (meaning that they are conventional and have long been in existence). The Grim Reaper is one such case. It is a fixed symbol and phrase; it is, on the analogy of the term *dead metaphor*, a "dead blend" (if there is one).

Blends in Material Culture and Cultural Practice

The blends that members of a culture produce are not only conceptual in nature. That is to say, they are not just "figures of thought." Many blends appear in the social-physical reality of a culture. As a matter of fact, the two examples we saw in the previous section have obvious physical manifestations. The angry person with smoke coming out of his or her ears can frequently be found in cartoons (see, e.g., Forceville, 2005) and the Grim Reaper is commonly drawn or painted. However, in such cases we could still claim that the physical events or entities are mere "expressions" of particular conceptual integrations—and not the "real thing." But the point is that there are many physical entities and events in every culture that members of the culture consider to be the "real thing"—and not some secondary expression or manifestation of something primarily conceptual. The list of such items includes clocks, graves, money, cathedrals, writing, speech, and many others (see Fauconnier and Turner, 2002). Several of these were first analyzed as blends by American anthropologist Edwin Hutchins (Hutchins, in preparation). Hutchins calls such objects material anchors, in the sense that they "anchor" complex conceptual blends in the physical-material reality of cultures.

Clocks

As a first example of such material anchors, consider clocks, as described by Fauconnier and Turner (2002), who in turn base their analysis on Hutchins's work. The clock assumes a complex network of spaces, which is a mirror network. The network consists of a series of input spaces for the days. There are as many input spaces as there are days: one for day1, one for day2, one for day3, one for dayX, ad infinitum. This is structured by the rising and setting of the sun in a cyclical manner (see chap. 5). The times like dawn, morning, noon, dusk, evening, and night are connected by "analogy connectors" that link morning to morning, dusk to dusk, and so on, in each individual day.

The input spaces for days are compressed into a blended space, where the times that correspond to every individual dawn, morning, noon, and the like are experienced as the *same* dawn, morning, noon, and so on. In other words, say, the individual dawn of yesterday, today, and tomorrow are compressed into a single entity—the time of the dawn—in the blend. The blend is remarkable because it compresses the infinity of time (as divided up by the infinity of days) into a unit of time that human beings can easily experience—that of a single day. This is the Cyclic Day blend.

There are interesting differences between the input spaces for the individual days and the blended space for day. Perhaps the most important of these is the idea that whereas time is linear in the input spaces for the individual days, it is cyclical in the blend. As Fauconnier and Turner (2002: 195) put it, "a single day runs its course just once." This means that the individual times of a day occur only once and then a new series of them begins. By contrast, *the* day of the blend runs its course "perpetually" and we experience the day in the blend as going through the same progression of the times of day, such as dawn, morning, and noon.

But the network for the clock consists of more. We have another input space that maps onto the blend. This is the face of the clock with its usually two thin rods rotating, where one rod is long and the other is short. The rods move around, which shows that the input space for the face of the clock is also cyclical. There are mappings that connect the Cyclical Day blend with the face of the clock. Interestingly, one cycle of the Cyclical Day corresponds to two cycles of the movement of the shorter rod and to twenty-four cycles of the movement of the longer rod. Furthermore, each moment of the Cyclic Day corresponds to a particular position of the rotating rods. Given these mappings between the Cyclic Day blend and the face of the clock, it will follow that an interval of time (e.g., the time interval for morning) is the length of an arc covered by a rod on the face of the clock.

In sum, we saw that the clock is a physical object that assumes a complex network of spaces and is a material anchor for that network. Now let us turn to another example of material anchors that is a physical event.

Trash-Can Basketball

We routinely construct blended spaces in the most mundane activities we perform. As an example, consider one such mundane activity, trash-can basketball, which was first analyzed by Seana Coulson (2000). Let us look at some of the features that make this game a blend. (The following description is based on Fauconnier and Turner, 2002.)

Imagine that you are tired and frustrated with studying and doing homework and, to have some fun, instead of simply dropping a piece of wastepaper into the trash can you crumple up the paper into a spherical shape, take up a basketball player's position, carefully take aim at the trash can, move your arm, wrist, and hand like a basketball player in the course of a shot, and slowly release the crumpled-up paper, which travels majestically through the air and lands in the trash can. Your roommate or friend sees this, gets up from the chair, and does the same thing with another piece of paper. He misses the trash can and comments: "You're one up." Soon you have a game going. This is trash-can basketball.

It is clear that the game is composed of two domains: BASKETBALL and the DISPOSING OF PAPER INTO A WASTEBASKET (see fig. 15.10). In this case, the input spaces are structured by the frame (domain) of BASKETBALL and the frame (domain) of DISPOSING OF WASTEPAPER. There are some obvious mappings between the two domains: The person disposing of the paper corresponds to a basketball player, the crumpled-up paper to the ball, the wastebasket to the basket, and so forth. This structure looks like a conceptual metaphor, in which we have the game of basketball structured by disposing paper into the wastebasket. But there is more than that to trash-can basketball.

First, how can we explain the mappings between the two domains? On what basis do the mappings emerge? In the theory of conceptual integration, in addition to the two input spaces (source and target) we used in metaphor theory we assume the existence of a generic space that contains what is shared by the source and target. In the case of trash-can basketball, it is the putting of a vaguely spherical object into a receptacle, or container. This generic-level structure is shared by disposing paper and basketball. On the basis of this generic-level structure, we can easily construct the mappings between the two activities.

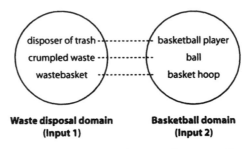

Waste disposal domain   **Basketball domain**
       (Input 1)   **(Input 2)**

Figure 15.10 Mappings between the "waste disposal" domain and the "basketball" domain

Second, in addition to the generic space and the two input spaces we have a blended space: This is trash-can basketball. In it, we have a crumpled-up-paper-basketball, bored and frustrated students as basketball players, a waste-paper-basketball basket, throwing the wastepaper-basketball in basketball fashion, and so on. All of these emerge from the projection of certain elements in the input spaces to the blended space and the fusion of the elements in that space. Moreover, we also have elements in the blend that derive from one of the inputs but are not fused with other elements. One example of this is the counting of shots and keeping score that comes from the BASKETBALL domain and is used in the blend.

Third, it is not the case that everything that we find a counterpart for in the two inputs is projected into the blend. Take placing wastepaper into the wastepaper basket and the corresponding element of placing the ball into the hoop in basketball. Although the two elements match each other perfectly, they are not projected into the blend. In trash-can basketball, we do not have the simple placing of the crumpled-up-paper-basketball into the wastebasket in the blended game. This action would be too easy for the purposes of playing the game. In other words, as soon as we begin to play the new game that is based on some of the mappings between the inputs, new structure emerges. This is called "emergent structure" in the blend. In this particular example, a certain move that has counterparts in the inputs is left out of the game. In other examples, the players in the blend will learn that they have to adjust the nature, intensity, and such of their movements due to the physical environment and the social interaction in the blend. For example, because of the lightness of the "new ball" in the blend, they have to adjust the strength of their arm movements in throwing the "ball" into the "basket."

In sum, we get the integration network for trash-can basketball in figure 15.11.

The point of this example was that blends are not esoteric abstract structures in the mind. True, they can be found in the way we make sense of counterfactual conditionals, but they also can be found in the way we construct mundane physical activities such as trash-can basketball. The conceptual apparatus we need to account for both examples is the same; we need

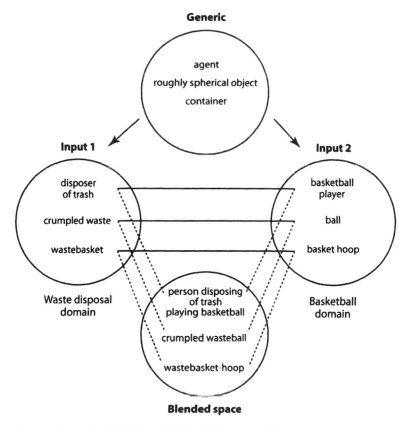

Figure 15.11 The "Trash-can basketball" network

input spaces, generic and blended spaces, mappings between the spaces, projections from the input spaces to the blend, and so forth. Another main conclusion that we can draw from this example is that material anchors can also
be physical events, not just physical objects. Physical objects and events that
are material anchors make up a large part of any culture. The serious study
of any culture is incomplete and unimaginable without the study of such
blends.

Conclusions

Conceptual blends are not simply mappings between two domains or spaces.
They are cases where input spaces contribute some conceptual material to a
blended space on the basis of a generic space. Conceptual integration is a
cognitive process that typically involves four spaces: two input spaces,
a blended space, and a generic space. Such an interacting system of mental
spaces is called a Network Model.

Four major types of conceptual integration have been identified: simplex networks, mirror networks, single-scope networks, and double- and multiple-scope networks. Simplex networks involve frames with various roles defined in them and elements (or values) that fit the roles of the frames. The frames and the sets of elements that fit the roles are input spaces. Mirror networks have a single organizing frame that structures all the frames in the network: the inputs, the generic space, and the blend. Single-scope networks employ input spaces that can be regarded as source and target in the theory of conceptual metaphor. Single-scope networks have a blended space that is structured by one of the input spaces (either the source or the target). In double-scope networks, the target domain also contributes to the frame structure of the blend. The blend is created by the selective projections into the blend from both source and target. The emergent frame that is so created can be "run," that is, further developed given the new blended frame.

Many conceptual blends also appear as physical objects in a culture. Such physical objects are termed *material anchors*. Cultural artifacts as material anchors constitute the cultural-physical aspect of cognitive blends. In these cases, cognitive processes and cultural artifacts mutually presuppose each other. Blending results in material objects, and the material objects so created will maintain, reinforce, and change the cognitive process that may again materialize in physical form. Conceptual integration also appears in cultural practices—ranging from religious rituals to mundane activities like trash-can basketball. The material anchors and the cultural practices that are based on conceptual integration make up a large part of what we take to be culture. The study of culture would be impoverished without paying attention to such material anchors and cultural practices and to the way they contribute to the maintenance and development of culture.

Exercises

1. Consider the following blends and identify the target and source domains of each. Note the relevant mappings or correspondences as well.

- social architecture
- social ladder
- a drinking spree
- a shopping spree
- dance-away lover
- table tennis
- Carmageddon

2. The great Austrian skier Herman Meier got the nickname Herminator from his fans. In terms of conceptual integration, what kind of process is going on here? Try to come up with the input spaces and the mappings/correspondences between them. Then describe the blend itself.

3. Imagine a situation where a manager says to another, "My chainsaw consultant is a Jack the Ripper, rather than a Boston Strangler. He is a real butcher." These two sentences are full of various types of blending. Try to give an account of the blends, their respective input spaces, and the mappings or correspondences between them.

4. Conceptual Metonymies versus Conceptual Metaphors versus Conceptual Integration: Examine the following examples. Try to determine whether they are blends or simpler structures:

   a. If I were you, I would like me more.
   b. Is Albany another Vietnam?
   c. Violet is the grandniece of Mervin and of Jessica.
   d. The Johnson Administration's War on Poverty is a churning
       Disneyland of administrative chaos.
   e. He has been entangled in the Kafkaesque web of criminal charges.

5. An adult says about a boy at Halloween, "We have a small Darth Vader here." What goes on here in terms of the relevant input spaces and blending?

16

Cognition and Grammar

The Cognitive Structure of Language

The discussion of the relationship between language, mind, and culture would not be complete without dealing with the issue of grammar. For those who have a primary interest in language, this chapter comes too late, but for those who study fields other than linguistics, this chapter comes at the right place. It is only now that I can present grammar in its complexity to students in anthropology, sociology, English, art, rhetoric, communication, public affairs, and so on, that is, to people whose primary interest is not in language and the structure of language.

The main idea of this chapter is to show that many of the cognitive processes that we find in cognition and culture can be found in what we call grammar. My goal is thus to show that grammar is a complex cognitive system but that its principles and processes are operative in our cognitive system at large, not only in the organization of linguistic structure. It will be claimed that what are called constructions are a major part of this. Furthermore, it will be suggested that the theory of constructions in grammar goes against the still-dominant view of grammar—generative grammar.

Much of the work to be described in this chapter goes back to the foundational work of Ronald Langacker (see Langacker, 1987, 1991a, b) and George Lakoff (1987), whose many ideas we have encountered in previous chapters. A large number of scholars have taken inspiration from this body of work and have applied it to a variety of issues in the grammatical description of human languages.

I begin my survey with the question of how the cognitive processes we have looked at so far in the book can contribute to our understanding of the complex phenomenon we call grammar.

Cognition and Grammar

Categorization and Radial Categories

In the chapter on prototypes, I noted that we have categories for everyday concepts, senses of words, and linguistic concepts. Linguistic categories include NOUN, VERB, ADJECTIVE, ADVERB, and so on.

According to the *traditional view*, linguistic categories must be set up on the basis of meaning. Thus, for example, traditional grammars often defined the category of NOUN along the lines of something like the following: *Nouns are words that denote people, animate and inanimate things, and places.* That is, the definition of linguistic categories was based on meaning, or conceptual content. The traditional view was rightly criticized for its inability to handle many cases, such as *invitation*, where we have a *noun* that denotes an action.

The *structuralist view* of linguistic categories maintains that linguistic categories must be set up on the basis of distributional criteria; that is, on the basis of the behavior of words in sentences—not on the basis of their conceptual content. Thus, it is claimed that, say, *invitation* is a noun (despite its meaning) because it can be preceded by the definite article, it can be pluralized, it can be moved to certain structural slots in the sentence, and so forth. This way of defining linguistic categories was the exact opposite of the traditional view: It attempted to set up linguistic categories on the basis of formal properties—to the exclusion of meaning.

The *cognitive linguistic view* of linguistic categories returns to the traditional view in that it is meaning based, but it recognizes that linguistic categories, just like categories in general, are organized around prototypes. Thus, it attempts to set up linguistic categories by making use of the machinery of categorization I dealt with in chapter 2. In particular, it suggests that linguistic categories, similar to other categories, have central and less central instances. Thus, for example, central cases of nouns include *table, ball, water, boy,* and *girl,* while less central, or less prototypical, cases include *invitation, fear, running,* and *collapse.* Prototypical verbs are *run, work, hit,* and *kick,* whereas *collapse* and *fear* as verbs are less prototypical.

Frames

As work by Charles Fillmore (1975, 1977a, b, 1982, 1985) shows, frames can account for how we understand particular grammatical constructions. Take the use of the word *fax* as a verb (Petruck, 1996):

(1)   Sara faxed Jeremy the invoice.

The original meaning of the noun *fax* is as follows: 'a machine for or system of transmitting documents via telephone wires'. However, when we understand this sentence, we have to take into account not only the noun's meaning but also the frame-based meaning of the construction that it evokes: that is, that of the ditransitive construction (i.e., V NP NP) in which someone gives someone something (e.g., give/ send/ take/ . . . someone something). The verb *fax* makes use of this frame-based meaning. This is why we can fill out the roles associated with the frame with *Jeremy* and *the invoice* in the example. As we will see, the notion that schematic constructions have a meaning and that this meaning is crucial in the understanding of sentences is one of the key ideas of cognitive grammar.

Another useful application of the notion of "frame" is in the understanding of texts. Some texts differ minimally from each other in terms of the linguistic forms they contain, but their interpretation may be significantly different. Consider the difference between the primary interpretations of the situations described by the following two sentences (Petruck, 1996):

(2)   The children played on the bus.

(3)   The children played in the bus.

In the first, we have a situation in which the bus moves and the children who travel on it play. By contrast, the second typically describes a situation in which the bus is permanently stationary and the children play in it. The differences in interpretation are signaled by the minimally contrasting prepositions *on* and *in*.

Metaphor

There are many ways in which metaphor interacts with grammatical aspects of a language. I will mention some that have to do with some of the issues I have discussed so far. The cases to be discussed are all "force-dynamic" situations, but they can be conceived as products of metaphorical conceptualization as well.

First, we can take sentence pairs in which the first sentence contains objects that follow the verb (both indirect and direct) and the second sentence contains a prepositional phrase after the verb (examples taken from Lakoff and Johnson, 1980, and Croft and Cruse, 2004, respectively):

(4)   a. I taught Harry Greek.

b. I taught Greek to Harry.

(5)   a. The dog chewed the bone.

b. The dog chewed on the bone.

We can observe that the first sentence in each pair expresses a greater degree of affectedness than the second. In the first example, the person involved (indicated by the indirect object) is assumed to have learned more Greek than what the second sentence indicates. We can account for this by a conceptual metaphor that links meaning with syntactic form: STRENGTH OF EFFECT IS CLOSENESS OF FORM. In other words, the affectedness of the (indirect) object (in terms of learning Greek) is indicated by the closeness of the linguistic forms that participate in the process of teaching: *I* and *him*. By contrast, the second sentence places these participants at a distance from each other: the forms (words) *I* and *him (Harry)* are distant in that they are placed at the beginning and the end of the sentence respectively, thereby showing that the affected-ness of the latter by the former is much weaker.

Second, several modals can be interpreted force-dynamically (Talmy, 2000a). Let us take *must* and *may*. Many modals have both a root sense and an epistemic sense. In the case of *must*, the root sense is a social force that compels one to act. The epistemic sense involves logical necessity. The two following examples illustrate this:

(6) John must be home by ten. (said by mother)

(7) John must be home by now. (said by someone who can see John's coat)

The first sentence is said by someone who has the appropriate social force (like mother) to compel John to be at home by ten. The speaker of the second sentence makes a logical inference given the evidence concerning John's presence at home.

The question is: Why does the epistemic sense derive from the root sense historically? Eve Sweetser (1990) argues that the root sense of *must* reflects a social force external to the speaker, whereas the epistemic sense reflects an internal force. This follows the pattern that the MIND-AS-BODY metaphor establishes: Internal events and states are conceptualized as external ones. According to the epistemic sense of *must*, there is some knowledge (as evidence) the speaker has that compels the speaker to come to the conclusion that John is at home. The evidence in this particular case is that his coat can be seen. The evidence thus serves as a kind of psychological force. This is based on the primary sense of *must*, which is a social force acting on someone. In other words, a psychological force is metaphorically based on a social one.

This still leaves us with the question: Where does the social force come from? It is obviously based on physical forces. The entire idea of social force is a metaphorically conceived notion that derives from physical force. Thus, we have three levels of forces:

A. Physical force
B. Social force
C. Psychological force

B is metaphorically based on A and C is metaphorically based on B:

SOCIAL IS PHYSICAL
PSYCHOLOGICAL IS SOCIAL.

We can represent this account in figure 16.1.

The same kind of account goes for *may*, with the difference that *may* can be characterized force-dynamically as involving the removal of a barrier in the course of action. So when we say

(8)   John may leave

we are removing a "social barrier" and allow John to leave. However, when we say

(9)   John may be at home

a "psychological, or internal, barrier" is removed from the path of concluding that John is at home. It is the force of evidence (the light is on in his room, etc.) that removes the barrier. As before in the case of *must*, we have a force-dynamic construal and we have the extension of the root sense to the epistemic sense based on the PSYCHOLOGICAL IS SOCIAL (INTERNAL IS EXTERNAL) metaphor.

Force Dynamics

Force dynamics (without metaphor) can also provide clear explanations for some of the choices that we make in producing and understanding sentences (Talmy, 1988a). As illustrations, two such cases will be briefly considered here.

We can think of a prototypical dynamic situation as a transfer of energy that goes from an agent to a patient. Langacker (1991a) calls this an action chain, where the patient is an "energy sink." The transfer of energy from agent to patient may be mediated by an instrument. In addition, sentences may have an entity in a "beneficiary" role. As the name implies, this is an entity that somehow benefits from the situation identified by the verb. Thus, many sentences that describe dynamic situations will mention either the beneficiary or the instrument, as shown by the following sentences taken from Croft and Cruse (2004):

(10)   I baked brownies for Mary.

(11)   I beat the eggs with a fork.

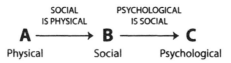

Figure 16.1 Various kinds of forces in modals

As can be seen, the beneficiary (the entity outside the action chain) is linguistically indicated by the preposition *for,* whereas the instrument (the intermediate participant on the chain) is indicated by the preposition *with.*

Given such force-dynamically construed situations, how do we select what becomes the subject and object of sentences that describe such situations? Let us take the following sentences (based on Fillmore's work):

(12)   John opened the door.

(13)   John opened the door with a key.

(14)   The key opened the door.

(15)   The door opened.

Out of the four sentences, three are transitive ones, where the verb is followed by a direct object. The fourth sentence is intransitive; the verb is not followed by an object. Notice that the first two sentences have to do with external causation (John opens the door), the third highlights the instrument (the key) in the force-dynamic chain, and the last sentence represents a case of internal causation (i.e., it mentions no external force: The door opens). This suggests a certain hierarchy in the selection of subject and object in the sentences:

> If the agent is mentioned, then the subject is the agent.
> If there is no agent mentioned, then it is the instrument.
> If there is neither agent nor instrument mentioned, then it is the patient.
> If either the agent or the instrument is mentioned, then the patient is the object.

At least in default cases, such a hierarchy can provide a reasonable explanation of why certain entities become the subjects and objects of sentences.

Iconicity

When a sign (word or phrase, or gesture in sign languages) resembles what it is a sign for, we talk about iconicity. A well-known set of examples includes cases of sound iconicity, where a word form is similar to the sound it signifies. Thus, for example, the word (sound sequence) *meow* is similar to the sound made by cats.

Other cases of iconicity are important in the description of several grammatical phenomena (see, e.g., Haiman, 1985). We can have a more complicated type of iconicity in which there is an isomorphism between conceptual structure and linguistic structure. We can think of this type of iconicity as a form of metaphorical conceptualization. In fact, this is how we treated certain grammatical phenomena earlier, when we relied on the metaphor STRENGTH OF EFFECT IS CLOSENESS OF FORM (Lakoff and Johnson, 1980).

But iconicity may also be viewed as being independent of metaphor. We will follow this latter strategy in this section.

First, consider the sentences

(16)   John killed Bill.

(17)   John caused Bill to die.

When we use a single word for a complex concept, it suggests a unitary construal. The verb *kill* implies both the action (which is unspecified) and the result of the action (death). When two or more words are used for the same complex concept, it suggests a nonunitary construal. In other words, when the action and the result are conceptualized as tightly connected (e.g., John stabs Bill in the heart and, as a result, Bill dies), we decide to use a single word. The single word *kill* iconically represents the tight connection between the action and the result. If, however, the connection between the two is not so tight, we iconically represent that construal by means of several words, such as *cause someone to die*. This is what it means that in cases of iconicity the conceptual structure (the conceptualization) is reflected by the linguistic structure (the linguistic expressions used).

We can find many such examples of iconicity in the use of language. Let us look at the examples we saw earlier:

(4)   a. I taught Harry Greek.

      b. I taught Greek to Harry.

(5)   a. The dog chewed the bone.

      b. The dog chewed on the bone.

In both of these pairs, the first sentence employs a single word (*taught* and *chewed*) and thus indicates a closer conceptual connection of some kind between an action and its result (that of affectedness in the examples) than the second one, where we have *taught . . . to . . .* and *chewed on. . . .*

Iconicity is not limited to transitive sentences that describe dynamic situations. It can also apply to noun phrases. As an example, consider the following noun phrase taken from Radden (1992):

(18)   The famous Italian pepperoni pizza
       *The Italian famous pepperoni pizza
       *The pepperoni famous Italian pizza

What makes the first sentence the most natural choice for the description of the entity (i.e., the pizza)? It makes sense to suggest that the reason is that the principle of iconicity is more closely observed in the first sentence than in the others. This principle says: Make the linguistic phrasing as similar (isomorphic) to the conceptual content as possible. What could this possibly mean here? We can ask if the features of being famous and being Italian are just as much part of our concept of "pizza" as the actual ingredients of pizza. Obviously, they are not. The actual ingredients, such as pepperoni, are more intimately involved in our idea of what pizza is than either origin (Italian) or general evaluation (famous). Given this, it makes sense to place the conceptually most distant feature (famous) at the greatest physical distance from the word that represents the entity and the conceptually closest feature (pepperoni) at the smallest distance from it.

As a matter of fact, we can now account for one set of examples I dealt with in connection with mental spaces in chapter 14. Let us see the examples again:

(19)   a. The trees get taller as you go up the mountain.

       b. ??The trees grow as you go up the mountain.

(20)   a. The cars get three feet longer when you enter Pacific Heights.

       b. ??The cars lengthen by three feet when you enter Pacific Heights.

(21)   a. Every time he buys a new car, it goes faster.

       b. ??Every time he buys a new car, it accelerates.

It was pointed out in the discussion of the examples that certain verbs, like *grow*, *lengthen*, and *accelerates*, have only a value interpretation, but their multiword counterparts have both a value and role interpretation. Why should this be the case? Eve Sweetser (1997) suggests that the answer has to do with iconicity. Since, as we saw earlier, the use of single words (such as *kill*) assumes a unitary interpretation of a situation, we can understand why the verbs *grow*, *lengthen*, and *accelerates* only have a value interpretation. These verbs refer to a single specific change of state, in which something actually grows, lengthens, and accelerates. The multiword expressions, however, are not restricted to such a situation; their reference is primarily to a subjective process of conceptualization in which no actual change of state occurs. It is only the comparison of the differences in the conceptualizer's head that is interpreted as change. This is what we called the role interpretation of the sentences. Because of the principle of iconicity, the single word forms are used for the unitary value interpretation and cannot be used for referring to the nonunitary role interpretation.

Mental Spaces

The theory of mental spaces has many obvious points of contact with grammar, as Gilles Fauconnier's work amply illustrates (1985/1994, 1997). It will suffice to show the relevance of mental spaces to the study of grammar by returning to some of the examples that were discussed in the chapter on mental spaces. The examples in this section are taken from David Lee (2001: 105–106).

Consider again the sentences with *hope* and *wish* as space builders.

(22)   I hope Jean has green eyes.

(23)   I wish Jean had green eyes.

As was observed in chapter 14, the verb *hope* builds what is called a "real hypothetical" space, which is not incompatible with reality; that is, Jean may actually have green eyes. By contrast, *wish* builds an "unreal (or counter-factual) hypothetical" space, which is incompatible with reality. If we wish that something were the case, we know that it is not the case in reality. The contrast between the different spaces is indicated in English by the present versus the past tense. Thus, we can explain the occurrence of the different tenses in such sentences by relying on the theory of mental spaces.

The grammatical category of MOOD can be given a similar account. We can distinguish, among others, indicative and subjunctive mood. As we saw in chapter 14, in French the distinction between the indicative and the subjunctive mood is made by means of different verb forms, as in the following sentences:

(24)   Jeanne veut epouser quelqu'un qui **est** Norvegien.

(25)   Jeanne veut epouser quelqu'un qui **soit** Norvegien.

Both sentences mean something like 'Jean wants to marry a Norwegian'. The French sentences grammatically mark two different interpretations. In the first, there is a specific Norwegian in reality space that Jean wants to marry. This is marked grammatically by the indicative mood. In the second, there is no specific individual whom Jean wants to marry. The sentence makes use of the subjunctive mood (by means of the verb *soit*, as opposed to *est*). In other words, we have the specific, or value, interpretation for the first sentence but the generic, or role, interpretation for the second. Mental space theory provides a straightforward explanation of the two different grammatical moods.

Conceptual Integration

We saw a number of different types of conceptual integration, or blending, in chapter 15. What does blending have to do with grammar? As I will show later in this chapter, blending is at the heart of grammar as well.

In this section, I will look at a single example of a grammatical phenomenon: compounding. I will show that compounds require an analysis that makes heavy use of conceptual integration. The particular example I will briefly describe here to illustrate the necessity of analyzing compounds in terms of blending is that of *chainsaw consultant*, a [noun + noun] compound that has the meaning 'a consultant hired specifically to reduce employee headcount, thus allowing the company's top executives to remain blameless'. The analysis, with slight modifications, is based on work by Réka Benczes (2005).

There are two specific questions we need to ask in connection with the meaning of this compound. One is: Why is the word *chainsaw* used to modify the head *consultant* to express (the first part of) this particular meaning? The second question is: How can we account for the second part of the meaning, 'thus allowing the company's top executives to remain blameless'?

The use of the word *chainsaw* is based on certain conceptual metaphors, specifically, PEOPLE ARE TREES, which is a special case of the PEOPLE ARE PLANTS metaphor. The PEOPLE ARE TREES metaphor is part of (that is, a mapping of) the A COMPANY IS A GROUP OF TREES metaphor (that is, A FOREST), which in turn is a member of the generic-level metaphor ABSTRACT COMPLEX SYSTEMS ARE PLANTS (Kövecses, 2002). An entailment of the metaphor is that the reduction in the size of the plant corresponds to the reduction in the size of the abstract complex system, that is, the company. The tool that is used for this kind of physical reduction in the source domain of FORESTRY is the chainsaw. And corresponding to the chainsaw in the source domain is the consultant in the target.

The two domains share generic-level structure. The shared structure is what Langacker (1991a) calls an "action chain" that consists of Agent–Instrument–Patient; an agent uses an instrument to affect a patient who undergoes a change. Both the source and the target domains have this abstract structure.

But how can we account for the second part of the meaning of *chainsaw consultant*, that is, 'thus allowing the company's top executives to remain blameless'? There seem to be several ways of accounting for this meaning, two of which will be considered here (based on Benczes, 2005). Both explanations require a blended space with projections from the two input spaces: The trees are fused with the employees, the cutting down of the trees with the reduction of workforce, and the chainsaw with the consultant. To show the network structure that underlies this compound, Benczes (2005) provides figure 16.2.

According to one explanation, the blended chainsaw/consultant will inherit the most obvious properties that chainsaws have in input 1, namely, that they are quick and efficient high-precision instruments for cutting down the trees. As a result, chainsaw consultants will appear in the blend as ruthless people who can be blamed for cutting down the workforce.

The other explanation makes use of an additional metonymy. Benczes (2005) suggests that the metonymy that we can also rely on in interpreting the compound is INSTRUMENT FOR AGENT in the source domain (i.e., input 1). Given this metonymy, the instrument (chainsaw) will be seen as performing the action of tree cutting—not the people who cut the trees. Since in the cross-space mappings the people cutting trees correspond to the executives and the chainsaw to consultants, the metonymy will work on the other input space as well, resulting in the consultants—rather than the executives—performing the job of reducing the workforce. This way, the executives will be seen as less responsible for their action than the consultants.

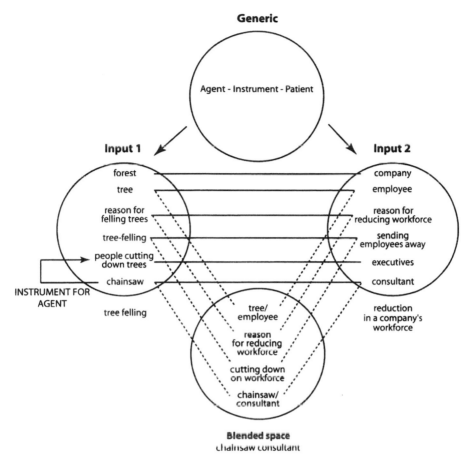

Figure 16.2 The blend analysis of *chainsaw consultant* (from Benczes, 2005, by permission)

Benczes (2005) analyzes many additional cases of creative compounds in English. She shows very clearly that an account of such compounds would not be complete without relying on the process of blending and on conceptual integration networks.

A Sketch of Cognitive Grammar

Let us now turn to the theory of cognitive grammar and see what it actually consists of and how it operates. The definitive work in this regard is Ronald Langacker's two-volume book (1987, 1991b). What we have seen of this work in the book so far is only glimpses of some of his ideas. At this point I will try to provide a sketchy outline of cognitive grammar as a coherent system of explanation of the phenomenon of language, making use of Langacker's work and that of others.

Symbolic Units

Let us begin with the notion of the "linguistic sign." Since the beginnings of modern linguistics (see Saussure, 1916/1959), linguistic signs have been defined as pairings of form and meaning. By *form* is meant the phonological shape/form (sound shape/sequence) of a word, and meaning is the conceptual content that is associated with that particular sound shape or sequence of sounds. An example that is perhaps most commonly given to demonstrate this kind of pairing of form and meaning is the word *tree* (an example introduced by Saussure himself).

The word *tree* has a sound shape /tri:/ and a conceptual content that we designate as "tree." The latter can be equated with the concept that corresponds to tree. The major claim about the relationship between sound shape and meaning in most of modern linguistics is that it is an arbitrary relationship. Its arbitrariness is demonstrated by the fact that in different languages different sound shapes correspond to essentially the same meaning. In English the sound shape is /tri:/, in Hungarian it is /fa/, in German it is /baum/, and so on. In other words, sound shapes do not resemble the meanings associated with them; the relationship between two is entirely arbitrary.

However, cognitive grammarians think about this issue in a significantly different way. For one thing, cognitive linguists suggest that linguistic signs include not just words but other units of language as well. They suggest that the category of LINGUISTIC SIGNS includes much more than just words; specifically, there are two types of extension from words that make the category much more inclusive (Taylor, 2002). It is this broader conception of "linguistic signs" that cognitive linguists call symbolic units (Langacker, 1987).

On the one hand, linguistic signs are extended "horizontally," including a diverse range of linguistic units, such as bound morphemes (like -ed, -s, -ing), fixed expressions like *how do you do?*, *how are you?*, *good morning!*, and idioms of all kinds, like *add fuel to the fire*, *digging your own grave*, and *spill the beans* (Taylor, 2002).

The significant issue that this more inclusive view of the linguistic sign raises is whether the relationship between form and meaning is indeed arbitrary. It can be claimed that, for example, in the case of bound morphemes when we add them to particular word stems that have a meaning (e.g., *walk + ed*), we actually add more meaning to the word. For instance, if we add *–ed* to *walk*, then the word form *walked* will have more meaning than *walk* by itself; it will include the meaning that the action of walking took place before the time of speaking. If we add the third-person verbal *–s* to *walk*, the new form *walks* will have more meaning than *walk* by itself; it will indicate the third-person simple present tense. Since when we speak we add these various morphemes to word stems, it can be suggested that the arbitrariness of the linguistic sign is a rather narrow view of the actual situation. It is true that the sound shapes of word stems in isolation have nothing to do with their meanings, but it is also true that when we actually use language for communication, we constantly add morphemes of various kinds to the word stems—a process that results in adding meaning to the meaning of the words in isolation. It follows from this that we can observe an iconic relationship between word forms and meanings in a huge number of cases: As we add more form to words, we create more meaning. This is what I called iconicity earlier. As we saw, we can capture the iconic relationship between word form and meaning by means of the metaphor MORE OF CONTENT/ MEANING IS MORE OF FORM. In sum, the thesis of the arbitrariness of the linguistic sign in earlier approaches to language is a very partial truth. In the majority of cases of actual language use, the relationship between the word form and the meaning is highly motivated—not arbitrary.

The category of LINGUISTIC SIGN is also seen as being extended "vertically" in cognitive linguistics (Taylor, 2002). This means that words are viewed as instances of word classes such as N(oun), V(erb), Adj(ective), and so on, and the combinations of words are seen as instances of more general syntactic categories and phrases, such as DET(ERMINER) + N = NP (NOUN PHRASE), ADJ N = NP, and NP + V + NP + NP = THE DITRANSITIVE CONSTRUCTION, and so on. Such categories as N, V, NP, and NP + V + NP + NP are regarded as being devoid of any meaning in most modern approaches to grammar. They are taken to be meaningless abstract symbols defined by structural properties. But, as we saw previously (see chap. 13 and this chapter), even such categories as NOUN, VERB, and the DITRANSITIVE CONSTRUCTION have meaning. On the cognitive linguistic view, nouns are "things" and verbs are "processes." But it could be asked: Does the ditransitive construction made up of symbols like NP VP NP NP have any meaning of its own? As was pointed out earlier, the verb *fax* has the meaning it has in part in virtue of the meaning of this construction, that is, 'the transfer of an entity from one participant to another'. Consider some typical examples of the ditransitive construction, where the transfer of an entity is physical:

(26) She threw me the ball.

(27) She tossed me a drink.

It is precisely this meaning that these sentences share. Less prototypical cases have a similar meaning:

(28) I taught him Russian.

(29) I baked her a cake.

(30) I faxed her a letter.

All of the sentences have the structure NP + V + NP + NP, which has the general meaning 'the transfer of an entity to another participant'. This suggests the conclusion that linguistic units such as noun, verb, the ditransitive construction, and so forth are not meaningless abstract symbols, as most modern approaches have it. On the contrary, these abstract categories appear to have meaning—no matter how schematic this meaning is.

Another conclusion that we can draw from this is that there is much less arbitrariness in linguistic units than previously thought. There seems to be iconicity in the ditransitive construction as well (as we saw, for instance, in the example *I taught Harry Greek*). As I pointed out in the discussion of iconicity earlier, contrasted with the prepositional phrase version of the sentence (*I taught Greek to Harry*), we find that the more "compact" ditransitive construction reflects a construal of the situation in which the agent entity has exerted more influence on the patient entity than in the case of the construal described by the prepositional phrase construction. By contrast, the construction with the prepositional phrase indicates less influence on the patient; thus, to this extent, this construction bears meaning as well.

As a final observation based on the preceding examples, we may note that cognitive linguists consider the particular linguistic expressions as instances of more general "constructional schemas." That is to say, there is a constructional schema, such as N, V, NP, that underlies the expressions we use; the expressions are said to be "sanctioned" by the schemas. This means that we can use the particular expressions because we have the underlying constructional schemas that sanction them. The expressions we use are instantiations of higher-level schemas. This view of how language works leads to what is known as "construction grammar"—designating a more specific version of grammar within the broader category of cognitive grammar (see, e.g., Fillmore, 1988; Goldberg, 1995; Lakoff, 1987; Langaker, 1987).

In a construction grammar, each linguistic expression is an instance of a higher-level constructional schema that sanctions the use of the expression. Cognitive grammar is essentially a construction grammar in this sense, where constructions are form-and-meaning pairs. Figure 16.3 shows some examples of such constructions extending both horizontally and vertically.

Earlier in this chapter, I called the broad category of FORM-AND-MEANING PAIRS symbolic units. It should be noticed that this was my initial definition of the linguistic sign: 'A linguistic sign is a combination of form and meaning'. I have thus set up the category of CONSTRUCTIONS, which includes all the linguistic signs in the traditional view (i.e., words), as well as other horizontally and vertically extended linguistic units (such as morphemes, idioms, noun, the ditransitive construction). As we will see shortly, the theory of constructions has far-reaching implications for how we think about grammar.

The Notion of "Core Grammar"

Modern approaches to grammar, like *generative grammar*, operate with rules. A grammar, on such views, is rule based; that is, it consists of a system of rules. An important class of rules is phrase structure rules. These rules account for the ways words are put together to form larger phrases. Thus, for

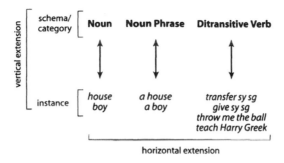

Figure 16.3 The linguistic sign vertically and horizontally extended

example, we have the rules NP → DET N or NP → ADJ N or VP → V NP, and so forth. The goal of such rules is to characterize the grammatical phrases and sentences of a language. In English, for instance, we cannot say *dog the because the definite article can only precede nouns. This fact about English is given in the phrase structure rule NP → DET N.

In general, the rules of a language are claimed to characterize a large portion of language—the part that is fully regular. (What follows in this section is based primarily on Taylor, 2002.) The rules in a way "produce" only the grammatical phrases and sentences of a language. The main assumption is that language and grammar are essentially rule based in this sense and that the regular patterns that we can characterize with the help of such rules form a fully predictable and regular core of grammar. The notion of "core grammar" that is fully predictable and regular lies at the heart of generative grammar.

If valid, this is an extremely important idea. It would reveal human language as being characterizable by a generative grammar in terms of a system of rules that employs "empty" abstract symbols (like N, VP, etc.) much in the same way as a computer does. The human linguistic capability would be describable as the software of a sophisticated computer-like machine that can produce an infinite number of grammatical sentences. Such a program could be regarded as somehow prewired in the brain. This could be the case, because we can learn our first language without any effort and without any formal teaching on the basis of very fragmented, distorted, and incomplete linguistic data we receive from our environment as children. According to the view of generative grammar, the emergence of a rule-based grammar by the age of five to ten based on such data is only imaginable if we are born with the prewired ability to learn language. We must assume, the argument goes, that we have the ability to develop core grammar as something innate and prewired in the brain. As the core grammar develops, we come to be equipped with a unique linguistic module of the mind: a set of rules that can "generate" the regular and predictable patterns of a language.

Let us now consider this possibility of how grammar operates. Let us take a particular pattern and see how "productive" it is, that is, how reliably a set of rules produce grammatical sentences that share the pattern. What is called in English the resultative construction is a reasonably productive pattern. Here are some example sentences to demonstrate it (Taylor, 2002):

(31) They shot him dead.

(32) They painted the house green.

(33) They beat her unconscious.

(34) They stripped him naked.

(35) He slammed the door shut.

The resultative construction consists of an NP functioning as an agent (which is its semantic or theta role), a verb, another NP in the semantic role of the patient, and a result (another semantic role) in the form of an AdjP. Thus, the semantics of the sentence can be given as agent-verb-patient-result. The syntactic characterization of the pattern is also straightforward; it is NP-V-NP-ADJ.

However, when we try to apply the pattern to some other cases, we get ungrammatical sentences:

(36) *They shot him wounded.

(37) *They beat her dead.

(38) *They undressed him naked.

This is a problem for the view of a rule-based core grammar because although the pattern we set up to account for the grammatical sentences fit the new instances, the new sentences are ungrammatical nevertheless.

It seems, then, that we have to know what instances are possible in the construction and what instances are not. It is not sufficient to rely on general principles of syntax and semantics. The syntactic rules of core grammar fit, but the result is ungrammatical. Moreover, the semantics is also the right one, in that we combine an agent with a verb with a patient with a result, and yet the new sentences do not work. To put it simply, instead of the rules generating an open-ended number of grammatical sentences, they fail to do this. In this sense, the resultative construction appears to be an idiomatic construction, in that it is not fully regular and predictable.

The larger question that this situation raises is if there is a clear-cut distinction between what's idiomatic and what's regular in language. In the core grammar view, there must be such a clear-cut distinction. There is a core grammar that characterizes only the grammatical, or well-formed, sentences of a language by means of a set of rules that produce fully regular and predictable sentences. What is not fully regular and predictable is not a part of core grammar and therefore is of much less interest for a theory of language. By contrast, cognitive linguists argue that "regularity" is a relative notion; some constructions appear to be more regular (i.e., apply to a large number of cases), while some other constructions appear to be less regular, or idiomatic (i.e., apply to a limited number of cases or, as a limiting case, to just one case). In general, cognitive linguists doubt if there is such a thing as a core grammar, where everything is completely regular and predictable.

But I based this conclusion on the study of a single pattern, the NP-V-NP-ADJ pattern, which may indeed be less productive and regular and hence a marginal one. So let us take another pattern in English that probably everyone would agree is highly productive, regular, and predictable and hence a central one, belonging to the core: the transitive construction. The account of the construction that follows is again based on Taylor (2002).

It could be suggested that the transitive construction has the following semantics: An agent acts on and affects a patient. There are many verbs in English that we use to describe such a situation, including *kill, hit, push, kick, write,* and so on. The syntactic pattern can be given as NP-V-NP. The syntax and the semantics are matched in the following way:

NP-V-NP
Ag-Act-Pat

As it happens, most languages have this construction for verbs like *kill, hit, push, kick,* and so on. The characterization of the transitive pattern offered here applies to a large number of cases, but it does not fit a large number of others. One such case where it does not fit is that of verbs of perception. The verbs *see, hear, remember, feel* in English have the NP-V-NP pattern, but they do not have the matching semantics. They do not indicate an agent acting on a patient, as is the case for verbs like *push.* Furthermore, in many languages the situations in which such verbs are used are not construed by means of the transitive pattern. In Hungarian, for example, you would say

(39) Emlékszem arra.
      remember-I it-on (LOC)
      I remember it.

Another category of cases involves examples such as the following:

(40) My car burst a tire.

(41) The book sold 1 million copies.

(42) The fifth day saw our departure.

(43) The tent sleeps six people.

Here, instead of an agent noun in subject position we have words that express location and setting as the subject of the process. What makes these examples very much unlike the cases discussed first (*kill, push*) is that although they display a transitive pattern, they do not allow passivization (i.e., there is no sentence such as *A tire was burst by the car* or *Six people are slept by the tent*). In short, the sentences do not have a passive version—a major feature of truly transitive situations.

We can conclude from this brief description of the transitive pattern that it seems that the transitive construction has a central core that is regular and predictable. However, other cases of it appear to be less regular and predictable. These latter cases display either semantics that is divergent or syntax that is unlike the syntax of the central core. In other words, even the transitive construction displays idiomatic features in that it is not fully regular! This shows that the idea of a core grammar that is fully regular is one that evidence does not seem to bear out.

The two examples I have discussed earlier, the resultative and transitive constructions, also remind us that constructions, similar to categories, are organized around prototypical cases. The central and noncentral cases of constructions form radial categories of the kind I discussed in chapters 2 and 6. Prototype-based categorization thus appears to be an important aspect of grammar as well.

The "Caused Motion" Construction in English

As another example of a construction, let us now take what is known as the "caused motion" construction, analyzed in detail by Adele Goldberg (1995) in a cognitive linguistic framework. There are two points we will be making in connection with this construction. One is to show through another case study how constructions can be analyzed using the apparatus of cognitive linguistics. The other is to demonstrate alternative ways in which the construction has been studied within cognitive linguistics.

First I will provide a general characterization of the caused motion construction. Semantically, the construction can be described in the following way: An agent does something, and as a result an object moves. As a prototypical example of this situation, we can take the sentence

Sentence:	Jack	threw	the ball	over the fence.
Semantic roles:	AGENT	ACT	PATIENT	RESULT
Syntactic structure:	NP	V	NP	PP

In the sentence, Jack is the agent who throws the ball (does something) and the action causes (produces a result) the ball to move over the fence (the object moves).

The form of the sentence can be given as NP-V-NP-PP, where *Jack* is the first NP, *throw* is the V, *the ball* is the second NP, and *over the fence* is the PP (prepositional phrase).

It is clear that in the prototypical case the verb must be a transitive verb, such as *throw, kick, toss, push, fling, flip*, and many others. This is the characterization of the prototype of the construction.

But there are many other cases, including:

She sneezed the napkin off the table.
I walked him to the door.
I'll talk you through the procedure.
They teased him out of his senses.
I read him to sleep.
They let Bill into the room.
We ordered them out of the house.
They laughed him off the stage.

The major difference between these examples and the prototype of the construction is that the latter verbs either are not transitive (*sneezed, talk*) or are not verbs that describe actions as a result of which objects are regularly moved (*sneezed, walked, talk, teased, read, let, ordered, laughed*).

Thus, we have the following problem: Which verbs can be used in this construction, and which ones cannot?

One way of going about answering the question is offered by David Lee (2001: 84–90), who in turn bases his analysis on Goldberg's study. Lee suggests that those verbs can participate in the construction that meet a basic condition of use: It is that the verb must refer to a process that has the potential to cause the movement. Furthermore, he finds other more specific conditions of use as well to explain the construction. These can be illustrated with the following pairs of sentences (Lee, 2001: 84–88), where the second sentence in each pair is not acceptable or natural:

One specific condition for the appropriate use of the construction is that the direction of the moving object must be completely determined by the action that causes the object to move:

(44)   a. He nudged the ball into the hole.

        b.*He nudged the ball down the hill.

In the second sentence, it is not the nudging action that determines this; rather, it is the force of gravity operating on the ball that causes it to roll down the hill.

A second specific condition is that the causing action must take direct effect on the object that moves:

(45)   a. We ordered them out of the house.

        b. *We instructed them out of the house.

In the case of *order*, this is met, but in the case of *instruct*, which is much weaker than *order*, the entity that is caused to move (*them*) has more discretion to obey. Thus, there may be no direct effect on the entity, or object.

A third condition is that the causing event must be done by an agent or force, not by an instrument:

(46)   a. *She* helped him into the car.

     b.*The cane helped him into the car.

The cane is an instrument in the second sentence, and as such it is difficult to construe it as directly causing the object to move.

Lee suggests that the three specific conditions can be seen as instantiations of a more general condition: namely, that the subject of the event described by the verb must be construable as the "immediate cause" of the movement of the object.

A particular example of the construction may rely on several of these conditions:

(47)   a. They laughed him off the stage.

     b.*They laughed him into the car.

Here both the first and the second conditions may be at work. On the one hand, the direction of the movement is conventionally determined in the first sentence but not in the second: While it is normal that we get off the stage when people laugh at us, there is no such convention to get into the car as a result of people laughing at us. On the other hand, in a situation that involves, say, an actor or speaker on the stage, laughter and ridicule leave no option concerning what to do. The person has no discretion to decide what to do. In the situation that involves the car, however, the target of laughter and ridicule may have many different options at his or her disposal other than getting into the car.

Lee provides more conditions for the appropriate use of the caused motion construction, but the ones we have seen so far will suffice. My goal here was to illustrate how this type of analysis proceeds in an attempt to account for the wealth of data that needs to be explained.

The "Blending" Account of the Caused Motion Construction

Another, very different, type of analysis of the caused motion construction comes from the theory of conceptual integration, or blending. Fauconnier (1997) proposes that it is best to analyze the construction as a blend. On this view, the blend emerges from two input spaces:

   1.   The basic construction that is found in many languages:

NP	V	NP	PP
a	d	b	c
John	threw	a ball	to me.

2. A "causal sequence"
   { [a' acts] causes [b' move to c'] }

There is a straightforward set of cross-space mappings between the two input spaces that can be given as follows:

Mappings between input 1 and input 2:
a → a'
b → b'
c → c'

In the basic, that is, prototypical, construction, the verb has all three elements in one: ACTS, CAUSES, MOVE. For example, *throwing* involves a particular kind of action (ACTS), the moving of an object (MOVE), and the causal link between the throwing action and the moving of the object (CAUSES). For this reason, d (e.g., *throw*) in the first input space may map to any one of these elements in the second input, which is represented as the following set of mappings:

d → ACTS   ⎫
d → MOVE   ⎬ three different blends with d
d → CAUSES   ⎭

Thus, we get three different blends: d with ACT, d with MOVE, and d with CAUSE. Fauconnier (1997: 172–175) illustrates these blends with the following examples:

d → ACTS: The sergeant waved the tanks into the compound.
d → MOVE: Junior sped the car around the Christmas tree.
d → CAUSES: The sergeant let the tanks into the compound.

This is shown in figure 16.4. The three different blends inherit the syntactic structure of input 1. This means that we have the same syntactic pattern in all three cases: NP-V-NP-PP. However, their conceptual structure derives from input 2, in which a' does something that causes b' to move to c'. As we saw, in the prototypical case the doing, the cause, and the moving are all present in one verb (such as *throw*), but in many nonprototypical cases (such as *wave, speed, let*) the complex d verb maps to and forms a blend with only a single element.

Although there is no syntactic innovation in this particular blended construction (the blend inherits the syntactic structure of input 1), there can be semantic innovation. Verbs that can be mapped to either ACT, MOVE, or CAUSE can appear in the caused motion construction. Fauconnier (1997: 176) mentions some innovative examples used in the construction:

(48) The psychic will think your husband into another galaxy.

(49) They prayed the boys home.

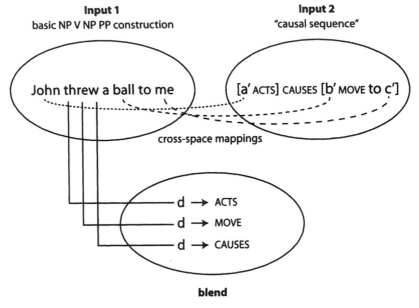

Figure 16.4 The blending account of the caused motion construction

The verbs *think* and *prayed* map to the ACT element but leave the CAUSE and MOTION elements unspecified. Which particular verbs can be used in the construction in novel ways is an open question. This is what the other approach (by David Lee) attempts to formulate by means of lists of conditions of use. Another factor that plays a role may be the issue of which actions are situationally interpretable as causing the motion in question. For example, in the case of *prayed* (describing missing boys in a news item) the action of praying is situationally interpretable as an immediate cause of the motion. It may be that the two approaches must complement each other in a full account of the construction.

Some Additional Basic Ideas of Construction Grammar

The following list of some additional features of construction grammar is based on Taylor (2002).

Symbolic units are at various "levels of schematicity" (or detail). For example, we can have the transitive construction either at a level of great detail in construal or at a highly schematic level with no detail given. Consider a sentence such as

(50)   The woman slapped the man.

The sentence exemplifies, or instantiates, in great detail the schematic transitive construction. The schematic construction can be represented as follows:

Form: NP-VP-NP
Meaning: 'agent affects patient'

Thus, we have a "schema-instance relation" here, in which the schema provides no or hardly any detail in connection with the construction, whereas the instance does provide a great deal more detail (by specifying the elements and the relation between them).

The transitive construction consists of a number of additional schemas and instances, given the sentence cited earlier. The nouns *woman* and *man* are instances of the NOUN schema and the phrases *the woman* and *the man* are instances of the NP (NOUN PHRASE) schema. The verb *slap* is an instance of the VERB schema and the verbal phrase *kicked something* is an instance of the VP (VERB PHRASE) schema. Finally, as was observed earlier, we also have the particular sentence *The woman slapped the man* as an instance of the general TRANSITIVE SITUATION schema, which has its formal side: NP-VP-NP, and its meaning side: 'agent affects patient'.

Moreover, even the schematic forms have meaning. In line with what has been said in this chapter and a previous one (chapt. 13), NOUN has the schematic meaning 'thing'; VERB has the schematic meaning process; and NP-VP-NP has the schematic meaning 'agent affects patient'. In addition, the main meaning of the NP is that it designates a "grounded" instance of a type of THING; in the example, it grounds an instance of the types WOMAN and MAN with respect to the speech situation, that is, in the domain of shared knowledge between speaker and hearer (i.e., *the*, rather than *a*, is used; on this, see chap. 13). The main meaning of VPs is to ground verbs with respect to the speech situation, in this case, to ground it as an event that preceded the time of speaking. All this information can be presented as follows:

man, woman—NOUN ("thing")
the man, the woman—NOUN PHRASE ("grounded thing")
slap—VERB ("event/process")
slapped—INFLECTED VERB ("grounded event/process")
The woman slapped the man—TRANSITIVE CONSTRUCTION / SITUATION
    (consisting of a form and a meaning: NP-V-NP / 'agent affects patient')

Two conclusions present themselves that reinforce my previous observations. First, abstract schemas sanction the use of the specific instances. Second, even abstract schemas have meanings. This contrasts markedly with the empty abstract symbols of formal theories (such as generative grammar).

Another feature of construction grammar is the way it deals with what is known as "embeddedness." This means that constructions can be embedded within other constructions. For example, the NP construction is embedded within the larger NP-V-NP transitive construction.

Furthermore, we can account for the embeddednes of a construction within the same type of construction. This is called recursion. Examples such as the following illustrate recursion:

NP's N – my father's hat
NP's (→NP's N's) N – my father's father's hat

Recursion is taken to be the defining feature of human language in generative grammar. We can easily account for it within the construction grammar approach.

Finally, we can observe that schemas are productive to various degrees: from the most productive to the least productive. Very productive schemas include the TRANSITIVE CLAUSE schema, which has the form NP-V-NP. This schema has a huge number of instances in the language. Less productive is the RESULTATIVE construction schema, which has the form NP-V-NP-ADJ. It has far fewer instances than the transitive construction that can exemplify it in various ways. The least productive are constructions like the idiom *by and large*. They cannot be brought under any abstract schema of the kind we have seen earlier. Many fixed idioms in language are like this.

Grammar and Compositionality of Meaning

Perhaps the most important principle in many modern approaches to the relationship between grammar and meaning is the "principle of compositionality." The principle can be illustrated by a simple example.

(51)   The boy found the black puppy.

In generative grammar, the sentence (S) can be described as having the phrase structure s → NP VP, NP → det (adj) N, and VP → V NP. Or the sentence can be shown in diagrammatic form, as in figure 16.5.

But how do we figure out what the sentence means? We simply put together the meanings of the constituents of the sentence. We compose the meaning of the phrase *the boy* by putting together the meanings 'the' and 'boy',

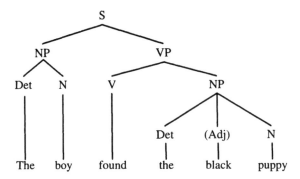

Figure 16.5 Tree diagram for "The boy found the black puppy"

the meaning of *found the puppy* by putting together the meanings 'found', 'the', and 'puppy'. The grammatical structure of the sentence tells us how to combine the meanings that can be "inserted" into the lexical categories, such as N, V, ADJ, and so on.

This way of composing the meanings that make up the sentence is based on the principle of compositionality. This is the idea that *the overall meaning of a phrase or sentence derives from the meanings of the constituent parts and the particular grammatical ways in which the constituent parts are put together*. Compositionality can be conceived in two ways: in its strict and its loose sense. The previous formulation defines strict compositionality because it describes how the meaning of a complex expression is fully determined by its constituent parts and the ways in which the parts are combined. In the example, the meaning of the sentence *The boy found the black puppy* is fully determined by the meanings of the constituent parts and the phrase structure rules that characterize the sentence.

Cognitive linguists do not accept the principle of *strict* compositionality on which to base the interaction of grammar and meaning. There are several reasons for this that I will discuss later. They work with only the *loose version* of compositionality in which it is assumed that the constituent parts of a complex expression and its grammar do *contribute* to the meaning of the expression but do not fully determine it. Cognitive linguists assume that the meanings of the component words do play an important role in the meaning of the whole. For example, the sentence cited earlier could not mean 'the man read the blue book' or 'the river flooded its steep banks'. What cognitive linguists have doubts about is whether the constituents and the way they are put together *fully* determine the overall meaning. They have doubts based on a great deal of evidence summarized by Taylor (2002) and briefly discussed in the next section.

Problems with Strict Compositionality

Idioms

The most obvious kinds of cases that argue against the notion of strict compositionality are idioms like *to be at a crossroads* (an expression that means 'facing a decision or choice'). Here the constituent meanings simply do not add up to what the idiom means; in this example the phrase *being at a crossroads* makes no mention of "facing a decision or choice." The usual solution to this problem on the part of the defenders of the strict view of compositionality is to relegate such idioms to the status of "lexical items" and suggest that idioms of this kind are nothing but complex expressions with a specific meaning; that is, they function just like any other lexical item (i.e., word) that has a meaning.

Metaphor and Other "Figures of Speech"

Strict compositionality also fails in the large area of figurative language. Metaphor, hyperbole, irony, metonymy, and several other "figures of speech" are all cases where compositionality in the strict sense does not apply. Consider the following examples taken from Taylor (2002):

Metaphor: *Defend* the argument; time *passes*
Hyperbole: Have a *thousand and one* things to do
Irony: A real *genius* he is!
Metonymy: It's 2 a.m. and the *city* is asleep.

Time does not really move, so the meaning of *time* and that of *pass* do not add up to what *time passes* means. The same also goes for the other instances of figures of speech.

Pragmatic Interpretation

When we ask someone to pass the salt by saying, "Can you pass the salt?" we do not really ask the person whether he or she is *able* to pass the salt, although this is exactly what the question is doing (literally) by making use of the word *can*. We do not figure out the meaning of the question in a strict compositional fashion. When someone says, "Can you pass the salt?" we know exactly that it is a *request* and not a question about whether we are able to pass the salt. The notion of strict compositionality runs into difficulty with what are called "indirect speech acts" of various sorts.

Active Zone

I discussed the phenomenon of "active zone" as described by Langacker in connection with metonymy. Active zone phenomena constitute another area where strict compositionality breaks down. Consider some examples taken from Taylor (2002):

(52)   John fed/painted/called the puppy.

(53)   The football under the table.

(54)   This car needs washing.

Each of the cases in the sentence requires a different construal of the situation. To understand the sentence, it is not sufficient to know what *puppy* means. We have to know *how* the verb affects the entity. A different part of *puppy* is activated when we feed it, paint it, or call it. Our construal of the situation requires the activation of a different active zone in each case. That is, to figure out the meaning of these sentences, we cannot simply add the meaning of *puppy* to that of the verb. Similar considerations apply to the other examples.

Mental Space Phenomena

Many mental space phenomena cannot be handled by making use of the principle of strict compositionality. Take again the example I dealt with in chapter 14:

(55)   The girl with the blue eyes has green eyes.

By using strict compositionality in our interpretation of the sentence we would end up with a semantically anomalous sentence; someone who is truly described as having blue eyes cannot in the same breath be truly described as having green eyes. But we do not interpret the sentence as anomalous. The way out was to suppose two different mental spaces (a REALITY space and a PICTURE space) for the construction of the meaning of the sentence.

Constructions

Finally, constructions provide perhaps the clearest counterexamples to the principle of strict compositionality.

One type of construction I have discussed in this chapter was the noun-noun construction. We have seen that the meaning of *chainsaw consultant* does not arise from mechanically adding the meaning of *chainsaw* to that of *consultant*. The same applies to adjective-noun combinations. A red pen is not necessarily a pen that is externally red; it can be one that writes in red. In other words, we can have a red pen that is externally blue but writes in red. A beautiful dancer may not be a dancer who is beautiful but one who dances beautifully. Such examples could be multiplied indefinitely.

As we have seen earlier, all the constructions I have dealt with in this chapter defy analysis in terms of strict compositionality. The transitive, resultative, and caused motion constructions are all additional cases where strict compositionality does not apply. Compound nouns, adjective-noun combinations, transitive sentences, and the like are at the heart of grammar in generative conceptions of grammar. But if strict compositionality does not apply to such common constructions that many grammarians take to be fully regular and predictable, we can legitimately ask: Isn't idiomaticity (i.e., the lack of regularity and predictability) the norm rather than the exception in the grammar of natural languages?

Cognitive grammar is a theory of language that makes and empirically justifies just this claim. In doing this, it achieves a new level in understanding the cognitive structure of language.

Grammar and Beauty

The innovative use of grammar may account for what we find beautiful in language. Poetic language commonly exploits grammar to create aesthetically effective and pleasing lines. As a matter of fact, underlying some of the most beautiful lines in English poetry we find several of the grammatical devices we have seen in this chapter and some earlier ones. In *Hamlet*, Horatio says this at the prince's deathbed:

> Now cracks a noble heart. Good night, sweet prince,
> And flights of angels sing thee to thy rest!

Many people believe that these lines are the most beautiful lines in English poetry (see, e.g., Hogan, 2003). Although we know that such judgments are extremely subjective, it makes sense to raise the issue of why the lines have acquired such a reputation. What makes the lines so highly appreciated? First, the lines employ a variety of conceptual metaphors and metonymies. "Now cracks a noble heart" is based on the LIFE IS A FLUID IN A CONTAINER metaphor and the HEART FOR THE PERSON metonymy. "Good night, sweet prince," employs three metaphors: DEATH IS NIGHT, THE OBJECT OF LIKING/LOVE IS SWEET, and THE OBJECT OF LOVE IS A YOUNG CHILD. Moreover, the expression *sing thee to thy rest* relies on the DEATH IS SLEEP/REST metaphor. Second, and more obviously to do with grammar, we have an innovative case of the caused motion construction in the phrase *And flights of angels sing thee to thy rest*. Primarily *sing* is an intransitive verb, like *sneeze* and *walk*. It is used innovatively in the construction. Where does its innovative character come from? It seems to map onto the ACT element with CAUSE and MOVE unspecified. What is especially interesting about it is that it can only appear in the construction in a particular cultural context; namely, it assumes a Christian worldview with angels who sing, heaven as our eternal resting place, and so on. Thus, the example illustrates two points. First, it shows that grammar can contribute to the aesthetic pleasure we feel in connection with poetry. Second, it shows that culture is very much a part of grammar.

Linguistic Relativity and Grammar

Finally, in this chapter, let us return to the issue of linguistic relativity. This return to the issue is all the more important since the linguistic relativity hypothesis was originally formulated by Whorf on the basis of the differences between grammars of radically different languages. In Whorf's own wording (1956: 221):

> The "linguistic relativity principle" . . . means, in informal terms, that
> users of markedly different grammars are pointed by the grammars
> toward different types of observations and different evaluations of
> externally similar acts of observations, and hence are not equivalent as
> observers but must arrive at somewhat different views of the world.

Do "markedly different grammars" shape the cognition of the speakers of such languages? Several researchers have tried to answer this question in recent decades (see, e.g., Enfield, 2002, for a useful collection)—with usually negative results (see Lucy, 1992, 1996, for references). However, systematic new investigation of the issue is just beginning, and the new results are much more promising. Among other work, John Lucy's research is especially noteworthy (see, e.g., Lucy 1992, 1996). Lucy's research focuses on some grammatical constructions and their potential influence on cognition in Yucatec Maya (spoken in Mexico) and American English. One of the constructions he examined in this connection is the plural marker on nouns. In English, it is obligatorily marked on all count nouns and it is obligatorily not marked on mass nouns. In Yucatec Maya, however, the marking of plural is optional and when it is marked it is only marked on nouns that are animate count nouns. Thus, while English obligatorily marks plurality on all count nouns when this is called for, Yucatec Maya only optionally marks it on those count nouns that denote animate beings. This means that English pluralizes a more extensive set of nouns than Yucatec Maya and pluralizes them obligatorily, while Yucatec Maya does so optionally on a certain group of count nouns. The obvious similarity between the two very different languages concerning pluralization is that neither of the languages marks plurality on mass nouns and that they both mark plural on animate count nouns (with Yucatec doing this optionally).

The most exciting issue, of course, is whether this difference in grammar has any impact on aspects of cognition in the two groups of speakers. Lucy (1996: 49–50) summarizes his findings in this regard in the following way:

> In nonverbal experimental tasks involving complex pictures, Americans and Mayans were sensitive to the number of various types of objects in accordance with the patterns in their grammar. The pictures showed scenes of everyday Yucatec village life and contained different numbers of referents of the various types. Speakers performed tasks which involved remembering the pictures (recall and recognition) and sorting them on the basis of similarity. In remembering and classifying, English speakers were sensitive to number for animate entities and objects but not for substances. By contrast, Yucatec speakers were sensitive to number only for animate entities.

In other words, the two groups of speakers performed differentially on the cognitive tasks they had to handle. More specifically, what was remarkable about this experiment was that English speakers attended to the number of both animate beings and inanimate objects in the pictures, whereas Yucatec speakers were sensitive to number only for animate beings, and even here they were less consistent than English speakers were. Their differential performance in cognitive tasks seems to follow from the differences embedded in the different "fashions of speaking" the grammatical systems of the two languages embody. Lucy's experiments thus shed new light on the linguistics relativity hypothesis by providing testable experimental evidence in its favor. In addition, Lucy's results can be found in an area of language where Whorf most explicitly predicted such effects from grammar to cognition. The new results are promising; however, as Lucy (1996) himself observes, much more confirming evidence is needed before the final word can be said about the precise status of the Sapir-Whorf hypothesis.

Conclusions

We have seen in this chapter that a number of cognitive processes are involved in grammar. These include categorization, frames, metaphor, force dynamics, mental spaces, conceptual integration, and others. Without relying on such processes it would be difficult to account for many grammatical phenomena. In this sense, they form an integral part of the cognitive structure of grammar.

The basic elements of cognitive grammar are constructions. Constructions are combinations of form and meaning. Constructions include both vertically and horizontally extended linguistic signs. In the new view, particular morphemes and highly schematic grammatical structures can both be thought of as constructions.

Constructions are based on prototypes and thus form radial categories. To account for them, we do not need rules in the traditional generativist sense. (Peter Gardenfors argues from an evolutionary perspective that rules of this kind are not necessary to develop language. See Gardenfors, 2003.) In cognitive grammar, instead of rules, schemas are used. Schemas can be said to "sanction" linguistic expressions.

Cognitive grammarians reject the notion of a core grammar, the part of grammar that characterizes only the grammatical sentences of a language by means of a set of rules that produce fully regular and predictable sentences. By contrast, cognitive grammar operates with the notion that regularity is relative and that some constructions are more regular, while some other constructions are less regular, (i.e., idiomatic). Cognitive linguists doubt the existence of a core grammar, where everything is completely regular and predictable.

This rejection of core grammar goes together with a rejection of theories of language acquisition that are based on a hard-wired "language instinct." Michael Tomasello (2003) argues that children acquire language on the basis of what they hear around them, as well as some general cognitive abilities. Children, he suggests, learn language as they form linguistic constructions from what they hear repeatedly. In this view, the acquisition of language is usage- and construction-based.

The relationship between grammar and meaning in most modern approaches is predicated on the idea of compositionality: the view that *the overall meaning of a phrase or sentence derives from the meanings of the constituent parts and the particular grammatical ways in which the constituent parts are put together.* Strict compositionality has been shown to be unacceptable, and cognitive grammar operates with a looser version of the principle. This is because in many cases, such as idioms, metaphor, metonymy, active zone phenomena, mental space phenomena, and, importantly, constructions, strict compositionality simply does not work. Given such evidence, we can legitimately suggest that idiomaticity (as opposed to regularity and predictability) is the default feature of natural languages.

Finally, new empirical evidence seems to point to the conclusion that the grammatical structure of language plays a constraining role on the way we think. As Benjamin Whorf claimed, aspects of cognition seem to be affected by the "background linguistic system"—that is, our grammar.

Exercises

1. What principle of cognitive grammar is at work in the following sentences and in what ways does it "operate" in each case? Briefly discuss how the principle contributes to the meaning and in what ways:

a. She talks, talks, talks.
b. The music got louder and louder.
c. I taught him to play the piano *versus* I taught playing the piano to him.
d. a big yellow French leather hat
e. "Words, words, words" (Hamlet)
f. He was getting farther and farther from his hometown as he walked.

2. In this chapter I have argued against the strict interpretation of the compositionality of meaning, maintaining that the complex meaning of idioms and metaphors is more than and different from the meanings of its component parts. In their *Introduction to Cognitive Linguistics* (1996), Frederick Ungerer and Hans-Jorg Schmid also concern themselves with a similar phenomenon. They claim that many noun-noun compounds have additional meanings that are not derivable from the component nouns of the compound. They call these nonderivable attributes and argue that the more there is of these, the more likely it is for a compound to assume the status of an independent lexical item (i.e., cease to be felt to be a compound). Your task here is as follows:

A. Determine the nonderivable attributes of the following compounds (i.e., attributes that are not the attributes of either of the component nouns).

B. Discuss at some length if the compound in question may—in your opinion—be considered as having assumed the status of an independent category of its own. State your reasons (supporting arguments in favor or against):

streetcar
newspaper
bean soup
skylight
drugstore

3. Metaphor as a cognitive process is very much present in everyday grammar and is the major engine behind many conventions of politeness, such as

the frequent use of past tense forms to refer to the present. For example, a desk clerk may ask a hotel guest to repeat his/her name (when not understood clearly) when he/she is checking into the hotel as follows: "What was your name again?" What kind of metaphor is at work here? What does it tell us about the nature of politeness? Can you think of other examples in the same vein?

4. In this chapter we saw that cognitive linguists claim that grammar is construction based rather than generated by a set of finite rules. What kind of non productive construction of a highly constrained use do the following phrases illustrate? What do you think contributes to the "marked" stylistic effect of these phrases?

- *time immemorial*
- *presents galore*
- *the world over*
- *beauty incarnate*
- *body politic*
- *notary public*
- *Friday last/next*

5. In your native language (if it is other than English), try to find a construction similar to the caused motion construction we have looked at in detail in this chapter. Try to apply the general constraint and the subconstraints and see if they work similarly in your native language. Are the constraints completely the same or did you have to add any others (or take some away)? Ask other native speakers to confirm your intuitions about the grammatical acceptability of your examples.

17

Summing It Up

An Account of Meaningful Experience

In this book, three general issues were examined. First, what cognitive processes play a role in making sense of the world around us? Second, how do these cognitive processes contribute to our understanding of issues in language? Third, how do the same cognitive processes provide an account of meaning in a wide range of social and cultural phenomena?

To begin, we have found that we make use of a relatively small number of cognitive processes in making sense of our experience. We categorize the world, organize our knowledge into frames, make use of within-frame mappings (metonymy) and cross-frame mappings (metaphor), build image-schemas from bodily experience and apply these to what we experience, divide our experience into figures and grounds, set up mental spaces and further mappings between them in the on-line process of understanding, and have the ability to skillfully and creatively integrate conceptual materials from the mental spaces that we set up. We do not do most of this in a conscious way; our cognitive system operates unconsciously most of the time. It is these and some additional cognitive processes that participate in our unconscious meaning-making activity.

With the help of such cognitive processes we can account for many (or perhaps most) of the phenomena of meaning in language in a coherent fashion. The theory that emerges from the application of these cognitive processes to our understanding of meaning in language will be very different from other theories of language. Most important, the theory will be a theory of meaning and not one of form. On this view, even highly abstract and schematic forms (such as N, V, NP-V-NP, and NP-V-NP-PP) are seen as having meaning; as a matter of fact, the only justification for the existence of such abstract and schematic forms is their role in the expression and understanding of meaning as being part of "symbolic units," which consist of combinations of meaning and form (Langacker, 1987). On the cognitive linguistic view, the scientific study of language cannot be the study of the manipulation of such abstract and schematic forms (i.e., syntax); the only legitimate and scientific goal in the study of language is the study of *meaning* in language (including the meaning of abstract symbolic units) and how the cognitive processes discussed earlier play a role in this.

But most important for the purposes of this book, we have seen that the same cognitive processes help us make sense of a wide range of social and cultural phenomena. Understanding the nature of debates about art, the issue of motherhood, setting up ideals and stereotypes to function in the world, the structure of political thought, the understanding of literature, the use of material objects, participating in mundane activities and rituals, and other topics discussed in this book are only some of the issues that we can make sense of by making use of such cognitive processes. The cognitive processes utilized by cognitive linguistics are not merely ways of accounting for meaning in language; they are ways of accounting for meaning in many aspects of our social and cultural reality. (Such a suggestion is in the spirit of Turner, 2001, which discusses the issue in relation to conceptual integration, and Kövecses, 2005a, which discusses it in relation to conceptual metaphor.)

As we have seen, our main meaning-making organ, the mind/brain, is shaped by both bodily and social/cultural experience. Image-schemas, correlation-based metaphors, and the like arise from bodily functioning and are at the same time imbued by culture (e.g., by applying alternative frames to the "same" aspect of reality). Both the mind/brain and its product, meaning, are embodied and culture-dependent at the same time (see Kövecses, 2005a; Yu, 2003). It is the goal of the cognitive linguistic enterprise to characterize the functioning of such an embodied and cultured mind in relation to language and beyond it in our social and cultural world at large.

How Do Our Main Questions Get Answered?

Let us now return to some of the questions that I raised at the beginning of the book in chapter 1. Now I am in a position to provide more detailed and, I hope, more meaningful answers to them.

What Is the Nature of Reality? Does the World Come in a Structured or Unstructured Form?

Reality does not come in a prestructured form; it does not come in well-defined categories. Categories are defined with respect to prototypes and have a "family resemblance" structure. One of our most essential abilities to survive is the ability to categorize the objects and events around us. By *creating* conceptual categories we make sense of the world; when we encounter new objects and events we assign them to already-existing categories or create new ones to accommodate them.

How do we mentally represent categories in our heads? I have considered three models of the mental representation of categories: classical categorization, prototype categorization, and exemplar models. The classical model is based on rulelike definitions of categories that operate with semantic features. The mental representations for categories can be taken to be minimal definitions given in terms of essential features. The model of prototype categorization claims that instead of necessary and sufficient conditions, categories are represented in the mind as prototypes, or best examples, for categories. These are abstract idealizations of category members. Prototype-based categories do not possess single sets of essential features to define them. The members of such a category are held together by family resemblances to a prototype. Prototypes are not abstract and static mental structures; prototypes are created in specific contexts for specific goals and thus cannot be conceived as abstract stable mental representations. Prototypes are culturally determined as well.

The classical theory of hierarchic categories operates with the notion of logical feature inclusion. However, on such a view, it would be difficult to explain why the middle of the hierarchy has a distinctive status for speakers. Basic-level categorization accounts for the psychological primacy of the middle level by claiming that this is the level where categories can simultaneously meet two basic demands: the pressure for maximal similarity among category members and the pressure of maximal dissimilarity between neighboring categories.

Categorization in general and levels of categorization for particular people is just as much a matter of culture as it is a matter of cognition. The cultural contexts in which the categorization takes place play a crucial role in why people categorize particular objects and events at particular levels of abstraction.

In sum, the world does not come in a prestructured fashion; categorization is an imaginative act that relies on human cognition and culture.

What Is the Relationship between the Mind and External Reality? Does the Mind Reflect or Create Reality?

The mind is not a mirror of reality; it reflects the world *as* we experience and perceive it. The world is built up by the mind in an imaginative way, as we just partly saw for prototypes and hierarchies of categories. We have additional cognitive processes at our disposal to create a "projected" reality—a reality of our imaginative powers, such as frames, metonymy, metaphor, mental spaces, blending.

The knowledge we have about the world is given to us in highly schematic, or idealized, form: in frames. Frames capture our prototypes for conceptual categories. They are cultural products shared by smaller or larger groups of people. They can take the form of folk and expert theories. Much of our knowledge about the world comes in the folk theories we possess. One extremely important feature of frames is that they help us account for multiple understandings of the same situation. Alternative construal made possible by multiple frames for the same "thing" is the norm in our meaning-making activity.

Metonymies are within-domain mappings, in which an entity is mapped onto another entity within the same frame, or domain, or ICM. Metonymies are inherently cognitive and cultural at the same time. Metonymy underlies many forms of cultural behavior. People often find meaning in their diverse activities because of the conceptual metonymies that underlie their activities.

Metaphors are systematic cross-domain mappings. Metaphor is not only linguistic but also conceptual, social-cultural, neural, and bodily at the same time. The connections between the two domains are set up either because the two domains share generic-level structure or because they are correlated in our bodily experience. What we find "similar" between domains is highly culture-dependent. In other words, culture is inherent in the creation of metaphor. Metaphors often define what's real for us.

Mental spaces are partial conceptual structures that we build up on-line in the course of communication. Mental spaces are created with the help of space builders. In actual discourse, mental spaces are connected by mappings between the elements of different but related mental spaces. A large part of our understanding of discourse involves our ability to keep track of which mental spaces are set up and what the mappings are between the elements of the spaces that we build. Similar to frames, mental spaces often involve multiple construals of situations. Meaning is constructed on-line in context by means of mental spaces and the mappings that connect the elements of mental spaces. Meanings are not in the words or sentences; they are creatively constructed by speakers and hearers. Finally, mental space theory gives us a way to begin to make sense of our ability to manage discourse. We can account for many aspects of how we understand everyday discourse in context, as well as the local and global structure of literary works.

Conceptual integration networks include four distinct frames or spaces: a generic space, at least two input spaces, and a blended space. The input spaces contribute conceptual material to the blended space on the basis of the generic space. Conceptual blends can become material blends.

Given such imaginative processes of the mind, we can conclude that a large part of reality is actually defined by the mind.

What Is the Relationship between the Mind and the Body? Is the Mind Independent of the Body (Is It Transcendent, Abstract?) or Is It Based on the Body?

Thought is *not* independent of the body, it is *not* abstract, and it is *not* like an abstract machine that manipulates abstract symbols. In a very real sense, thought is embodied. The categories of mind are defined by interactional properties; this is especially clear in the case of basic-level categories.

Image-schemas are recurring, dynamic patterns of our perceptual interactions and motor programs that give coherence to our experience (Johnson, 1987). Image-schemas arise from our most basic bodily experiences, and we use them to make sense of the world around us. The CONTAINER schema, the

WHOLE-PART schema, the LINK schema, the CENTER-PERIPHERY schema, and the SOURCE-PATH-GOAL schema, which are all body-based schematic structures, are projected onto nonbodily experiences, thus helping us understand the world outside the body. Furthermore, image-schemas structure our conceptual system in general. We have an embodied understanding of the structure (form) of our conceptual system. These ideas provide us with the notion of an embodied mind. (David M. Johnson problematizes this connection between the body and the mind in the experientialist program. See Johnson, 2005.) Providing the most recent statement on the issue, in a wide-ranging study, Raymond Gibbs (2005) supplies further evidence for the inherently embodied nature of the human mind.

Is the mind essentially and inherently literal? Some objectivist philosophers like John Searle claim that it is essentially and inherently literal. However, we have convincing evidence to the effect that abstract meanings are always *constituted* by figurative meanings; that the *comprehension* of abstract meanings does, in fact, recruit metaphoric mappings; and that figurative abstract meanings in one language are always *expressed* as figurative abstract meanings in another. This leads me to conclude that the mind (and the meanings that it generates) is both literal and figurative—and not essentially and predominantly literal.

Cultural models for abstract concepts can only be metaphor based. Figurative abstract meaning seems to be just as much a design feature of thought as literal concrete meaning is.

What Is Language? Is It Mostly a Matter of Form or Conceptualization?

Language uses many of the same operations that other cognitive faculties of the mind use. Aspects of attention, figure-ground organization, force dynamics, metaphor, metonymy, blending, and so on are a part and parcel of grammar. This suggests a holistic, rather than modular, structure for the mind.

Grammar reflects the ways we conceptualize the world at a highly schematic level. There are no rules of the Chomskyan kind in cognitive grammar. They are replaced by schemas. The basic elements of cognitive grammar are constructions. Constructions are combinations of form and meaning. Constructions include both vertically and horizontally extended linguistic signs. In the new view, particular morphemes and highly schematic grammatical structures can both be thought of as constructions. Constructional schemas also have meaning; their meaning is constituted by commonly occurring scenes in a culture (such as the meaning of 'agent affects patient' in the transitive construction).

Cognitive grammar operates with the notion that regularity is relative and that some constructions are more regular than others, while some other constructions are less regular, or idiomatic. Cognitive linguists doubt the existence of a core grammar, where everything is completely regular and predictable.

What Is Meaning? What Is Meaningfulness? Can It Be
Defined in Terms of Truth Conditions? How Does
Meaning Arise? How Does Language Acquire Meaning?

The symbol grounding problem receives an elegant solution if we take into account the role of image-schemas in making sense of experience. Abstract symbols and linguistic expressions get their meaning through image-schemas. Image-schemas are based on our bodily experience; this ensures the meaningfulness of symbols and expressions. We rely on our bodily experience in understanding the world around us.

Construals are particular ways of understanding the world. The relationship between language (linguistic expressions), construal, and the world is manifold. We can construe the same situation in different ways and indicate this by using different expressions, we can construe different aspects of the same thing by means of the same expression, and we can construe different situations by means of the same expression.

There are many cognitive operations at our disposal to conceptualize the world in alternate ways. Alternative construal adds a new dimension to our conception of "meaning." In the new view, meaning is not simply some conceptual content but also some construal of that conceptual content. The way we construe some conceptual content may be more important than the conceptual content itself.

The meaning of complex linguistic (and nonlinguistic) units is taken to be compositional in most modern approaches. This is the idea that the overall meaning of a phrase or sentence derives from the meanings of the constituent parts and the particular grammatical ways in which the constituent parts are put together. However, we saw that strict compositionality cannot be right and has to be replaced by a looser version in order to account for the meaning of complex units. Since in most cases this weaker version of compositionality is the only available (and reasonable) option, I suggest that idiomaticity is the default feature of natural languages and the meaningful (nonlinguistic) complex units of cultures.

Universality and Relativity

Perhaps the best way to term my stance on the issue of universality versus relativity of human knowledge is to use the apparently contradictory phrase *relative universality*. It is intended to suggest that knowledge and meaning are always relative to some context, even if there is a strong universal basis that underlies them. It seems that universality as regards knowledge and meaning is never complete; and given the manifold and fundamental presence of context in acquiring knowledge and making meaning, it cannot ever be (see Alverson, 1991). I will spell out this idea in more detail.

Speakers of different languages and members of different cultures have at their disposal a set of universal cognitive processes by means of which they make meaning. These meaning-making processes include categorization, framing, metonymy, metaphor, figure-ground alignment, force dynamics, perspective taking, attention, mental spaces, blending, and several others. Such processes are universally available for all human beings, but they may not put these processes to use to the same degree. For example, as Ning Yu's (1998) work shows, speakers of Chinese tend to conceptualize some of their emotions more along metonymic lines, while speakers of English tend to use predominantly metaphorical understanding for the same emotions. But we should not conclude from this that Chinese is predominantly metonymy oriented, while English is metaphor oriented. The reverse of this situation may apply in other domains. Jonathan Charteris-Black (2003) discusses the conceptualization of the main speech organs (mouth, lip, tongue) for various speech activities in English and Malay. He found that speakers of English primarily make use of metonymies and speakers of Malay primarily employ metaphorical conceptualization with regard to these speech organs when they talk about speaking. The point is that although the cognitive processes of metaphor and metonymy are available to Chinese, Malay, and English speakers, they do not utilize them in the same way and to the same degree. We have potential universality that is realized partially and differentially in different cultures.

In light of what we have seen in this book, it seems most reasonable for us to adopt a version of relativity that is based on the universality of embodiment. Relativity does not exclude universality in human knowledge and meaning making. *Embodiment* refers to basic bodily processes and action, such as physiological processes, perception, motor activities, and the like (Gibbs, 2005). These are all processes that all human beings share. Embodiment provides the motivation for large segments of our conceptual systems. We saw how this works in several chapters. One example is the discovery of basic colors and basic color terms. Berlin and Kay also discovered that the emergence of basic color terms in the world's languages follows an evolutionary sequence from *black*, *white*, *red*, and so on, to *pink*, *orange*, and *gray*. The basic colors may be at least partially based on universal aspects of color physiology.

A second example is basic-level categorization. Basic-level categorization depends on interactional properties—properties that are based on bodily experience. However, categorization in general and levels of categorization in particular are just as much a matter of culture as they are a matter of cognition. The cultural contexts in which the categorization takes place play a crucial role in why people categorize particular objects and events at particular levels of abstraction.

Metaphors might serve as our third example. Some conceptual metaphors may be universal because the bodily experiences on which they are based are universal. Many of the same conceptual metaphors may reflect certain culture-specific features at a more specific level of conceptualization. Other conceptual metaphors may be entirely based on unique cultural phenomena. However, even those conceptual metaphors that are based on universal embodiment may receive culture-specific meanings in different cultures. The SEX

IS HEAT metaphor may be universal or at least widespread due to its obvious universal embodiment, but it seems to possess different cultural meanings in different cultural contexts (see Emanatian, 1995; Kövecses, 2005a).

Metaphors provide a major source of variation in conceptualizing the world. For example, we saw that it is very common for languages to display alternative ways of conceptualizing spatial relations. As Heine's work indicates, there appear to be three major alternatives for doing this. In one, differential body parts are used; in another, either the body, environmental landmarks, or the immediate human environment is made use of; and in a third, the animal body, as opposed to the human body, is the basis of conceptualization. All of these are highly motivated. Spatial relations are conceived in terms of human beings in the center of a humanly interpreted universe. The human being speaking a language uses his or her own body and its relationship to the surrounding natural and cultural environment as a basis to conceptualize spatial relations. Many of our metaphors vary because our experiences as human beings vary and because the cognitive processes we put to use for the creation of abstract thought may also vary.

Language and Cognition: Linguistic Relativity Again

What is the relationship between language and cognition? I have considered two possible ways of interpreting the relationship: (1) cognition shapes language and (2) language shapes cognition. The second interpretation is known as the linguistic relativity hypothesis. The first one is the commonsense assumption entertained by those who believe that we have an internal representation system (or conceptual system) and that this system manifests itself in a variety of ways—one of them being language. Indeed, this was one of my main working hypotheses throughout this work: I tried to arrive at a characterization of the conceptual system by looking at language (although I have taken into account a large amount of other evidence as well). Now the question is whether (1) and (2) are mutually exclusive hypotheses. Another underlying assumption of this work was that they are not. We can resolve their apparent conflict if we think of them as both being a part of a larger process, in the course of which cognition gains expression through (shapes) the use of language, but at the same time language exerts an influence on (shapes) the way we think.

In early influential work, Berlin and Kay showed that basic colors may be based on universal aspects of color physiology. This may point to the possibility that it is color perception that determines/shapes the naming of colors. This conclusion goes against the linguistic relativity hypothesis, which states that it is language that determines/shapes what we perceive. However, in light of what was said in the previous paragraph, the two do not necessarily contradict each other. As a matter of fact, Paul Kay himself noted this possibility in an interview with him mentioned in chapter 2.

But the strong "anti-Whorfian" effects obtained in the domain of COLOR were not found in many other domains. Boroditsky studied the gender-marking system of several languages. Her basic research question was: Can we assume that, for instance, inanimate nouns that are marked for a particular gender do not play any role in the way speakers of such a language think about the world? Boroditsky's experimental studies show that the gender-marking system of a language does shape the way people mentally represent inanimate objects. Thus, language does seem to have an effect on how people think about things in the world.

In general, the languages we speak appear to make us attend to different aspects of experience through grammatically encoding different aspects of experience. That is to say, "we think for the way we speak," as Dan Slobin and his associates (Slobin, 1996, 2003) have repeatedly shown.

"Thinking for speaking" represents a relatively weak influence on the part of language on cognition. Langacker's suggestions concerning different grammatical forms for the expression of the same conceptual content are in line with this weak form of the influence of language on thought and experience. He claims that the use of different grammatical structures in different languages does not mean that the different ways of speaking shape the way we think or feel at a deeper level. However, the different ways of speaking do imply *different construals* of the same experiential content for that purpose.

But work by John Lucy, Stephen Levinson, and others suggests a stronger kind of influence from language to cognition. Their proposal, based on hard experimental evidence, is that differences in language structure result not only in differences in construal but also in differences in the successful performance of a variety of nonlinguistic tasks and activities. These results gain especial importance (1) because the Whorfian effects are shown in the area of grammar, where Whorf originally predicted them, and (2) because the effects were produced in tasks and domains that cannot be brought into direct correspondence with language.

It seems that after many years of misunderstanding and ridicule the Sapir-Whorf hypothesis has a good chance of being taken seriously and maybe even being proven right.

Meaning and Culture

We can take culture to be a large set of meanings shared by a group of people. To be a member of a culture means to have the ability to make meaning with other people. This requires, of course, for people to have the organ of meaning making, the brain, the cognitive processes of meaning making, the body that makes linguistic and nonlinguistic signs meaningful and that imbues with meaning all objects and events that are not signs themselves (e.g., a tree that we conceptualize as being vertical and tall), and the physical and social environment in which the brain and the body jointly evolve. On this view, then, particular cultures consist of the particular meaning-making processes that a group of people employs and the particular sets of meanings produced by them, in other words, a particular conceptual system. The meaning-making organs of the body and brain are shared universally and thus they do not belong to particular cultures. They are thus responsible for universal meanings—meanings shared by all groups of people (though, as we have seen, universal meanings always have culture-specific aspects to them; hence the notion of "relative universality" discussed earlier). However, as targets of conceptualization, both the body and the brain may be imbued with culture-specific meanings in particular cultures.

As noted earlier, a key component of meaning making is the physical and social environment. Cultures differ considerably relative to their physical and social environment. What this means in our terms is that the environment contributes a large portion of the meanings that members of groups use to understand other aspects of their world. This influence of the environment is most obvious in metaphorical conceptualization (see Kövecses, 2005a).

Also on this view, language can be regarded as a repository of meanings shared by members of a culture. This lends language a historical role in stabilizing and preserving a culture—due, in part, to "linguistic relativity," the notion that language shapes thought. Language is thus a part of culture because it gives us clues for meaning. At the same time, however, language often underdetermines interpretation; we create particular meanings (construals) in context (in other cases, particular construals are explicitly indicated by language).

In the course of their interaction for particular purposes, members of a culture produce particular discourses. Such discourses can be thought of as particular assemblies of meanings concerning particular subject matters. When discourses provide a particular perspective on especially significant subject matters in a culture and when they function as latent norms of conduct, the discourses can be regarded as ideologies (see, e.g., Charteris-Black, 2004; Goatly, forthcoming; Musolff, 2004), which may have an impact on other discourses within the culture. (On the issue of ideology in cognitive linguistics, see, e.g., Dirven, Polzenhagen, and Wolf, in press.) Discourse in this sense is another source of making meaning. A large part of socialization involves the learning of how to make meaning in a culture.

Some Examples of Meaning Making

In this book, I have surveyed a large number of cases where, in some form, people engage in the process of cultural meaning making. As a last reminder, I will now review some of them briefly here.

First, a large part of cultural meaning making consists in negotiating situations that arise from people having different and contradictory cultural/cognitive models of the "same" area of experience. People often call into question each other's conceptions of reality. I used the concept of "art" to demonstrate the point. The dominant folk theory of art is given as either a "classical" definition or one based on basic-level categorization. The classical definition attempts to provide the essential features of art, that is, the necessary and sufficient conditions that we need to call something art. However, my analysis of art showed that there are no essential features in terms of which the concept could be defined. The concept of "art" can be debated because it has no essential features; hence its features can be challenged, negated, and replaced. In short, then, meaning making occurs in both establishing what art is and making sense of the debates that surround it.

Second, classification systems can be thought of as being based on frames. Framing, as we saw, is one of our most important meaning-making devices. Part of frames' significance derives from the fact that, as Boroditsky's studies indicate, the gender-marking system of a language shapes the way people mentally represent certain objects. Frames are also crucially involved in how we form categories. For example, due to frame-based, as opposed to similarity-based, categorization, cultures may differ in terms of the ways they classify experience. We saw an instance of this in the operation of the "domain principle" in the case of Dyirbal.

Third, meaning making may be involved in cases where we are trying to establish the identity of people or objects. This can be an especially sensitive issue when it comes to identities that involve sex, ethnicity, social or political roles, and so on. In such situations, we are confronted with difficult questions, such as "Who is she?" and "Who am I?" This may become an issue even when we think we cannot have a problem in deciding it. The particular example I discussed in this connection centered around the identity of motherhood.

Fourth, we also need the meaning-making process to understand symbols. The understanding of symbols often depends on various cognitive processes I have studied in this book. Metaphor, metonymy, blending, and others are especially important in comprehending symbols. A cultural symbol, like the Statue of Liberty, may evoke particular conceptual metaphors, such as ACTION IS MOTION and KNOWING IS SEEING, for its interpretation.

Fifth, the understanding of many actual historical events may require metaphorical understanding—not only on the part of an observer but also on the part of a participant. As an example of the latter, the Mormons moved to the Salt Lake City area in the nineteenth century as a result of following through the metaphor that their journey to the west corresponds to the movement of the Jews to the Promised Land (see Kövecses, 2002). This is the metaphor that made the action meaningful for them.

Sixth, how do we understand the sentences that describe a certain plot in a piece of literature? One important way to see them connected is given by being able to connect them on the basis of image-schemas. We saw this in Michael Kimmel's analysis of *Heart of Darkness* by Joseph Conrad. Image-schemas, such as CONTAINER, SOURCE-PATH-GOAL, FORCES, help us understand and remember the plot of the novel. That is, we can make meaning of a certain kind by means of image-schematic understanding.

Seventh, cultures consist of not only abstract meanings in the head but also material objects and physical events. Even the simplest objects and events can have complex culturally specific meanings. Material anchors are a case in point. Certain material anchors can be regarded as the cultural-physical counterparts of cognitive blends. Material objects of this kind help maintain, reinforce, and change the cognitive processes that were used to create them.

This list provides some examples of cases discussed in this book where cultural meaning making in my sense plays an important role. Indeed, without engaging in (unconscious) meaning making along the lines I have suggested it would be difficult to claim that we function as culturally competent beings.

But given such a wide scope of the field as conceived here, we need to ask what the appropriate general name of such an enterprise could be. Clearly, cognitive linguistics is too narrow. Perhaps terms such as *cognitive social science* (Turner, 2001), *cognitive semiotics* (Brandt, 2004), and *cultural semantics* would be more appropriate labels. They would reflect the nature ("cognitive," "semantics") and the scope of the enterprise ("social," "semiotics," "cultural"). By accepting such designations for the field, we would indicate that the study of language, and especially meaning in language, is just a part (a small part) of a more general meaning-making activity that we as human beings are all engaged in—no matter which language we speak and which society we live in. In other words, after working out all the connections among the components of the meaning-making process (including embodiment, language, discourse, mind, and culture) in a much more detailed and comprehensive way than I have been able to do in this book, we might arrive at a "unified science" of meaning making that would allow us to make sense of, say, semantic anomaly and trash-can basketball by utilizing the same cognitive apparatus in human beings.

Solutions to Exercises

*A*lthough the title of this part of the book is "Solutions to Exercises," a word of caution is in order. First, the particular "solutions" we (Koller Bálint, Noémi Endrődi, Sarolta Komlósi, Rita Tóth, and Zoltán Kövecses) offer should not be taken as the only possible solutions to the exercises; in many of the cases, several other good solutions are possible. Several such solutions came to us from students in a course on the topic in the Department of American Studies at Eötvös Loránd University, Budapest, but, for lack of space, we cannot present all of them that could also be accepted in an introductory course. Second, the "good solutions" presented here are typically just the beginning or a part of a solution. In most cases, the solutions could be worked out much more fully and precisely (e.g., by making use of elaborate diagrams and figures). We judged the solutions on the basis of whether they contain the right ideas and whether they point in the direction of a good solution, rather than insisting on completeness and/or precision in working them out. Third, each instructor may have his or her preferred way of dealing with the problems in the exercises and may place emphasis on aspects of the problems and solving them that are different from the way we approached them.

Chapter 2

1. Possible solution: *At least in a Euro-American (Western) climatic and cultural context, you will be likely to find certain answers (like carrot and hammer) occurring more than others. People you ask will probably not be able to explain why they have mentioned exactly these words, but you, having read chapter 2, should be able to account for the phenomenon in a cognitive linguistic framework. The answers given are more frequent because they are more salient, "better" examples of their category than other members (prototype effects). Of course, the answers may vary greatly depending on your respondent's cultural background, the climate of the region where he or she lives (i.e., that region's staple agricultural produce), and to some extent by his or her personal eating habits.*

2. Possible solution: *Given the experiments mentioned in the chapter, most people are likely to agree that it is sentence a that captures the prototype of the noun* ring. *The noun in b differs from it in that it denotes an object where the circular object is not worn on the finger but surrounds a napkin. However, it shares the features of being material and being circular in shape with* ring *in a. In c the extension of the sense is based on metaphor. This usage does not have the feature of either being material or being circular in shape.*

3. Possible solution: *First, one should secure a satisfying number of participants, approximately in the same age group. Our hypothesis is that the category of* TOYS *is not simply characterized by prototype effects (more central and more marginal category members), but it also shows variation cross-culturally and along the lines of gender (girls and boys will probably pick different toys as their "best examples"). The explanation for this lies in culture and the process of socialization. Girls are given dolls to play with, while boys are given cars and toy trains from an early age. This is true at least in a Western (Euro-American) cultural context. Children growing up in essentially different cultures may have different prototypes in the category of* TOYS.

    To support the claim about the differences between the structure of girls' and boys' concept of "toys," one can use different methods (production of examples, rating, sentence verification, priming), and their high internal consistency is the guarantee that the results are reliable (e.g. which is a better example of toy—doll vs. car?).

4. Possible solution: *When Hungarian students of cognitive linguistics did this task (in the Department of American Studies at ELTE, Budapest), they found interesting results. As they mostly had Hungarian and American respondents at their disposal, it was these two cultures that they could compare with regard to the internal structuring (prototype effects) of the concept "house." Most typically, uppermost on their lists were items like a detached house (in Hungarian, "family house"), condominium, and high-rise block. Words like* hut, church, *and* barn *consistently occupied the last places on the lists. They found significant correlation between what kind of building a respondent inhabited and what building he or she mentioned among the first examples. The only major difference they found between Hungarian and American people's concept of "house" was that many of their American respondents included the word* home *as an item on their list. This shows that the words* house *and* home *in American English are much more closely related than the equivalent words-concepts in Hungarian.*

5. Possible solution: *The chances are that people will mention mostly males. If so, the linguistic relativity hypothesis is confirmed even in its strong version. If the distribution of males and females is more or less equal, the hypothesis is disconfirmed.*

Chapter 3

1. Possible solution: *As we would expect, it is the words denoting basic-level categories that are easiest to guess in a parlor game like Activity. This is especially and conspicuously true for drawing and miming but to a lesser extent to verbal explanations as well. In the first case, our drawing will reflect prototype effects: Chances are that people will draw a schematic representation of the category prototype (which, as we now know, has the most distinguish-*

able overall shape). Miming makes use of the fact that it is in relation to cat-egory members at the basic level that we perform the greatest number of typi-cal motor actions—thus, miming the action of turning the steering wheel will probably evoke the image of a car (and the concept/word car*) and most people will not think of* vehicle *or* Porsche. *Likewise, miming cutting movements performed in relation to a pipe-shaped edible object will make* sausage *pop up in the hearer's mind rather than* food *or* pepperoni. *Another factor that contributes to the fact that basic-level members are easier to guess than superordinate or subordinate ones is that we simply have more knowledge about these items and they come to mind more effortlessly and naturally than the other two levels (especially in a neutral context like the one Activity offers). Thus, all the four areas that distinguish basic-level categories from other levels (overall shape, motor actions, language, and knowledge) predispose these items to be more easily guessed in a parlor game like Activity than categories at either the more generic or more specific levels.*

2. Possible solutions:
A. *See table S.1.*
B. *Theoretically, the last task should have been more difficult. Since basic-level terms are what we most commonly use, it should be harder to specify which subordinate category of the basic-level term (for example,* BUS*) we are talking about (i.e., Bus Nr. 102 or Bus Nr. 11). That rules the subordinate category out. The superordinate category should also be difficult to mime, as there usually is no one typical motor action or no one set overall shape and when the mime starts to mime instances of the category with, for example, motor actions the guessers are more likely to think of the basic-level terms directly in connection with that particular motor action. That is, when the mime tries to act out* vehicle*, he or she is likely to grab hold of an imaginary steering wheel and rotate it in order for us to call to mind the action of driving. How-ever, the most typically evoked object in relation to the wheel-rotating move-ment is* car*, not* vehicle*.*

3. Possible solution:

Superordinate level: computer; PC
Basic level: laptop, personal organizer, palmtop, cell phone; processor
*Subordinate level: Nokia 3310; Intel Inside Celeron Processor, Pentium
    III Processor*

With the invention of newer and newer technical devices, there might be a general tendency of upward shift in the horizontal categories, earlier basic-level categories becoming less and less specific. For example, earlier COMPUTER *might have been a basic-level category; now, with a lot of new specific items appearing on the subordinate level, it has shifted up to the superordinate level.*

Table S.1. Possible Elements of Chart

Superordinate level	*VEHICLE*	GAME	*STATIONERY*
Basic level	*BUS*	*COMPUTER GAME*	PEN
Subordinate level	BUS NR.102	*MARIO BROTHERS*	PARKER-PEN

A more recent example is Pentium. Originally, this was the name of a specific type of processor. Now that there are more than three versions of it, it has become a basic-level term. We say, "My laptop has a Celeron, but I like my Pentium at home" to distinguish between the two processor types, not, "My laptop has a Celeron, but I like my Intel Inside Pentium IV/2003 Processor."

4. Possible solutions:
   A.

   a. N
   b. N
   c. B
   d. N
   e. N

   B.

   Brunette = N
   Blue = B
   Pink = B (however, the status of this may vary across languages and may be debated in some languages other than English, e.g., in Hungarian)
   Dark brown = N
   Blue-violet = N
   Black = B
   Ocher = N
   Saffron = N
   Buff = N

5. Possible solutions:
   A. Coffee. We use this word in everyday language, but to people who work in a café or drink coffee every morning, it may be a superordinate category. To them, coffee has many subcategories according to various features: where the coffee beans come from, how they were processed, what types of sweeteners and dairy products were added at which particular stage of boiling, and so on.
   B. Other highly specialized subcultures and terms: mechanics utilizing car types (Suburban, sedan, etc.) to talk about cars; architects using house types ("I don't know when I last saw a good, tornado-proof steel frame": here, steel frame is used to denote the whole house, not simply the structuring elements.); falconers using the names of species, like the Latin Falco peregrinus or peregrine falcon, to denote something that a layperson would only name a falcon or bird of prey.

6. Possible solution: *Depending largely on who our respondents are and in what actual situational context we do the experiment, we may get different results. The most likely outcome is that most respondents will say "stork" when they take a look at this picture (native speakers, that is, or non-native speakers who know this word and easily recall it from memory). However, we might find city dwellers who do not know this particular species or people who come from a climatic/geographical region where the stork is unknown. They might easily say "bird" as their automatic response. Conversely, ornithologists in a professional context (e.g., at a conference) might refer to it by its Latin name.*

This experiment may reveal that basic-level status is not something fixed and carved into stone forever. Not only may it shift with time (as in the case of computers), but it may also vary according to situational circumstances and people having different background knowledge, cultures, and places of origin.

Chapter 4

1. Possible solution: *(Some ideas from* Routledge Encyclopedia of Philosophy: *You should probably go beyond this discussion in the encyclopedia and make more use of Gallie's criteria.) Love is usually understood to be a powerful emotion that involves an intense attachment to the object of desire accompanied by a high evaluation of it (romantic/erotic love; loving deities). In some cases, however, love does not involve extreme emotions at all (motherly love) but only an active interest in the well-being of the object of one's love (love of principles, concepts). On other accounts, love is essentially a relationship that involves mutuality and reciprocity, rather than a relationship governed by extreme emotions (e.g., love in a marriage of fifty years).*

   One can conclude that there are many varieties of love, including erotic/romantic love, motherly love, love of humanity, and others. Different cultures also recognize different types of love. Because it is closely related to early experiences of attachment, it can exist in several levels within a single individual: Love may be present in various degrees of articulacy and depth—posing special problems for self-analysis and knowing one's own self. Moreover, love has been understood by many philosophers to be a source of great richness and energy in human life. However, even those who praise its contribution acknowledge it as a potential threat to spiritually healthy or even virtuous living. With so many contradictory factors, it is a mistake to try to give too precise an account of such a complex phenomenon—one is bound to be amiss somewhere.

2. Possible solution: *For example, if we think of freedom, this term has several different interpretations throughout the (political and nonpolitical) world. Even dictionaries emphasize different aspects of freedom as relevant. However, one will probably find a central definition (a common feature from most of the definitions) with several noncentral ones. Apart from the fact that contested concepts are internally complex, other factors, such as culture, political systems, accepted traditions, and more, cause these concepts to be contested ones. If one expects to pinpoint these factors, cross cultural experiments need to be carried out to discover how different communities interpret the (political) terms in question.*

3. —

Chapter 5

1. Possible solution: *When Hungarian university students of cognitive linguistics did this exercise, most of them came up with roughly the following solution.* Spinster *in the componential view is defined in terms of essential features such as* −MALE, + ADULT, + BEYOND CONVENTIONAL AGE OF MARRIAGE, −MARRIED, *whereas* bachelor *is defined by the same characteristics except it is* +MALE *in his case. Strictly in terms of a componential view, thus, the two concepts are each other's mirror images and are therefore also each other's counterparts.*

Therefore, if componential analysis were sufficient for a good understanding of categories, we would expect the two concepts to have an equal status in our minds. However, the cultural knowledge we inherit and that surrounds us (at least in a Euro-American, "Western" cultural context), tells us that this is not the case. A large amount of background cultural knowledge is needed to understand the two frames. For example, the frame of SPINSTER *is laden with negative connotations. Spinsters are usually frowned upon as instances of social failure who have only themselves to thank for for not having "found" a husband. They are usually portrayed as negative "characters." Conversely, the cultural connotations of* BACHELOR *tend to be the opposite. Middle-aged unmarried men are considered to be "unrealized potentials" and generally good candidates for husbands rather than failures. When we think of the prototypical bachelor, the figure we have in mind is either someone who decides to enjoy life rather than tying himself down in a lifelong commitment or someone who focuses on his career too much and thus has not had much time for romantic relationships and establishing a family. The fact that we have a bachelor's degree but no spinster's degree is a further confirmation of the asymmetry of the two frames.*

2. Possible solution: *Though there will be many similarities across different cultures (for example, a woman, the bride, and a man, the groom, are being joined "in holy matrimony[?]"), there are various differences that can be found. From the colors that are put to use (e.g., Europeans and Americans adorn the bride with white clothes, signaling innocence) to the number of previously wed women that a Muslim may have, through the feasting customs and the type of festivities that are held before and after the marriage ceremony itself, or the superstitions (e.g., the groom may not see the bride dressed up in her wedding gown until the ceremony, etc.). The task is to find specific instances of these differences between the cultures.*

3. Possible solution: *The HOTEL frame: You go to the reception desk of the hotel, tell the desk clerk your name and address, give him or her your ID, tell him or her how long you want to stay and what kind of a room you want, with or without breakfast, and so on. The desk clerk gives you the key to your room and you sign your name in the check-in book. The bellboy takes care of your luggage. You find your room and settle in.*

    Checking in may evoke several additional frames as well: You can check into a library or check into a dormitory you live in, you can check in at your workplace or check in to see one's mother, or you can check in at the airport, and so on, all constituting very different frames.

4.
   —

5. Possible solution: *This is a frame-external negation, since it does not negate the actual semantic content of the sentence; it only negates the frame itself and the applicability of the frame and offers another frame to be activated (skinny typically has a negative connotation, while slim typically has a positive connotation). This is only an apparently contradictory sentence.*

Chapter 6

1. Possible solution: *When asked to do this creative exercise, Hungarian students of cognitive linguistics came up with lots of different schemes, but all of*

these plans agreed in some respects. For example, almost everyone mentioned that they would make use of category levels in the following way. They would put up signs with superordinate category names on them above the different sections, with the purpose of giving a general direction to the customer as to where he or she should orient him/herself for the desired article. Then, they argued, within the different departments they would make further subdivisions, this time by using basic-level categories as more specific guidance to the customer. Within these subsections, the different kinds of items (at the subordinate level) would be arranged according to price, size, quality, and so on. There are goods that would be difficult to categorize due to the fact that products are not necessarily categorized with the principle of family resemblances in mind. There is an alternative principle, namely frame-based categorization, where it is entities belonging to the same frame that we group together rather than entities sharing characteristics. In frame-based categorization, we take practical life and its situations as the basis of organization. For example, men's colognes would be put on the shelves of the toiletries department if we were to go by resemblance-based categorization alone. However, the frame of which men's colognes are a part is the FORMAL MEN'S WEAR *frame: We imagine a man dressing up for an occasion (perhaps wearing a suit, a tie, and elegant leather shoes) and the script of this event, for many men, includes putting on cologne as one of the last steps. Innumerable instances of such ambiguous categorization are bound to crop up when we design a department store. Which principle we prefer to apply in each case will determine our choice of arrangement.*

2. Possible solution: *B. Prototypical or paradigmatic stories are easier to remember because they fit into a classic schema shared by most people. Even children like these kinds of stories, for they help the children react to their own problems, since paradigmatic stories contain everyday conflicts—perhaps in a peculiar form. People are used to these prototypes, they categorize their own world according to prototypes, and the most easily recognizable emotions are also prototypical, together with their eliciting conditions.*

3. Possible solution: *There are many elements of folk tales in Star Wars, such as the poor peasant boy who wins out in the end; a princess, a dark lord, and even an evil mastermind. Aside from the Euro-American folk tale traits, we can also find elements of diverse cultures in it, such as Asian ones: martial arts and Eastern philosophy (i.e., self-discipline, keeping fit physically as well as mentally). Struggle for power (on the emperor's side), struggle for love (Han Solo and Leia), family feuds (Luke and Anakin), death of a fatherlike mentor (Obi-Wan) . . . anything that can be said to be stereotypically emotionally moving is featured in the story.*

4. Possible solution: *For example, marriage, if viewed according to the Christian (Catholic) laws and morals, cannot be nullified. What has been joined before the eyes of God should not be separated by man. Therefore, if one applies the Christian frame to marriage by using such words as* joined in holy matrimony, sacred marriage, wedding vow (or oath), blessed union, or holy wedlock, *one evokes the whole frame of the religion of Christianity, where Man is inferior to God and whatever God has approved of should not and cannot be made ineffectual by Man. However, putting to use such phrases as* the institution of marriage, mutual engagement, marriage settlement, or we gave each other our word *can have a different effect:* institution *implies a*

man-made thing; therefore, it can be revoked. Stressing mutuality in mutual engagement *gives way to nullifying the "agreement" (marriage) if one of the signatories does not keep his or her part of the promises included in the "treaty." The same is the case with* marriage settlement: *"It is sort of like a contract," which can be broken if one of the parties fails to deliver. In the last phrase, if one of the two goes back on his or her word, the other is no longer under the obligation of keeping her/his own, as in the days of knightly oaths (note that Christianity's oath giving is being distorted here).*

5. Possible solution: *Naturally, those who like animals are more inclined to personify them using pronouns like* he *or* she. *The underlying metaphor for these people might be that animals are beings with feelings, just like humans. They tend to refer to animals as having habits, like people. It is much easier to picture the animals as having personalities and even—though limited—intelligence. This type of framing is very close to how we frame humans. Killing or harming an intelligent being, one that feels, is much more easily looked upon as a crime. Members of the opposing group, however, often look upon animals as living beings but do not attribute feelings to them (or habits or any kind of human-like behavior that may give the animals some kind of personality). Their framing is closer to something like a plant. And we have no problem accepting "cutting down a plant," "trimming a plant," or "bending it" to our own needs. Another possibility for framing animals is to consider them as "wild beasts of nature." This would also provide those who do not care for animals with a frame that would make the acceptance of harming animals easier.*

6. Possible solutions:

   - *An example for differential framing in school would be the notion of test taking. The teacher may view it as merely "a means of grading," whereas the students taking the test may look upon it as a "nerve-wracking battle" with the institution.*
   - *Another example: Mr. X is commonly called the boss in the* OFFICE *frame but dad or husband in the* HOME *frame, where son and wife would have different choices to refer to the person.*

7. —

8. —

Chapter 7

1. Possible solution: *When this task was assigned to Hungarian students of cognitive linguistics, they came up with various different linguistic metonymies for the conceptual metonymies listed here, using recent publications of the American, British, and Hungarian presses alike. Also, they made quite a few interesting observations about what these metonymies reveal. Some examples are as follows:*

   PLACE FOR INSTITUTION:
   The Pentagon attempts to plan for the aftermath of the U.S.-led invasion two years ago . . . (=Department of Defense)

Yet a month later, the White House is still no closer to its goal of passing legislation . . . (=the President and the policy-making bureaucracy of the executive)
In the concluding sections of "An American Way of War," Mr. Fisher contrasts how Washington dealt with the prisoners of war . . . (=the State Department, or American foreign policy-makers)
It is political London's favorite parlor game: who would Prime Minister Tony Blair vote for? (=the British political institutions)

CONTROLLER FOR THE CONTROLLED:
Bush actually blitzed Iraq. (=the U.S. army)
Some of these problems may have been inevitable consequences of the war to topple Saddam Hussein. (=Saddam Hussein's regime and its supporters)

CONTROLLED FOR THE CONTROLLER:
The United States sees North Korea as an equal in nuclear talks. (=the American government)
Mr. Bush publicly stated convictions about the need to disarm Saddam Hussein, insisting that Iraq had prohibited weapons that presented a "serious and current" threat. (=the Iraqi government)
The U.S. spy agency relented this month and agreed in principle to release more documents. (=the leaders of the spy agency)
Medicare will cut the payment for each physician service next year. (=the decision-making body of Medicare)

   One observation in connection with the PLACE FOR INSTITUTION metonymies was that locations like the Pentagon, the city of Washington, and the White House abounded in American and non-American presses alike, suggesting that these places are known worldwide to be the centers of U.S. policy decision making and are therefore effortlessly identified as such. Some of the students commented on the frequency of the CONTROLLER FOR THE CONTROLLED metonymy as a proof for the centralized nature of Western democracies, where a group of people responsible for following the instructions of a leader is easily overshadowed and thus mentally conveniently accessed through the leader him- or herself. The metonymic configurations available in the CONTROL ICM are not simply linguistic or even conceptual phenomena; they also reveal much about the very hierarchical structure of Western societies.

2. Possible solutions:
   a. A WHOLE-PART metonymy, where the school, as a whole, stands for parts of it (i.e., teachers, homework, fellow students, and so on). Of course, school can also be a PLACE FOR INSTITUTION metonymy, since one rarely means exclusively the building itself even if it is the venue of most events connected to school. It may also be seen as an instance of the phenomenon called active zone, in which a larger, more general conceptual category (SCHOOL) may conveniently stand for the most typical event or process that takes place there. In this case, the active zone is learning (as the predominant purpose and activity of the school as an institution from the perspective of the student). If the same sentence, however, is uttered by a teacher, the active zone may well be teaching instead of learning.

b. *Smith using only his hands evokes a performance that may be good at first sight but surely lacks some deep emotional extra, which supposedly comes from his heart or soul. This involves the background understanding of an artistic rendering of a score.* However, Brahms *stands for a piece of music written by the famous composer Johannes Brahms; thus a whole-part relationship or* COMPOSER-FOR-THE-PIECE *metonymy is also involved (more generally,* ARTIST FOR WORK OF ART *or* PRODUCER FOR PRODUCT).

3. Possible solutions:

   a. WHOLE THING FOR A PART OF THE THING: *house (vehicle) for the walls (target) that were actually painted. ("active zone" phenomenon)*

   b. PART OF THE THING FOR THE WHOLE THING: Big Stomach *(vehicle) for the person (target) who ate all the food.*

   c. PROPERTY FOR THE CATEGORY: White Rose, Red Rose *(vehicles) for the Houses of Lancaster and York, who used these symbols to identify themselves (targets).*

   d. PROPERTY FOR THE CATEGORY: Redshirts *(vehicle) stands for a group of people (target) wearing shirts of red color.*

   e. PLACE FOR THE INSTITUTION: Harvard *(vehicle) stands for the whole university (target), including the staff (faculty), the students, the grounds, the campus, and so forth.*

4. Possible solution: *When Hungarian students of cognitive linguistics were assigned this task, they gave roughly the following answer: All of the examples here have the* CAUSATION *ICM as their common frame. The metonymies are all types of the* EFFECT FOR CAUSE *metonymy. In the first example, the effect of slow-moving traffic stands for the either the bad condition or the congested nature of the particular route. The book cannot be sad because it does not have feelings—the contents of the book can make us sad—the effect of the book stands for its ability to cause sadness. In the third and fourth examples, too, "ruin" and "failure" are effects (end results) of certain causes—thus* She caused my ruin *and* He caused his own failure *have roughly the same meaning as the original, metonymic sentences here. These two latter also constitute a special subtype of the* EFFECT FOR CAUSE *metonymy, in which a state/event stands for the thing/person/state that caused it ("she was a success" and "he was a miracle" are further examples).*

5. Possible solution: *One large area where metonymy-based cultural practices can be found is advertisements. In one type of advertisement, cosmetics products are regularly used by beautiful young people. The underlying metonymy seems to be:* BEAUTIFUL YOUNG PEOPLE FOR PEOPLE IN GENERAL. *The idea seems to be that "if the product makes them beautiful, it will make me beautiful, too."*

Chapter 8

1. Possible solutions:

   a. *Metaphor:* THEORIES/ARGUMENTS ARE BUILDINGS. _____

   b. *Mappings:*

i.	*foundation*	→ *basis that supports the entire theory*
ii.	*framework*	→ *overall structure of the elements that make up the theory*

      iii. *stability of the building* → *the strength of a theory/argument*
      iv. *process of building* → *constructing the theory/argument*
      v. *the person building the* → *the person constructing the theory/*
          house   *argument*
    and so on

2. Possible solution:

   Metaphor: PEOPLE ARE PLANTS.
   Mappings:
      i. *the plants*   → *the people (central mapping)*
      ii. *cutting down a plant* → *ending a human life*
      iii. *plants in their prime* → *young people*
      iv. *cutting down the plant* → *killing a person in a violent way*
          in a violent way
    and so on

3. Possible solutions:

   a. MORAL IS UP; IMMORAL IS DOWN
   b. HIGH SOCIAL STATUS/POWER IS UP; LOW SOCIAL STATUS/LACK OF POWER IS DOWN
   c. HAPPY IS UP; SAD IS DOWN
   d. HEALTHY IS UP; SICK IS DOWN

   In general, upward orientation is assigned to positive things, while downward orientation is used to speak about negative things. Thus, we have the generic-level metaphors GOOD IS UP *and* BAD IS DOWN.

4. Possible solution: *In all of the excerpts, Britain is conceptualized as a mother/ parent. Thus, American colonies are seen as dependent children in need of nurturance and guidance from the mother. These entailments not only establish a clear power hierarchy between the colonies and Great Britain (with the latter occupying the superior position) but also circumscribe the rightful sphere of action for colonists. The colonies are thought of as not capable of defending themselves and therefore in need of the protection of Britain ("protectress"). In excerpt a, an alternative metaphor of the British Empire is also established besides the* MOTHER *metaphor. According to this metaphor, the* BRITISH EMPIRE IS A HUMAN BODY. *The most important mapping of this conceptual metaphor is that Britain itself is the head (the center) and the colonies are body parts directed by the head. One important entailment of this particular metaphor is that the colonies (just like body parts) are under the control of the head and carry out its "orders." In other words, this metaphor further strengthens the power hierarchy established by the* MOTHER *metaphor.*

5. Possible solution: *There are several ways in which Emily Dickinson extends and quite profoundly transforms the common* LIFE IS A JOURNEY *and* DEATH IS DEPARTURE *metaphors in this poem. In fact, part of the special poetic quality of her lines seems to come from her novel uses of these metaphors: she brings in new elements of the source domain and uses them to structure the domains of* LIFE *and* DEATH *in new, unusual, surprising and poetic ways. The mappings are not always clear, but the fuzziness of the target is what poetry in part is*

about. The LIFE IS A JOURNEY *metaphor is fused with the* DEATH IS DEPARTURE *metaphor so that the* JOURNEY OF LIFE *becomes the* DEPARTURE OF DEATH. *This is my interpretation, but others might interpret the poem in a very different way.*

Chapter 9

1. Possible solution: INFOTAINMENT *may be regarded as an example of the target domain actually becoming the source domain and the fusion turning into social-physical reality. This fusion is signaled by the morphological blending of the two words* information *and* entertainment. *Within this broad area, we can find many instances that prove that the process is indeed happening. For example, we routinely talk about the random skipping from one piece of (interesting) information to the next in terms of an entertaining sport, namely, surfing. But other, nonlinguistic examples also come to mind. Documentaries with the original purpose of informing/educating the public can only hope to succeed if they are also entertaining and contain show elements. It is enough to think of documentaries about the natural world, in which the world of wild animals is brought to the audience in a deliberately entertaining way (e.g., the famous* Desert Show *documentary). Cartoons that are meant to educate children about environmental protection are also presented as funny adventure tales. The "trivia-book" industry has become a field in itself, and many people are entertained by picking up otherwise completely useless pieces of information.*

2. Possible solution: *Throughout American history, the changing self-conceptualization of Americans has been influencing the country's actions and policy decisions. For example, the* MELTING POT *metaphor that was dominant in the nineteenth and early twentieth centuries entailed that America saw itself as a nation of immigrants, whose aim is to transform its newcomers with diverse cultural, ethnic, and racial backgrounds into one homogenous amalgam, where everyone adopts the same Anglo-Saxon Protestant heritage and conforms to this dominant culture. This metaphor gave rise to policy measures whose aim was to heavily Americanize immigrants and replace their original identity with a new American identity rooted in Anglo-Saxon Protestant values, the English language, and the country's democratic institutions (those established by the Founding Fathers). The more recent* SALAD BOWL *and* MOSAIC *metaphors have just the opposite entailments. A salad is made up of different components with different flavors, and all of these ingredients add their unique touch to the composite taste of the salad. Similarly, a mosaic is made up of tiny parts of different colors, and all of these contribute to the harmony of the whole picture. It will follow that people who share these latter metaphors of American society will not push for forceful integration and homogenization. Rather, they will encourage cultural diversity and all the different ethnic, cultural, and racial groups' preserving their own special cultural heritage.*

    Another field where such differences in framing have had policy consequences in the United States is that of health care. Politicians who advocate universal health care as a right of every citizen will talk about "health care" and "the repairing of the safety net provided by Medicare or Medicaid." Through talking about health issues in terms of individuals and their needs, these politicians foreground humane concerns. Conversely, there are politicians who routinely talk about a "health-care business," the "medical marketplace," and "consumers who can purchase whatever service they want" there. This business-minded framing will foreground strictly economic and financial perspectives, and the policy decisions made on its basis will take into account the needs of individual citizens to a lesser extent.

3. Possible solution: *"Road movies" as a uniquely American phenomenon may stem from the quintessential American experience of the first settlers, who traveled to a new, unknown land to begin a new life. This first journey was followed by many journeys across the continent with the aim of populating and "civilizing" it. Even today, Americans still tend to be notorious movers who often do not develop any binding attachment to any particular geographical location in their country. Thus, it is no surprise that all these experiences condense in the American psyche as a dominant metaphor for life. From novels like Kerouac's* On the Road *through a great number of road movies (Thelma* and Louise, *for example), the journey on the road may be interpreted as the beginning of a new life or an escape from the past toward a different future. The essence of life is not departing or arriving but "being on the road," always "on the go," involved in a quest after meaning, the discovery of the world's opportunities, self-discovery, and self-fulfillment. In other words, there seems to be a heavy reliance on the part of Americans on the metaphor* LIFE IS A JOURNEY.

4.

—

Chapter 10

1. Possible solution: *One consequence of such basic differences in spatial conceptualization is that native speakers of L1 will inevitably transfer their L1 conceptualization to L2. Precisely because these spatial conceptualizations are so deeply ingrained, errors in foreign language learning like these are the most difficult to avoid or weed out. One way to do so still would be to explain the difference in cognitive linguistic terms rather than just giving L1 and L2 equivalents with equation marks between them, leaving the apparent difference unaccounted for. Once the student realizes that these differences are not random but can be systematized (or at least compiled into a finite list), he or she will be able to handle them better. Moreover, teaching the L2 conceptualization rather than the linguistic item might be effective. This could be done via graphic illustrations as well. For example, a Hungarian student of English should be confronted with a drawing of the "English" sky as a three-dimensional thing (figs S.1 and S.2).*

2. Possible solution: *Though the examples are not abundant, we could say that the motive of journey is in them; namely, the* LIFE IS A JOURNEY *conventional conceptual metaphor is present in a special form:* CANCER IS AN OBSTACLE IN LIFE'S JOURNEY. *Verbs like* move into *and* walking off *suggest that a kind of traveling is involved in the metaphors (note the container and source-path-goal schemas). Life is a kind of trip, and cancer is a roadblock on the road of life, detouring the person, which results in moving her in another direction, unfortunately sometimes toward negative ends.*

    For example, a new phase may be a phase where one has no other choice but to walk the road the "roadblock" of cancer has detoured her onto . . .

Figure S.1 The "Hungarian" sky

toward an inevitable death. Walking off the face of the earth *is a phrase that definitely has negative and alienating connotations. At the same time, these metaphors contain the element of movement: Cancer forces a person to alter her course, move somewhere, often downward ("I hit rock bottom"), inward, or toward a center ("to the core of life"; "I coiled up"; "inner part"). Another view of cancer was* CANCER IS A (NEGATIVE/POSITIVE) FORCE: *It pulls you down, forces you to strip away a lot of things that don't matter; at the same time there were opinions that* CANCER IS A SIGNAL: *It makes one concentrate on the more important things in life. One other conceptual metaphor can be* EMOTIONAL EFFECT IS PHYSICAL IMPACT. *Cancer is an entity, the embodiment of pain that results in emotions.*

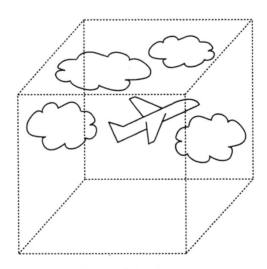

Figure S.2 The "English" sky

3. Possible solution: *Metaphors in the text:* go further down the road, look down the road, snowball effect, floating down the river. *These metaphors can be grouped under the conceptual metaphor* LIFE IS A JOURNEY; *however, Howard's conceptualization of "life" also includes going down.* → LIFE IS GOING DOWN. *When Judy, on the one hand, uses the expression* snowball effect *she tries to capture how Howard might feel (evoking the picture of a snowball rolling downward on a hill, getting bigger and bigger and becoming more and more unstoppable). Howard, on the other hand, chooses to liken it to "floating down the river," which not only shows the uncontrollability of the situation but also evokes the slow stagnation, the slackness, and the slump quality of his state. This example proves that one's own personal history influences what metaphors one uses. For a psychologically ill person life can be very different from that experienced by healthy people.*

4. Possible solutions:
a. *The teacher conceptualized as a "pipe" has probably arisen as an instance of a rich imagistic metaphorical extension of the conventionalized* ANGER IS A HOT SUBSTANCE IN A CONTAINER *metaphor. In other words, the abstract, somewhat generic original metaphor was specialized, in that the container was given the concrete/specific "value" of a pipe and, accordingly, the contents came to be instantiated by the burning tobacco in the pipe. In other words, the original, schematic source domain was replaced by a more detailed and specific source (one that could be derived from the original source) and the elements of this new source came to be mapped onto the target domain. Moreover, in the Hungarian sentence, the "pipe-container" metonymically stands for the anger the "pipe container" contains (cf.* She was fuming with rage*). This Hungarian variation on the aforementioned near-universal metaphor is similar to the variations in Chinese and Japanese that were discussed in this chapter. Those, too, modified the original, more generic and abstract source domain by structuring it with some culture-specific content.*
b. GIVING OUT F GRADES IS PLANTING TREES—*in Hungarian, this metaphor is based on an objective resemblance between the figure 1 and some common physical entities that recall the schematic vertical shape of the figure (maybe even with the little "hook" at the top also taken into consideration). Hence, the figure 1 is easily understood in terms of trees, stakes, hoes, or harpoons. Once that resemblance is set up and the metaphorization happens, the "tree" element of the source domain immediately entails a great deal of general knowledge about the frame it evokes. As is usually the case, some entailments map onto the target, whereas some do not. For example, "planting trees" is mapped onto the target, and it becomes the teacher "handing out Fs." However, the entailment that trees have leaves and consist of several parts is not mapped onto the target in this particular metaphor (i.e., not all entailments are utilized).*

Chapter 11

1. Possible solution: *The finding that many of the function words in grammar derive from morphological items that used to (or in some form still do) denote concrete physical entities says a lot about the nature of language. For one thing, it is yet another proof for the argument that abstract grammatical*

meanings were originally conceived figuratively (through metaphor and metonymy). If we look at prepositions, for instance, we find that many of them etymologically derive from the names of body parts (back and ahead are examples in English). Meaning is thus "embodied" and the mental is intimately and inextricably connected to the "bodily" and "physical." In Hungarian, for instance, the preposition for "next to" (mellett) is related to the word for "breast/chest" (mell). Like "back," in Hungarian hátra (hát is the Hungarian word for the body part "back"). Moreover, the Hungarian prefix for "inner" is bel, which can historically be traced back to the word for "bowels" (bél).

2.
   —

3.
   —

4. Possible solutions:
   a.

i.	theory	⇒	Gr. theoria *contemplation, speculation, sight.* f. theoros *spectator*
ii.	fear	⇒	OS. faron *lie in wait,* OHG. faren *plot against, lie in wait*
iii.	life	⇒	OHG. lib *life* (Ger. leib *body*), ON. lif *life, body*
iv.	sad	⇒	OE. saed, OHG. sat (Ger. satt), L. sat, satis *enough,* satur *sated*
v.	succeed	⇒	L. succedere *come close after, go near*
vi.	comprehend	⇒	f. COM- + prehendere *seize*
vii.	anger	⇒	OE. enge, OS., OHG. engi *narrow*

   b.

   i. *Theory has to do with* KNOWLEDGE; *"knowing is seeing," therefore spectator.*
   ii. *Lying in wait correlates with an emotion (fear) and can therefore stand for it metonymically.*
   iii. *The body is living, and it is only functional when it is alive, so this is a metonymy* LIVING ORGANISM FOR LIVING.
   iv. *Sated suggests that someone's "emotion container" is full, thus* STRONG FEELING IS FULLNESS OF CONTAINER—*later on, the strong feeling might have been narrowed down to an intense bad feeling, for example, sadness*
   v. *Development is growth/going (development: succeed; going: go near).*
   vi. *"Understanding is grasping" seize.*
   vii. ANGER IS A PRESSURIZED CONTAINER; *maybe narrow suggests the pressurized state of the container, although the underlying conceptual metaphor is difficult to identify. Maybe this is metonymically motivated: "cause of anger for anger itself."*

(Source: Oxford Concise Dictionary of English Etymology)

Chapter 12

1. Some hints:

- *Structural elements: a starting point; duration of events; ending point (which is the same as the starting point)*
  - *Logic: symmetrical (you always get back to the same starting point and the phases in a cycle are always the same)*
  - *Temporal: life cycle (nature: the cycle of the seasons, the months of the year, ebb and tide, the moon cycle, the menstruation cycle of women, the energy cycle, history as a spiral [Hegel])*
  - *Spatial: traveling (starting from one point and returning to it)*

2. Possible solutions:

  a. CONTAINER *image-schema*
  b. SOURCE-PATH-GOAL *image-schema;* LINK *image-schema*
  c. CENTER-PERIPHERY *image-schema;* PART-WHOLE *image-schema*
  d. SOURCE-PATH-GOAL *image-schema*
  e. CENTER-PERIPHERY *image-schema;* SOURCE-PATH-GOAL *image-schema;* LINK *image schema*
  f. SOURCE-PATH-GOAL *image-schema;* LINK *image-schema*
  g. CENTER-PERIPHERY *image-schema;* PART-WHOLE *image-schema;* SOURCE-PATH-GOAL *image-schema;*
  h. CONTAINER *image-schema: full-empty*
  i. WHOLE-PART *image-schema: center-periphery*
  j. PATH *image-schema: front-back*
  k. WHOLE-PART *image-schema: matching*
  l. WHOLE-PART *image-schema: center-periphery/matching*
  m. PATH *image-schema: cycle—up and down*

3. Possible solutions:

- *Heads of governments or boards typically sit or stand in the middle.*
- *Gold medalists are in the middle (and at the highest point)—between the silver and the bronze medalists.*
- *In movies (and their billboard posters), the important faces or objects tend to be up close.*
- *World maps in Europe typically have Europe in the middle—those published in America often have the American hemisphere in a central position, with the rest of the world on the peripheries.*
- *In geopolitics, some countries are regarded as central with respect to certain cultural-political establishment, while others belong to the periphery zone—this may shift to a certain extent and the center-periphery alignment in a geopolitical sense does not necessarily coincide with center-periphery in a geographical-physical sense. For example, America's Heartland is taken to be the Midwest; however, in terms of industrial production and business, America's centers (New York and Los Angeles) are located at the geographical peripheries. Still, capitals of countries typically occupy not only a central role but*

often a geographically central position in the country (e.g., Hungary, Spain, France, the states of Indiana, Colorado, etc.).

4. Possible solutions:
   a. *See table S.2.*
   b. *Some metaphors in language for* EMOTION IS A BURDEN:

"he is plagued by heavy thoughts"
"her grief weighed her down"
"every man has to carry his cross"
"I feel relieved now"

5.
   —

Chapter 13

1. Possible solutions:
   A.

I'm in the phone book. (subj.)
The teacher is standing in front of Jerry. (obj.)
The teacher is standing in front of me. (subj.)
You can be sure that your grandma loves you. (obj.)
Why don't you love me? (subj.)
The teacher is standing in front of her desk. (obj.)

   B.

    i. *Figure-ground alignment: the football is the figure and the background with respect to which we relate it is the table.*

ii–iii. *Profiling/attention: In ii. "in the field" profiles a small, pointlike spot somewhere in the field; in contrast, in iii. the scene profiles a more extensive area all over which there are corpses scattered.*

 iv–v. *Dynamic versus static scene: iv. is sequential scanning (dynamic), while v. is summary scanning. (static).*

  vi. *Viewing the same situation from a different perspective: vi. the optimist's perspective, vi. the pessimist's perspective.*

 vii. *Case of structural schematization: temporally unbounded-bounded.*

Table S.2. Possible Elements under Force-Dynamic Interpretation of Emotions

Metaphorical Mapping	Agonist's Force Tendency	Antagonist's Force Tendency	Result Action
Source	*Person: to hold the burden*	*Burden: to cause physical pressure on person*	*Person experiences physical difficulty*
Target	*Self: to withstand emotional stress*	*Emotion: to cause emotional stress on self*	*Self experiences emotional stress*

c.

Sue walked across the road (complex relation; several relations along the path).

Sue is sitting across the table from Jim (simple relation; only one—at the end of the imaginary path).

- *Distinction between "simple" and "complex relations"*

    i. *First you as trajectory are in an entity (landmark); then you move through a series of locations to a place that is out of the landmark entity. Dynamic verbs are good examples of words that construe the situation in terms of multiple relations between the trajector and landmark (road)—the situation is conceptualized as a complex relation*

    ii. *There is only a single relation—a simple one—between Sue and Jim. As noted earlier, this is characteristic of static verbs like* sit

2. Possible solution: *The examples listed here are all cases of focus of attention versus scope of attention. When we apply "focus of attention" we focus on certain facets of a frame. For example, a means the education at the university, b focuses on the building, c the institution, d. the institution/education (in that special institution), e the building.*

    However, c' and c" are those that have "scope of attention" phenomena, specifically, that Europe is peripheral if we think of departments. We usually do not establish a direct link between Europe and (university) departments, because Europe in this case is not in the immediate scope, but in a distant one. Even in c" the two aspects cannot be brought together to yield an immediately acceptable sentence.

3. Possible solution: *The words are examples of different degrees of schematization. In all three cases, a more general category is given first and then a specific example of that general category is presented. We have learned in this chapter that schematization is a kind of scalar adjustment that views things at a higher, more abstract level ignoring some determining features at a lower level. For example,* ANIMAL *ignores several determining characteristics of the specific animal,* cat, *for example, that it is not really attached to humans and that although it is a domestic animal it likes to wander in the wild.* ANIMAL *is a unifying category/schema that contains several distinct properties at the same time. The same is true for* QUADRANGLE. *It is a more general category that does not specify specific properties; thus, the object can still be a rectangle or perhaps a parallelogram. The same relation is characteristic of the last example.*

    These show that schematization, as a kind of categorization, generalizes things by emphasizing certain features, while ignoring others. Thus, it makes the world simpler and helps cognitive information processing and orientation in the world but avoids individual differences of the things and thus homogenizes them to some extent.

a. *count noun*   ← *individuated, bounded entity*
b. *the same*
c. *uncount, mass noun* ← *individuated entity*
    (unbounded entity)

4. Possible solutions:
   A.

   A fly is under the president's nose. (fly = figure, nose = ground)
   **The president('s nose) is above the fly. (size)*
   The car was behind the Coliseum. (mobility)
   **The Coliseum was behind the car.*
   Car = figure, Coliseum = ground
   A toy car was next to a millionaire's Ferrari. (complexity)
   **The Ferrari was next to a toy car.*
   Toy car = figure, Ferrari = ground

   B.

   i.   *Book = figure, newspaper/pencil = grounds (we have two grounds with respect to which we locate the figure).*
   ii. *This is a more complicated figure/ground alignment, with two figure/ground alignments combined – book is a figure and it is located with respect to the newspaper (ground). However, the newspaper also functions as figure with respect to the pencil (ground). Moreover, the original figure is also aligned with respect to the other ground (pencil).*

   ## Chapter 14

1. Possible solutions:

   a.   *My mother believes that Kate is ugly. (belief space)*
   b.   *My mother thinks Kate was not so ugly thirty years ago. (space for past)*
   c.   *Just imagine, I cheated the last time we played. (imagination space)*
   d.   *If I had not cheated, I would have lost two thousand dollars (counterfactual hypothetical space)*
   e.   *My would-be husband is my elementary school friend. (hypothetical future space)*

2. Possible solution: *The first sentence establishes a base/reality space with two elements, a boy and the puppy. The second sentence adds another element to the base space, the "frog in the open jar." The third sentence complicates the situation in that the word* thinks *creates the boy's belief space. In this belief space, we have a frog that "doesn't know it can get out of the jar." This element of the belief space requires the setting up of an imagined future space embedded in the belief space. Namely, in this imagined future space, the frog will not get out of the jar; it will stay there and won't escape. Having established these two spaces, the next sentence,* So he goes to sleep, *takes us back to the base space, into which a new frame, that of* SLEEPING, *is introduced. However, this base space is not the same as that with which the paragraph began. The belief space and the imagined future space entail a modified base space, one in which the frog is actually able to get out of the jar (since in reality, the frog can do this, only it is not aware of this ability). In the last sen-*

tence, a future space is established, now a factual future space. The space builder here is going to, and in this future space the frog gets out of the jar. Thus, the point of the paragraph is the contradiction between the imagined future space (embedded in the boy's belief space) and the actual future space.

3.   —

4. Possible solutions:

a. *Sentence is correct: Sentence i. has a role interpretation and sentence ii. has a value interpretation. However, the verb* expand *does not allow a role interpretation; it can only have a value interpretation.*

b. *Similarly, i. is correct because the verb* lessen *only allows for a value interpretation*

c. *Sentence ii. is correct because the verb* grow *only allows for a value interpretation.*

Chapter 15

1. Possible solutions:

- *Social architecture: The principles of designing and a conscious "construction" of society and its structure are meant here. The source, as always, is something more concrete; here the domain of* ARCHITECTURE *is utilized to structure the domain of* SOCIETY *in the blend. This kind of structuring makes it possible to view society as having pillars, for example, the three pillars of society: the judicial, executive, and legislative branches.*
- *Social ladder (e.g., climb the social ladder): This expression evokes at least three conceptual metaphors:* SOCIETY IS A STRUCTURED OBJECT (BUILDING), HIGH SOCIAL STATUS IS UP, *and* ACHIEVING HIGH SOCIAL STATUS IS UPWARD MOVEMENT. *This last metaphor is also possibly based on* LIFE IS A JOURNEY. *In terms of conceptual integration, all of these source and target domains have to be taken into account as input spaces that yield a blended space in which someone has acquired high social status, as described by the sentence "He's climbed the social ladder."*
- *A drinking spree: A spree is characterized by behavior that does not take into consideration what will happen next as a consequence of these actions—a foolish way of acting without responsibility. This frame is blended with the* DRINKING *frame.*
- *A shopping spree: Similarly, the* SHOPPING *frame is blended with the spree.*
- *Dance-away lover: The* DANCING *frame (there are two partners, corresponding to a loving couple) and the lover role are blended here. The* DANCING *frame can be viewed as a script of a relationship (meeting each other, eye contact, the dance itself as the main part of the relationship, and finally leaving each other or—if the pair happen to stay together—the "endless dance," meaning an eternal relationship). Someone who dances away means that he/she is not dancing with the other one anymore (i.e., it means separation, splitting up).*
- *Table tennis: In table tennis one of the inputs contains the* TENNIS *frame (two players with their rackets, a net dividing the court into*

*two equal parts, a ball), while the other contains a simple table,
resulting in a "miniaturizing" table version of tennis in the blend.*
- *Carmageddon (a famous car-demolition computer game; car +
Armageddon): Armageddon here means any catastrophic event,
destructive battle. The blend expresses that this destructive battle is
fought by cars. The blend embodies the essence of the game as well:
Cars get wasted throughout the game.*

2. Possible solution:

- *Input space 1 has Meier, the skier, who is relentless and strong,
usually wins, and is able to recover from injuries a normal human
being cannot overcome.*
- *Input space 2 has the Terminator, a robotic character from the movie
Terminator, with all the characteristics of an artificial robot: exceptionally strong, capable of deeds humans are incapable of, able to
"heal" (fix mechanically) itself, with set aims/goals to which it strictly
holds itself (concentrating only on its mission, carrying it out no
matter what difficulties might come).*
- *In the blended space we have a skier who outdoes his fellow competitors by far, simply because he is endowed with special talent. He is
almost impossible to beat and always gets up when others think there
is no chance of him getting up anymore. Combining the two names
and the characteristics of the real athlete and the imaginary movie
figure, we have "Herminator," who is more than just a perfect robot
and more than simply a talented athlete. He is a blend of the two.
Moreover, on a final note, it may be said that the blend is motivated
by the fact that the actor Arnold Schwarzenegger, who has played
Terminator in a number of movies, also happens to be an Austrian.*

3. Possible solution: *In the first part of the sentence, input space 1 contains the
woods, the lumberjack, the chain saw, and the trees that are to be cut down
by the lumberjack. Input space 2 contains the company, the consultant, the
job, and the redundant people who are to be fired by this consultant.*

*From the second part of the sentence, we have a third input space (3), namely,
a "value domain," that contains the two individuals Jack the Ripper and the
Boston Strangler (both of whom were notorious killers), and the elements of
this frame fill the roles of the fourth input space. This input space 4 is the
MURDER domain, which contains the means and rituals for the homicides the
killers mentioned earlier commit.*

*The second sentence prompts a fifth space, input space 5, containing butch-
ery, its means, tools, the person, the carcass that butchers work with, and so
forth, which will account for the bloody handling of a job (a similar instance
of this phrase is detailed in the chapter that deals with the blend of a surgeon
and a butcher).*

*All these input spaces are merged in the blend space, creating a person who
is hired to find those employees in the company whose job is not rationally
necessary to the company and fire them swiftly, impersonally—since s/he (the
chain-saw consultant) has no real connections to the company and definitely
not to its employees. Because of this fact, s/he can make objective judgments*

on who is needed and who is not needed at the company—without his or her emotions being involved. This is why he or she is seen as a ruthless, unfeeling, somewhat hidden or detached person, with a systematicity that is based on nothing but sheer, cold logic. Thus, in the new emergent structure, we deal with a person whose characteristics are merged/blended from five different input spaces.

4. Possible solutions:

    a. *If I were you, I would like me more. (blending of reality space, counterfactual space)*

    b. *Is Albany another Vietnam? (metonymy, Vietnam being the symbol of long-lasting, undeclared, unpopular war—based on the metonymy* SALIENT MEMBER FOR THE WHOLE CATEGORY)

    c. *Violet is the grandniece of Mervin and of Jessica. (simplex blending —associating kinship roles with specific values [individuals])*

    d. *The Johnson administration's War on Poverty is a churning Disneyland of administrative chaos. (blend of elements of Disneyland and those of bureaucracy)*

    e. *He has been entangled in the Kafkaesque web of criminal charges. (blend, Kafkaesque-nightmarish* WEB OF CRIMINAL CHARGES *is a metaphor)*

5. Possible solution: *It is a "physical/material blend," as it were, a conceptual integration made "real." The small boy puts on the clothes that are roughly identical to the clothes that Darth Vader wore in the Star Wars series. Though the boy is not tall, strong, or evil, he still evokes the name Darth Vader. This is a blend, in a sense that the two input spaces both contribute to the resulting "small Darth Vader":*

    • *input space 1: the boy, with all his characteristics, for example, being small.*

    • *input space 2: Darth Vader, with his own attributes (tall, strong, evil lord wearing black robes and a cape).*

    • *the resulting blended figure: more than just a boy and more than just Darth Vader. He is a boy version of Darth Vader (small "lord" wearing black robes and a cape).*

Chapter 16

1. Possible solution: *All of the examples in one way or another illustrate the phenomenon and principle of iconicity. Essentially, the principle of iconicity is based on a generic metaphor to the effect that MEANING IS FORM. The consequence of this is that more form (more words, repetition) suggests more meaning (greater intensity etc.). It is precisely this that explains why sentences a, b, e, and f carry a more emphatic meaning than they would if the words were not repeated. For example, the phrase* louder and louder *suggests a progressive increase of the volume in an imagistic way, as it were. Its meaning is definitely more expressive than* progressively louder *would be. The same applies for* farther and farther *in sentence f. In sentences c and d, the proximity of form correlates with closeness (inherence) of meaning (or strength of ef-*

fect). In c, the first sentence implies that learning has definitely taken place. In d, this is not implied. In d, the adjectives that are placed closer to the noun they modify are more inherent properties of the noun and are therefore more salient in its characterization (i.e., the material something is made of defines it more than its color or size, etc.).

2. Possible solutions: *In the case of* streetcar, *the nonderivable attributes would be "runs on tracks in cities," "old-fashioned," "(usually) powered by electricity," a "vehicle for public rather than private transportation." None of these attributes can be derived from either* street *or* car. *This word has come to mean such a well-defined category of vehicles that it may be thought of as an opaque compound: that is, it is no longer felt to be a compound, although the component parts have not merged phonetically.*

   Newspaper *is perhaps a less clear-cut example. The nonderivable attributes include "having sections and articles," "published regularly," and so on. However, the expression* online newspaper *would suggest that* NEWSPAPER *has become a category on its own and is no longer felt to be a compound word.*

   For bean soup *one would be hard-pressed to find any nonderivable attributes. Even the ones that offer themselves (like other ingredients such as carrot or meat) are not enough to treat* bean soup *as a category on its own. Bean soup is a type of soup, but newspaper is not a type of paper.*

   Skylight, *as meaning a window cut into the roof, is largely made up of nonderivable attributes. Actually, it is a kind of window rather than a kind of light. Thus, it may rightly be claimed to constitute a category of its own, and its component parts add relatively little to its aggregate meaning.*

   Drugstore *in its American sense may have started out as a "store where drugs are sold," but through time it has acquired a lot of nonderivable attributes (e.g., "general goods available," "usually a small-town establishment"), but it is questionable if this development qualifies it to assume a category status of its own and cease to be a kind of "store."*

3. Possible solution: *In a sentence like* What was your name again, please? *the speaker is definitely not referring to the past. Still, the verb form is a past form. This is because of the metaphor politeness or social distance is temporal distance; that is, the desk clerk is trying to be polite by signaling the maximum social distance between him and the new guest. For this purpose, the desk clerk has the option to change the present tense verb form into the past, temporally distancing the question from the immediacy of the present. Other similar examples abound in everyday language. For example, when we want to make polite requests, we often use hypotheticality (the conditional). Thus, a sentence like* If you could please spell your name *takes away the "edge" of a request by assigning the value of hypothetical to it when in reality both the speaker and the hearer know that what is meant is completely real and factual.*

4. Possible solution: *This construction has very limited use in the English language, in which the default case is that (adjectival) modifiers precede (and do not follow) the nouns whose meanings they modify. The examples here are rather isolated, and their rarity and the fact that the construction is just the opposite of the regular sequencing of nouns and modifiers in English contributes to their stylistic markedness (used for creating both an elevated and a mock-serious, ironic effect). The noun phrases with* immemorial, incarnate, politic, *and* public *are adaptations of the Latinate construction (still the de-*

fault constructions in languages such as French), whereas galore, over, *and* last/next *may have been formed on the analogy of this kind of construction at a stage in the history of language when both orders (modifier + noun, noun + modifier) were productive. If we want to generalize the difference in meaning between the constructions "Modifier-Noun" and "Noun-Modifier," we can say that the latter has an added meaning of stylistic markedness, being the less frequent construction.*

5. —

Glossary

Active zone. An active zone is the aspect, or facet, of an entity that is focused on (or profiled) by a relation (e.g., verb, preposition) in which the entity participates. For example, in the expression *Wash the car!* it is only the external body of the car that is focused on. *See also* Conceptual metonymy.

Alternative conceptualization/construal. A situation, or state of affairs, can be conceptualized, or construed, in several distinct ways. When this happens, we have to do with alternative conceptualization, or construal. *See also* Construal and Construal operations.

Aspects of conceptual domains. Both source and target domains are characterized by a number of different dimensions of experience, such as purpose, function, control, manner, cause, shape, size, and many others. These are called aspects of domains. Each such aspect consists of elements: entities and relations. Metaphorical mappings between a source and a target obtain between these elements. *See also* Conceptual domain.

Aspects of metaphor involved in metaphor variation. Conceptual metaphors consist of a variety of aspects, or components, such as source and target domains, mappings, linguistic expressions, experiential basis, cultural models, and others. These aspects are involved in variation in different ways. *See also* Dimensions of metaphor variation and Causes of metaphor variation.

Basic mapping. *See* Central mapping.

Basic terms. These are words that are characterized by a number of properties: They are monolexemic; their meaning is not included in that of another word; their application is not limited to one or a small number of objects, and so on.

Basic-level categories. The basic level is the level where people can identify category members most readily; this is the highest level where category members have similar overall shapes; this is the highest level where we interact with members by making use of the same motor programs; and this is the highest level where we possess the most knowledge (in terms of features) concerning categories.

Basis of metaphor. *See* Experiential basis (of metaphor).

Blend(ing). *See* Conceptual integration and Mental spaces.

Bodily motivation (for metaphor). See Experiential basis (of metaphor).

Category. A category is a mental representation for a set of objects or events.

Causes of metaphor variation. There are several distinct factors that cause variation in metaphor. They can be grouped into two large classes: differential experience and differential cognitive preferences and styles. *See also* Aspects of metaphor involved in metaphor variation and Dimensions of metaphor variation.

Central mapping. A central mapping is a mapping that is involved in projecting the main meaning focus (or foci) of the source onto the target. *See* Main meaning focus (of conceptual metaphor) and Entailments, metaphorical.

Classical category/categorization. This is the view that a category can be defined by essential features, that is, in terms of a set of necessary and sufficient conditions.

Cognitive model. *See* Frame.

Cognitive operations/processes. These are largely unconscious mental acts and activities we perform in order to make sense of language (discourse, sentences, linguistic expressions) and the social-cultural world (institutions, objects, practices, rituals, and the like). *See also* Construal operations.

Combining. This is one way in which a conventional, ordinary metaphor can be reworked in literature. It works by combining several conventional conceptual metaphors in a few lines or even within a single line. Thus, the metaphorical linguistic expressions used within a small space can activate in the reader a number of distinct conceptual metaphors.

Complex metaphor. This is a metaphor that is composed of simple or primary metaphors. The latter function as mappings within the complex one. *See also* Mappings, Primary metaphor, and Simple metaphor.

Complexity of conceptual metaphor. Conceptual metaphors can be placed along a scale of complexity, yielding simple metaphors at one end and complex metaphors at the other. *See* Complex metaphor.

Compositionality. This is the idea that the overall meaning of a complex expression can be computed from the meanings of the constituent parts and the ways of their combination. *See also* Strict compositionality and Partial/ Loose compositionality.

Concept. *See* Category and Conceptual domain.

Conceptual category. *See* Category.

Conceptual domain. This is our conceptual representation, or knowledge, of any coherent segment of experience. We often call such representations concepts, such as the concepts of "building" and "motion." This knowledge involves both the knowledge of basic elements that constitute a domain and knowledge that is rich in detail. This detail-rich knowledge about a domain is often made use of in metaphorical entailments. *See also* Entailments, metaphorical, and Frame.

Conceptual integration. Conceptual integration, or blending, is a cognitive operation in which input spaces or domains contribute some conceptual material to a blended space or domain on the basis of some shared abstract structure in a generic space or domain. Conceptual integration is a process that typically involves four spaces or domains: two input spaces or domains, a blended space, and a generic space. Such an interacting system of mental spaces is called a Network Model.

Conceptual metaphor. When one conceptual domain is understood in terms of another conceptual domain, we are dealing with a conceptual metaphor. This understanding is achieved by seeing a set of systematic correspondences, or mappings, between the two domains. Conceptual metaphors can be given by means of the formula A IS B or A AS B, where A and B indicate different conceptual domains. *See also* Mappings and Correspondences.

Conceptual metonymy. This is a cognitive process in which one conceptual entity, the vehicle, provides mental access to another conceptual entity, the target, within the same frame, or ICM. It is important to note that in metonymy both the vehicle entity and the target entity are elements of one and the same conceptual domain. *See also* Active zone.

Construal. Construal is a particular way of conceptualizing, or understanding, a situation (or, more technically, a state of affairs). There are usually several distinct ways in which a situation can be conceptualized. *See also* Cognitive operations/processes and Construal operations.

Construal operations. Construal operations are cognitive processes whereby we understand particular situations. Such cognitive processes include categorization, metaphor, force dynamics, figure-ground alignment, blending, and several others. We can use several distinct construal operations to conceptualize the "same" situation. Construal operations have to do with attention, comparison/judgment, perspective, and overall structure. *See also* Cognitive operations/processes.

Conventional knowledge. This is everyday, nonspecialist knowledge about a particular domain that is shared by speakers of a linguistic community.

Conventionality of metaphor. Conceptual metaphors may be more or less conventional; that is, they can be placed along a continuum, or a scale of conventionality. Some conceptual metaphors are deeply entrenched and hence well known and widely used in a speech community (such as LOVE IS FIRE), whereas others are much less so (such as LOVE IS A COLLABORATIVE WORK OF ART). The less conventional ones can be called novel (conceptual) metaphors. Metaphorical linguistic expressions that reflect a particular conceptual metaphor can also be more or less conventional. These less conventional, or novel, metaphorical expressions are especially prevalent in poetry. Thus, although they both come from the conceptual metaphor LIFE IS A JOURNEY, the lines by Frost "Two roads diverged in a wood, and I / I took the one less traveled by" are more novel than the clichéd expression *I'm at a crossroads in life.*

Correlations in experience. *See* Experiential basis (of metaphor).

Correspondences. To understand a target domain in terms of a source domain means that we see certain conceptual correspondences between elements of the source domain and those of the target domain. *See also* Mappings.

Cultural model. *See* Frame.

Cultural prototypes. These are prototypes (which see) that are defined by the particular goal, context, and history of categorization.

Cultural variation (in metaphor). Conceptual metaphors may vary cross-culturally and within a single culture. The limiting case of within-culture variation is individual variation in the use of metaphor. In those cases where a conceptual metaphor is universal, its universality obtains at a generic level, while the same conceptual metaphor shows cultural variation at the specific level. *See also* Universality of metaphor.

Dimensions of metaphor variation. Conceptual metaphors vary along two general dimensions of experience: cross-cultural (intercultural) and within-culture (or intracultural). *See also* Aspects of metaphor involved in metaphor variation and Causes of metaphor variation.

Domain. *See* Conceptual domain and Frame.

Elaboration (in metaphor). This is one way in which a conventional, ordinary metaphor can be reworked in literature. It works by elaborating on an existing element of the source domain in an unusual way.

Elements (of aspects of domains). The aspects of domains are constituted by (conceptual) elements: entities and relations. Mappings between domains are based on these elements. *See also* Aspects of conceptual domains.

Embodiment. This is the notion that language, meaning, and mind rely on and arise from bodily experience, provided in large part by image-schemas (which see), basic-level categories (which see), and correlations in experience (*See* Experiential bases [of metaphor]).

Entailment potential, metaphorical. Source domains have a large set of potential entailments that can become actually used metaphorical entailments. These potential entailments constitute the metaphorical entailment potential of the source domains in structural metaphors.

Entailments, metaphorical. Metaphorical entailments arise from the rich knowledge people have about elements of source domains. For example, in the ANGER IS A HOT FLUID IN A CONTAINER metaphor we have rich knowledge about the behavior of hot fluids in a container. When such knowledge about the source domain is carried over to the target domain, we get metaphorical entailments.

Essential features. These are semantic features (which see) that are shared by each and every member of a category and hence define the category.

Essentially contested concepts. These are concepts, or categories, that are defined by a number of properties, such as the following: The category must evaluate an achievement; the achievement must be internally complex; the achievement must be capable of indefinite modification; the concept must derive from an original exemplar whose authority is acknowledged by all the contestant users of the concept; and some others.

Experiential basis (of metaphor). Conceptual metaphors are grounded in, or motivated by, human experience. The experiential basis of metaphor involves just this groundedness-in-experience. Specifically, we experience the interconnectedness of two domains of experience and this justifies for us conceptually linking the two domains. For example, if we often experience anger as being connected with body heat, we will feel justified in creating and using the conceptual metaphor ANGER IS A HOT FLUID IN A CONTAINER. The experiences on which the conceptual metaphors are based may be not only bodily but also perceptual, cognitive, biological, or cultural. The interconnectedness between the two domains of experience may be of several types, including correlations in experience, perceiving structural similarities between two domains, and so on.

Experientialism. As it is used here, experientialism is contrasted with objectivism (which see). Experientialism is a set of views that give systematically different solutions to such issues as the nature of mind, the nature of language, the nature of meaning, and so on. Some of its claims include that the mind is based on the body, that language is best thought of as a set of grammatical constructions each with its distinctive semantic, syntactic, and pragmatic properties, that meaning is embodied, and others.

Expert theories. Expert theories are defined in contrast to folk theories (which see), or understandings. Expert theories represent reflected, scientific knowledge about a domain of experience. Expert theories often conflict with folk theories, or understandings.

Extended metaphors. These occur mainly in literary texts. They are large-scale metaphors "behind" a text that underlie other, more local metaphors (called micrometaphors). Their cognitive function is to organize the local metaphors into a coherent metaphorical structure in the text.

Extension. This is one way in which a conventional, ordinary metaphor can be reworked in literature. In it, a conventional conceptual metaphor that is associated with certain conventionalized linguistic expressions is expressed by new linguistic means. This is typically achieved by introducing a new conceptual element into the source domain.

Family resemblance relations. If category A has members B, C, and D, B and C may share certain features, C and D may share certain features, but B may not share any features with D. In other words, there is no set of essential features that characterizes each and every member of a category. Family resemblance relations function relative to prototypes (which see).

Figure-ground alignment. *See* Trajector and Landmark.

Folk theories (of a conceptual domain). We have nonexpert, naive views about everything in our world. When this kind of naive, nonexpert knowledge comes in a more or less structured form, we call it folk understanding or folk theory. These folk understandings of the world include our knowledge about how we communicate meaning to each other, about how language can refer to objects and events, about the behavior of hot fluids in a closed container, about how machines work, about what a journey is, about what wars are, and a huge number of other things. Folk understandings often conflict with expert theories and a folk theory may conflict with another folk theory for the same "thing." *See* Conceptual domain and Expert theories.

Force dynamics. This is the view that a large part of meaning can be described in terms of two forceful entities in interaction. We conceptualize many situations as having two entities acting on each another with a particular result. Such conceptualizations are coded into language in particular ways. *See* Cognitive operations/processes.

Frame. Frames are structured mental representations of an area of human experience (i.e., objects or events). As such, they amount to representations of prototypes (which see). Framelike structures have received a variety of names in the literature, including model, idealized cognitive model, domain, script, scene, experiential gestalt, folk theory, and several others. Frames have roles (which see) that can be instantiated by particular values (which see). Frames are like schemas in that they sanction more specific instances. *See also* Image-schemas and Schemas.

Frame-based categorization. This is categorizing items on the basis of the items belonging to a particular frame, rather than on the basis of their similarity to prototypes (which see). *See* also Similarity-based categorization.

Function of conceptual metaphors. Different types of metaphor serve different cognitive functions. Three major types have been distinguished: structural metaphors, ontological metaphors, and orientational metaphors (all of which see).

Generic-level metaphors. These metaphors occupy a high level on a scale of generality on which conceptual metaphors can be placed and are composed of generic-level source and target domains. Generic-level metaphors are instantiated, or realized, by specific-level ones. Thus, the metaphor EMOTIONS ARE FORCES is instantiated, or realized, by the specific-level metaphor ANGER IS A HOT FLUID IN A CONTAINER. *See also* Specific-level metaphors.

Hiding. In hiding, of the several aspects of a target, only some will be focused on. The ones that are not in focus can be said to be hidden. *See also* Aspects of conceptual domains.

Highlighting. In highlighting, of the several aspects of a target domain, some will be focused on by the source domain. The source domain can be said to highlight these aspects of the target. *See also* Aspects of conceptual domains and Utilization.

ICM. *See* Frame.

Iconicity. This involves cases where there is an isomorphism (structural similarity) between conceptual structure and linguistic structure. *See also* Conceptual metaphor.

Idealized Cognitive Model. *See* Frame.

Image-schema metaphors. Image-schema metaphors are based on "skeletal" image-schemas, such as the path schema, the force schema, the contact schema, and so on. They are skeletal in the sense that these source domains do not map rich knowledge onto the target.

Image-schemas. Image-schemas are recurring, dynamic patterns of our perceptual interactions and motor programs that give coherence to our experience. They are highly schematic, or abstract, cognitive structures. *See also* Frame and Schemas.

Intercultural variation (in metaphor). *See* Cultural variation (in metaphor).

Intracultural variation (in metaphor). *See* Cultural variation (in metaphor).

Invariance principle. This principle states: Map as much knowledge from the source domain onto the target domain as is coherent with the image-schematic properties of the target. *See also* Main meaning focus (of conceptual metaphor).

Kinds of conceptual metaphor. Conceptual metaphors can be classified in a variety of ways. We can classify them according to their conventionality, function, nature, level of generality, and complexity (all of which see).

Landmark. In a situation the element with respect to which another element is seen as more prominent is the landmark. Alternative terminology for landmark in this book is *ground*. *See also* Trajector.

Level of generality of conceptual metaphor. Conceptual metaphors can be placed on a scale of generality: Some metaphors are at the specific level, while others at the generic level. Thus, we have specific-level metaphors and generic-level metaphors (both of which see).

Linguistic relativity. This is the view, proposed by a number of scholars but most eminently by Benjamin Lee Whorf, that language shapes cognition (used here in a broad sense to include a variety of cognitive processes, such as memory, categorization, and recognition).

Literary metaphors. These are metaphors that can be found in literary works. They are especially prevalent in poetry. As conceptual metaphors, they are commonly conventional; as linguistic expressions, they are commonly unconventional.

Loose compositionality. *See* Partial/Loose compositionality.

Main meaning focus (of conceptual metaphor). Each source domain is associated with a particular meaning focus (or foci) that is (are) mapped onto the target. This meaning focus (or foci) is (are) conventionally fixed and agreed upon within a speech community or subculture. For example, the main meaning focus of the source domain of FIRE is intensity. This is what is most commonly "imported" to target domains. *See also* Invariance principle.

Mappings. Conceptual metaphors are characterized by a set of conceptual correspondences between elements of the source and target domains. Such correspondences can also be found within a domain (between the vehicle and target of metonymy) and between two mental spaces. These correspondences are technically called mappings. *See* Conceptual metaphor, Conceptual metonymy, and Mental spaces.

Megametaphors. *See* Extended metaphors.

Mental spaces. Mental spaces are partial conceptual structures that we build up on-line in the course of communication. We set up mental spaces with the help of space builders. Space builders include adverbials of time, various adverbs, modal verbs, and several others. Mental spaces are cognitively real phenomena that we can think of as small activated areas of the brain/mind. Similar to frames, or domains, mental spaces also represent structured areas of experience, but they differ from frames in that they are smaller and more specific. At the same time, mental spaces may be structured by frames—often by several of them at the same time. *See also* Conceptual integration and Mappings.

Metaphor systems. Metaphor systems involve cases where a number of different individual source domains jointly characterize various aspects of a single target domain. This can happen at a specific level (e.g., at the level of concepts such as "argument" or "anger" characterized by their sources) or at a generic level (e.g., at the level of the superordinate concept of "event" characterized by its several source domains).

Metaphor. *See* Conceptual metaphor.

Metaphorical entailments. *See* Entailments, metaphorical.

Metaphorical linguistic expressions. These are words or other linguistic expressions (e.g., idioms) that come from the terminology of the conceptual domain that is used to understand another conceptual domain. For example, when we use *to be at a crossroads* to talk about life, it is a metaphorical expression that comes from the domain of JOURNEY. Usually there are many metaphorical linguistic expressions that reflect a particular conceptual metaphor, such as LIFE IS A JOURNEY. *See also* Nonlinguistic realization of metaphor.

Metonymy. *See* Conceptual metonymy.

Micrometaphors. These are local metaphors in a text that are organized into a coherent metaphorical structure by extended metaphors. *See also* Extended metaphors.

Motivation (of metaphor). *See* Experiential basis (of metaphor).

Nature of metaphor. Metaphors may be based on basic knowledge concerning conceptual domains (sometimes called propositional knowledge) and knowledge concerning images. Image-based metaphors include image-schema metaphors and one-shot image metaphors. *See* Image-schema metaphors and One-shot image metaphors.

Network model. *See* Conceptual integration.

Nonlinguistic realization of metaphor. Metaphors may appear not only in language but also in social-physical reality; that is, they can take social-physical form, such as institutions, objects, actions, and practices. *See also* Metaphorical linguistic expressions.

Objectivism. As it is used here, objectivism is contrasted with experientialism (which see). Objectivism is a set of views that gives systematically different solutions to such issues as the nature of mind, the nature of language, the nature of meaning, and so on. Some of its claims include that the mind is independent from the body, that language consists of abstract symbols and the rules for their manipulation, that meaning is disembodied, and so forth.

One-shot image metaphors. One-shot image metaphors are metaphors that involve the superimposition of one rich image onto another rich image. For example, when we compare the rich image we have of a woman's body with the rich image of an hourglass, we get a one-shot image metaphor. These cases are called "one-shot" metaphors because in them we bring into correspondence two rich images for a temporary purpose on a particular occasion.

Ontological metaphors. These conceptual metaphors enable speakers to conceive of their experiences in terms of objects, substances, and containers in general, without specifying further the kind of object, substance, or container.

Orientational metaphors. These conceptual metaphors enable speakers to make a set of target concepts coherent by means of some basic human spatial orientations, such as up-down, in-out, center-periphery, and so on.

Partial/Loose compositionality. The idea of partial/loose compositionality differs from that of strict compositionality in that in it the overall meaning of a complex expression is seen as being *partially* constituted by the meanings of the constituent parts. *See also* Compositionality and Strict compositionality.

Personification. This is a kind of conceptual metaphor that involves understanding nonhuman entities, or things, in terms of human beings. It thus imputes human characteristics to things. Personification can be regarded as a type of ontological metaphor (which see).

Prediction (of metaphor). The cognitive view of metaphor does not claim that we can predict what metaphors there are either within a single culture or cross-culturally. Instead, it claims that the metaphors that do exist are motivated, or have an experiential basis. *See* Experiential basis (of metaphor).

Primary metaphor. A primary metaphor is one that emerges directly from correlations in experience, for example, MORE IS UP, PURPOSES ARE DESTINATIONS, (ABSTRACT) ORGANIZATION IS PHYSICAL STRUCTURE, PERSISTENCE IS BEING ERECT, and so on. Several primary metaphors can be joined together to form complex metaphors, such as THEORIES ARE BUILDINGS, which is constituted by the last two primary metaphors. *See also* Complex metaphor and Simple metaphor.

Prototype category/categorization. This is the view that categories are not defined by essential features (which see) but by prototypes (which see) and family resemblance relations (which see) to the prototypes.

Prototypes. These are abstract mental representations of a category that define and hold together (the members of) a category.

Questioning. This is one way in which a conventional, ordinary metaphor can be reworked in literature. In it, the writer calls into question the appropriateness of a conventional conceptual metaphor.

Realizations of conceptual metaphors. Conceptual metaphors can become manifest in several ways. One major way is through language. However, they can also manifest themselves in nonlinguistic ways, such as in cartoons, social action, art, and so on. *See also* Nonlinguistic realization of metaphor.

Relations. Relations and things are the highest-level conceptual units. Relations are the products of sequential scanning (which see). *See also* Things.

Relativity of knowledge. This contrasts with universality of knowledge (which see) and is the view that our knowledge of the world derives primarily from experience and since experience is obtained "through culturally mediated conceptual schemes," knowledge is relative to particular cultures.

Roles. ROLES are generic categories as a whole that can be instantiated in many ways. Values (which see) are particular individual instantiations of the generic category. This is the role-value distinction. Interpretations of sentences may depend on whether we interpret an expression based on roles or on the values associated with those roles.

Sapir-Whorf hypothesis. *See* Linguistic relativity.

Scene. *See* Frame.

Schemas. In a construction grammar, each linguistic expression is an instance of a higher-level constructional schema that "sanctions" the use of the expression. Schemas are abstract representations that are instantiated by more specific expressions. *See also* Frame and Image-schemas.

Scope of metaphor. This is the entire range of target domains to which a given source domain, such as JOURNEY, WAR, PLANT, HUMAN BODY, FIRE, and so on, can apply.

Script. *See* Frame.

Semantic features. These are properties that characterize and can define (the meaning of) a category. *See also* Essential features.

Sequential scanning. When we observe a dynamic situation, or scene, dynamically, we have to deal with sequential scanning. The scene is dynamic because we can observe something happening through time. Typically, dynamic situations are construed by means of sequential scanning and are expressed by means of verb phrases in sentences. However, it is also possible to view a static situation by means of sequential scanning. *See also* Summary scanning.

Similarity-based categorization. This is categorizing an item by virtue of its similarity to a prototype. It contrasts with frame-based categorization (which see).

Simple metaphor. A simple metaphor is one that emerges from what we find important in connection with basic physical entities and events that make up the human world, such as BUILDING, FIRE, PRESSURIZED CONTAINER, WAR, JOURNEY, BODY, PLANT, MACHINE, SPORTS, and so on. All these entities and events have a main meaning focus (which see) for us within a culture. The mappings that constitute this meaning focus (or foci) are simple metaphors. For example, the central mapping (which see) (ABSTRACT) DEVELOPMENT IS PHYSICAL GROWTH derives from the PLANT source domain within the scope of the metaphor COMPLEX ABSTRACT SYSTEMS ARE PLANTS. *See also* Complex metaphor and Primary metaphor.

Source domain. This is a conceptual domain that we use to understand another conceptual domain (the target domain). Source domains are typically less abstract or less complex than target domains. For example, in the conceptual metaphor LIFE IS A JOURNEY the conceptual domain of JOURNEY is typically viewed as being less abstract or less complex than that of LIFE.

Specific-level metaphors. These metaphors occupy a low level on a scale of generality on which conceptual metaphors can be placed. They are composed of specific-level source and target domains. Specific-level metaphors are instantiations, or special cases, of generic-level ones. Thus, the metaphor ANGER IS A HOT FLUID IN A CONTAINER is an instantiation, or special case, of the generic-level metaphor EMOTIONS ARE FORCES. *See also* Generic-level metaphors.

Strict compositionality. The principle of strict compositionality maintains that the overall meaning of a complex expression can be *fully* computed from the meanings of the constituent parts and their combination. *See also* Compositionality and Partial/Loose compositionality.

Structural metaphors. These are conceptual metaphors that enable speakers to understand the target domain in terms of the structure of the source domain. This understanding is based on a set of conceptual correspondences between elements of the two domains.

Summary scanning. When we view a static situation, or scene, nondynamically or when we view a dynamic situaton, or scene, as a single static frame that somehow "summarizes" a whole series of events, we have summary scanning. Thus, it is possible to construe dynamic situations by means of summary scanning and express them by means of noun phrases that we do not use predicatively. *See also* Sequential scanning.

Target domain. This is a conceptual domain that we try to understand with the help of another conceptual domain (the source domain). Target domains are typically more abstract and subjective than source domains. For example, in the conceptual metaphor LIFE IS A JOURNEY the conceptual domain of LIFE is typically viewed as being more abstract (and more complex) than that of JOURNEY.

Taxonomic hierarchy. These are conceptual hierarchies in which members of the category can be found at different levels of abstraction or generality. The higher-level members include lower-level members by "logical inclusion," that is, by the lower-level members sharing features of the higher-level ones but also possessing additional ones.

Things. Things and relations are the highest-level conceptual units. Things are the products of summary scanning (which see). *See also* Relations.

Thinking for speaking. This is the idea that language makes us attend to certain aspects of experience through grammatically encoding these aspects (while ignoring other aspects).

Trajector. In a situation an element that is viewed as more prominent with respect to another element is the trajector. Alternative terminology for trajector in this book is *figure*. *See also* Landmark.

Unconventional metaphors. *See* Conventionality of metaphor.

Unidirectionality of conceptual metaphor. In conceptual metaphors, the understanding of abstract or complex domains is based on less abstract or less complex conceptual domains. With metaphors that serve the purpose of understanding, this is the natural direction; metaphorical understanding goes from the more concrete and less complex to the more abstract and more complex. The reverse direction can also sometimes occur, but then the metaphor has a special noneveryday function.

Universality of knowledge. This is the idea that human beings share the most significant knowledge about the world in the form of transcendental universal concepts. *See also* Relativity of knowledge.

Universality of metaphor. Conceptual metaphors that can be found in all languages are universal. Obviously, because of the large number of languages spoken around the world, it would be impossible to obtain conclusive evidence for the universality of any single conceptual metaphor. Some candidates for universal metaphors have been suggested, such as the EVENT STRUCTURE metaphor. The (potential) universality of conceptual metaphors largely exists at the generic level. *See also* Cultural variation (in metaphor).

Utilization. In metaphorical utilization, only some aspects of the source are utilized in metaphorical mappings, while the others remain unutilized. *See also* Highlighting.

Values. Values are particular individual instantiations of a particular role, or generic category. *See also* Roles.

References

Aitchison, Jean. 1987. *Words in the Mind*. London: Blackwell.

Alverson, Hoyt. 1991. Metaphor and experience: Looking over the notion of image schema. In J. Fernandez (ed.), *Beyond Metaphor: The Theory of Tropes in Anthropology*, 94–117. Stanford, CA: Stanford University Press.

Alverson, Hoyt. 1994. *Semantics and Experience: Universal Metaphors of Time in English, Mandarin, Hindi, and Sesotho*. Baltimore: Johns Hopkins University Press.

Andor, József. 1985. On the psychological relevance of frames. *Quaderni di Semantica*, 6(2, December), 212–221.

Barcelona, Antonio (ed.). 2000a. *Metaphor and Metonymy at the Crossroads*. Berlin: Mouton de Gruyter.

Barcelona, Antonio. 2000b. On the plausibility of claiming a metonymic motivation for conceptual metaphor. In Antonio Barcelona (ed.), 31–58. *Metaphor and Metonymy at the Crossroads*. Berlin: Mouton de Gruyter.

Barsalou, Lawrence. 1983. Ad hoc categories. *Memory and Cognition*, 11, 211–227.

Barsalou, Lawrence. 1992. *Cognitive Psychology: An Overview for Cognitive Scientists*. Hillsdale, NJ: Lawrence Erlbaum.

Barsalou, Lawrence. 1993. Structure, flexibility, and linguistic vagary in concepts: manifestations of a compositional system of perceptual symbols. In A. C. Collins, S. E. Gathercole, and M. A. Conway (eds.), *Theories of Memory*, 29–101. London: Lawrence Erlbaum Associates.

Benczes, Réka. 2005. Creative Compounding in English. Doctoral dissertation, Eötvös Loránd University, Budapest.

Berlin, Brent, and Paul Kay. 1969. *Basic Color Terms: Their Universality and Evolution*. Berkeley: University of California Press.

Boers, Frank, and Jeanette Littlemore. 2000. Cognitive style variables in participants' explanations of conceptual metaphors. *Metaphor and Symbol*, 15(3), 177–187.

Boroditsky, Lera. 2001. Does language shape thought? Mandarin and English speakers' conception of time. *Cognitive Psychology*, 43, 1–22.

Boroditsky, Lera. In press. Linguistic relativity. In *Encyclopedia of Cognitive Science*. New York: Macmillan.

Boroditsky, Lera, and Michael Ramscar. 2002. The roles of body and mind in abstract thought. *Psychological Science*, 13(2), 185–189.

Boroditsky, L., L. A. Schmidt, and W. Phillips. 2003. Sex, syntax and semantics. In D. Gentner and S. Goldin-Meadow (eds.), *Language in Mind: Advances in the Study of Language and Thought*, 61–78. Cambridge, MA, MIT Press.

Brandt, Per Aage. 2004. *Spaces, Domains and Meaning: Essays in Cognitive Semiotics*. Bern: Peter Lang.

Brdar, Mario, and Rita Brdar-Szabó. 2003. Metonymic coding of linguistic action in English, Croatian and Hungarian. In Uke-Klaus Panther and Linda Thornburg (eds.), *Metonymy and Pragmatic Inferencing*, 241–246. Amsterdam: John Benjamins.

Brdar-Szabó, Rita, and Mario Brdar. 2003. The MANNER FOR ACTIVITY metonymy across domains and languages. *Jezikoslovlje*, 4(1), 43–69.

Brown, Roger. 1958. How shall a thing be called? *Psychological Review*, 66, 14–21.

Cameron, Lynne, and Graham Low. 2004. Figurative variation in episodes of educational talk and text. *Cultural Variation in Metaphor*, special issue of *European Journal of English Studies (EJES)*, 8(3), 355–373. (Guest editor: Z. Kövecses.)

Charteris-Black, Jonathan. 2002. Second language figurative proficiency: A comparative study of Malay and English. *Applied Linguistics*, 23(1), 104–133.

Charteris-Black, Jonathan. 2003. Speaking with forked tongue: A comparative study of metaphor and metonymy in English and Malay phraseology. *Metaphor and Symbol*, 18(4), 289–310.

Charteris-Black, Jonathan. 2004. *Corpus Approaches to Critical Metaphor Analysis*. Houndmills, England: Palgrave Macmillan.

Chilton, Paul, and George Lakoff. 1995. Foreign policy by metaphor. In C. Schaffner and A. L. Wenden (eds.), *Language and Peace*, 37–59. Brookfield, VT: Dartmouth.

Cienki, Alan. 1998. Metaphoric gestures and some of their relations to verbal metaphoric expressions. In J.-P. Konig (ed.), *Discourse and Cognition: Bridging the Gap*, 189–204. Stanford, CA: CSLI.

Clark, Herbert H. 1996. *Using Language*. Cambridge: Cambridge University Press.

Coulson, Seana. 2000. *Semantic Leaps: Frame-Shifting and Conceptual Blending in Meaning Construction*. Cambridge: Cambridge University Press.

Croft, William, and Alan Cruse. 2004. *Cognitive Linguistics*. Cambridge: Cambridge University Press.

Cruse, Alan. 1977. The pragmatics of lexical specificity. *Journal of Linguistics*, 13, 153–164.

Csábi, Szilvia. 2005. Alternative conceptualization in English and Hungarian idioms. Doctoral dissertation, Eötvös Loránd University, Budapest.

Damasio, Antonio R. 1994. *Descartes' Error, Emotion, Reason, and the Human Brain*. New York: Avon Books.

D'Andrade, R. 1995. *The Development of Cognitive Anthropology*. Cambridge: Cambridge University Press.

Deignan, A., D. Gabrys, and A. Solska, 1997. Teaching English metaphors using cross-linguistic awareness raising activities. *ELT Journal*, 51(4), 353–360.

Dirven, René. 1994. *Metaphor and Nation: Metaphors Afrikaners Live By.* Frankfurt am Main: Peter Lang.

Dirven, René, and Ralph Pörings (eds.). 2002. *Metaphor and Metonymy in Comparison and Contrast.* Berlin: Mouton de Gruyter.

Dirven, René, Frank Polzenhagen, and Hans-Georg Wolf. In press. Cognitive linguistics, ideology, and critical discourse analysis. In *Handbook of Cognitive Linguistics.* Oxford: Oxford University Press.

Dirven, René, Hans-Georg Wolf, and Frank Polzenhagen. In press. Cultural studies. In *Handbook of Cognitive Linguistics.* Oxford: Oxford University Press.

Dixon, R. M. W. 1982. *Where Have All the Adjectives Gone? And Other Essays in Semantics and Syntax.* Berlin: Mouton de Gruyter.

Edelman, Gerald M. 1992. *Bright Air, Brilliant Fire: On the Matter of the Mind.* New York: Basic Books.

Emanatian, Michelle. 1995. Metaphor and the expression of emotion: The value of cross-cultural perspectives. *Metaphor and Symbolic Activity*, 10, 163–182.

Encyclopedia Britannica Ready Reference. 2003. Version on Dell computers.

Enfield, N. J. (ed.). 2002. *Ethnosyntax:. Explorations in Grammar and Culture.* Oxford: Oxford University Press.

Fauconnier, Gilles. 1985/1994. *Mental Spaces.* Cambridge: Cambridge University Press. (Originally published in 1985 by MIT Press.)

Fauconnier, Gilles. 1997. *Mappings in Language and Thought.* Cambridge: Cambridge University Press.

Fauconnier, Gilles, and Mark Turner. 1998. Conceptual integration networks. *Cognitive Science*, 22, 133–187.

Fauconnier, Gilles, and Mark Turner. 2002. *The Way We Think.* New York: Basic Books.

Fillmore, Charles J. 1975. An alternative to checklist theories of meaning. In C. Cogen, H. Thompson, G. Thurgood, K. Whistler, and J. Wright (eds.), *Proceedings of the First Annual Meeting of the Berkeley Linguistics Society*, 123–131. Berkeley, CA: Berkeley Linguistics Society.

Fillmore, Charles J. 1977a. The case for case reopened. In P. Cole and J. M. Sadock (eds.), *Grammatical Relations*, vol. 8: *Syntax and Semantics*; pp. 59–81. London: Academic Press.

Fillmore, Charles J. 1977b. Scenes-and-frames semantics. In Antonio Zampolli (ed.), *Linguistics Structures Processing*, 55–81. Amsterdam: North Holland Publishing.

Fillmore, Charles J. 1977c. Topics in lexical semantics. In Roger Cole (ed.), *Current Issues in Linguistic Theory*, 76–138. Bloomington: Indiana University Press.

Fillmore, Charles J. 1982. Frame semantics. In The Linguistic Society of Korea (ed.), *Linguistics in the Morning Calm*, 111–137. Seoul: Hanshin.

Fillmore, Charles J. 1985. Frames and the semantics of understanding. *Quaderni di Semantica*, 6(2), 222–254.

Fillmore, Charles J. 1988. The mechanisms of construction grammar. In Shelley Axmaker, Annie Jaisser, and Helen Singmaster (eds.), *Proceedings of the Fourteenth Annual Meeting of the Berkeley Linguistics Society*, 35–55. Berkeley, CA: Berkeley Linguistics Society.

Fillmore, Charles J., and B. T. Atkins. 1992. Towards a Frame-based organization of the lexicon: The semantics of RISK and its neighbors. In Adrienne Lehrer and Eva Kittay (eds.), *Frames, Fields, and Contrasts: New Essays in Semantics and Lexical Organization*, 75–102. Hillsdale, NJ: Lawrence Erlbaum.

Foley, William A. 1997. *Anthropological Linguistics. An Introduction*. Oxford: Blackwell.

Forceville, Charles. 1996. *Pictorial Metaphor in Advertising*. London: Routledge.

Forceville, Charles. 2002. Visual representations of the ICM of ANGER in comics. Paper presented at the conference Social Cognition and Verbal Communication, February 20–23, University of Pécs, Pécs, Hungary.

Forceville, Charles. 2005. Visual representations of the Idealized Cognitive Model of anger in the Asterix album La Zizanie. *Journal of Pragmatics*, 37(1), 69–88.

Gabler, Neil. 1998. *Life: The Movie: How Entertainment Conquered Reality*. New York: Vintage Books.

Gallese, Vittorio, and George Lakoff. 2005. The brain's concepts: The role of the sensory-motor system in conceptual knowledge. *Cognitive Neuropsychology*, 21, 1–26.

Gallie, W. B. 1956. Essentially contested concepts. In *The Proceedings of the Aristotelian Society*. Vol. 51, 167–198. London: Harrison and Sons.

Gardenfors, Peter. 2003. *How Homo Became Sapiens: On the Evolution of Thinking*. Oxford: Oxford University Press.

Geeraerts, Dirk, and Stephan Grondelaers. 1995. Looking back at anger: Cultural traditions and metaphorical patterns. In J. R. Taylor and R. MacLaury (eds.), *Language and the Cognitive Construal of the World*, 153–179. Berlin: Mouton de Gruyter.

Gentner, Dedre. 1983. Structure-mapping: A theoretical framework for analogy. *Cognitive Science*, 7, 155–170.

Gevaert, Caroline. 2001. Anger in Old and Middle English: A "hot" topic? *Belgian Essays on Language and Literature*, 89–101.

Gevaert, Caroline. 2005. The ANGER IS HEAT question: Detecting cultural influence on the conceptualization of anger through diachronic corpus analysis. In N. Delbecque ed., *Perspectives on Variation: Sociolinguistic, Historical, Comparative*, 195–208. Berlin: Walter de Gruyter.

Gibbs, Raymond W. 1994. *The Poetics of Mind. Figurative Thought, Language, and Understanding*. Cambridge: Cambridge University Press.

Gibbs, Raymond W. 1998. The fight over metaphor in thought and language. In A. Katz, C. Cacciari, R. W. Gibbs, and M. Turner (eds.), *Figurative Language and Thought*, 88–118. New York: Oxford University Press.

Gibbs, Raymond W. 1999. Taking metaphor out of our heads and putting it into the cultural world. In Raymond W. Gibbs Jr. and Gerard J. Steen (eds.), *Metaphor in Cognitive Linguistics*, 145–166. Amsterdam: John Benjamins.

Gibbs, Raymond W. 2002. Feeling moved by metaphor. In Sz. Csábi and J. Zerkowitz (eds.), *Textual Secrets: The Message of the Medium*, 13–28.

Budapest: School of English and American Studies, Eötvös Loránd University.

Gibbs, Raymond W. 2003a. Embodied experience and linguistic meaning. *Brain and Language*, 84, 1–15.

Gibbs, Raymond W. 2003b. Prototypes in dynamic meaning construal. In J. Gavins and G. Steen (eds.), *Cognitive Poetics in Practice*, 27–40. London: Routledge.

Gibbs, Raymond W. 2005. *Embodiment a Cognitive Science*. New York: Cambridge University Press.

Gibbs, Raymond W., Dinara Beitel, Michael Harrington, and Paul Sanders. 1995. Taking a stand on the meanings of *stand*: Bodily experience as motivation for polysemy. *Journal of Semantics*, 11, 231–251.

Gibbs, Raymond W., and Heather Franks. 2002. Embodied metaphor in women's narratives about their experiences with cancer. *Health Communication*, 14(2), 139–165.

Glucksberg, Sam, and Boaz Keysar. 1993. How metaphors work. In A. Ortony (ed.), *Metaphor and Thought*, 2nd edition, 401–424. Cambridge: Cambridge University Press.

Goatly, Andrew. Forthcoming. *Metaphor and Ideology*. Amsterdam: John Benjamins.

Goffman, Erving. 1974. *Frame Analysis: An Essay on the Organization of Experience*. New York: Harper and Row.

Goldberg, Adele. 1995. *Constructions. A Construction Grammar Approach to Argument Structure*. Chicago: University of Chicago Press.

Grady, Joseph. 1997a. Foundations of Meaning: Primary Metaphors and Primary Scenes. Doctoral dissertation, University of California at Berkeley.

Grady, Joseph. 1997b. THEORIES ARE BUILDING revisited. *Cognitive Linguistics*, 8, 267–290.

Grady, Joe, Todd Oakley, and Seana Coulson, 1999. Blending and metaphor. In Raymond W. Gibbs Jr. and Gerald J. Steen (eds.), *Metaphor in Cognitive Linguistics*, 101–124. Amsterdam: John Benjamins.

Győri, Gábor. 1998. Cultural variation in the conceptualization of emotions: A historical study. In A. Athanasiadou and E. Tabakowska (eds.), *Speaking of Emotions: Conceptualization and Expression*, 99–124. Berlin: Mouton de Gruyler.

Haiman, John. 1985. *Natural Syntax: Iconicity and Erosion*. Cambridge: Cambridge University Press.

Harnad, S. 1990. The symbol grounding problem. *Physica D*, 42, 335–346.

Haviland, John B. 1979. Guugu Yimithirr. In R. M. Dixon and B. Blake (eds.), *Handbook of Australian Languages*, 27–180. Canberra: ANU Press.

Hebb, Donald, O. 1949. *The Organization of Behavior: A Neuropsychological Theory*. New York: Wiley.

Heider, E. 1972. Universals in color naming and memory. *Journal of Experimental Psychology*, 93, 10–20.

Heider, Eleanor, and D. Olivier. 1972. The structure of the color space in naming and memory in two languages. *Cognitive Psychology*, 3: 337–354.

Heine, Bernd. 1995. Conceptual grammaticalization and prediction. In J. R. Taylor and R. MacLaury (eds.), *Language and the Cognitive Construal of the World*, 119–135. Berlin: Mouton de Gruyter.

Heine, Bernd. 1997. *Possession: Cognitive Sources, Forces, and Grammaticalization*. Cambridge: Cambridge University Press.

Heine, Bernd, and Tania Kuteva. 2002. *World Lexicon of Grammaticalization*. Cambridge: Cambridge University Press.

Heine, Bernd, Ulrike Claudi, and Friederike Hünemeyer. 1991. *Grammaticalization: A Conceptual Framework*. Cambridge: Cambridge University Press.

Hogan, Patrick Colm. 2003. *The Mind and Its Stories: Narrative Universals and Human Emotion*. Cambridge: Cambridge University Press.

Holland, Dorothy, and Naomi Quinn, eds. 1987. *Cultural Models in Language and Thought*. Cambridge: Cambridge University Press.

Holyoak, Keith, and Paul Thagard. 1996. *Mental Leaps: Analogy in Creative Thought*. Cambridge, MA: MIT Press.

Hutchins, Edwin. In preparation. Material anchors for conceptual blends. Retrieved from http://www.google.com/search?q=cache:4hxbrg77qwyj:hci .ucsd.edu/lab/hci_papers/eh2004-1.pdf+%22material+anchors%22 +hutchins&hl=hu&client=firefoxa.

Jakel, Olaf. 1995. The metaphorical concept of mind: "Mental activity is manipulation." In J. R. Taylor and R. MacLaury (eds.), *Language and the Cognitive Construal of the World*, 197–229. Berlin: Mouton de Gruyter.

Johnson, David M. 2005. Mind, brain, and the Upper Paleolithic. In C. E. Erneling and D. M. Johnson (eds.), *The Mind as a Scientific Object: Between Brain and Culture*, 499–510.Oxford: Oxford University Press.

Johnson, Mark. 1987. *The Body in the Mind*. Chicago: University of Chicago Press.

Johnson, Mark, and George Lakoff. 2002. Why cognitive linguistics requires embodied realism. *Cognitive Linguistics*, 13(3), 245–263.

Katz, J. J., and J. A. Fodor.1963. The structure of a semantic theory. *Language*, 39, 170–210.

Kay, Paul. 1987. Linguistic competence and folk theories of language: Two English hedges. In David Holland and Naomi Quinn (eds.), *Cultural Models in Language and Thought*, 67–77. Cambridge: Cambridge University Press.

Kay, Paul. 2004. Draining the language of color. Interview with P. Kay in *Scientific American*, April 2004. Retrieved from *www.sciam.com/ article.cfm?articleid=00055ee3-4530-1052-853083414b7f0000*.

Kay, Paul, and Luisa Maffi. 2000. Color appearance and the emergence and evolution of basic color lexicons. *American Anthropologist*, 10(4), 743–760.

Kimmel, Michael. 2002. Metaphor, Imagery, and Culture. Spatialized Ontologies, Mental Tools, and Multimedia in the Making. Doctoral dissertation, University of Vienna.

Kimmel, Michael. 2005. From metaphor to the "mental sketchpad": Literary macrostructure: and compound image schemas in *Heart of Darkness*. *Metaphor and Symbol*, 20(3), 199–238.

King, Brian. 1989. The conceptual structure of emotional experience in Chinese. Doctoral dissertation, Ohio State University.

Koller, Bálint. 2003. Metaphoricity and Metonymicity in Grammar: A Journey in Space. M.A. dissertation, Eötvös Loránd University, Budapest.

Kövecses, Zoltán. 1986. *Metaphors of Anger, Pride, and Love*. Amsterdam: John Benjamins.

Kövecses, Zoltán. 1988. *The Language of Love*. Lewisburg, PA: Bucknell University Press.

Kövecses, Zoltán. 1990. *Emotion Concepts*. Berlin: Springer-Verlag.

Kövecses, Zoltan. 1991a. Happiness: A definitional effort. *Metaphor and Symbolic Activity*, 6(1), 29–46.

Kövecses, Zoltán. 1991b. A linguist's quest for love. *Journal of Social Personal Relation*, 8, 77–97.

Kövecses, Zoltán. 1994. Tocqueville's passionate "beast": A linguistic analysis of American democracy. *Metaphor and Symbolic Activity*, 9(2), 113–133.

Kövecses, Zoltán. 1995a. American friendship and the scope of metaphor. *Cognitive Linguistics*, 6, 315–346.

Kövecses, Zoltán. 1995b. Understanding the Statue of Liberty. In Zoltán Kövecses (ed.), *New Approaches to American English*, 129–138. Budapest: Eötvös Loránd University.

Kövecses, Zoltán. 1999. Does metaphor reflect or consitute cultural models? In Raymond W. Gibbs and Gerald J. Steen (eds.), *Metaphor in Cognitive Linguistics*, 167–188. Amsterdam: John Benjamins.

Kövecses, Zoltán. 2000a. *American English. An Introduction*. Peterborough, Canada: Broadview Press.

Kövecses, Zoltán. 2000b. *Metaphor and Emotion*. New York: Cambridge University Press.

Kövecses, Zoltán. 2000c. The scope of metaphor. In Antonio Barcelona (ed.), *Metaphor and Metonymy at the Crossroads*, 79–92. Berlin: Mouton de Gruyter.

Kövecses, Zoltán. 2002. *Metaphor. A Practical Introduction*. Oxford: Oxford University Press.

Kövecses, Zoltán. 2003. Language, figurative thought, and cross-cultural comparison. *Metaphor and Symbol*, 18(4), 311–320.

Kövecses, Zoltán. 2005a. *Metaphor in Culture. Universality and Variation*. Cambridge: Cambridge University Press.

Kövecses, Zoltán. 2005b. Is thought (meaning) essentially literal? The relationship between literal-figurative and concrete-abstract meanings. In Seana Coulson and Barbara Lewandowska-Tomaszczyk (eds.), *The Literal and Nonliteral in Language and Thought*, 201–217. Frankfurt am Main: Peter Lang.

Kövecses, Zoltán, and Günter Radden. 1998. Metonymy: Developing a cognitive linguistic view. *Cognitive Linguistics*, 9(7), 37–77.

Köves, Nikoletta. 2002. American and Hungarian dreamworks of life. Term paper, Eötvös Loránd University, Budapest.

Krzeszowski, Tomasz P. 2002. From target to source: Metaphors made real. In B. Lewandowska Tomaszczyk and K. Turewicz (eds.), *Cognitive Linguistics Today*, 139–158. Frankfurt am Main: Peter Lang.

Lakoff, George. 1987. *Women, Fire, and Dangerous Things: What Categories Reveal about the Mind*. Chicago: University of Chicago Press.

Lakoff, George. 1990. The invariance hypothesis: Is abstract reason based on image schemas? *Cognitive Linguistics*, 1(1), 39–74.

Lakoff, George. 1992. Metaphors and war: The metaphor system used to justify war in the Gulf. In M. Putz (ed.), *Thirty Years of Linguistic Evolution*, 463–481. Amsterdam: John Benjamins.

Lakoff, George. 1993. The contemporary theory of metaphor. In A. Ortony (ed.), *Metaphor and Thought*, 2nd edition, 202–251. Cambridge: Cambridge University Press.

Lakoff, George. 1996. *Moral Politics: What Conservatives Know That Liberals Don't*. Chicago: University of Chicago Press.

Lakoff, George, and Zoltán Kövecses, 1987. The cognitive model of anger inherent in American English. In Dorothy Holland and Naomi Quinn (eds.), *Cultural Models in Language and Thought*, 195–221. Cambridge: Cambridge University Press.

Lakoff, George, and Mark Johnson. 1980. *Metaphors We Live By*. Chicago: University of Chicago Press.

Lakoff, George, and Mark Johnson. 1999. *Philosophy in the Flesh*. New York: Basic Books.

Lakoff, George, and Raphael Nunez. 2000. *Where Mathematics Comes From*. New York: Basic Books.

Lakoff, George, and Mark Turner. 1989. *More than Cool Reason. A Field Guide to Poetic Metaphor*. Chicago: University of Chicago Press.

Langacker, Ronald. 1987. *Foundations of Cognitive Grammar*, vol. 1: *Theoretical Prerequisites*. Stanford, CA: Stanford University Press.

Langacker, Ronald. 1991a. *Concept, Image, and Symbol*. Berlin: Mouton de Gruyter.

Langacker, Ronald. 1991b. *Foundations of Cognitive Grammar*, vol. 2: *Descriptive Applications*. Stanford, CA: Stanford University Press.

Lee, David. 2001. *Cognitive Linguistics: An Introduction*. New York: Oxford University Press.

Levinson, Stephen C. 1992. Language and Cognition: The Cognitive Consequences of Spatial Description in Guugu Yimithirr. Working paper No. 13. Nijmegen: Cognitive Anthropology Research Group.

Levinson, Stephen C. 1996. Relativity in spatial conception and description. In J. Gumperz and Stephen C. Levinson (eds.), *Rethinking Linguistic Relativity*, 177–202. Cambridge: Cambridge University Press.

Littlemore, Jeannette. 2003. The effect of cultural background on metaphor interpretation. *Metaphor and Symbol*, 18(4), 273–288.

Lucy, John. 1992. *Grammatical Categories and Cognition: A Case Study of the Linguistic Relativity Hypothesis*. Cambridge: Cambridge University Press.

Lucy, John. 1996. The scope of linguistic relativity: An analysis and review of empirical research. In J. Gumperz and Stephen C. Levinson (eds.), *Rethinking Linguistic Relativity*, 37–69. Cambridge: Cambridge University Press.

Maalej, Zouhair. 2004. Figurative language in anger expressions in Tunisian Arabic: An extended view of embodiment. *Metaphor and Symbol*, 19(1), 51–75.

Maalej, Zouhair. In press. The embodiment of fear expressions in Tunisian Arabic: Theoretical and practical implications. In G. Palmer and F. Sharifian (eds.), *Applied Cultural Linguistics*. Amsterdam: John Benjamins.

Mandler, J. M., and P. J. Bauer. 1988. The cradle of categorization: Is the basic level basic? *Cognitive Development*, 8, 247–264.

Mandler, J. M., P. J. Bauer, and L. McDonough. 1991. Separating the sheep from the goats: Differentiating global categories. *Cognitive Psychology*, 23, 263–298.

Matsuki, Keiko. 1995. Metaphors of anger in Japanese. In J. R. Taylor and R. MacLaury (eds.), *Language and the Cognitive Construal of the World.* Berlin: Mouton de Gruyter.

McMullen, Linda, and John Conway. 2002. Conventional metaphors for depression. In S. Fussell (ed.), *Verbal Communication of Emotion: Interdisciplinary Perspectives,* 167–181. Mahwah, NJ: Lawrence Erlbaum.

McNeill, David. 1992. *Hand and Mind: What Gestures Reveal about Thought.* Chicago: University of Chicago Press.

Murphy, G. L., and D. L. Medin. 1985. The role of theories in conceptual coherence. *Psychological Review,* 92, 289–316.

Musolff, Andreas. 2001. Political imagery of Europe: A house without exit doors? *Journal of Multilingual and Multicultural Development,* 21(3), 216–229.

Musolff, Andreas. 2004. *Metaphor and Political Discourse. Analogical Reasoning in Debates about Europe.* London: Palgrave Macmillan.

Oatley, Keith. 1992. *Best Laid Schemes: The Psychology of Emotions.* Cambridge: Cambridge University Press.

Özçalıskan, Seyda. 2003a. "In a caravanserai with two doors, I am walking day and night": Metaphors of death and life in Turkish. *Cognitive Linguistics,* 14(4), 281–320.

Özçalıskan, Seyda. 2003b. Metaphorical motion in crosslinguistic perspective: A comparison of English and Turkish. *Metaphor and Symbol,* 18(3), 189–228.

Özçalıskan, Seyda. 2004a. Encoding the manner, path and ground components of a metaphorical motion event. *Annual Review of Cognitive Linguistics,* 2, 73–102.

Özçalıskan, Seyda. 2004b. *Time can't fly, but a bird can:* Learning how to think and talk about time as spatial motion in English and Turkish. *European Journal of the English Language,* 8(3), 309–336. (Guest editor: Zoltán Kövecses.)

Özçalıskan, Seyda. 2005. Metaphor meets typology: Ways of moving metaphorically in English and Turkish. *Cognitive Linguistics,* 16(1), 207–246.

Palmer, Gary. 1996. *Toward a Theory of Cultural Linguistics.* Austin: Texas University Press.

Panther, Uwe-Klaus, and Günter Radden (eds.). 1999. *Metonymy in Language and Thought.* Amsterdam: John Benjamins.

Panther, Uwe-Klaus, and Linda Thornburg (eds.). 2003. *Metonymy and Pragmatic Inferencing.* Amsterdam: John Benjamins.

Petruck, Miriam R. L. 1996. Frame Semantics. In J. Verschueren, J-O. Östman, J. Blommaert, and C. Bulcaen (eds.), *Handbook of Pragmatics,* 1–13. Philadelphia: John Benjamins.

Pinker, Steven. 1994. *The Language Instinct: How the Mind Creates Language.* New York: William Morrow.

Pontoretto, Diane. 1994. Metaphors we can learn by [Electronic version]. *Forum,* 32(3). Retrieved from *http://exchanges.state.gov/forum/vol5/vol132/no3/p2.htm.*

Pullum, Geoffrey K. 1991. *The Great Eskimo Vocabulary Hoax and Other Irreverent Essays on the Study of Language.* Chicago: University of Chicago Press.

Qi, Donald. 2001. Identifying and bridging cross-cultural prototypes: Exploring the role of collaborative dialogue in second language lexical meaning acquisition. *Canadian Modern Language Review*, 58(2, December). Retrieved from *http://www.utpjournals.com/jour.ihtml?lp=product/cmlr/582/582-Qi.html.*

Quinn, Naomi. 1987. Convergent evidence for a cultural model of American marriage. In Dorothy Holland and Naomi Quinn (eds.), *Cultural Models in Language and Thought*, 173–192. Cambridge: Cambridge University Press.

Quinn, Naomi. 1991. The cultural basis of metaphor. In J. Fernandez (ed.), *Beyond Metaphor: The Theory of Tropes in Anthropology*, 56–93. Stanford, CA: Stanford University Press.

Radden, Günter. 1992. The cognitive approach to natural language. In M. Pütz (ed.), *Thirty Years of Linguistic Evolution*, 513–541. Amsterdam: John Benjamins.

Radden, Günter, and Zoltán Kövecses. 1999. Towards a theory of metonymy. In Uwe-Klaus Panther and Günter Radden (eds.), *Metonymy in Language and Thought*, 17–59. Amsterdam: John Benjamins.

Reddy, M. 1979. The conduit metaphor—a case frame conflict in our language about language. In A. Ortony (ed.), *Metaphor and Thought*, 1st edition, 228–324. Cambridge: Cambridge University Press.

Riddle, Elizabeth M. 2001. The "string" metaphor of life and language in Hmong. Paper presented at the 7th International Pragmatics Conference, July, Budapest, Hungary.

Rosch, Eleanor. 1973. Natural categories. *Cognitive Psychology*, 4, 328–350.

Rosch, Eleanor. 1974. Linguistic relativity. In A. Silverstein (ed.), *Human Communication: Theoretical Explorations*, 95–121. New York: Halsted Press.

Rosch, Eleanor. 1975. Cognitive reference points. *Cognitive Psychology*, 7, 532–547.

Rosch, Eleanor. 1978. Principles of categorization. In Eleanor Rosch and B. B. Lloyd (eds.), *Cognition and Categorization*, 27–48. Hillsdale, NJ: Lawrence Erlbaum.

Rosch, Eleanor, and Carolyne Mervis. 1975. Family resemblances: Studies in the internal structure of categories. *Cognitive Psychology*, 7, 573–605.

Rosch, E., C. B. Mervis, W. D. Gray, D. M. Johnson, and P. Boyes-Braem. 1976. Basic objects in natural categories. *Cognitive Psychology*, 8, 382–439.

Ruiz de Mendoza Ibanez, Francesco. 2000. The role of mappings and domains in understanding metonymy. In Antonio Barcelona (ed.), *Metaphor and Metonymy at the Crossroads*, 109–132. Berlin: Mouton de Gruyter.

Saussure, Ferdinand de. 1916/1959. *Course in General Linguistics*. New York: McGraw-Hill.

Schank, Robert, and Robert Abelson. 1977. *Scripts, Plans, Goals, and Understanding*. Hillsdale, NJ: Lawrence Erlbaum.

Searle, John R. 1969. *Speech Acts*. Cambridge: Cambridge University Press.

Searle, John R. 1979. Metaphor. In A. Ortony (ed.), *Metaphor and Thought*, 1st edition, 92–123. Cambridge: Cambridge University Press.

Semino, Elena. 2003. Possible worlds and mental spaces in Hemingway's "A Very Short Story." In J. Gavins and G. Steen (eds.), *Cognitive Poetics in Practice*, 83–98. London: Routledge.

Shore, Bradd. 1996. *Culture in Mind. Cognition, Culture, and the Problem of Meaning*. Oxford: Oxford University Press.

Slobin, Dan I. 1987. Thinking for speaking. In *Proceedings of the Thirteenth Annual Meeting of the Berkeley Linguistics Society*, 435–444. Berkeley, CA: Berkeley Linguistics Society.

Slobin, Dan I. 1996. From "thought and language" to "thinking for speaking." In J. Gumperz and Stephen C. Levinson (eds.), *Rethinking Linguistic Relativity*, 70–96. Cambridge: Cambridge University Press.

Slobin, Dan I. 2003. Language and thought online: Cognitive consequences of linguistic relativity. In D. Gentner and S. Goldin-Meadow (eds.), *Language in Mind: Advances in the Investigation of Language and Thought*, 157–191. Cambridge, MA: MIT Press.

Smith, Linda B., and Larissa K. Samuelson. 1997. Perceiving and remembering: Category stability, variability, and development. In K. Lamberts and D. Shanks (eds.), *Knowledge, Concepts, and Categories*, 161–195. Hove: Psychology Press.

Steen, Gerard. 2003. "Love stories": Cognitive scenarios in love poetry. In J. Gavins and G. Steen (eds.), *Cognitive Poetics in Practice*, 67–82. London: Routledge.

Stockwell, Peter. 2002. *Cognitive Poetics: An Introduction*. London: Routledge.

Strauss, Claudia, and Naomi Quinn. 1997. *A Cognitive Theory of Cultural Meaning*. Cambridge: Cambridge University Press.

Susman, Warren I. 1984. *Culture as History: The Transformation of American Society in the Twentieth Century*. New York: Pantheon.

Sweetser, Eve. 1990. *From Etymology to Semantics*. Cambridge: Cambridge University Press.

Sweetser, Eve. 1997. Role and individual interpretations of change predicates. In J. Nuyts and E. Pederson (eds.), *Language and Conceptualization*, 116–136. Cambridge: Cambridge University Press.

Sweetser, Eve. 1998. Regular metaphoricity in gesture. Bodily-based models of speech interaction. In *Acts du 16e Congress International de Linguistes* (CD-ROM). Elsevier.

Sweetser, Eve. 1999. Compositionality and blending: Semantic composition in a cognitively realistic framework. In Gisela Redeker and Theo Janssen (eds.), *Cognitive Linguistics: Foundations, Scope and Methodology*, 129–162. Berlin: Mouton de Gruyter.

Talmy, Leonard. 1983. How language structures space. In Herbert L. Pick Jr. and Linda P. Acredolo (eds.), *Spatial Orientation: Theory, Research and Application*, 225–282. New York: Plenum Press.

Talmy, Leonard. 1988a. Force dynamics in language and cognition. *Cognitive Science*, 12, 49–100.

Talmy, Leonard. 1988b. The relation of grammar to cognition. In Brygida Rudzka-Ostyn (ed.), *Topics in Cognitive Linguistics*, 165–205. Amsterdam: John Benjamins.

Talmy, Leonard. 2000a. *Toward a Cognitive Semantics*, vol. 1: *Concept Structuring Systems*. Cambridge, MA: MIT Press.

Talmy, Leonard. 2000b. *Toward a Cognitive Semantics*, vol. 2: *Typology and Process in Concept Structuring*. Cambridge, MA: MIT Press.

Taub, Sarah. 2001. *Language from the Body: Iconicity and Metaphor in American Sign Language*. Cambridge: Cambridge University Press.

Taylor, John R. 1989/1995. *Linguistic Categorization*. Oxford: Clarendon Press.

Taylor, John R. 2002. *Cognitive Grammar*. Oxford: Oxford University Press.

Taylor, John R., and Tandi Mbense. 1998. Red dogs and rotten mealies: How Zulus talk about anger. In A. Athanasiadou and E. Tabakowska (eds.), *Speaking of Emotions: Conceptualization and Expression*, 191–226. Berlin: Mouton de Gruyter.

Tilley, Christopher. 1999. *Metaphor and Material Culture*. Oxford: Blackwell.

Tomasello, Michael. 2003. *Constructing a Language: A Usage-based Theory of Language Acquisition*. Cambridge, MA: Harvard University Press.

Turner, Mark. 1991. *Reading Minds: The Study of English in the Age of Cognitive Science*. Princeton, NJ: Princeton University Press.

Turner, Mark. 1996. *The Literary Mind*. New York: Oxford University Press.

Turner, Mark. 2001. *Cognitive Dimensions of Social Science*. Oxford: Oxford University Press.

Ungerer, Frederick, and Hans-Jorg Schmid. 1996. *Introduction to Cognitive Linguistics*. London: Longman.

Veale, Tony. 2001. The literalist manifesto. Retrieved from http://www.compapp.dcu.ie/tonyv/trinity/lit-manifesto.html.

Whorf, Benjamin Lee. 1956. *Language, Thought, and Reality. Selected Writings of Benjamin Lee Whorf*. John B. Carrol (ed.), Cambridge, MA: MIT Press.

Wilcox, Phyllis. 2000. *Metaphor in American Sign Language*. Washington, DC: Gallaudet University Press.

Wittgenstein, Ludwig. 1953. *Philosophical Investigations*. New York: Macmillan.

Yu, Ning. 1995. Metaphorical expressions of anger and happiness in English and Chinese. *Metaphor and Symbolic Activity*, 10, 59–92.

Yu, Ning. 1998. *The Contemporary Theory of Metaphor in Chinese: A Perspective from Chinese*. Amsterdam: John Benjamins.

Yu, Ning. 2003. Metaphor, body, and culture: The Chinese understanding of *gallbladder* and *courage*. *Metaphor and Symbol*, 18(1), 13–31.

Index

CPSIA information can be obtained at www.ICGtesting.com
Printed in the USA
BVOW07s1523101213

338684BV00002B/9/P